SB
Shojo Beat

Yona of the Dawn

11

Story & Art by
Mizuho Kusanagi

YONA OF THE DAWN

Story Thus Far

Hak

One of the greatest heroes in the nation, known as the "Thunder Beast." He'd obeyed King Il's orders and became bodyguard to his childhood friend, Yona. He walks away from his position as general in order to protect his tribe.

Yona

While on the run from her deceased father's political enemies, she comes to the realization that she's spent her life being protected by other people. She sets out to locate the Four Dragons in order to protect herself and the people who are most important to her.

Su-won

A young scion of the royal bloodline. To keep Kohka safe from invasion by the Kai Empire to the north or the nations of Xing and Sei to the south, he is trying to create a powerful nation by uniting and ruling over the Five Tribes.

Yun

Brilliant and intellectually curious. He may be a mouthy pretty boy, but he takes good care of people. He comes from a poor town in the Fire Tribe lands, and when he first met Yona, he was scornful of her because of her royal heritage.

The Blue Dragon of the Four Dragon Warriors. With the power of a dragon in his eyes, he can paralyze anyone he looks at. He grew up being hated and feared for his incredible power. He usually wears a mask.

Sinha

The White Dragon of the Four Dragon Warriors. His right hand contains a dragon's might and is more powerful than ten men. Though beloved by everyone in his village, he yearned for a master to serve. He adores Yona and finds fulfillment in his role as one of the Four Legendary Dragons.

Gija

The Yellow Dragon of the Four Dragon Warriors. He has the power of a dragon in his body...or at least he's supposed to! In practice, he's delicate and soft skinned. He left his village to go on a journey, and while traveling, he met and joined Yona's group.

Zeno

The Green Dragon of the Four Dragon Warriors. With the power of a dragon in his right leg, he can leap to tremendous heights. Due to his love of freedom and his hatred of his destined duty as one of the Four Legendary Dragons, he fled his village and joined a pirate crew.

Jaeha

The Four Dragon Warriors… In the Age of Myths, a dragon god took on human form and founded a nation. As the Crimson Dragon King, he was the first ruler of the Kingdom of Kohka. Four other dragons shared their blood with humans so that they could protect him. Those warriors became known as the Four Legendary Dragons, or the Four Dragon Warriors, and their power has been passed down for generations.

STORY

Yona, the princess of the Kingdom of Kohka, was raised by her kind, loving father, King Il. She has deep feelings for her cousin Su-won, a companion since childhood. On her 16th birthday, she sees her father being stabbed to death—by Su-won!

Driven from the palace, Yona and Hak meet a priest named Ik-su who tells Yona that her life will transform the nation and that she must locate the Four Dragon Warriors. And now, after overcoming many obstacles, she and the Four Dragon Warriors are together!

Yona decides to take up arms and defend her nation with the Four Dragon Warriors at her side. They go to the lands of the Fire Tribe, where the people are suffering horribly because their land is barren and they face crushing taxes. In order to protect them from the tax collectors, Yona and her friends masquerade as a group of bandits, calling themselves the Dark Dragon and the Happy Hungry Bunch and claiming the surrounding villages as their territory.

Tae-jun, the second son of the Fire Tribe chief, is tasked with the job of eliminating them. Believing that he had killed Yona in a valley in the northern mountains, Tae-jun had been feeling depressed, but now he is thrilled to be reunited with her. Eventually, he gains a desire to protect his subjects as well. Yona places her trust in Tae-jun to care for the Fire Tribe and sets out on a journey to find a crop that can grow in harsh environments to help people who are suffering from the food shortage.

*The Kingdom of Kohka is a coalition of five tribes: Fire, Water, Wind, Earth and Sky. The throne is held by the tribe with the greatest influence, so the current royal family are of the Sky Tribe. The royal capital is Kuuto. Each tribe's chief also holds the rank of general, and the Meeting of the Five Tribes is the nation's most powerful decision-making body.

Yona of the Dawn

Volume 11

CONTENTS

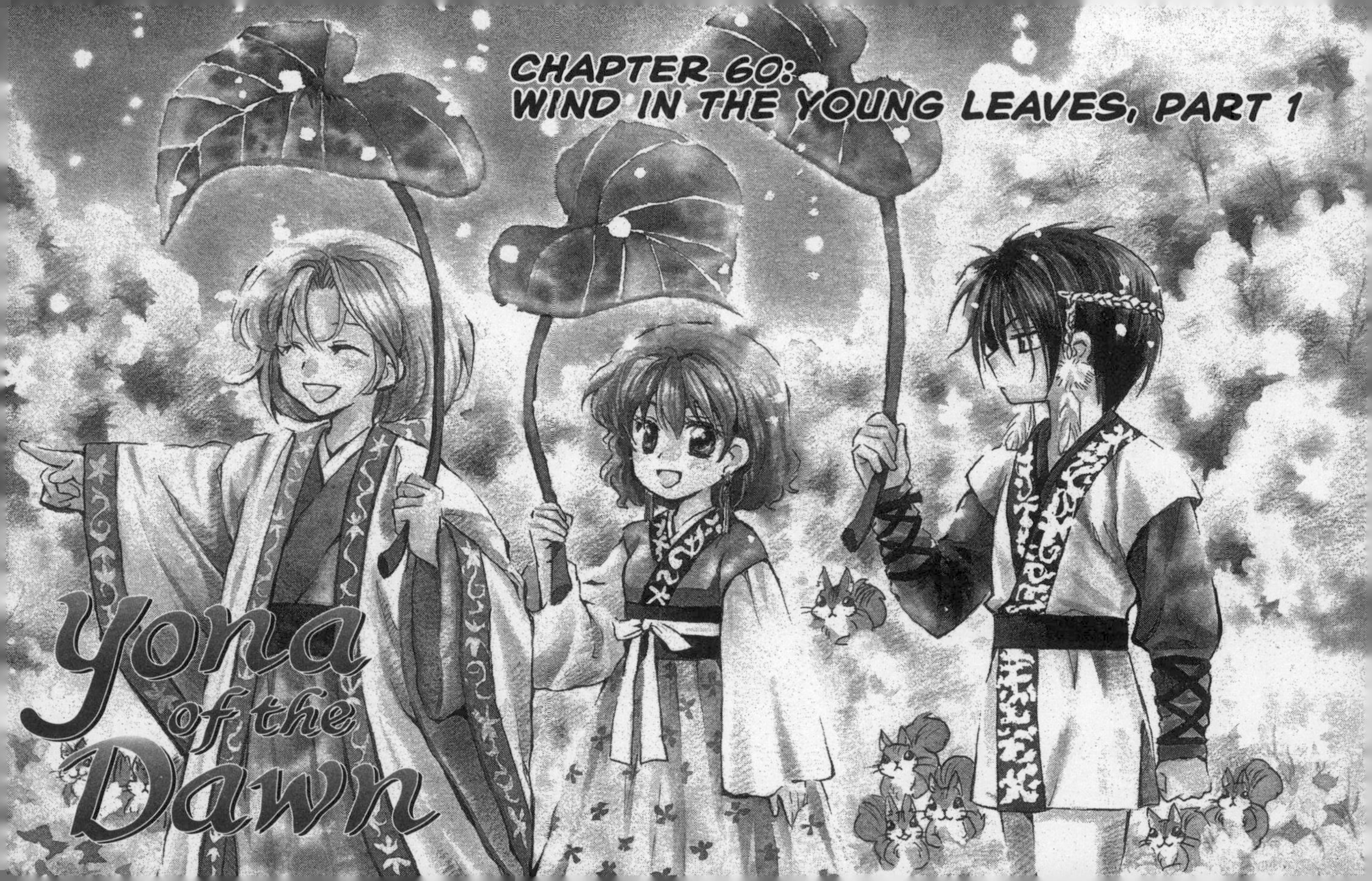
CHAPTER 60:
WIND IN THE YOUNG LEAVES, PART 1
Yona of the Dawn

Yona
of the
Dawn

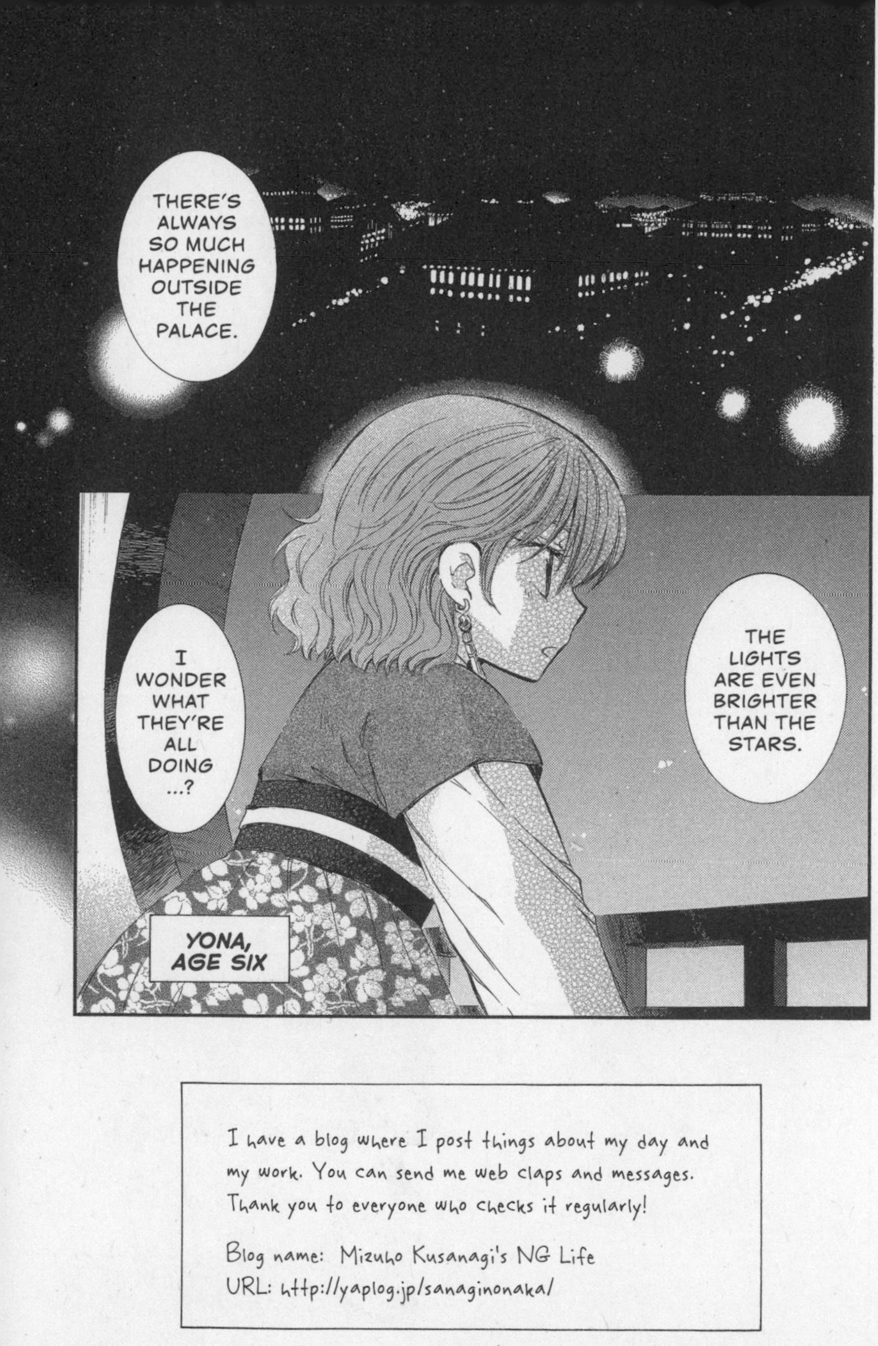
THERE'S ALWAYS SO MUCH HAPPENING OUTSIDE THE PALACE.
THE LIGHTS ARE EVEN BRIGHTER THAN THE STARS.
I WONDER WHAT THEY'RE ALL DOING ...?
YONA, AGE SIX

I have a blog where I post things about my day and my work. You can send me web claps and messages. Thank you to everyone who checks it regularly!

Blog name: Mizuho Kusanagi's NG Life
URL: http://yaplog.jp/sanaginonaka/

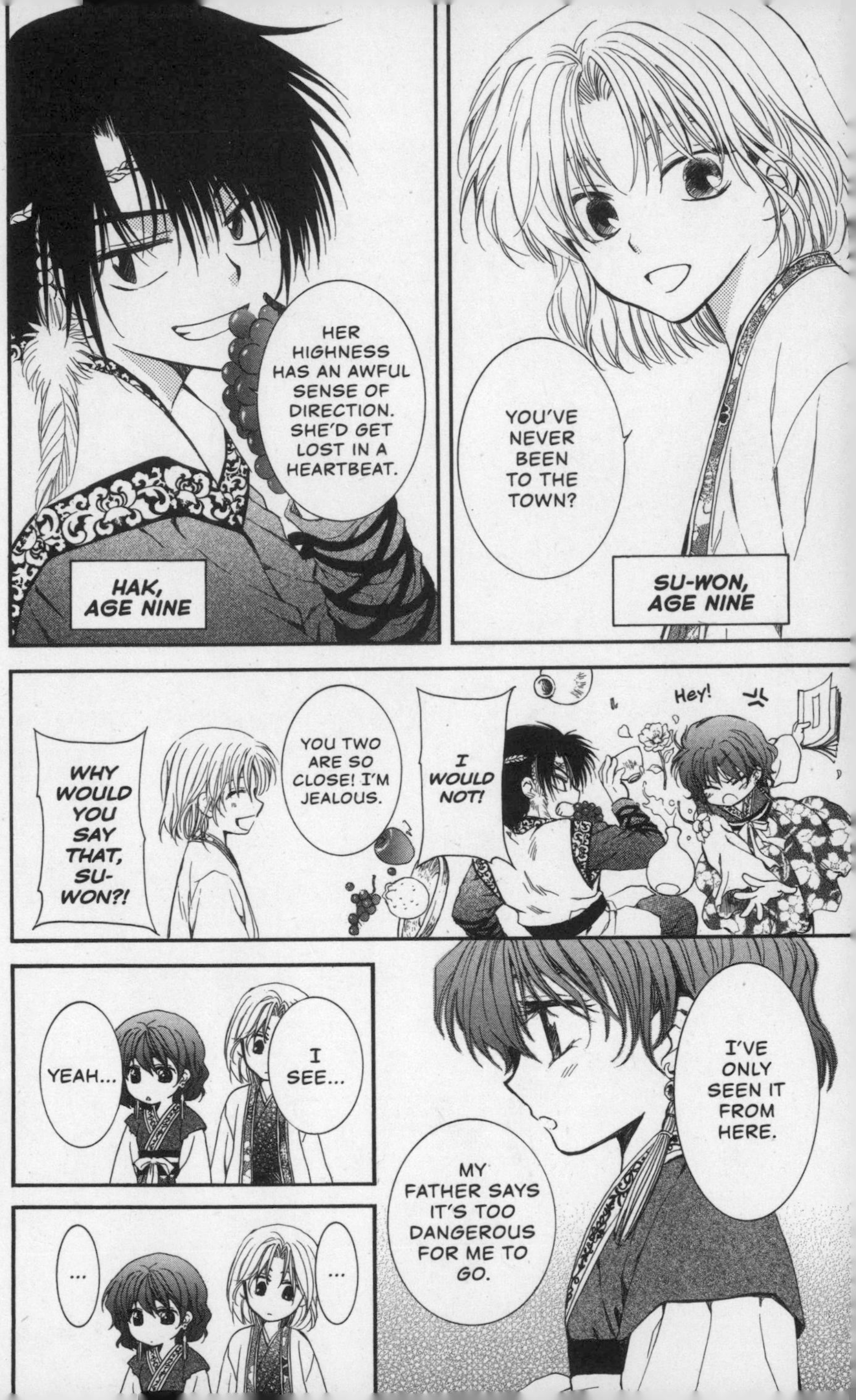
YOU'VE NEVER BEEN TO THE TOWN?
SU-WON, AGE NINE
HER HIGHNESS HAS AN AWFUL SENSE OF DIRECTION. SHE'D GET LOST IN A HEARTBEAT.
HAK, AGE NINE
Hey!
I WOULD NOT!
YOU TWO ARE SO CLOSE! I'M JEALOUS.
WHY WOULD YOU SAY THAT, SU-WON?!
I'VE ONLY SEEN IT FROM HERE.
MY FATHER SAYS IT'S TOO DANGEROUS FOR ME TO GO.
I SEE...
YEAH...
...
...

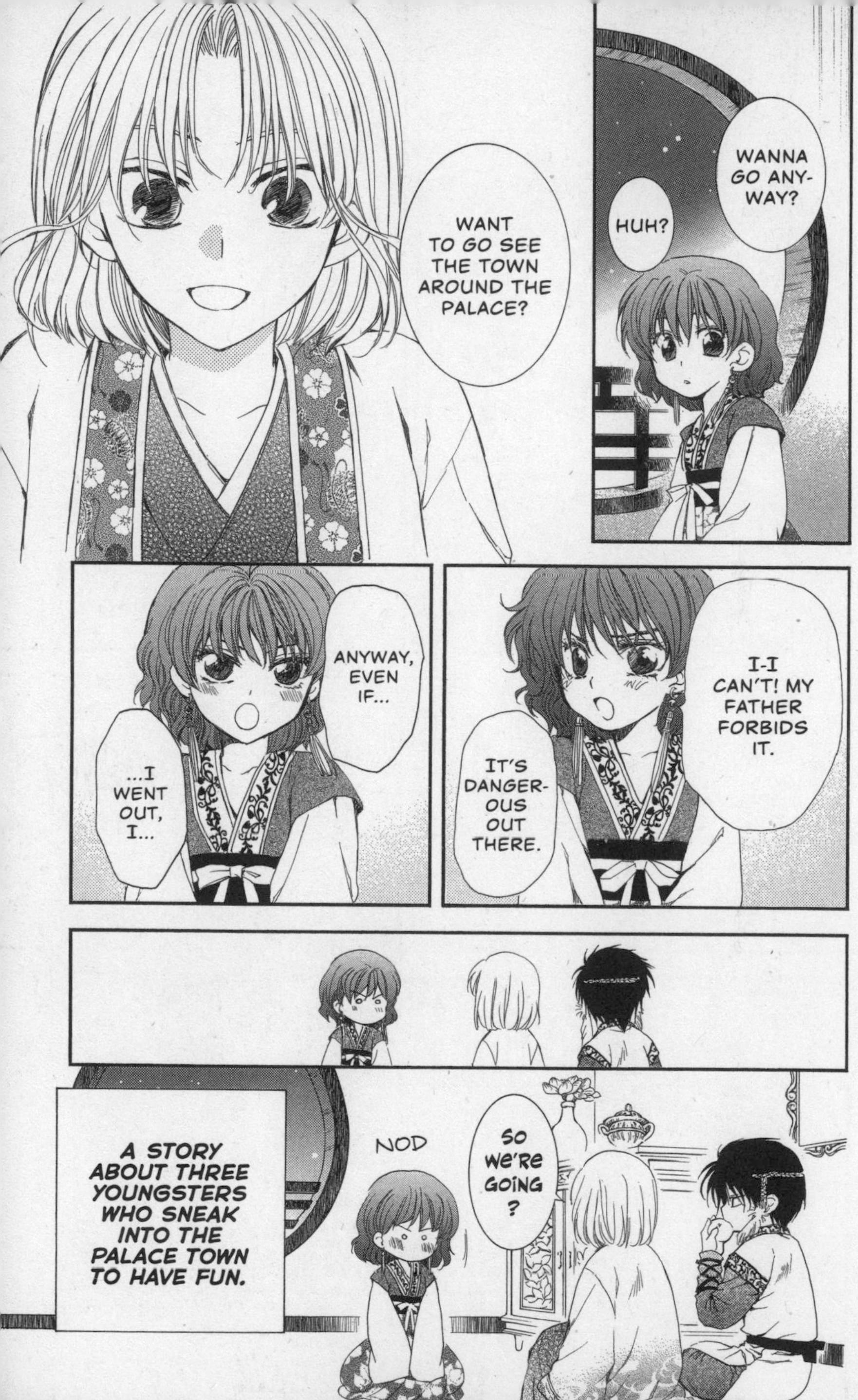
WANNA GO ANY-WAY?
HUH?
WANT TO GO SEE THE TOWN AROUND THE PALACE?
I-I CAN'T! MY FATHER FORBIDS IT.
IT'S DANGER-OUS OUT THERE.
ANYWAY, EVEN IF...
...I WENT OUT, I...
SO WE'RE GOING?
NOD
A STORY ABOUT THREE YOUNGSTERS WHO SNEAK INTO THE PALACE TOWN TO HAVE FUN.

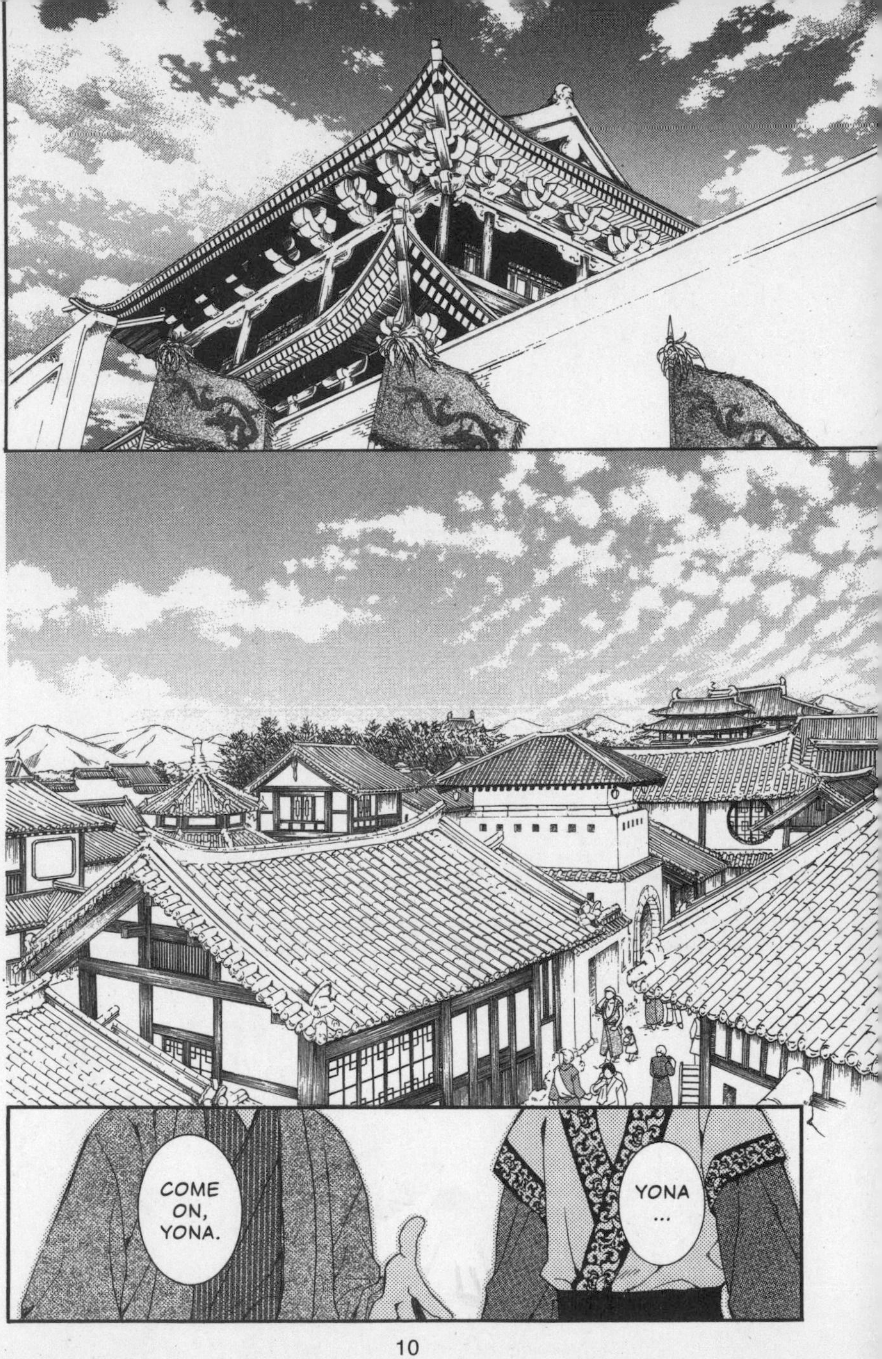
YONA ...
COME ON, YONA.

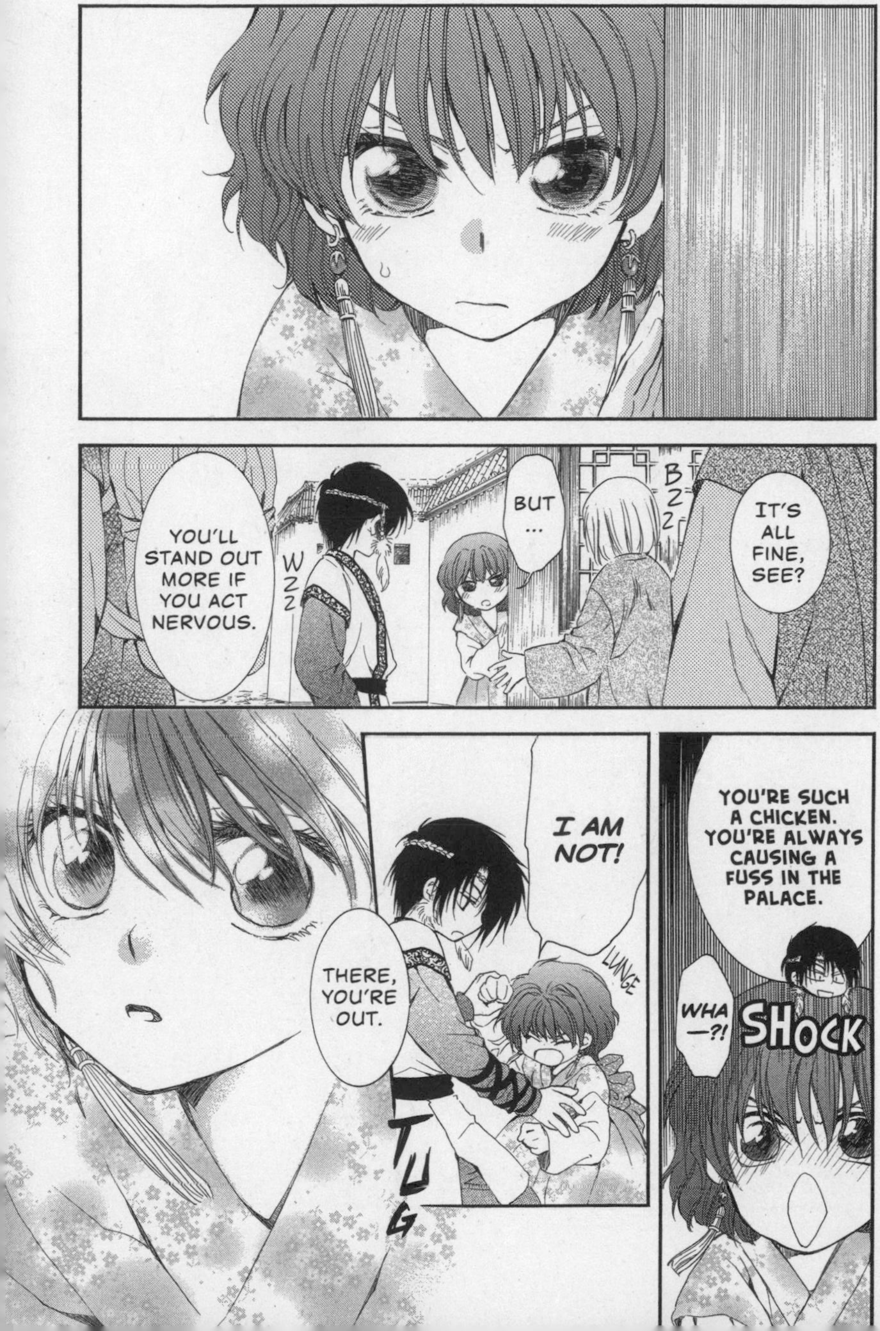
IT'S ALL FINE, SEE?
BZZ
BUT ...
WZZ
YOU'LL STAND OUT MORE IF YOU ACT NERVOUS.
YOU'RE SUCH A CHICKEN. YOU'RE ALWAYS CAUSING A FUSS IN THE PALACE.
SHOCK
WHA—?!
I AM NOT!
LUNGE
THERE, YOU'RE OUT.
TUG

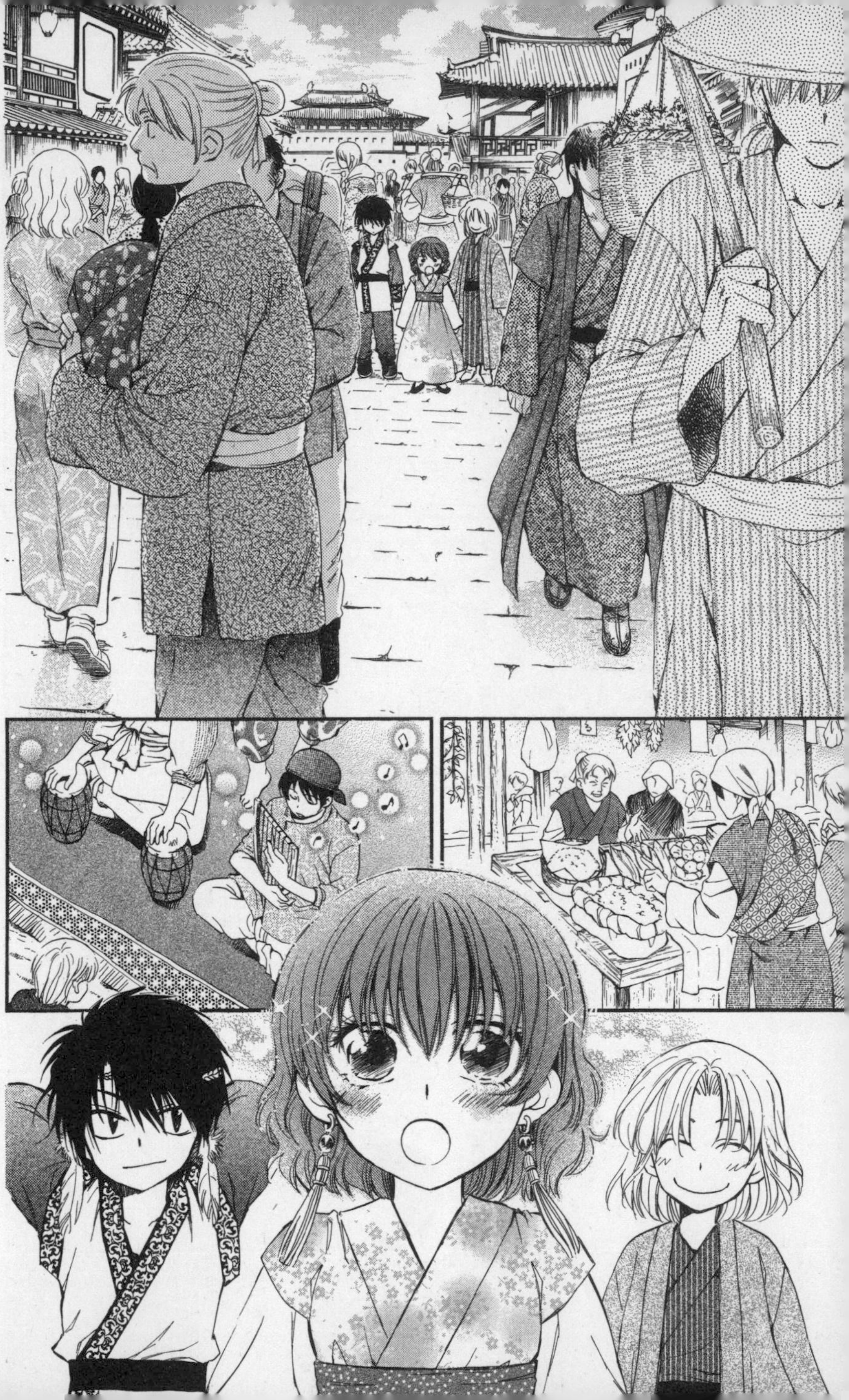

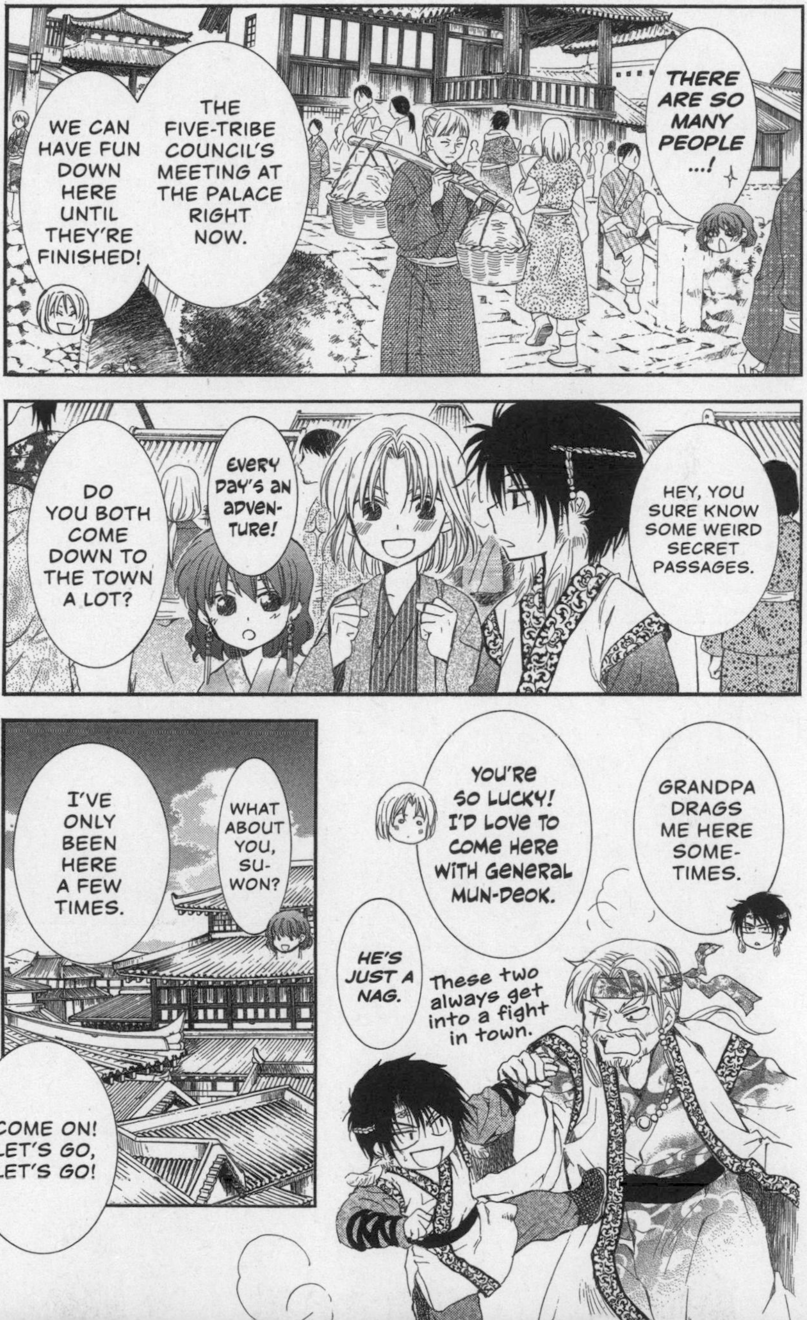
THERE ARE SO MANY PEOPLE ...!
THE FIVE-TRIBE COUNCIL'S MEETING AT THE PALACE RIGHT NOW.
WE CAN HAVE FUN DOWN HERE UNTIL THEY'RE FINISHED!
HEY, YOU SURE KNOW SOME WEIRD SECRET PASSAGES.
EVERY DAY'S AN ADVENTURE!
DO YOU BOTH COME DOWN TO THE TOWN A LOT?
GRANDPA DRAGS ME HERE SOME-TIMES.
YOU'RE SO LUCKY! I'D LOVE TO COME HERE WITH GENERAL MUN-DEOK.
HE'S JUST A NAG.
These two always get into a fight in town.
WHAT ABOUT YOU, SU-WON?
I'VE ONLY BEEN HERE A FEW TIMES.
COME ON! LET'S GO, LET'S GO!

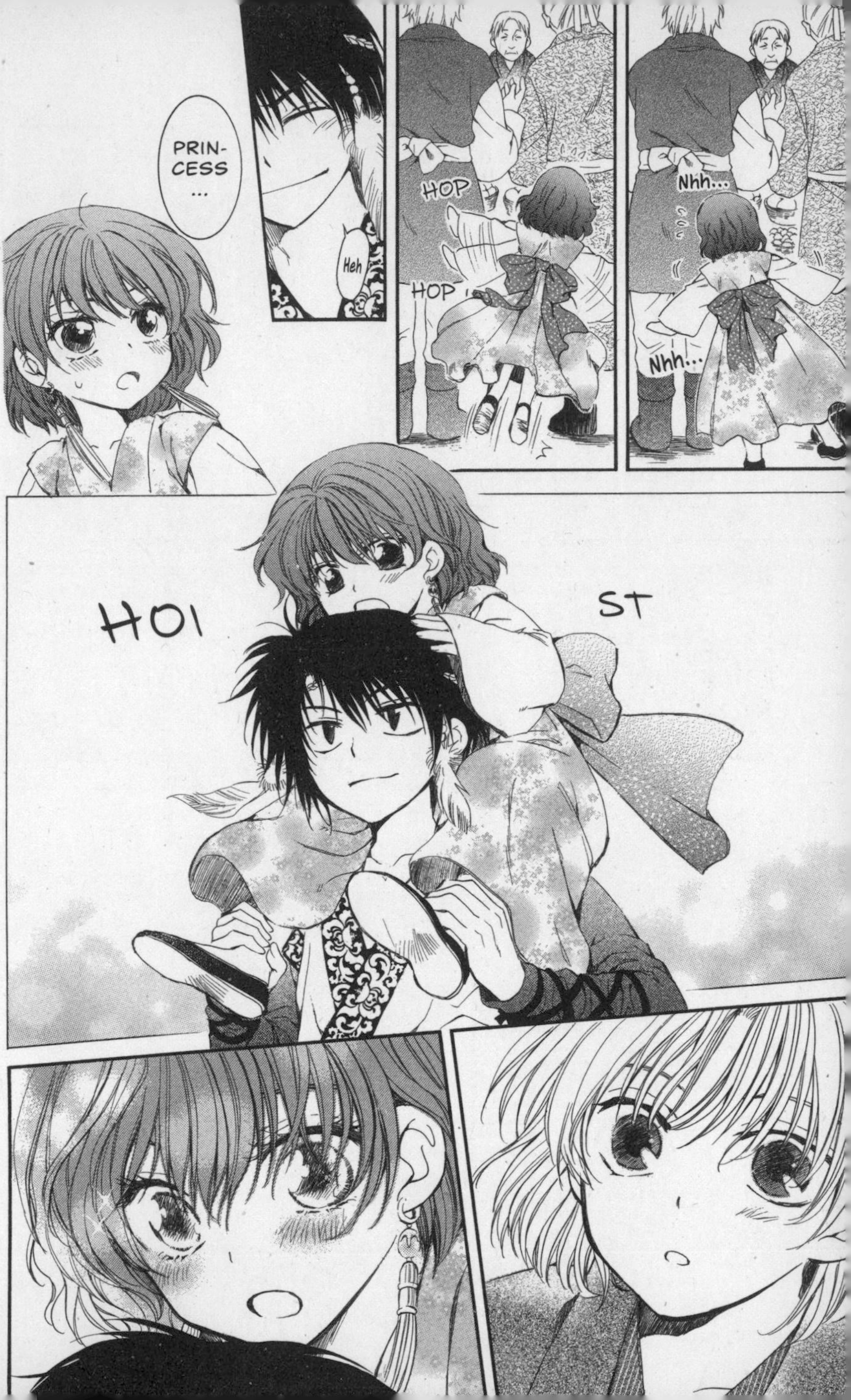
Nhh...
Nhh...
HOP
HOP
Heh
PRIN-CESS...
HOIST

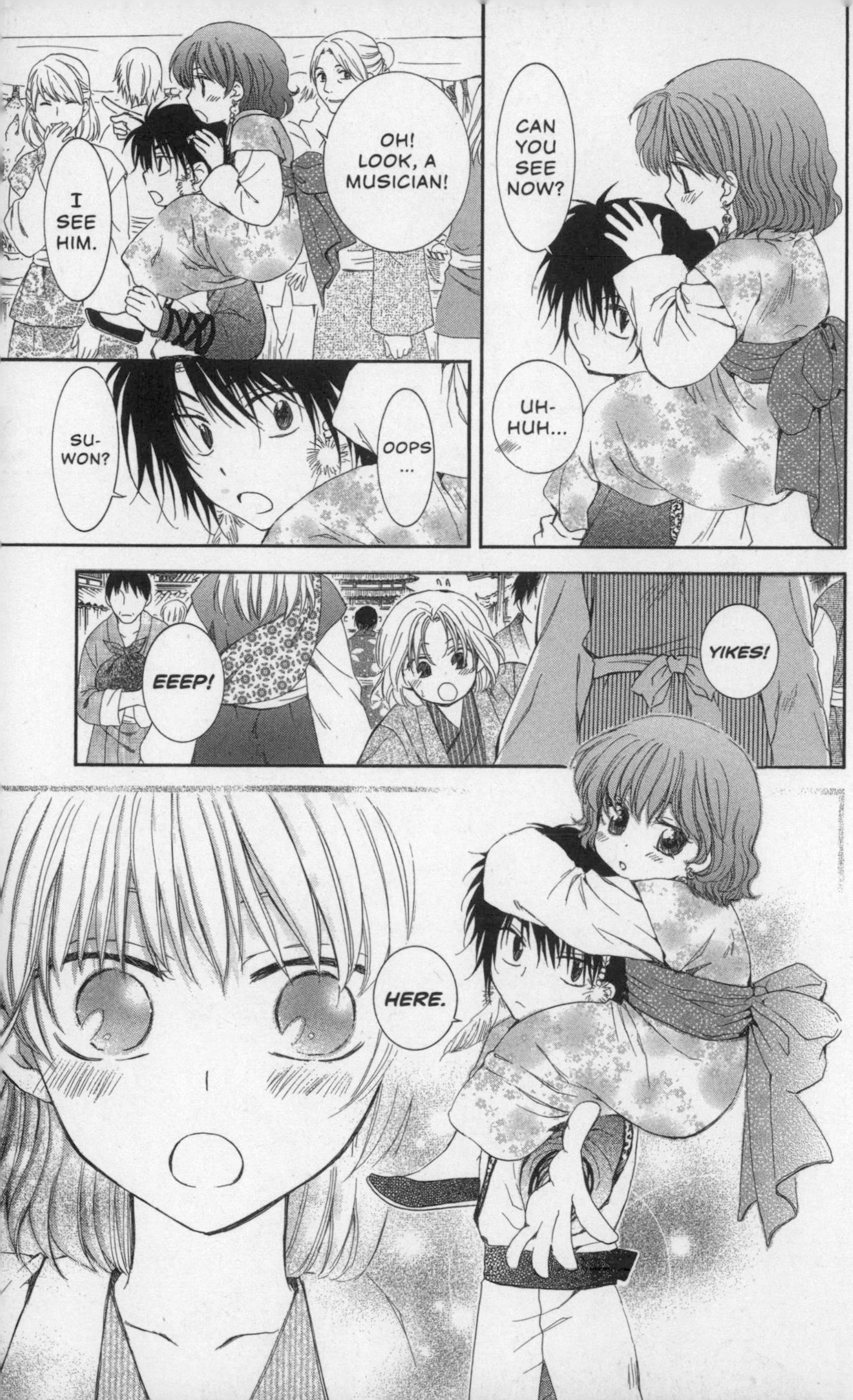

CAN YOU SEE NOW?
UH-HUH...
OH! LOOK, A MUSICIAN!
I SEE HIM.
OOPS...
SU-WON?
YIKES!
EEEP!
HERE.

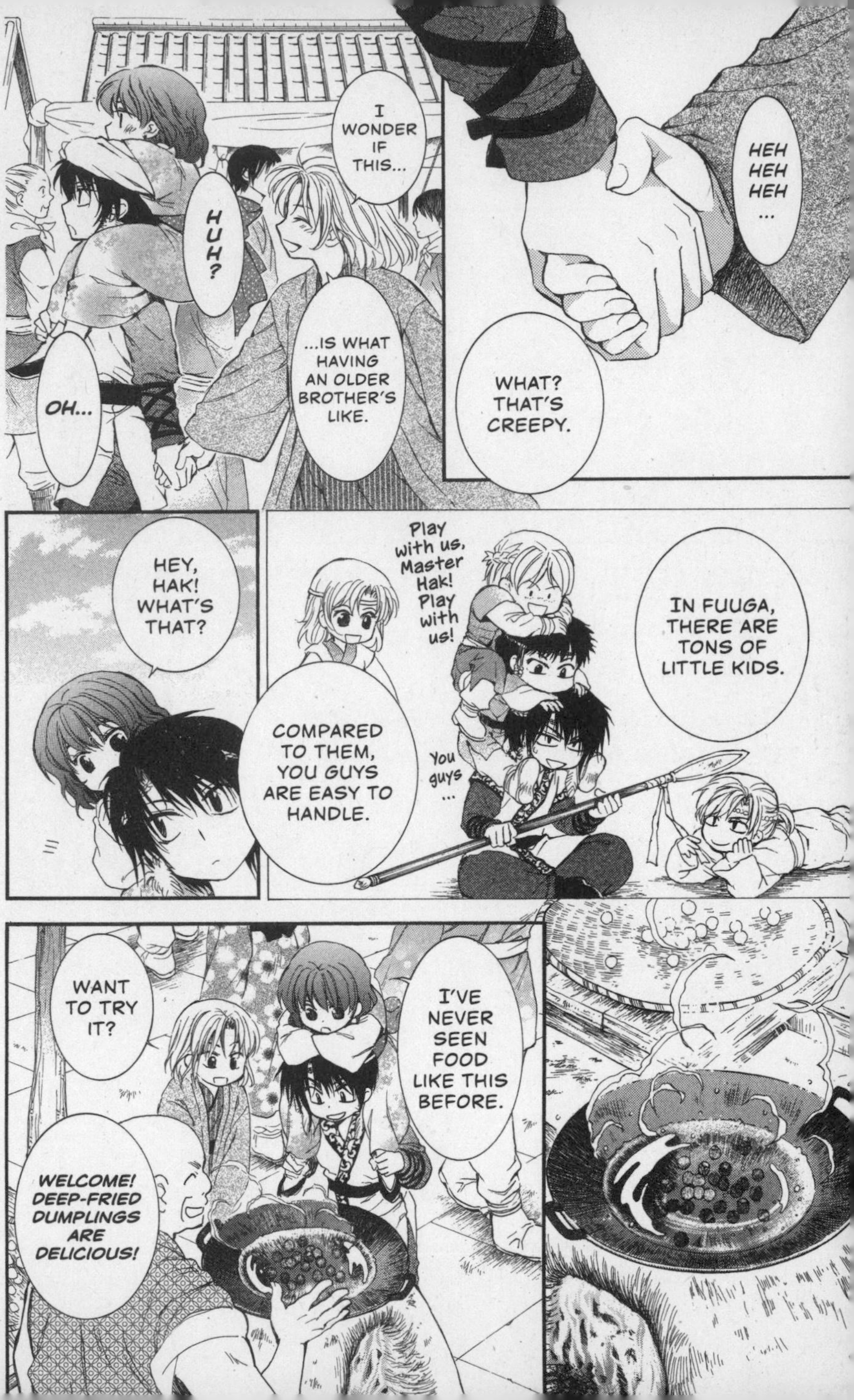
HEH HEH HEH ...
WHAT? THAT'S CREEPY.
I WONDER IF THIS...
HUH?
...IS WHAT HAVING AN OLDER BROTHER'S LIKE.
OH...
IN FUUGA, THERE ARE TONS OF LITTLE KIDS.
Play with us, Master Hak! Play with us!
You guys ...
COMPARED TO THEM, YOU GUYS ARE EASY TO HANDLE.
HEY, HAK! WHAT'S THAT?
I'VE NEVER SEEN FOOD LIKE THIS BEFORE.
WANT TO TRY IT?
WELCOME! DEEP-FRIED DUMPLINGS ARE DELICIOUS!

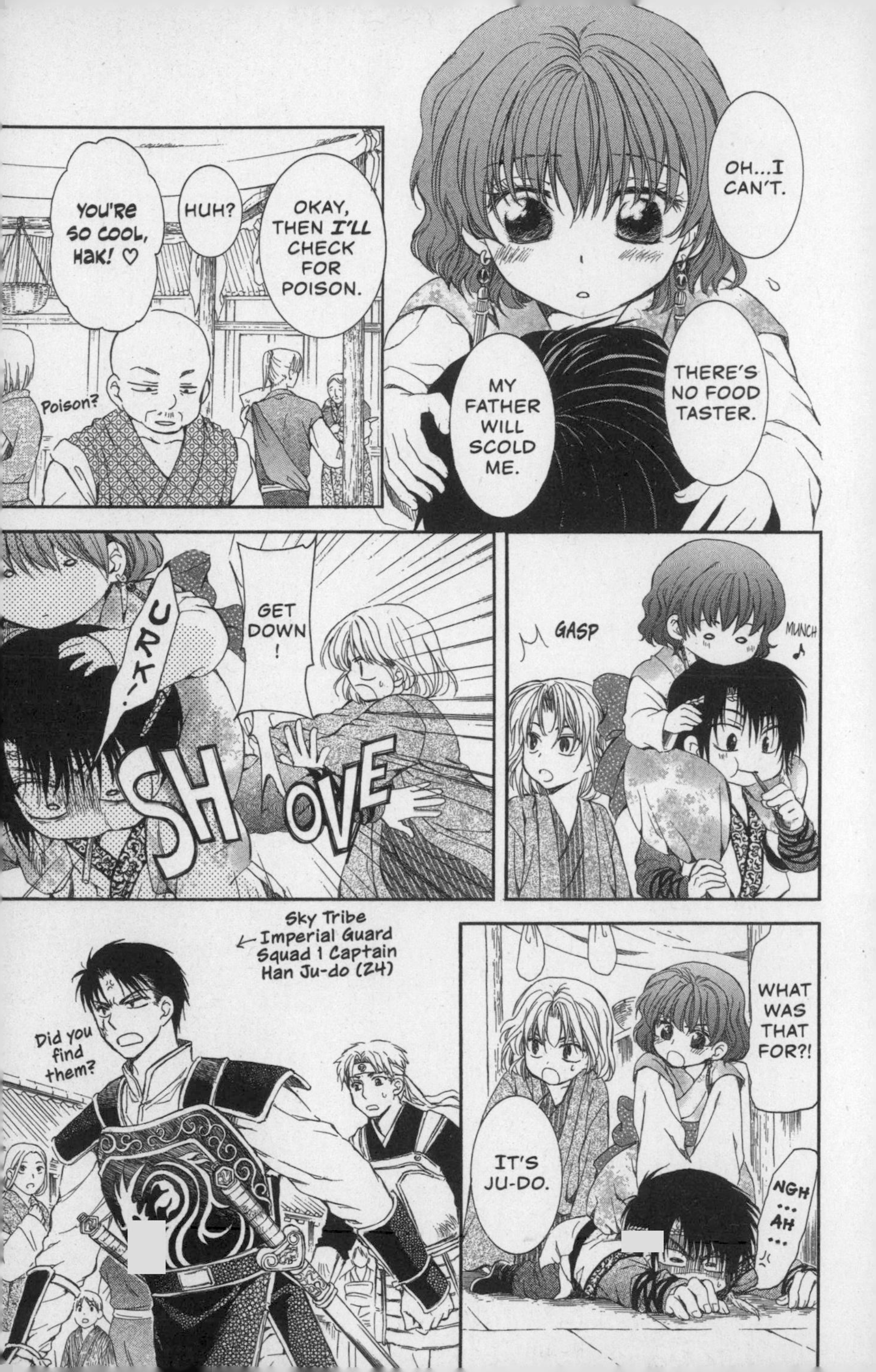
OH...I CAN'T.
THERE'S NO FOOD TASTER.
MY FATHER WILL SCOLD ME.
OKAY, THEN I'LL CHECK FOR POISON.
HUH?
YOU'RE SO COOL, HAK! ♡
Poison?
MUNCH ♪
GASP
GET DOWN!
URK!
SHOVE
WHAT WAS THAT FOR?!
IT'S JU-DO.
NGH... AH...
Sky Tribe Imperial Guard Squad 1 Captain Han Ju-do (24)
Did you find them?

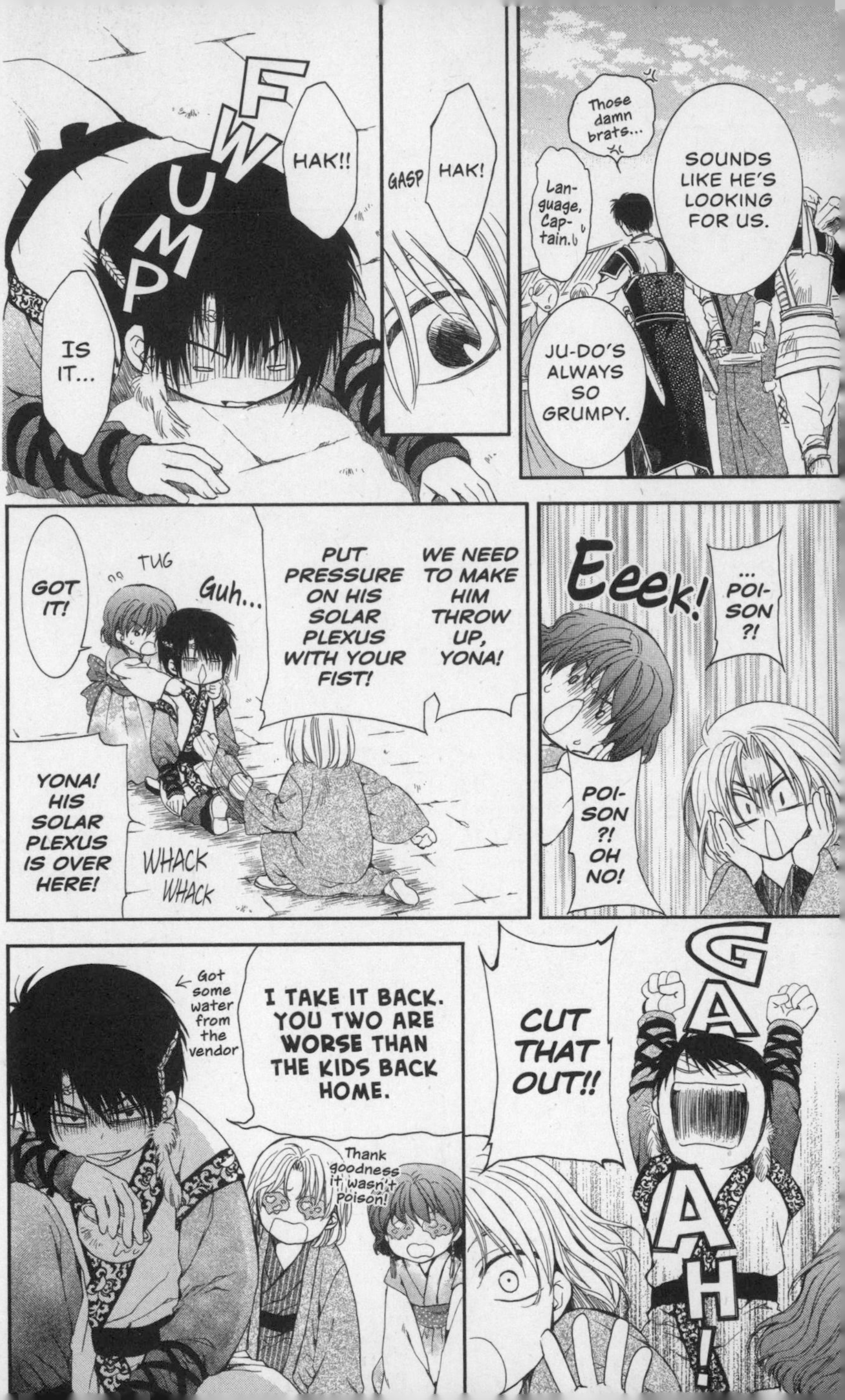
Those damn brats...
SOUNDS LIKE HE'S LOOKING FOR US.
Language, Captain.
JU-DO'S ALWAYS SO GRUMPY.
GASP
HAK!
HAK!!
FWUMP
IS IT...
Eeek!
...POISON?!
POISON?! OH NO!
WE NEED TO MAKE HIM THROW UP, YONA!
PUT PRESSURE ON HIS SOLAR PLEXUS WITH YOUR FIST!
GOT IT!
TUG
Guh...
YONA! HIS SOLAR PLEXUS IS OVER HERE!
WHACK WHACK
GAAH!
CUT THAT OUT!!
I TAKE IT BACK. YOU TWO ARE WORSE THAN THE KIDS BACK HOME.
Got some water from the vendor
Thank goodness it wasn't poison!

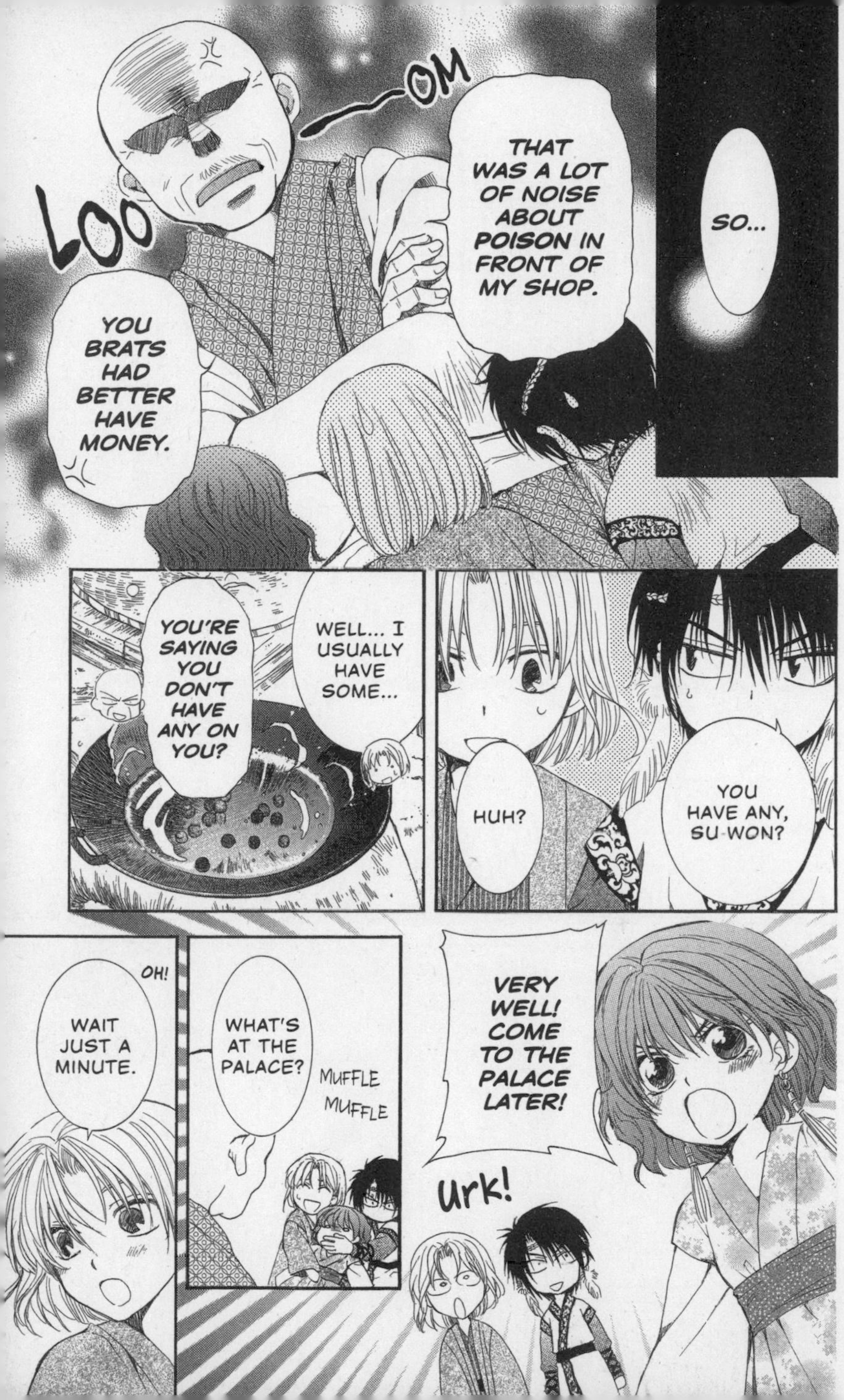
SO...
THAT WAS A LOT OF NOISE ABOUT POISON IN FRONT OF MY SHOP.
LOO—OM
YOU BRATS HAD BETTER HAVE MONEY.
YOU HAVE ANY, SU-WON?
HUH?
WELL... I USUALLY HAVE SOME...
YOU'RE SAYING YOU DON'T HAVE ANY ON YOU?
VERY WELL! COME TO THE PALACE LATER!
Urk!
WHAT'S AT THE PALACE?
MUFFLE MUFFLE
OH!
WAIT JUST A MINUTE.

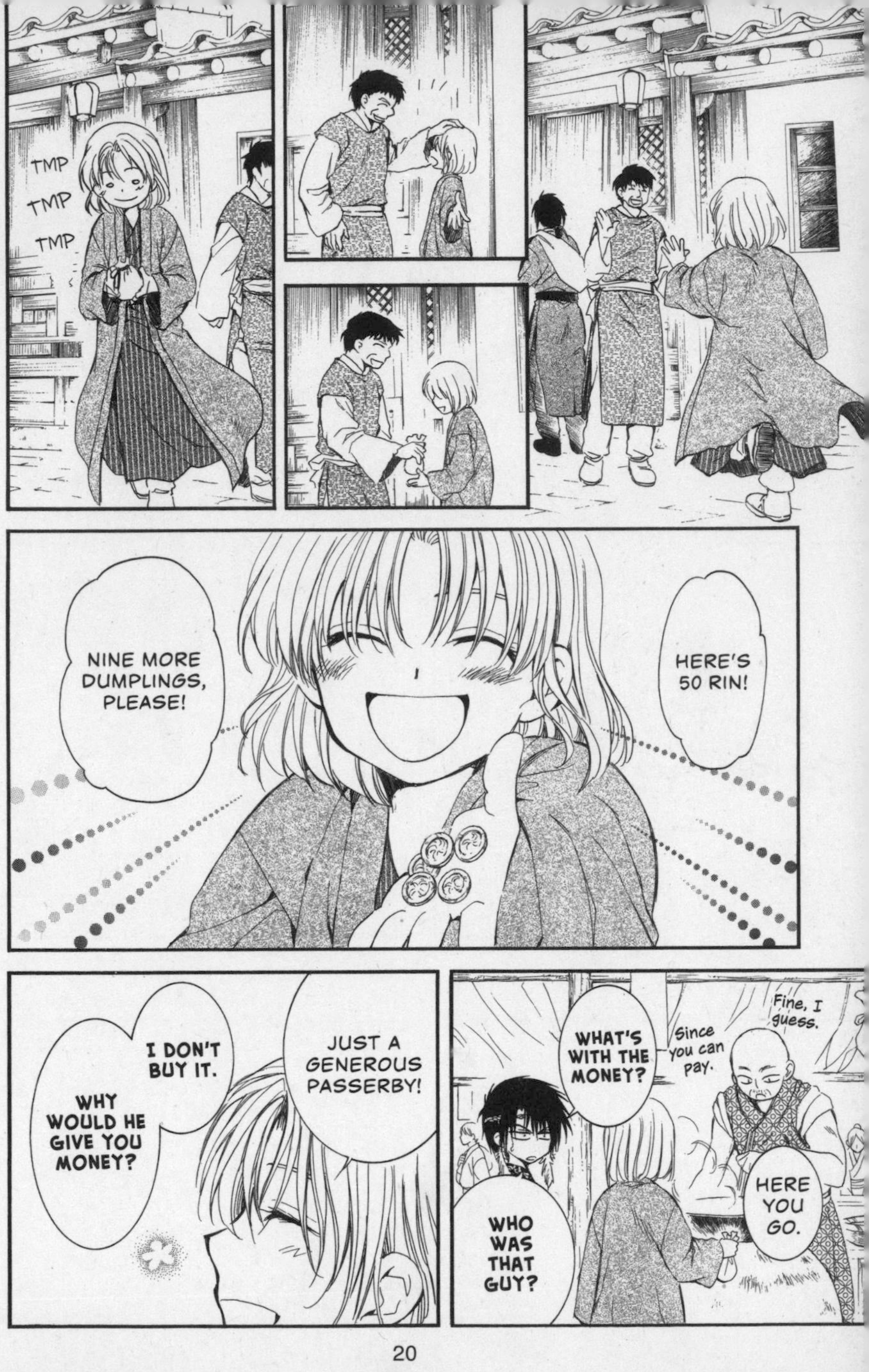
TMP
TMP
TMP
HERE'S 50 RIN!
NINE MORE DUMPLINGS, PLEASE!
Fine, I guess.
Since you can pay.
WHAT'S WITH THE MONEY?
HERE YOU GO.
WHO WAS THAT GUY?
JUST A GENEROUS PASSERBY!
I DON'T BUY IT.
WHY WOULD HE GIVE YOU MONEY?

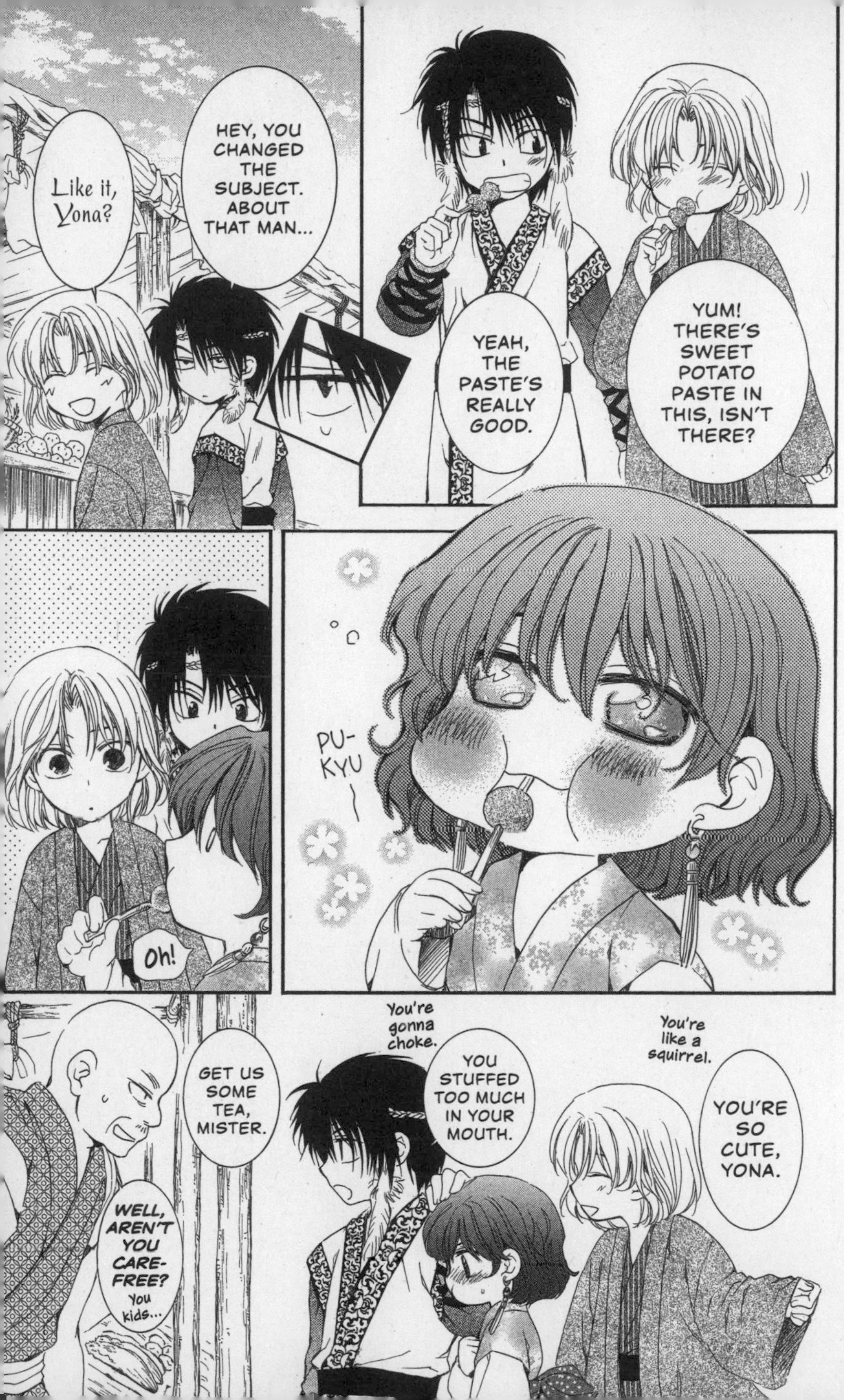
YUM! THERE'S SWEET POTATO PASTE IN THIS, ISN'T THERE?
YEAH, THE PASTE'S REALLY GOOD.
HEY, YOU CHANGED THE SUBJECT. ABOUT THAT MAN...
Like it, Yona?
PU-KYU
Oh!
YOU'RE SO CUTE, YONA.
You're like a squirrel.
YOU STUFFED TOO MUCH IN YOUR MOUTH.
You're gonna choke.
GET US SOME TEA, MISTER.
WELL, AREN'T YOU CAREFREE?
You kids...

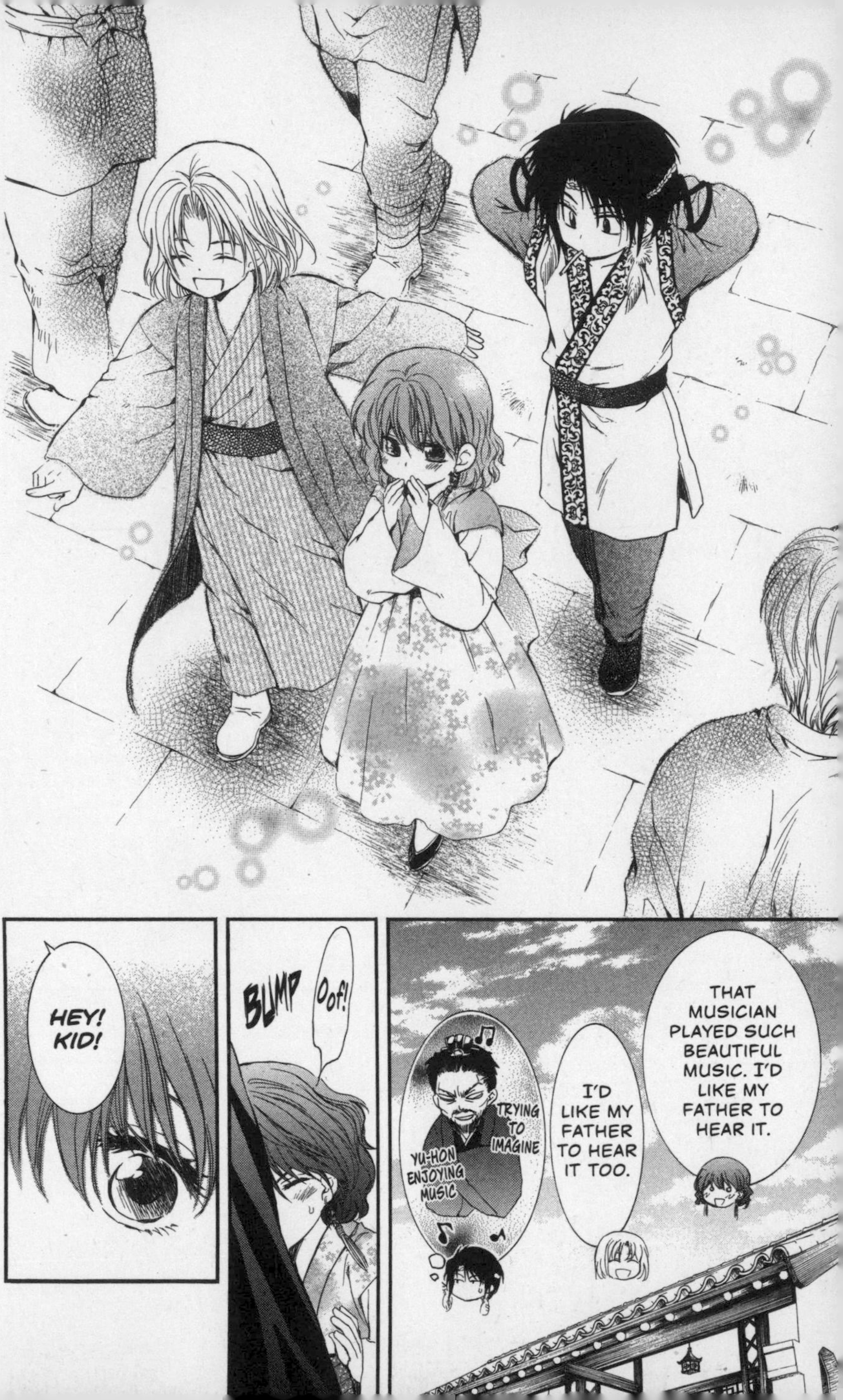
THAT MUSICIAN PLAYED SUCH BEAUTIFUL MUSIC. I'D LIKE MY FATHER TO HEAR IT.
I'D LIKE MY FATHER TO HEAR IT TOO.
TRYING TO IMAGINE YU-HON ENJOYING MUSIC
Oof!
BUMP
HEY! KID!

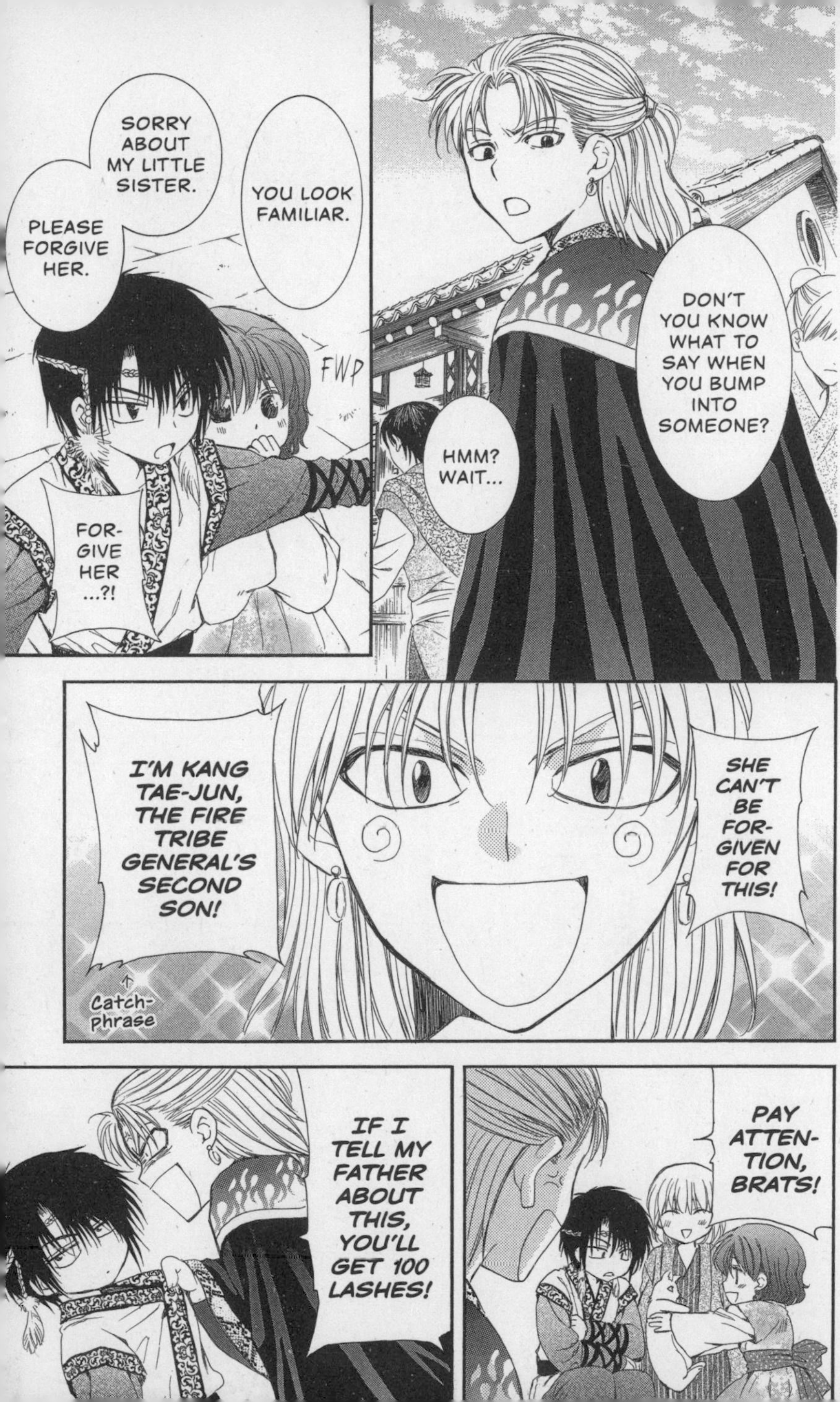
DON'T YOU KNOW WHAT TO SAY WHEN YOU BUMP INTO SOMEONE?
HMM? WAIT...
YOU LOOK FAMILIAR.
SORRY ABOUT MY LITTLE SISTER.
PLEASE FORGIVE HER.
FWP
FOR-GIVE HER ...?!
SHE CAN'T BE FOR-GIVEN FOR THIS!
I'M KANG TAE-JUN, THE FIRE TRIBE GENERAL'S SECOND SON!
Catch-Phrase
PAY ATTEN-TION, BRATS!
IF I TELL MY FATHER ABOUT THIS, YOU'LL GET 100 LASHES!

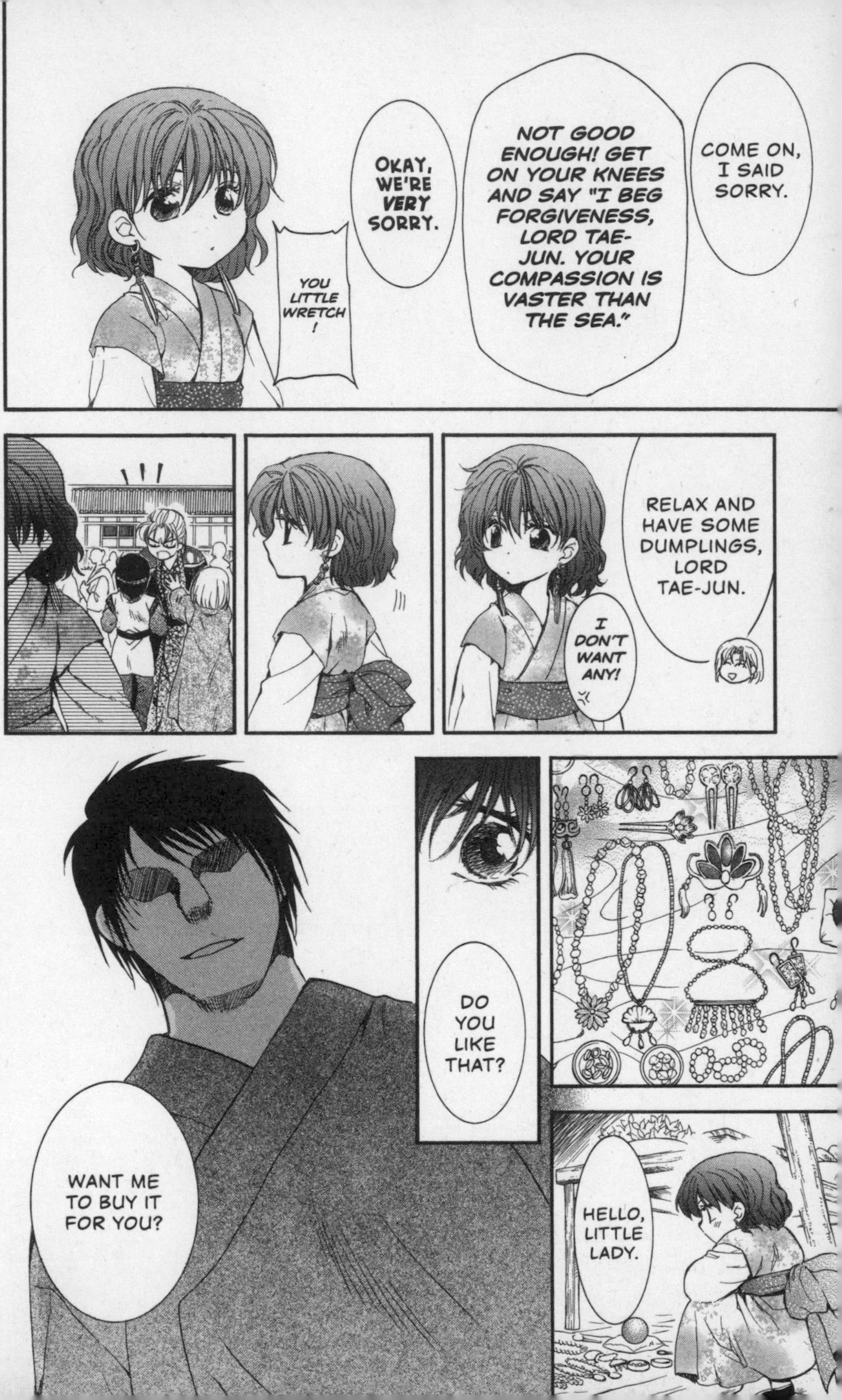
COME ON, I SAID SORRY.
NOT GOOD ENOUGH! GET ON YOUR KNEES AND SAY "I BEG FORGIVENESS, LORD TAE-JUN. YOUR COMPASSION IS VASTER THAN THE SEA."
OKAY, WE'RE VERY SORRY.
YOU LITTLE WRETCH!
RELAX AND HAVE SOME DUMPLINGS, LORD TAE-JUN.
I DON'T WANT ANY!
HELLO, LITTLE LADY.
DO YOU LIKE THAT?
WANT ME TO BUY IT FOR YOU?

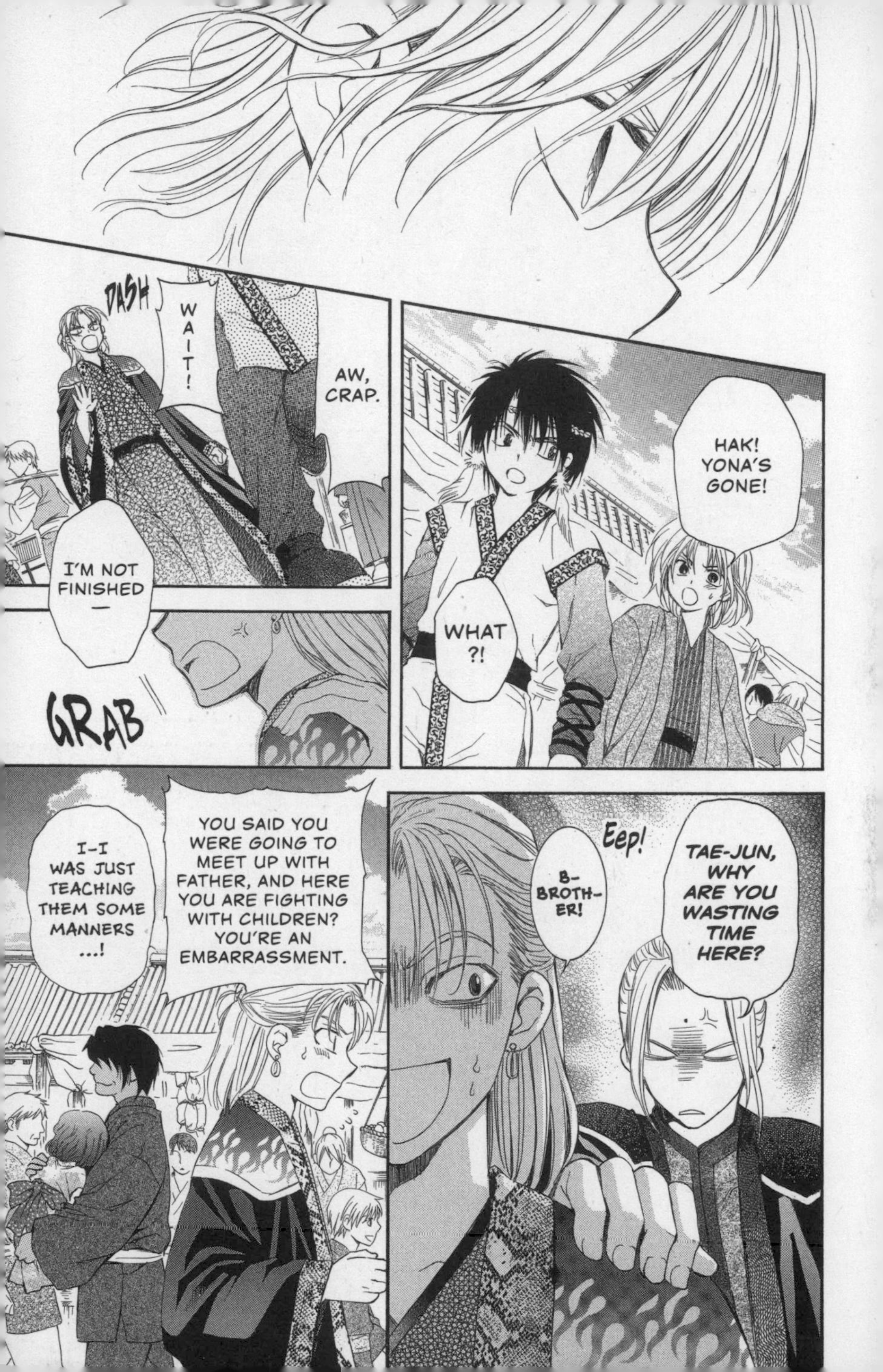
HAK! YONA'S GONE!
WHAT?!
AW, CRAP.
DASH
WAIT!
I'M NOT FINISHED—
GRAB
TAE-JUN, WHY ARE YOU WASTING TIME HERE?
Eep!
B-BROTHER!
YOU SAID YOU WERE GOING TO MEET UP WITH FATHER, AND HERE YOU ARE FIGHTING WITH CHILDREN? YOU'RE AN EMBARRASSMENT.
I-I WAS JUST TEACHING THEM SOME MANNERS ...!

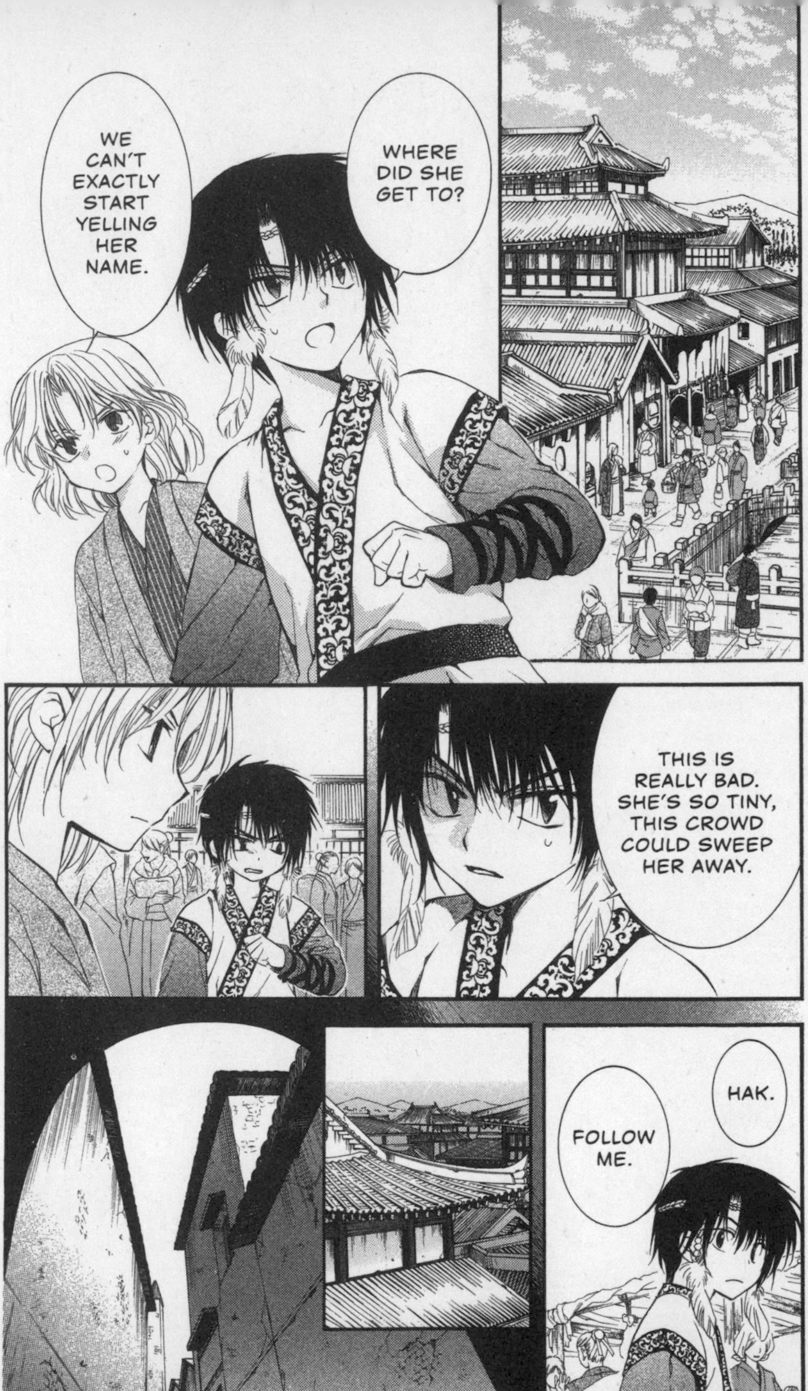
WHERE DID SHE GET TO?
WE CAN'T EXACTLY START YELLING HER NAME.
THIS IS REALLY BAD. SHE'S SO TINY, THIS CROWD COULD SWEEP HER AWAY.
HAK.
FOLLOW ME.

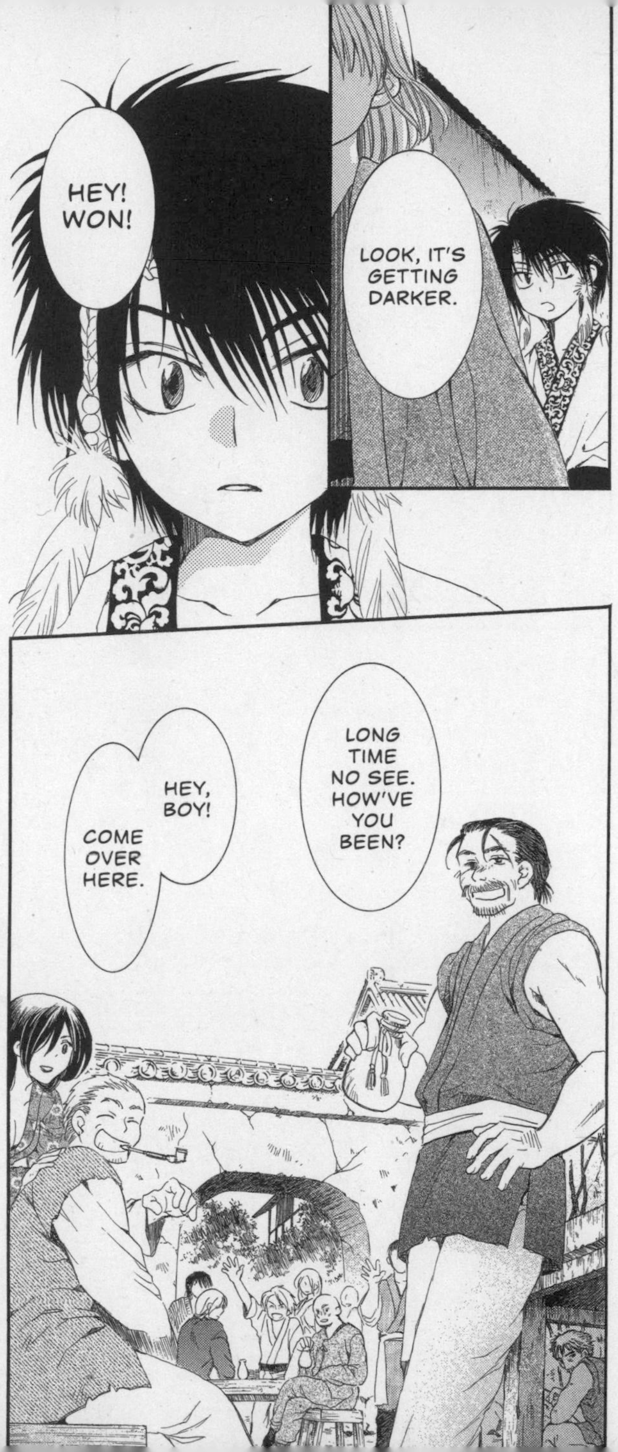
LOOK, IT'S GETTING DARKER.
HEY! WON!
LONG TIME NO SEE. HOW'VE YOU BEEN?
HEY, BOY! COME OVER HERE.

Hello! I'm Mizuho Kusanagi, and this is volume 11 of Yona. We're already 11 books in! I don't know how long I'll be able to tell this story, but I'll always do my best. Thank you so much to all of you who've been buying *Hana to Yume* too!

Sometimes I'm asked to illustrate covers or bonus fun things for *Hana to Yume*, like art postcards. If things like that interest you, please check it out.

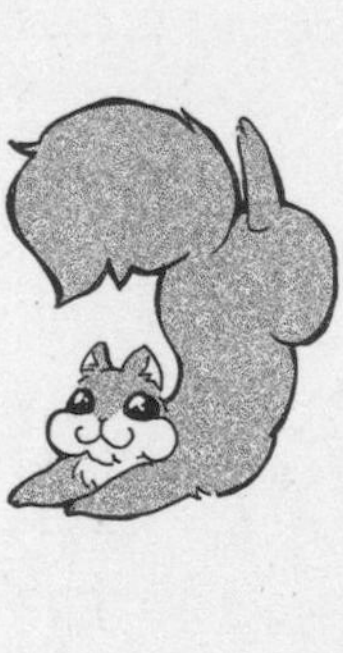

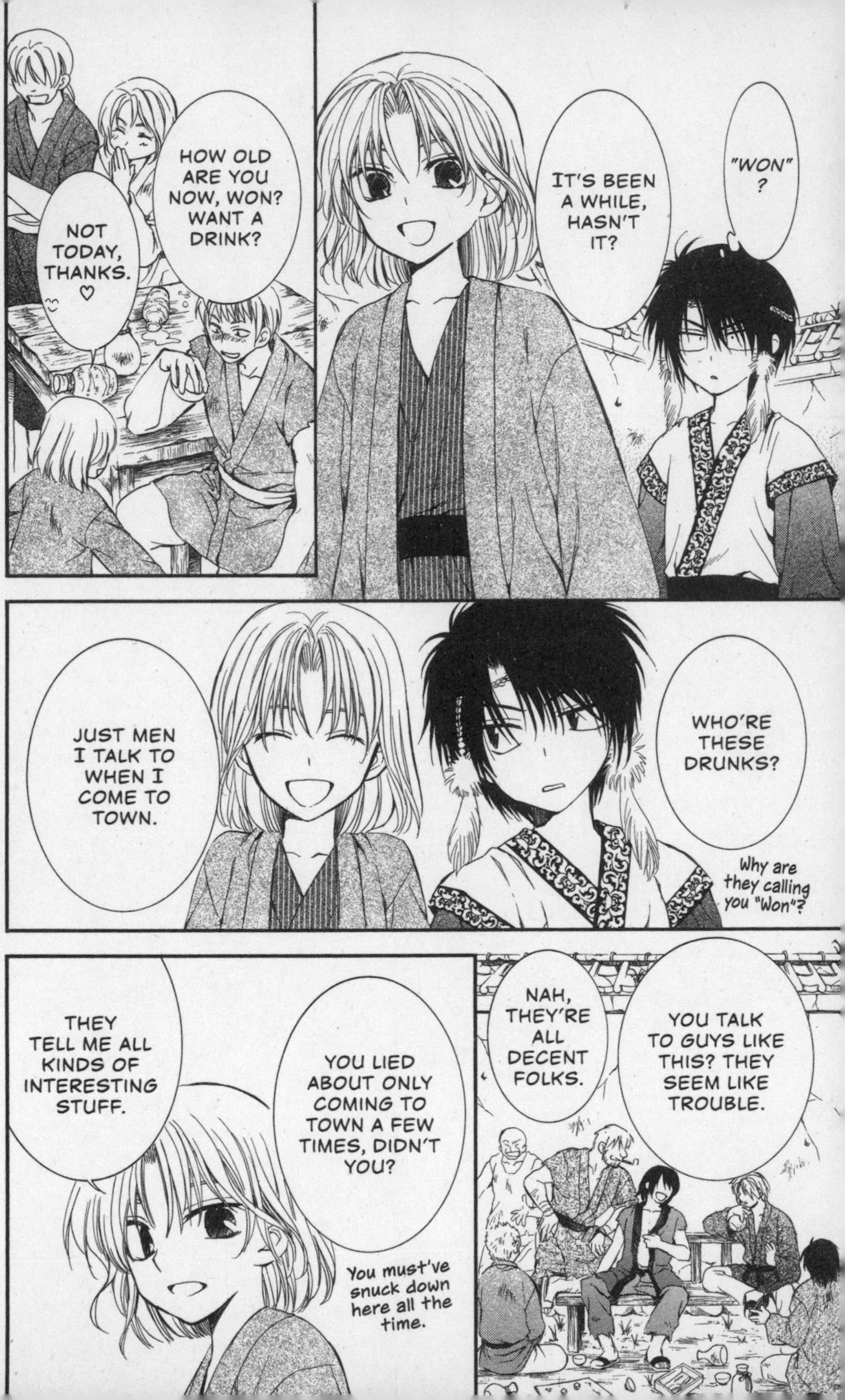
"WON"?
IT'S BEEN A WHILE, HASN'T IT?
HOW OLD ARE YOU NOW, WON? WANT A DRINK?
NOT TODAY, THANKS. ♡
WHO'RE THESE DRUNKS?
Why are they calling you "Won"?
JUST MEN I TALK TO WHEN I COME TO TOWN.
YOU TALK TO GUYS LIKE THIS? THEY SEEM LIKE TROUBLE.
NAH, THEY'RE ALL DECENT FOLKS.
YOU LIED ABOUT ONLY COMING TO TOWN A FEW TIMES, DIDN'T YOU?
THEY TELL ME ALL KINDS OF INTERESTING STUFF.
You must've snuck down here all the time.

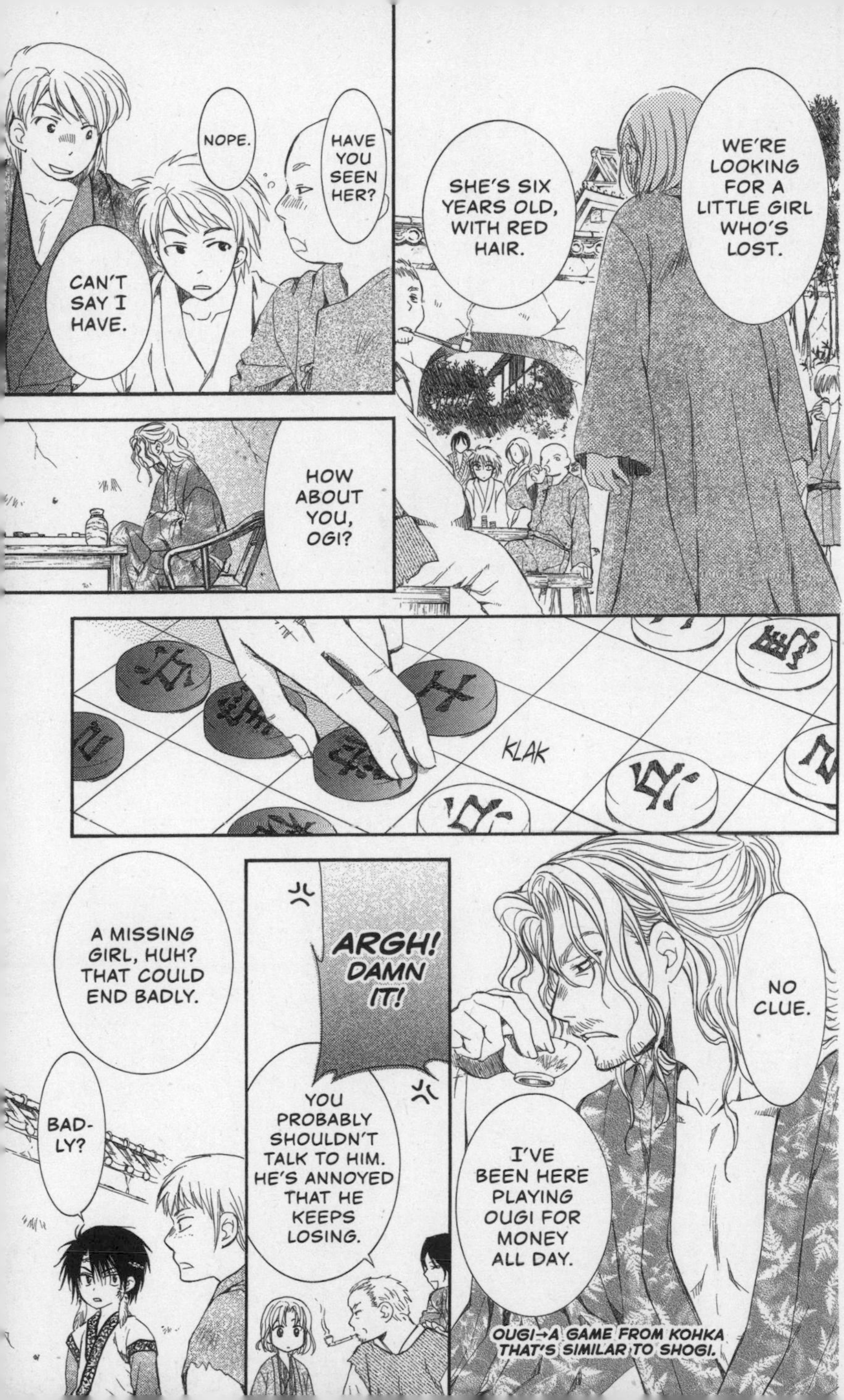
WE'RE LOOKING FOR A LITTLE GIRL WHO'S LOST.
SHE'S SIX YEARS OLD, WITH RED HAIR.
HAVE YOU SEEN HER?
NOPE.
CAN'T SAY I HAVE.
HOW ABOUT YOU, OGI?
KLAK
NO CLUE.
I'VE BEEN HERE PLAYING OUGI FOR MONEY ALL DAY.
OUGI→A GAME FROM KOHKA THAT'S SIMILAR TO SHOGI.
ARGH! DAMN IT!
YOU PROBABLY SHOULDN'T TALK TO HIM. HE'S ANNOYED THAT HE KEEPS LOSING.
A MISSING GIRL, HUH? THAT COULD END BADLY.
BADLY?

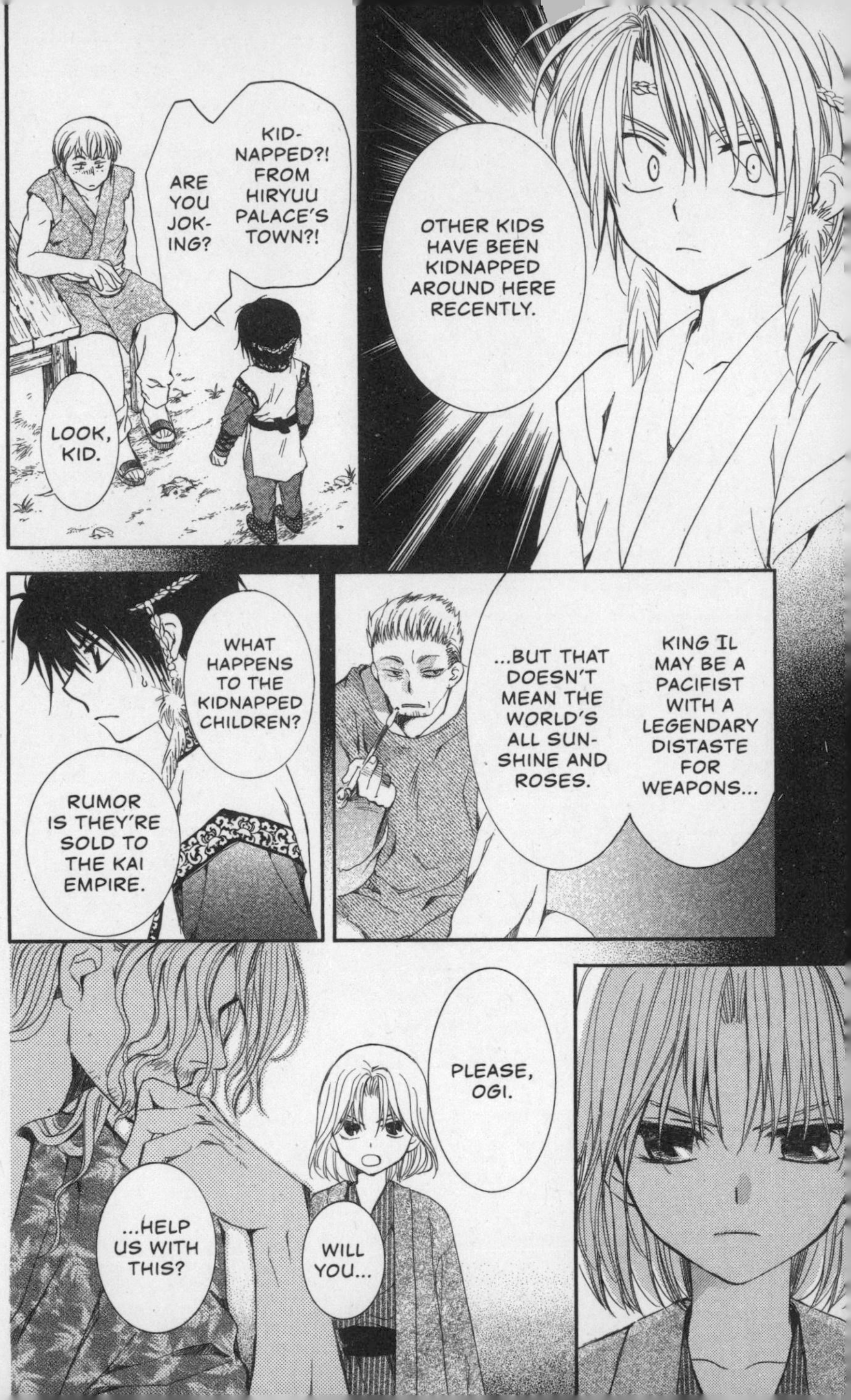
OTHER KIDS HAVE BEEN KIDNAPPED AROUND HERE RECENTLY.
KID-NAPPED?! FROM HIRYUU PALACE'S TOWN?!
ARE YOU JOK-ING?
LOOK, KID.
KING IL MAY BE A PACIFIST WITH A LEGENDARY DISTASTE FOR WEAPONS...
...BUT THAT DOESN'T MEAN THE WORLD'S ALL SUN-SHINE AND ROSES.
WHAT HAPPENS TO THE KIDNAPPED CHILDREN?
RUMOR IS THEY'RE SOLD TO THE KAI EMPIRE.
PLEASE, OGI.
WILL YOU...
...HELP US WITH THIS?

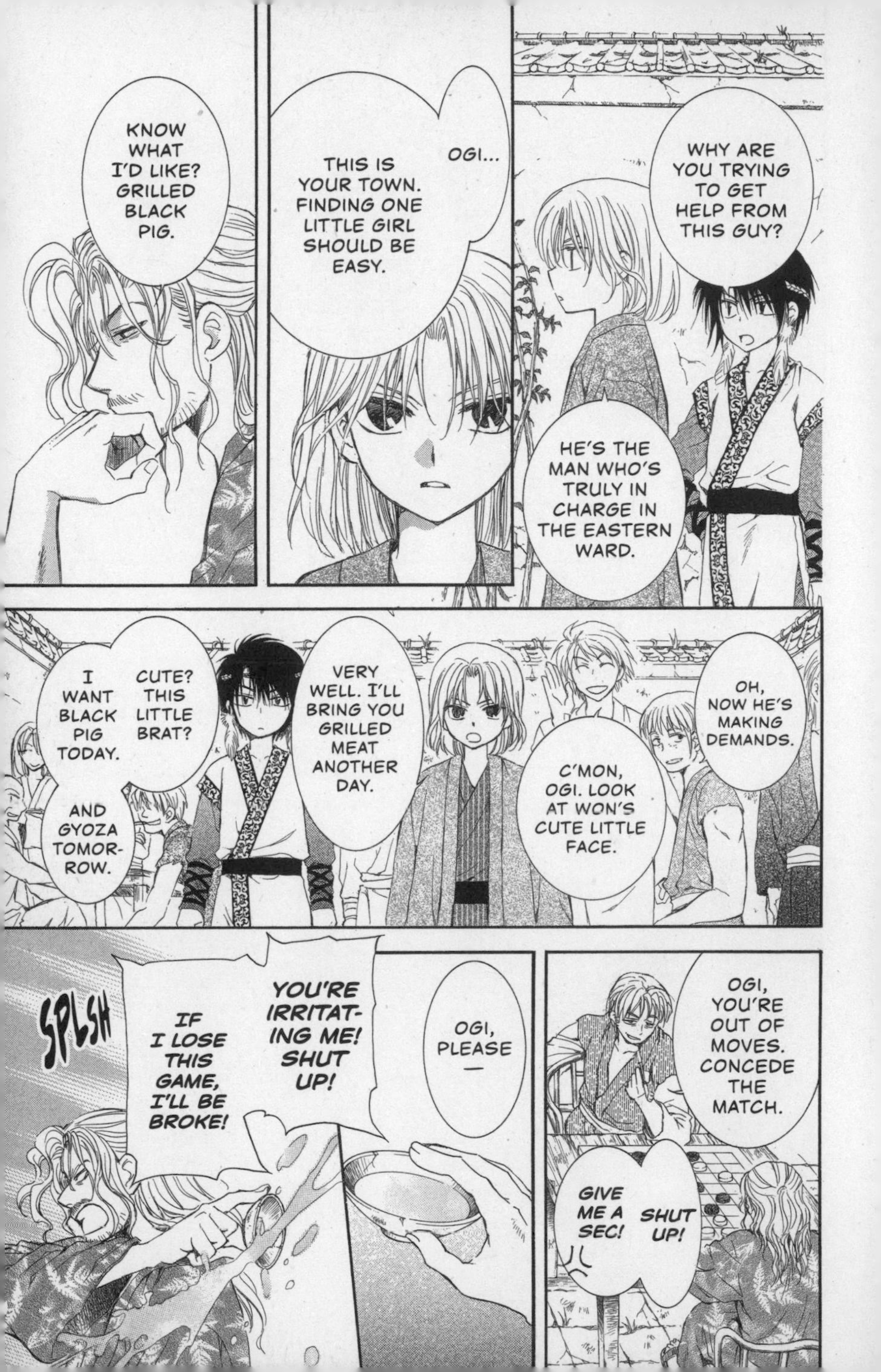
WHY ARE YOU TRYING TO GET HELP FROM THIS GUY?
HE'S THE MAN WHO'S TRULY IN CHARGE IN THE EASTERN WARD.
OGI...
THIS IS YOUR TOWN. FINDING ONE LITTLE GIRL SHOULD BE EASY.
KNOW WHAT I'D LIKE? GRILLED BLACK PIG.
OH, NOW HE'S MAKING DEMANDS.
C'MON, OGI. LOOK AT WON'S CUTE LITTLE FACE.
VERY WELL. I'LL BRING YOU GRILLED MEAT ANOTHER DAY.
CUTE? THIS LITTLE BRAT?
I WANT BLACK PIG TODAY.
AND GYOZA TOMORROW.
OGI, YOU'RE OUT OF MOVES. CONCEDE THE MATCH.
SHUT UP!
GIVE ME A SEC!
OGI, PLEASE —
YOU'RE IRRITATING ME! SHUT UP!
IF I LOSE THIS GAME, I'LL BE BROKE!
SPLSH

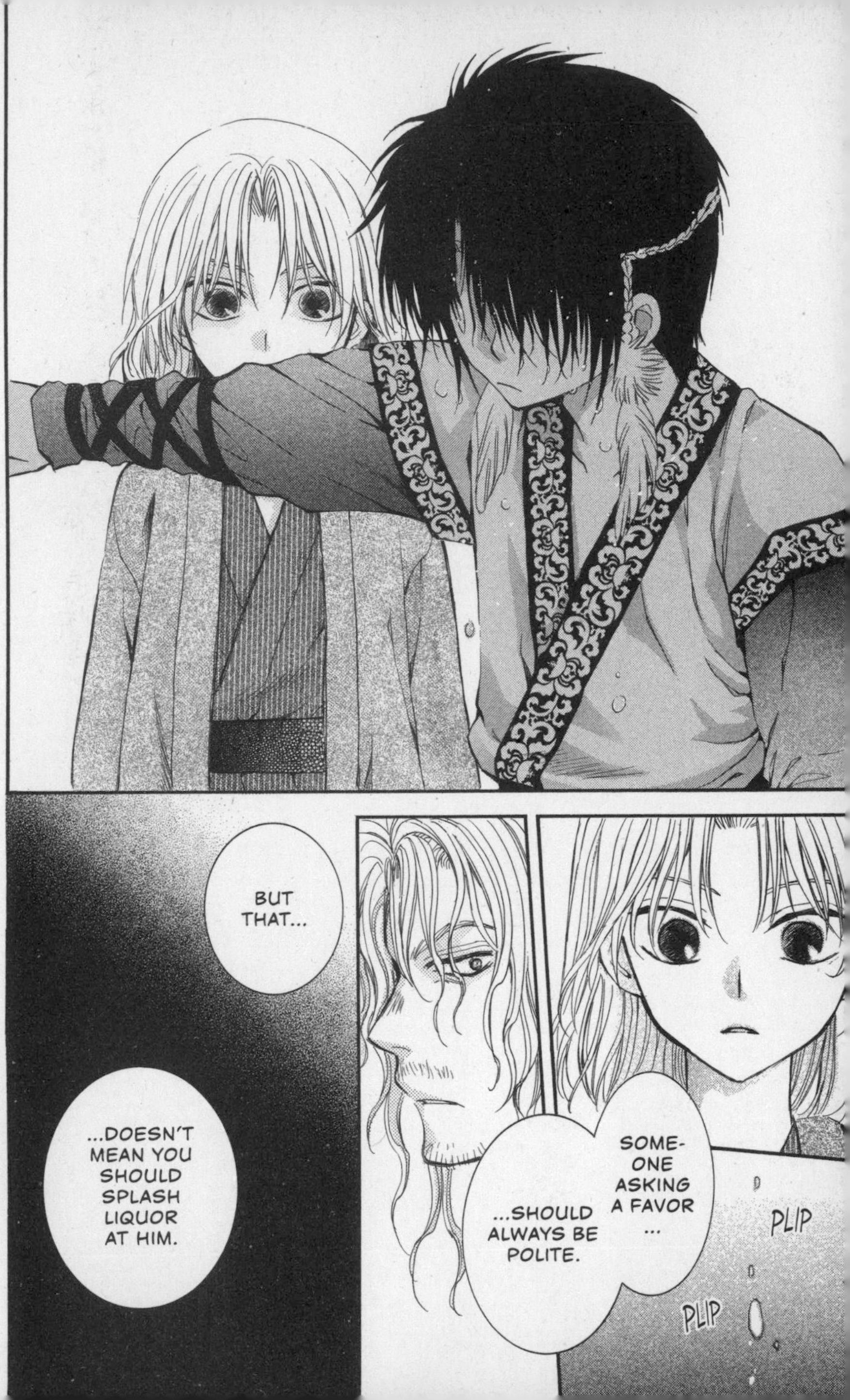
SOME-ONE ASKING A FAVOR ...
...SHOULD ALWAYS BE POLITE.
PLIP
PLIP
BUT THAT...
...DOESN'T MEAN YOU SHOULD SPLASH LIQUOR AT HIM.

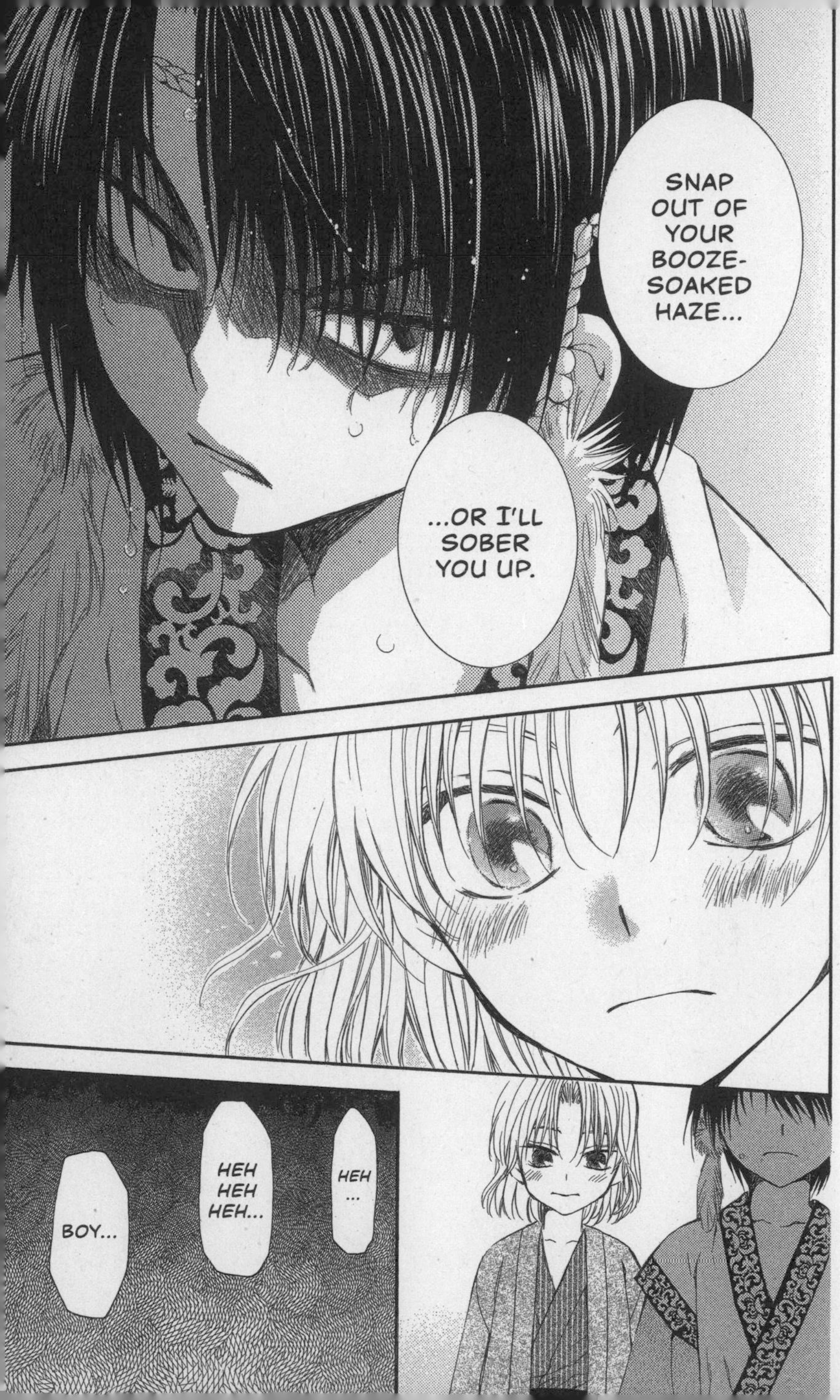
SNAP OUT OF YOUR BOOZE-SOAKED HAZE...
...OR I'LL SOBER YOU UP.
HEH ...
HEH HEH HEH...
BOY...

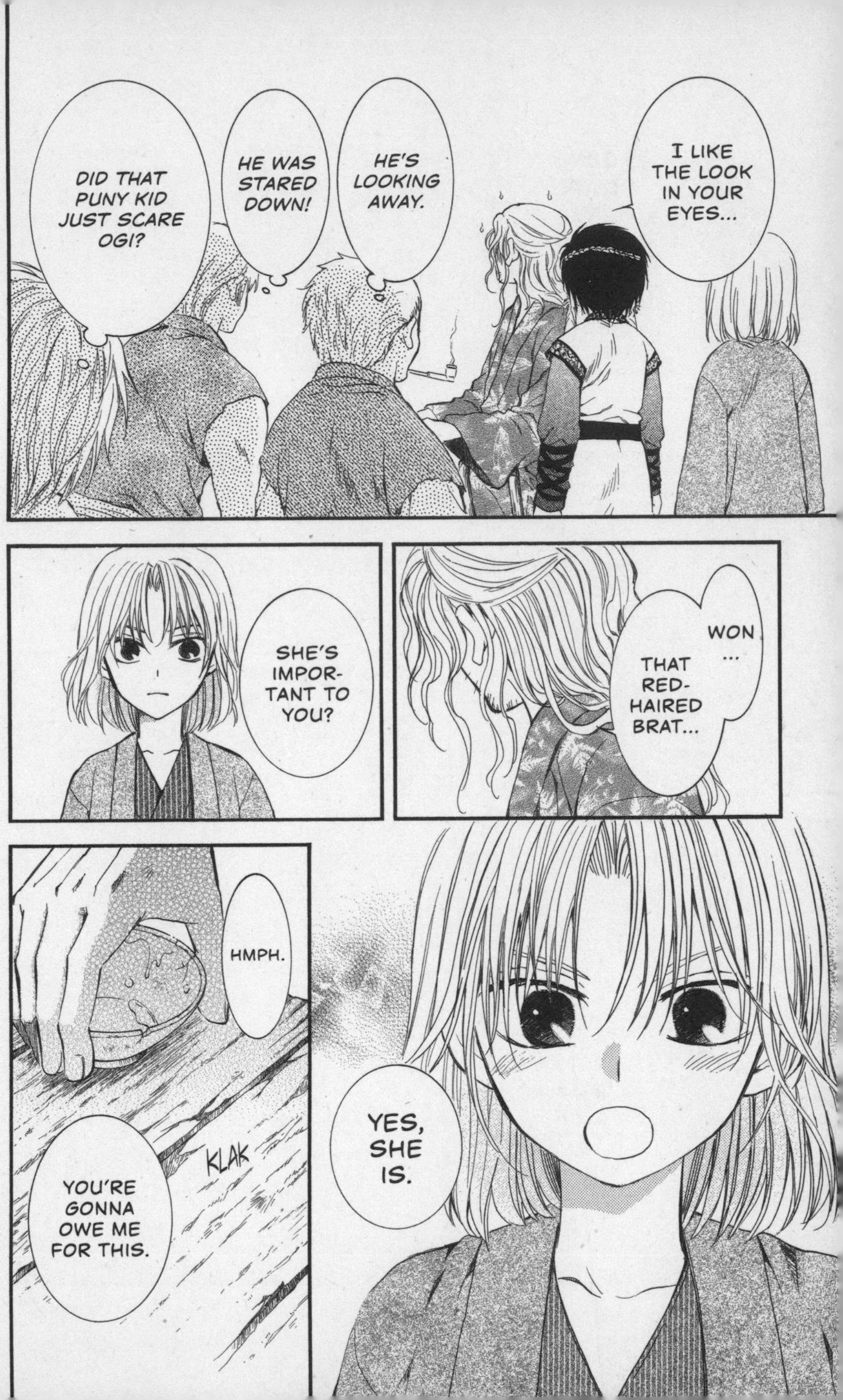
I LIKE THE LOOK IN YOUR EYES...
HE'S LOOKING AWAY.
HE WAS STARED DOWN!
DID THAT PUNY KID JUST SCARE OGI?
WON ...
THAT RED-HAIRED BRAT...
SHE'S IMPOR-TANT TO YOU?
YES, SHE IS.
HMPH.
KLAK
YOU'RE GONNA OWE ME FOR THIS.

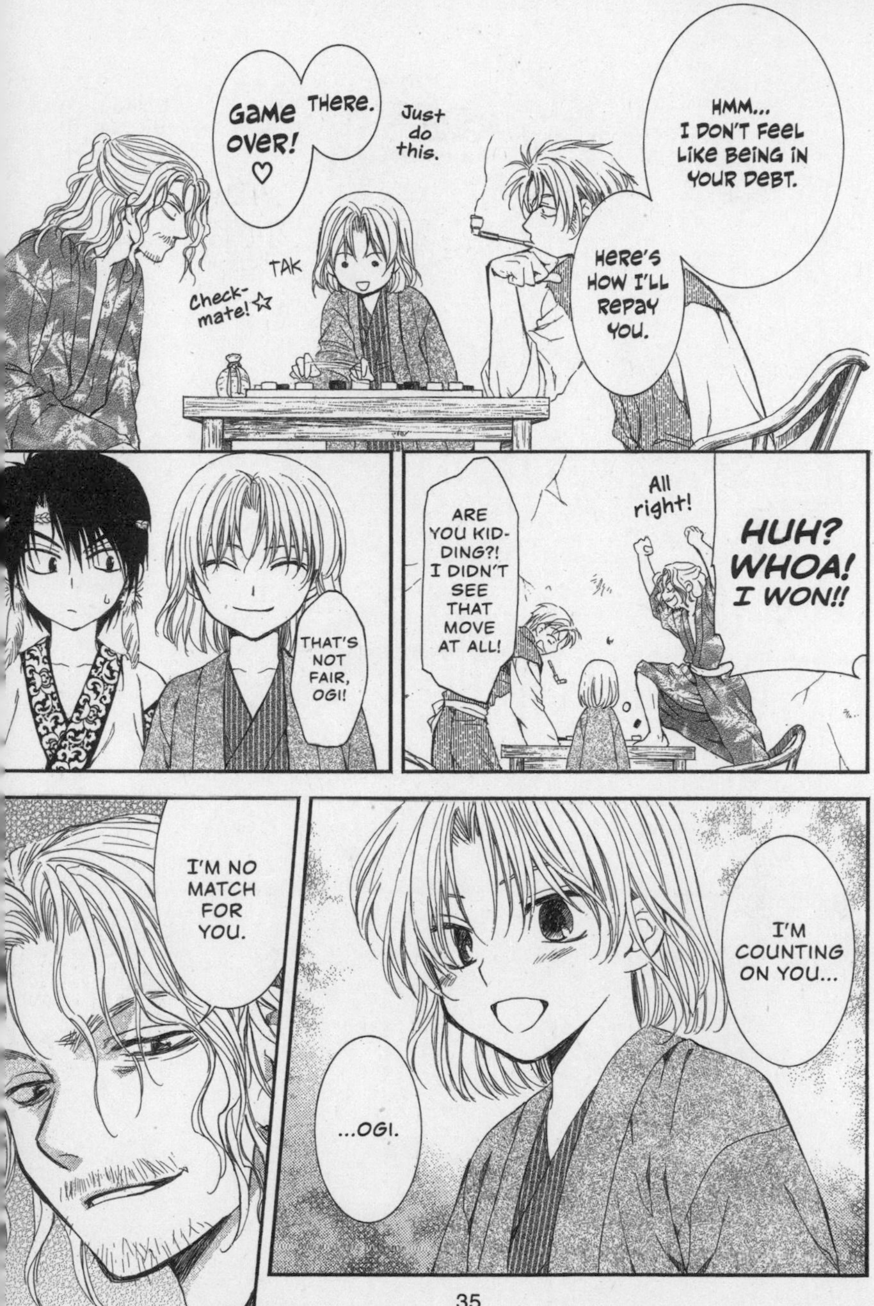
HMM... I DON'T FEEL LIKE BEING IN YOUR DEBT.
HERE'S HOW I'LL REPAY YOU.
Just do this.
THERE.
GAME OVER! ♡
TAK
Checkmate! ☆
HUH? WHOA! I WON!!
All right!
ARE YOU KIDDING?! I DIDN'T SEE THAT MOVE AT ALL!
THAT'S NOT FAIR, OGI!
I'M COUNTING ON YOU...
...OGI.
I'M NO MATCH FOR YOU.

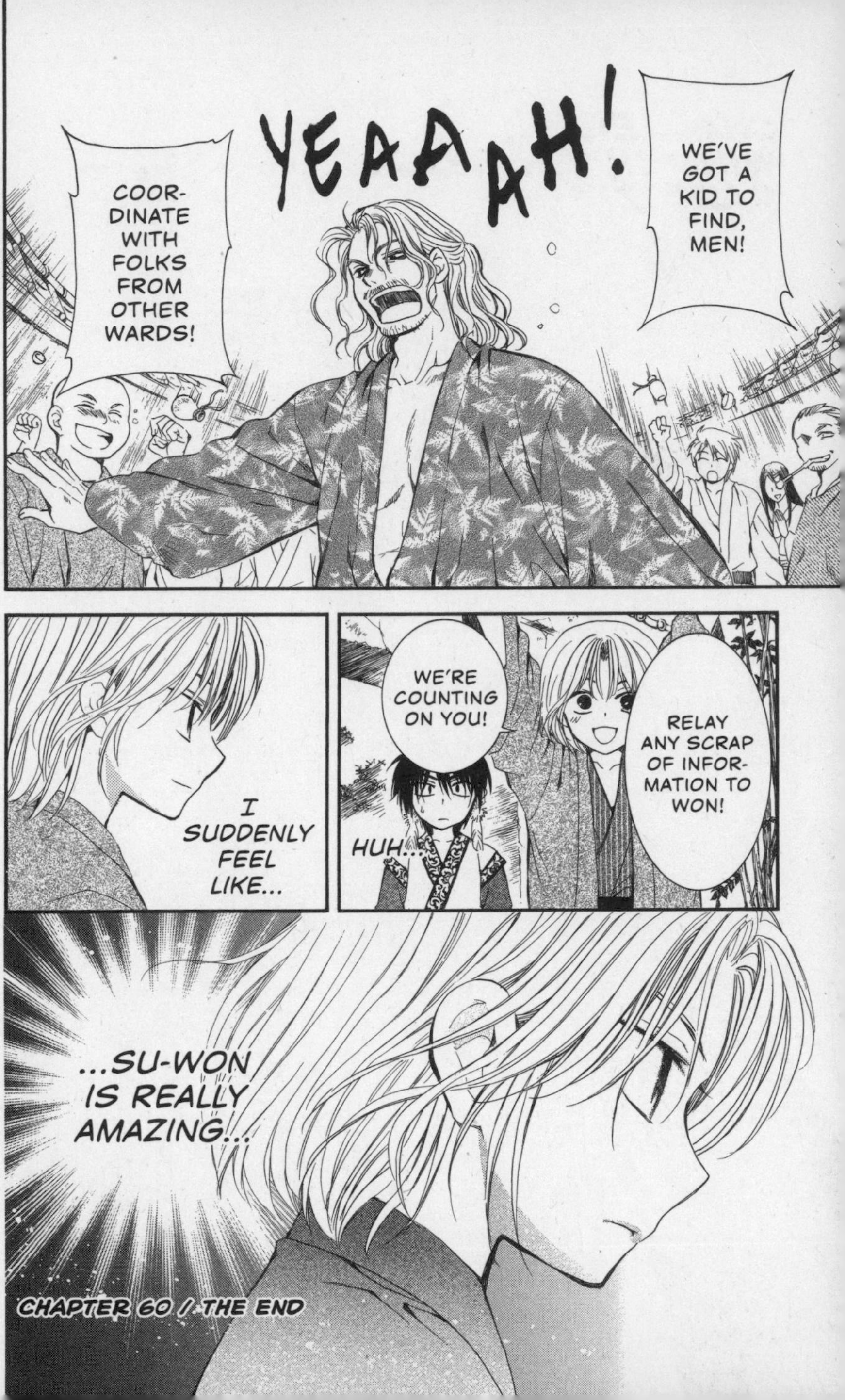
WE'VE GOT A KID TO FIND, MEN!
YEAAAH!
COOR-DINATE WITH FOLKS FROM OTHER WARDS!
RELAY ANY SCRAP OF INFOR-MATION TO WON!
WE'RE COUNTING ON YOU!
HUH...
I SUDDENLY FEEL LIKE...
...SU-WON IS REALLY AMAZING...
CHAPTER 60 / THE END

CHAPTER 61: WIND IN THE YOUNG LEAVES, PART 2

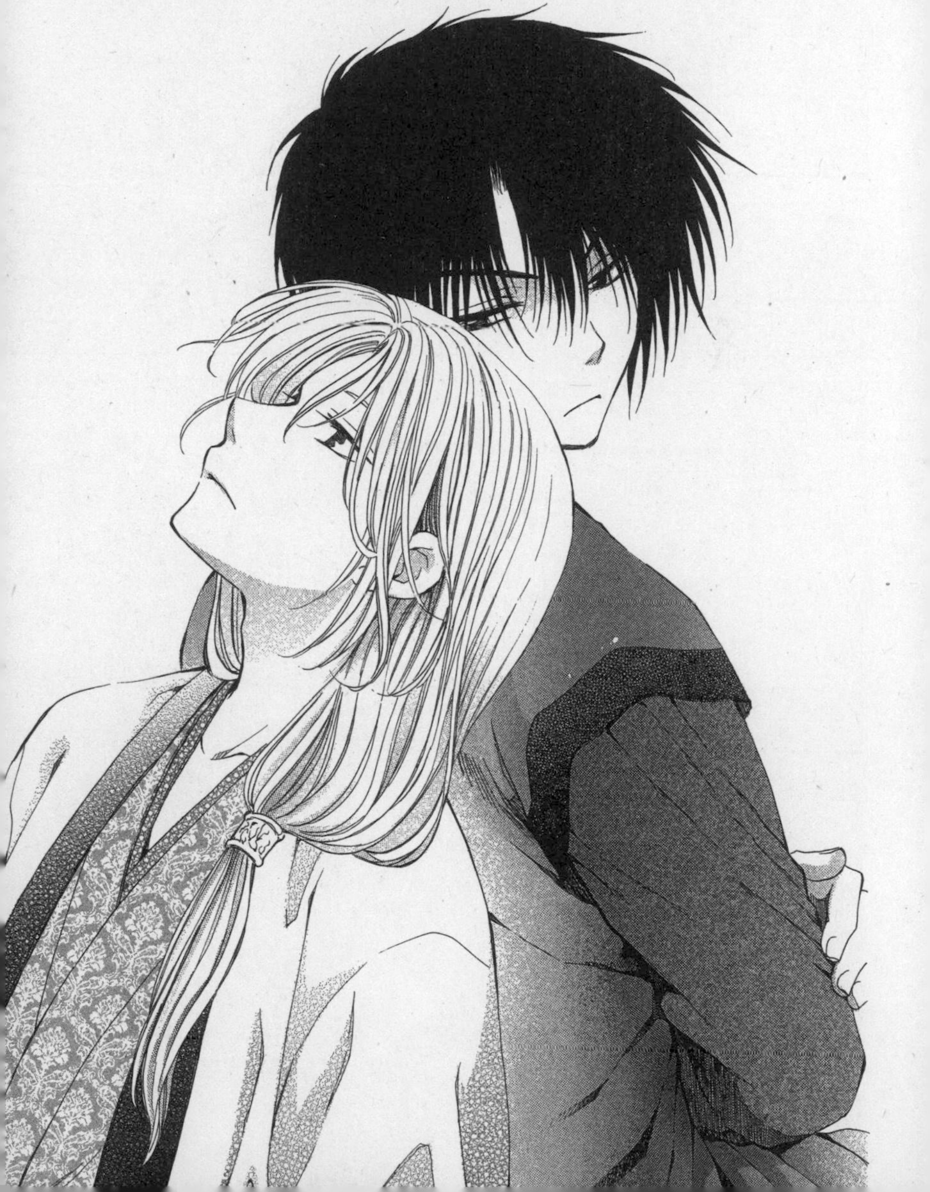

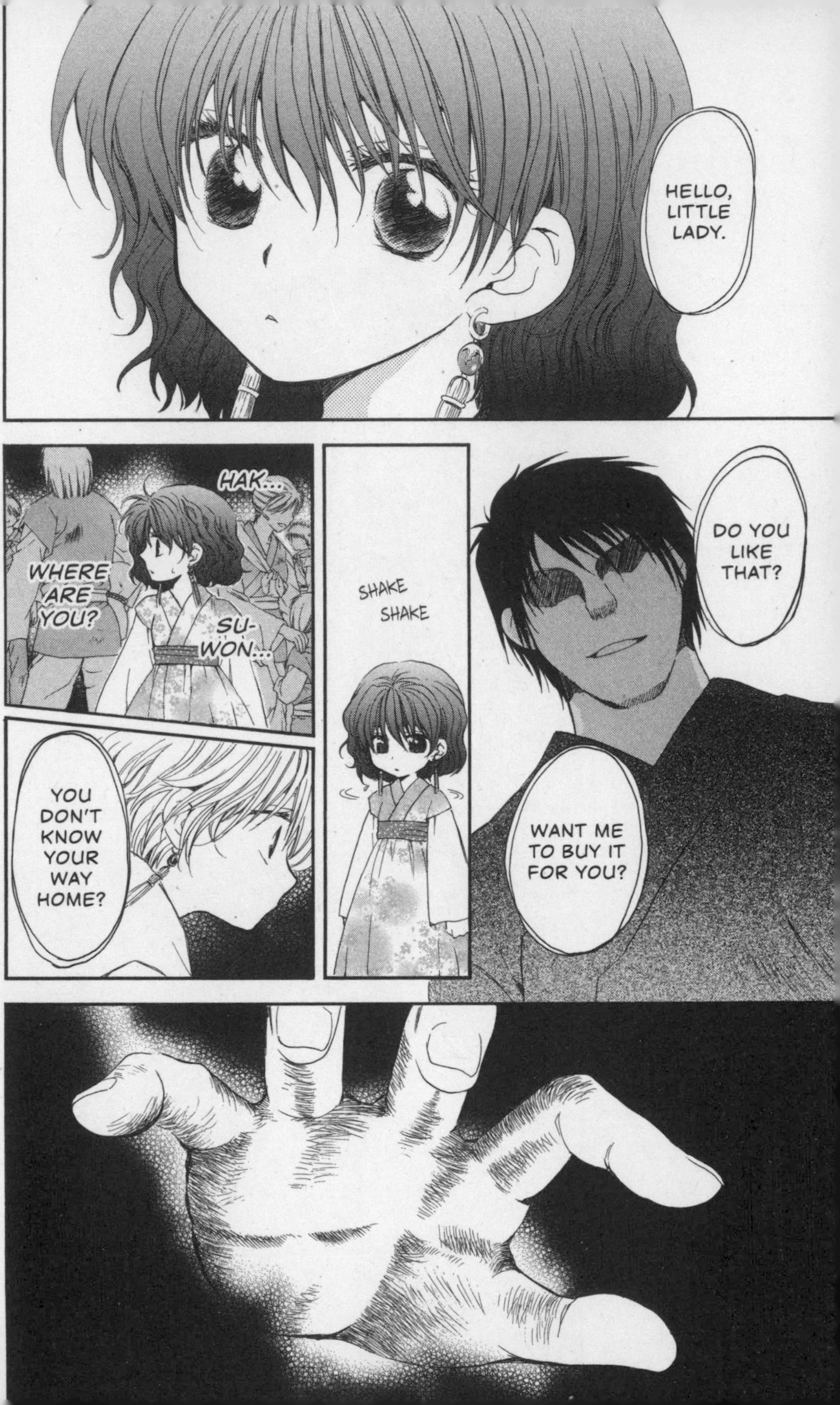
HELLO, LITTLE LADY.
DO YOU LIKE THAT?
WANT ME TO BUY IT FOR YOU?
SHAKE SHAKE
HAK...
SU-WON...
WHERE ARE YOU?
YOU DON'T KNOW YOUR WAY HOME?

During this story of Yona's childhood, Su-won's father, Yu-hon, is still alive. Sometime after this, something terrible happens and Yu-hon passes away.

Su-won was always bursting with curiosity. He'd go into town to learn more about the world. It was fun drawing past versions of various characters for this story.

Ogi is one of my favorite characters.

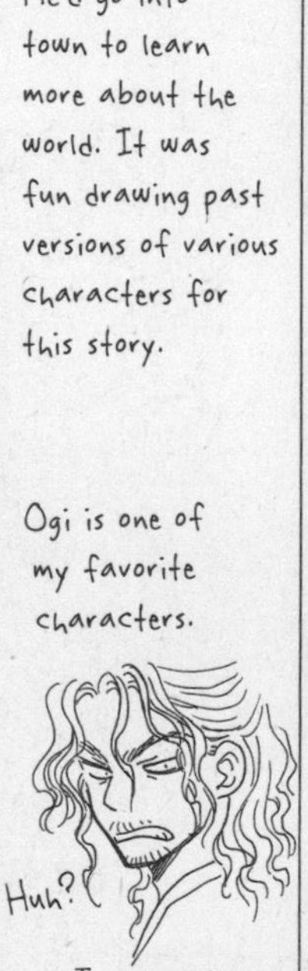

Huh?

The superstar of the backstreets!

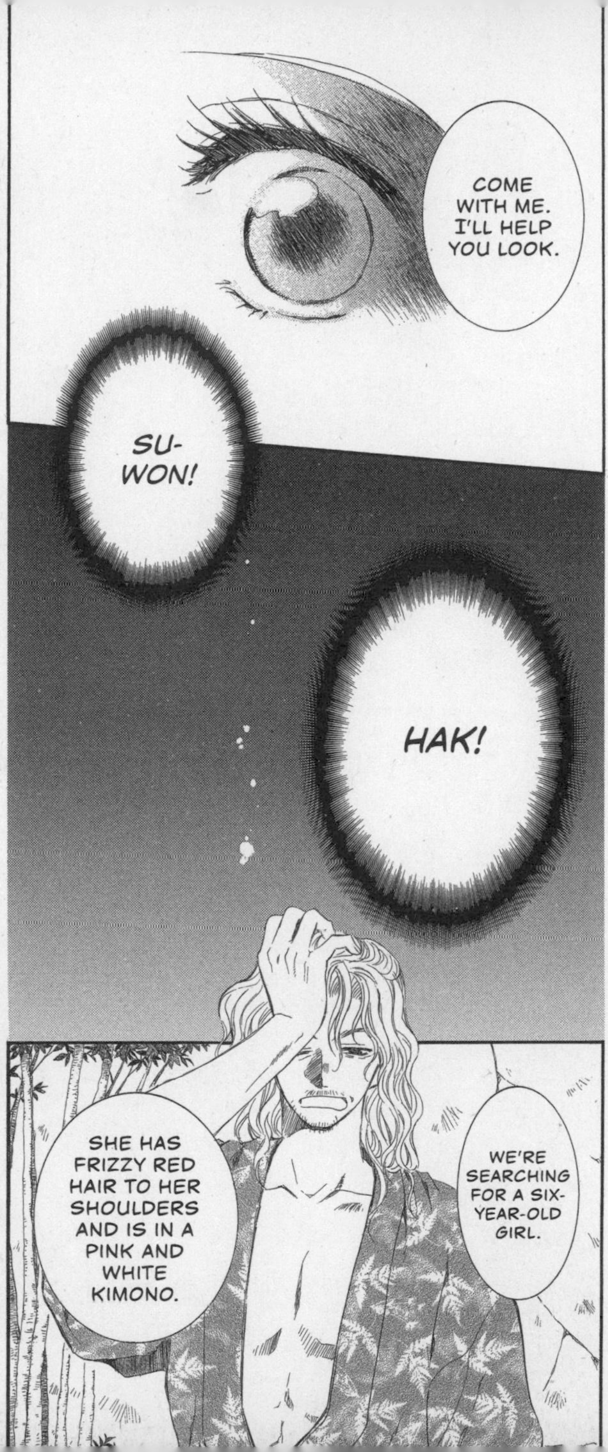

COME WITH ME. I'LL HELP YOU LOOK.
SU-WON!
HAK!
WE'RE SEARCHING FOR A SIX-YEAR-OLD GIRL.
SHE HAS FRIZZY RED HAIR TO HER SHOULDERS AND IS IN A PINK AND WHITE KIMONO.

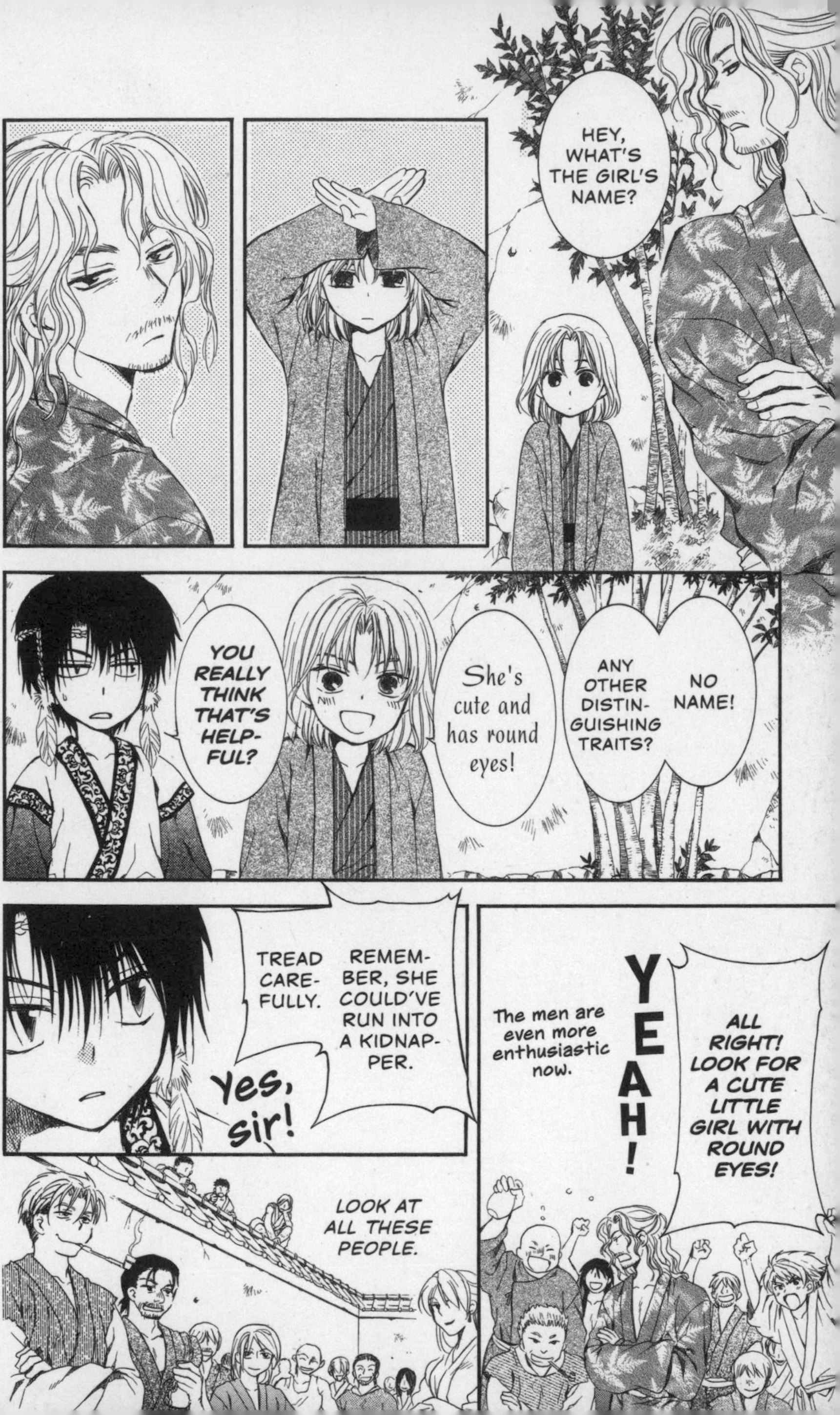
HEY, WHAT'S THE GIRL'S NAME?
NO NAME!
ANY OTHER DISTIN-GUISHING TRAITS?
She's cute and has round eyes!
YOU REALLY THINK THAT'S HELP-FUL?
ALL RIGHT! LOOK FOR A CUTE LITTLE GIRL WITH ROUND EYES!
YEAH!
The men are even more enthusiastic now.
REMEM-BER, SHE COULD'VE RUN INTO A KIDNAP-PER.
TREAD CARE-FULLY.
Yes, sir!
LOOK AT ALL THESE PEOPLE.

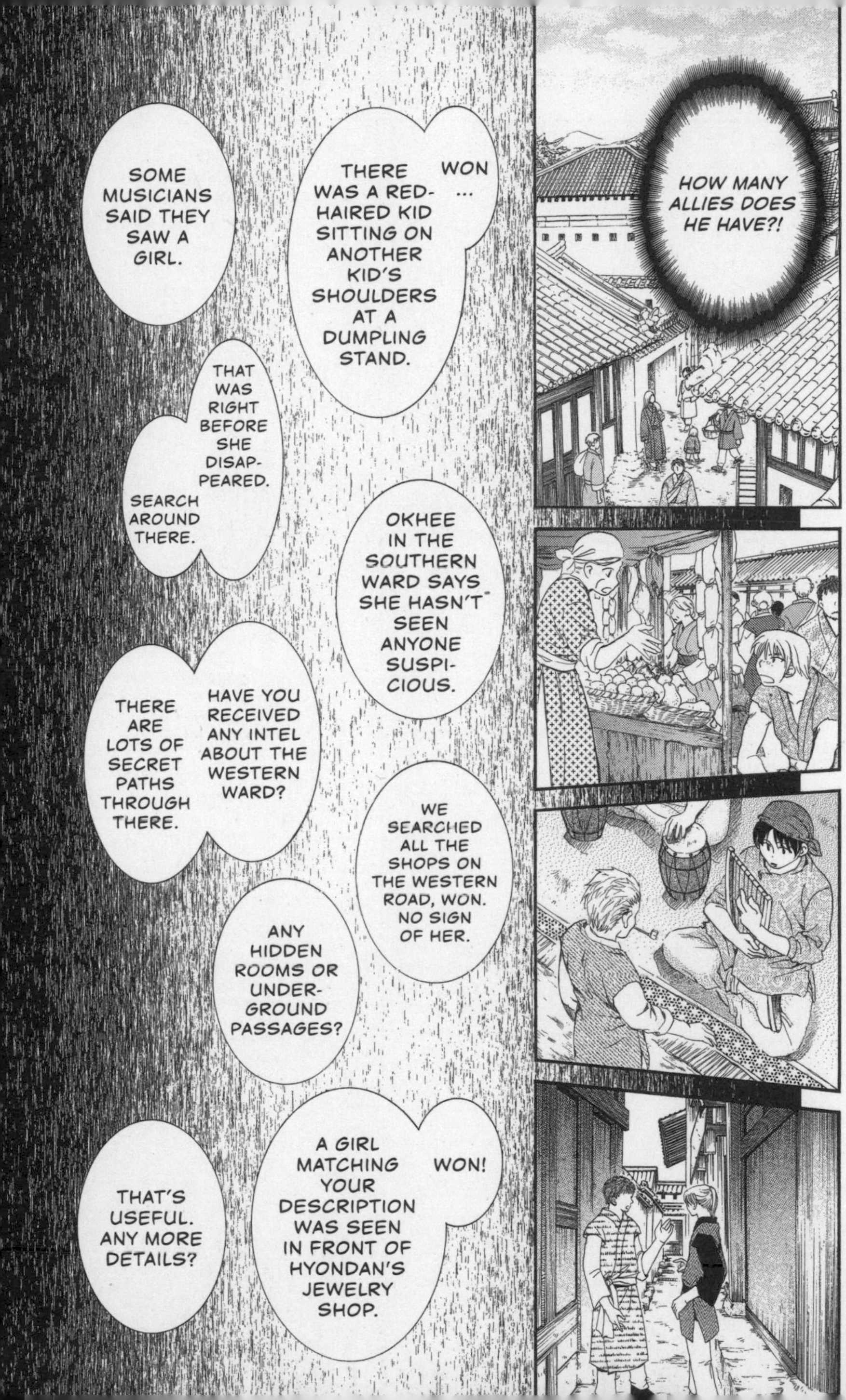
HOW MANY ALLIES DOES HE HAVE?!
WON ...
THERE WAS A RED-HAIRED KID SITTING ON ANOTHER KID'S SHOULDERS AT A DUMPLING STAND.
SOME MUSICIANS SAID THEY SAW A GIRL.
THAT WAS RIGHT BEFORE SHE DISAP-PEARED.
SEARCH AROUND THERE.
OKHEE IN THE SOUTHERN WARD SAYS SHE HASN'T SEEN ANYONE SUSPI-CIOUS.
HAVE YOU RECEIVED ANY INTEL ABOUT THE WESTERN WARD?
THERE ARE LOTS OF SECRET PATHS THROUGH THERE.
WE SEARCHED ALL THE SHOPS ON THE WESTERN ROAD, WON. NO SIGN OF HER.
ANY HIDDEN ROOMS OR UNDER-GROUND PASSAGES?
WON!
A GIRL MATCHING YOUR DESCRIPTION WAS SEEN IN FRONT OF HYONDAN'S JEWELRY SHOP.
THAT'S USEFUL. ANY MORE DETAILS?

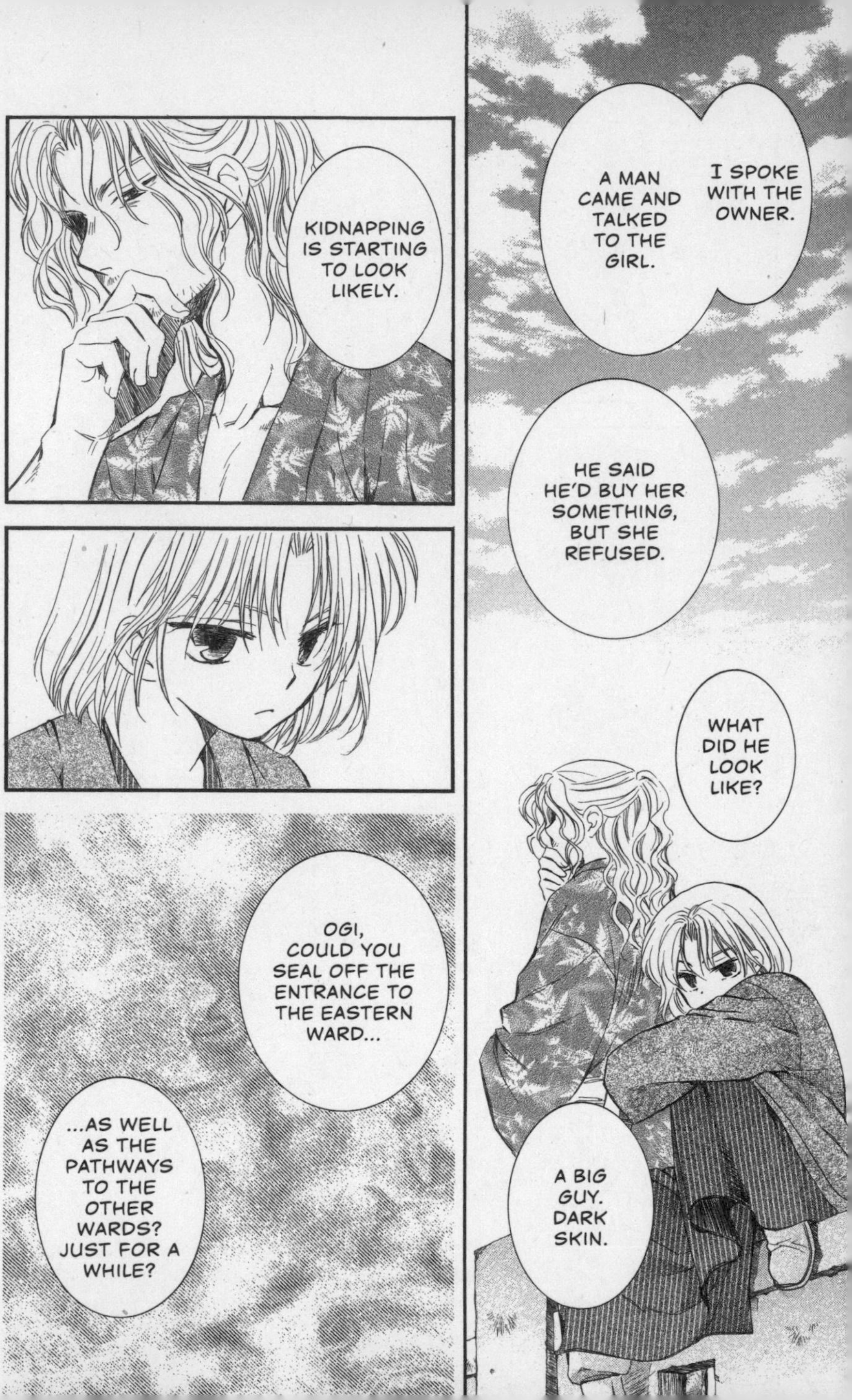
I SPOKE WITH THE OWNER.
A MAN CAME AND TALKED TO THE GIRL.
HE SAID HE'D BUY HER SOMETHING, BUT SHE REFUSED.
WHAT DID HE LOOK LIKE?
A BIG GUY. DARK SKIN.
KIDNAPPING IS STARTING TO LOOK LIKELY.
OGI, COULD YOU SEAL OFF THE ENTRANCE TO THE EASTERN WARD...
...AS WELL AS THE PATHWAYS TO THE OTHER WARDS? JUST FOR A WHILE?

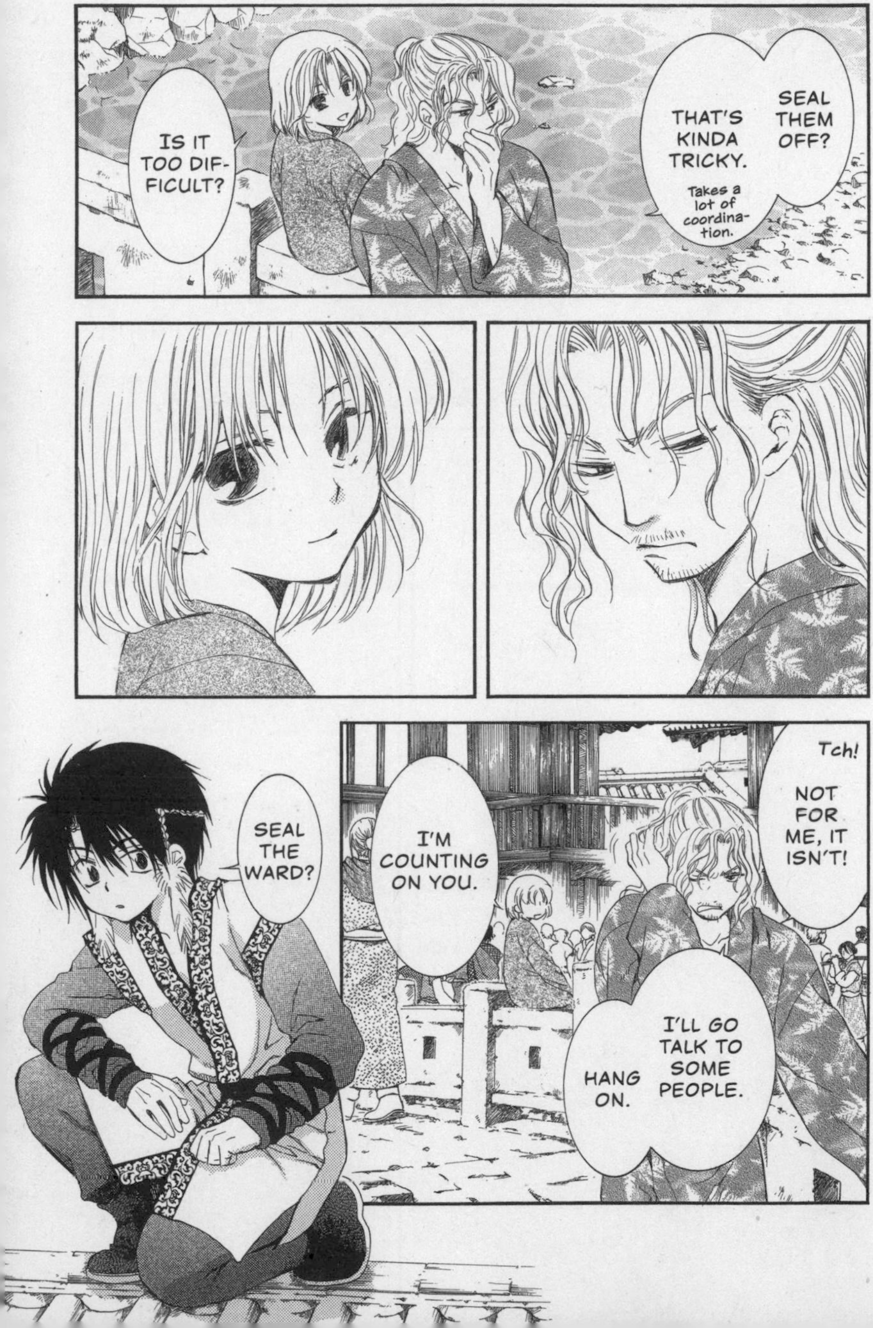
SEAL THEM OFF?
THAT'S KINDA TRICKY.
Takes a lot of coordination.
IS IT TOO DIFFICULT?
Tch!
NOT FOR ME, IT ISN'T!
I'LL GO TALK TO SOME PEOPLE.
HANG ON.
I'M COUNTING ON YOU.
SEAL THE WARD?

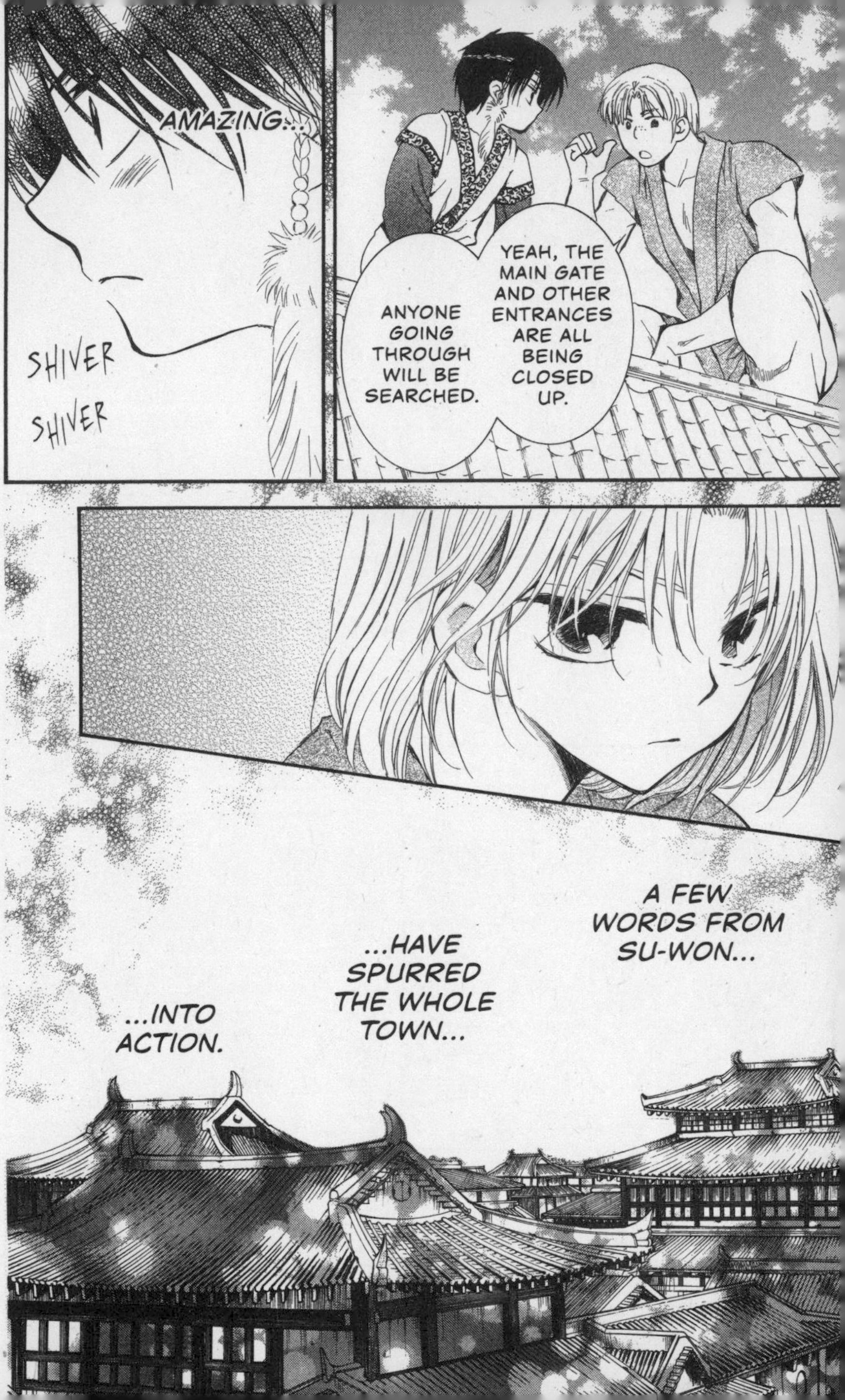
YEAH, THE MAIN GATE AND OTHER ENTRANCES ARE ALL BEING CLOSED UP.
ANYONE GOING THROUGH WILL BE SEARCHED.
AMAZING...
SHIVER
SHIVER
A FEW WORDS FROM SU-WON...
...HAVE SPURRED THE WHOLE TOWN...
...INTO ACTION.

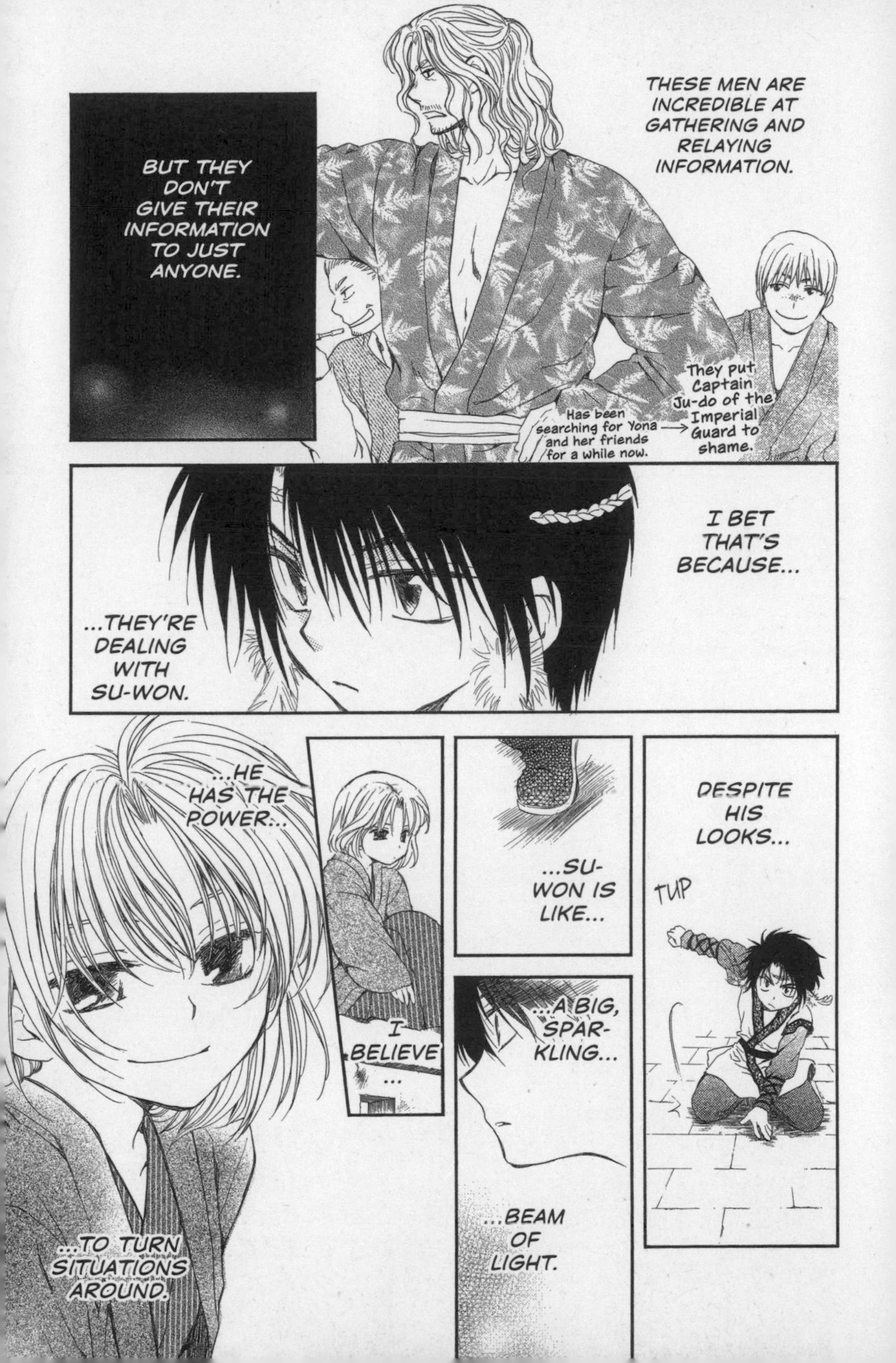
THESE MEN ARE INCREDIBLE AT GATHERING AND RELAYING INFORMATION.
They put Captain Ju-do of the Imperial Guard to shame.
Has been searching for Yona and her friends for a while now.
BUT THEY DON'T GIVE THEIR INFORMATION TO JUST ANYONE.
I BET THAT'S BECAUSE...
...THEY'RE DEALING WITH SU-WON.
DESPITE HIS LOOKS...
TUP
...SU-WON IS LIKE...
...A BIG, SPARKLING...
...BEAM OF LIGHT.
I BELIEVE...
...HE HAS THE POWER...
...TO TURN SITUATIONS AROUND.

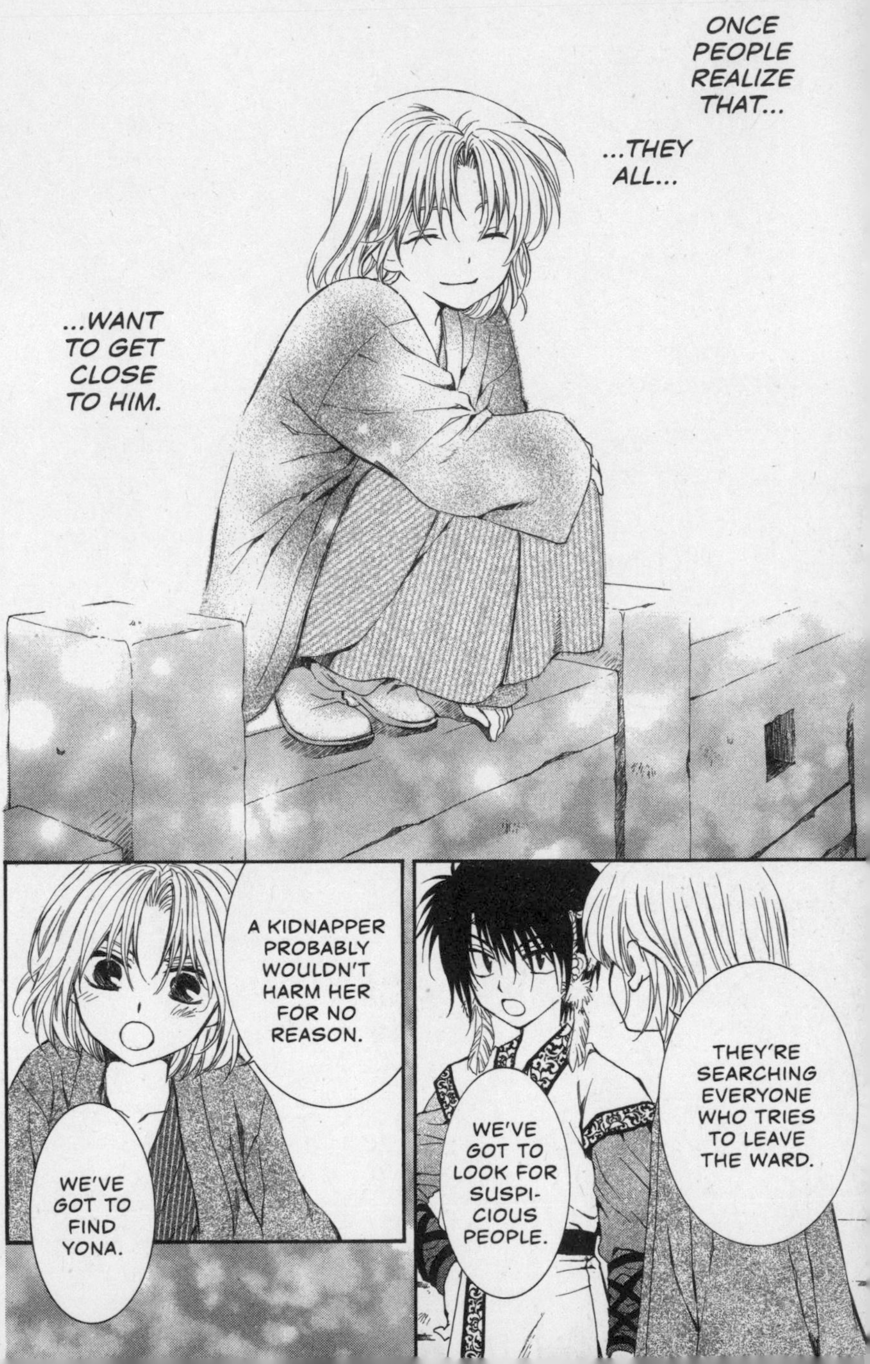
ONCE PEOPLE REALIZE THAT...
...THEY ALL...
...WANT TO GET CLOSE TO HIM.
THEY'RE SEARCHING EVERYONE WHO TRIES TO LEAVE THE WARD.
WE'VE GOT TO LOOK FOR SUSPICIOUS PEOPLE.
A KIDNAPPER PROBABLY WOULDN'T HARM HER FOR NO REASON.
WE'VE GOT TO FIND YONA.

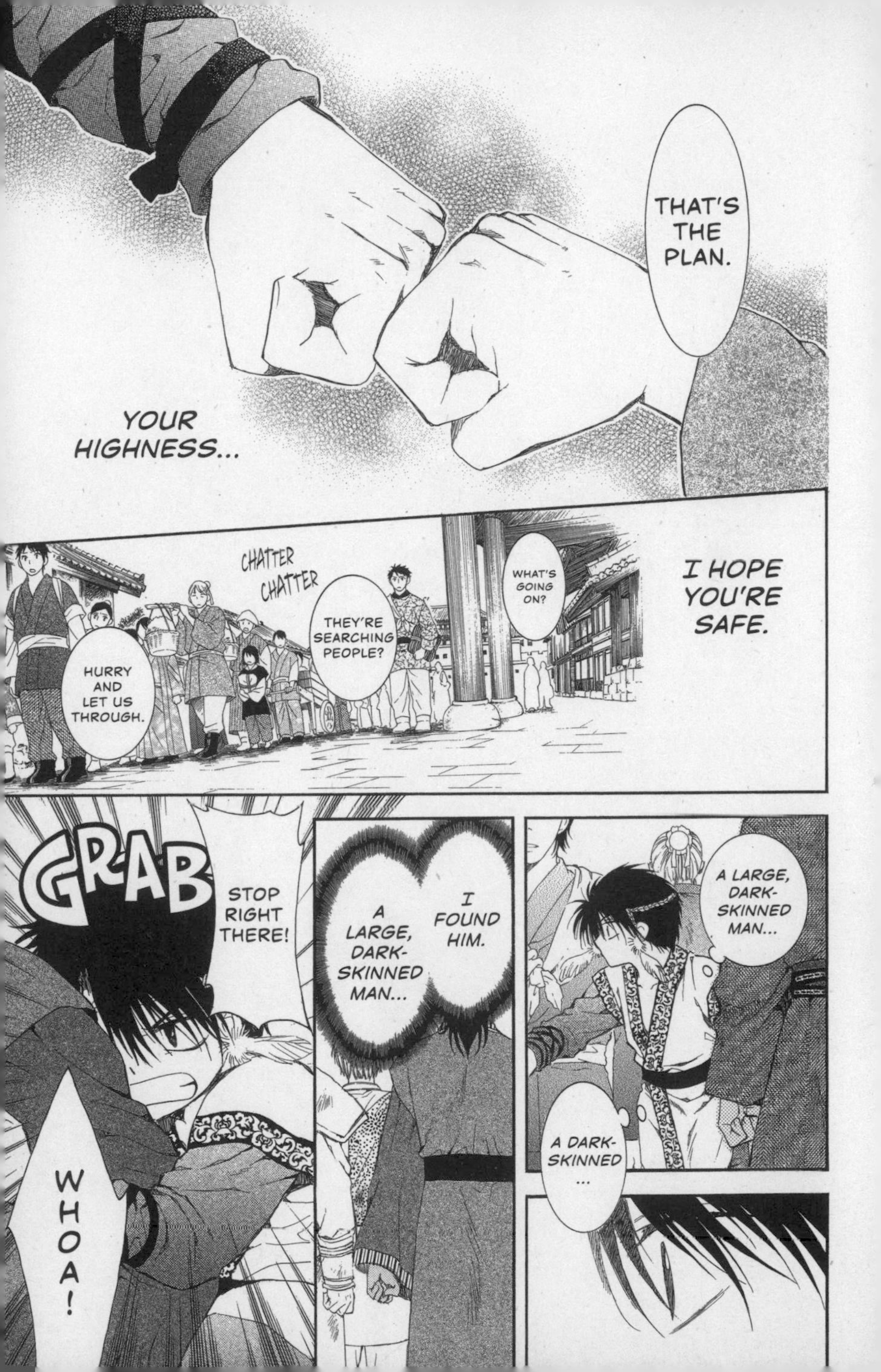
THAT'S THE PLAN.
YOUR HIGHNESS...
I HOPE YOU'RE SAFE.
WHAT'S GOING ON?
THEY'RE SEARCHING PEOPLE?
CHATTER CHATTER
HURRY AND LET US THROUGH.
A LARGE, DARK-SKINNED MAN...
A DARK-SKINNED ...
I FOUND HIM.
A LARGE, DARK-SKINNED MAN...
STOP RIGHT THERE!
GRAB
WHOA!

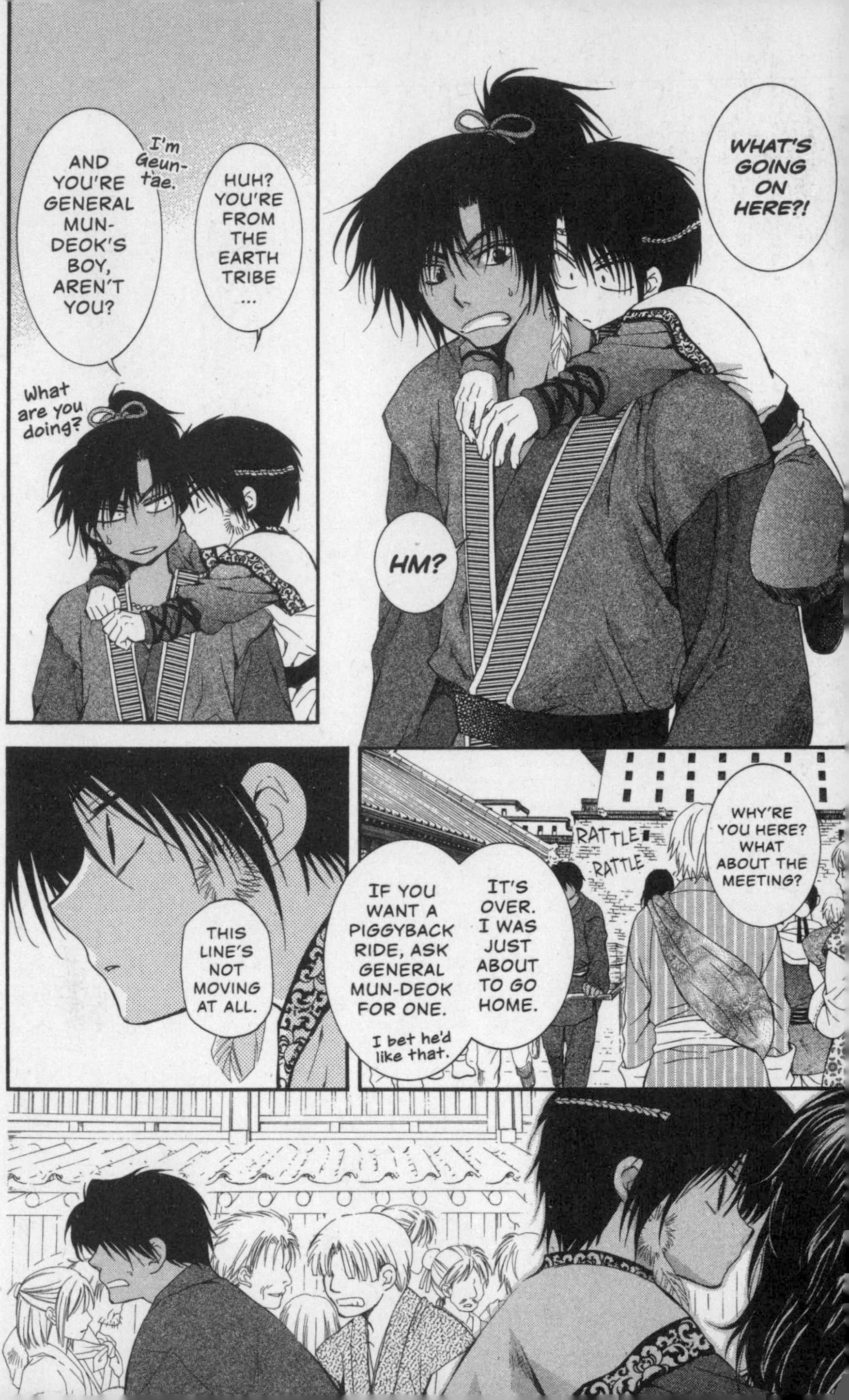
WHAT'S GOING ON HERE?!
HM?
HUH? YOU'RE FROM THE EARTH TRIBE ...
I'm Geun-tae.
AND YOU'RE GENERAL MUN-DEOK'S BOY, AREN'T YOU?
What are you doing?
RATTLE RATTLE
WHY'RE YOU HERE? WHAT ABOUT THE MEETING?
IT'S OVER. I WAS JUST ABOUT TO GO HOME.
IF YOU WANT A PIGGYBACK RIDE, ASK GENERAL MUN-DEOK FOR ONE.
I bet he'd like that.
THIS LINE'S NOT MOVING AT ALL.

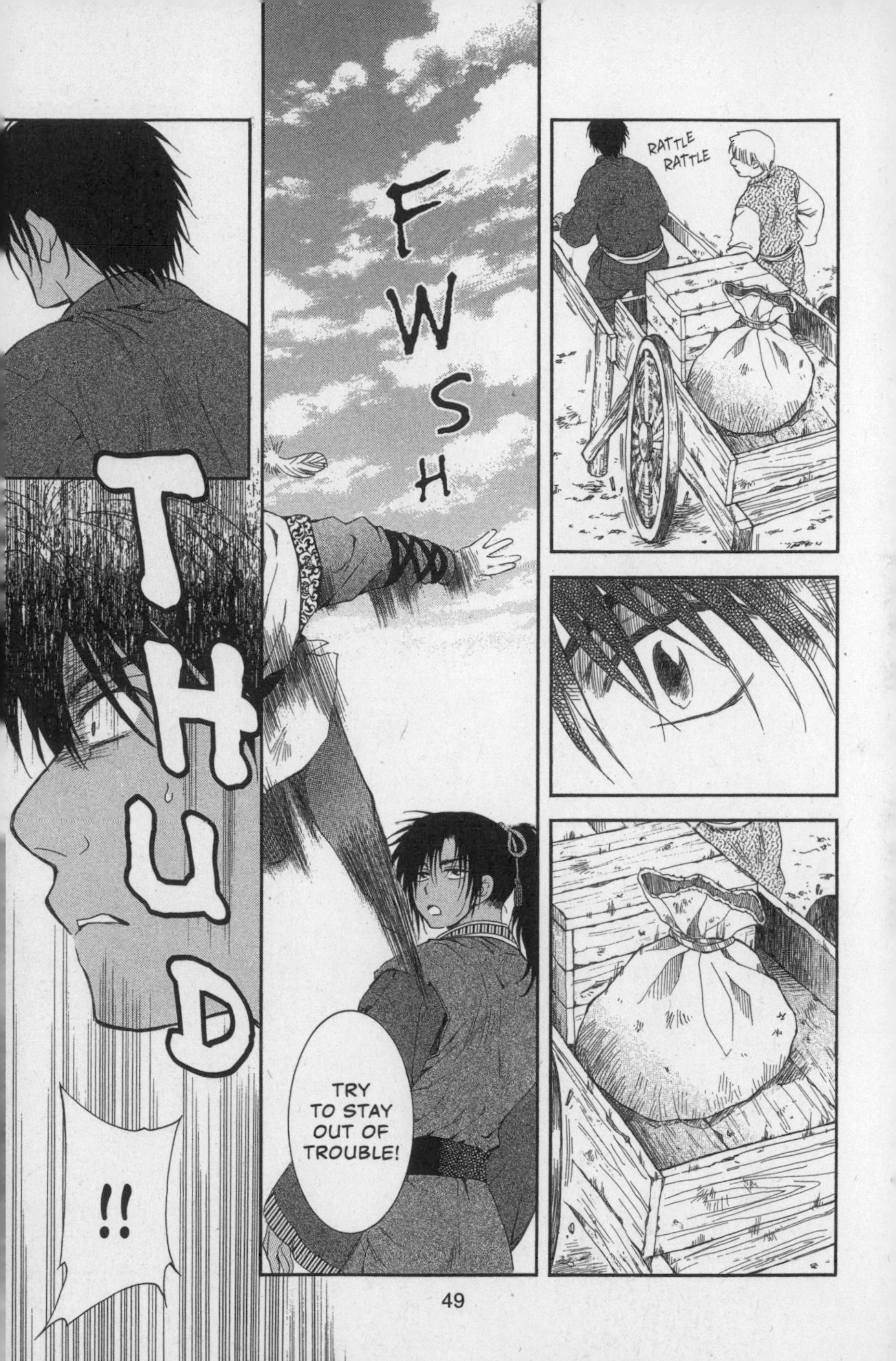
RATTLE RATTLE
FWSH
TRY TO STAY OUT OF TROUBLE!
THUD
!!

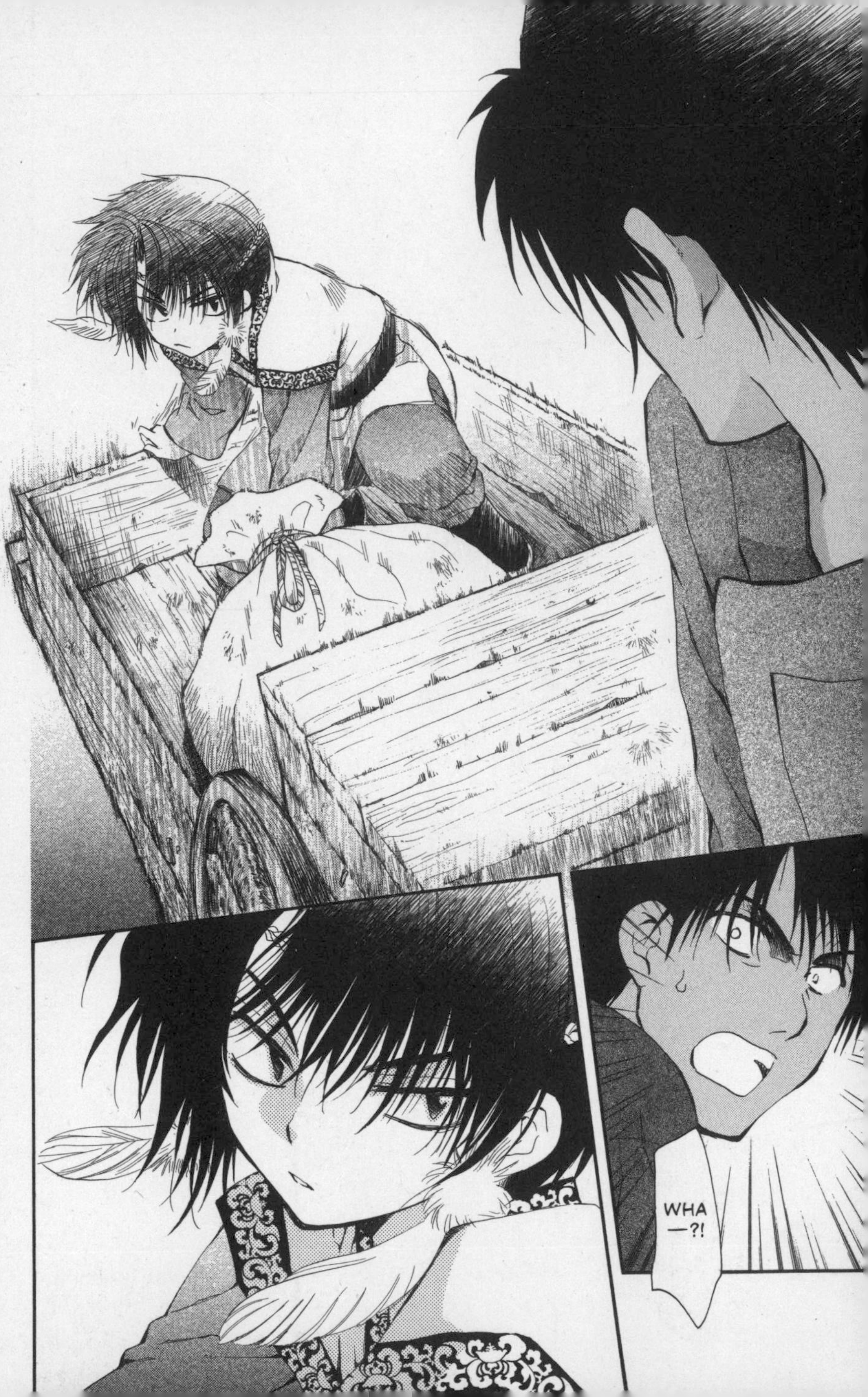
WHA
—?!

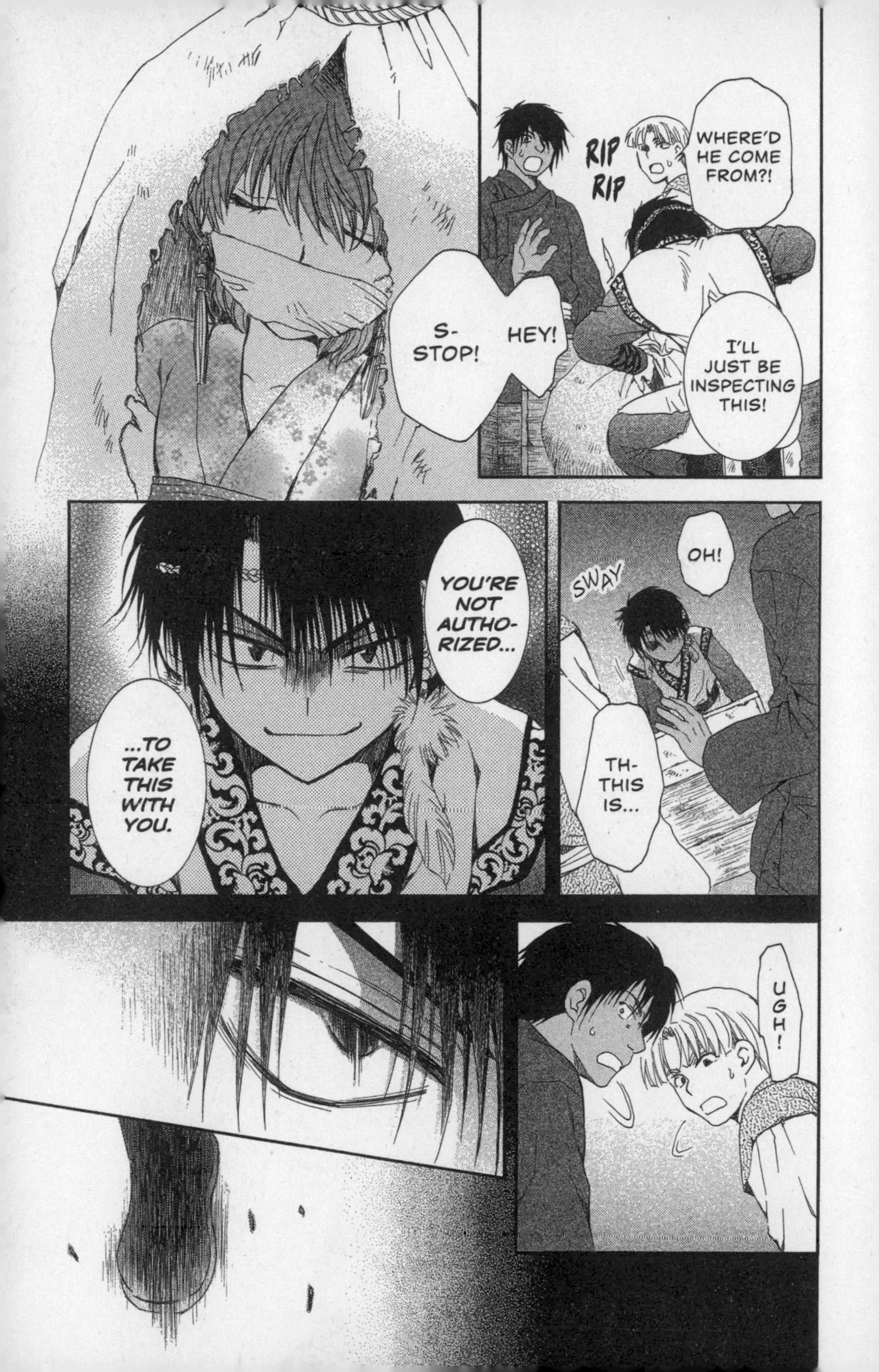
WHERE'D HE COME FROM?!
RIP RIP
HEY!
S-STOP!
I'LL JUST BE INSPECTING THIS!
OH!
SWAY
TH- THIS IS...
YOU'RE NOT AUTHORIZED...
...TO TAKE THIS WITH YOU.
UGH!

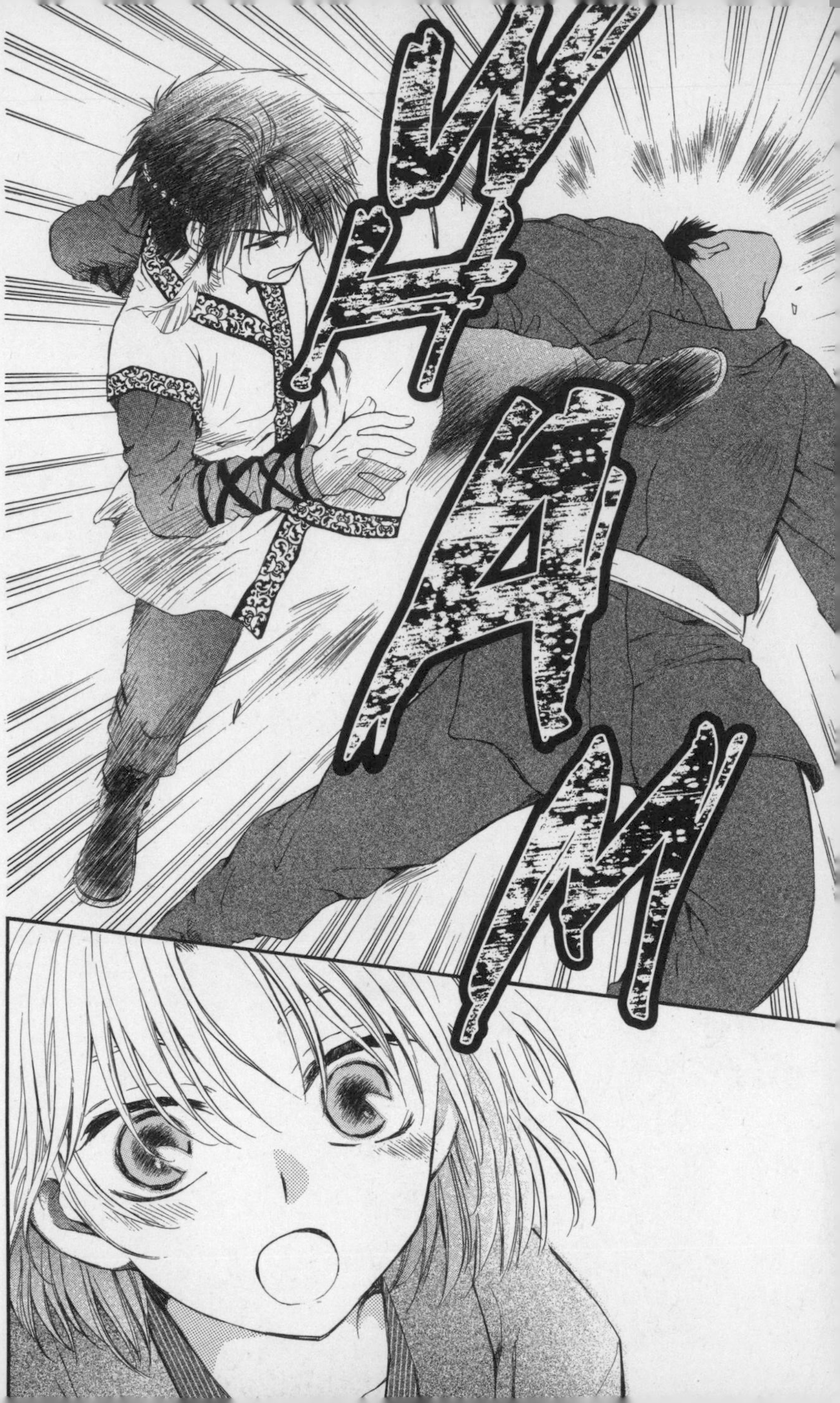
WHAM

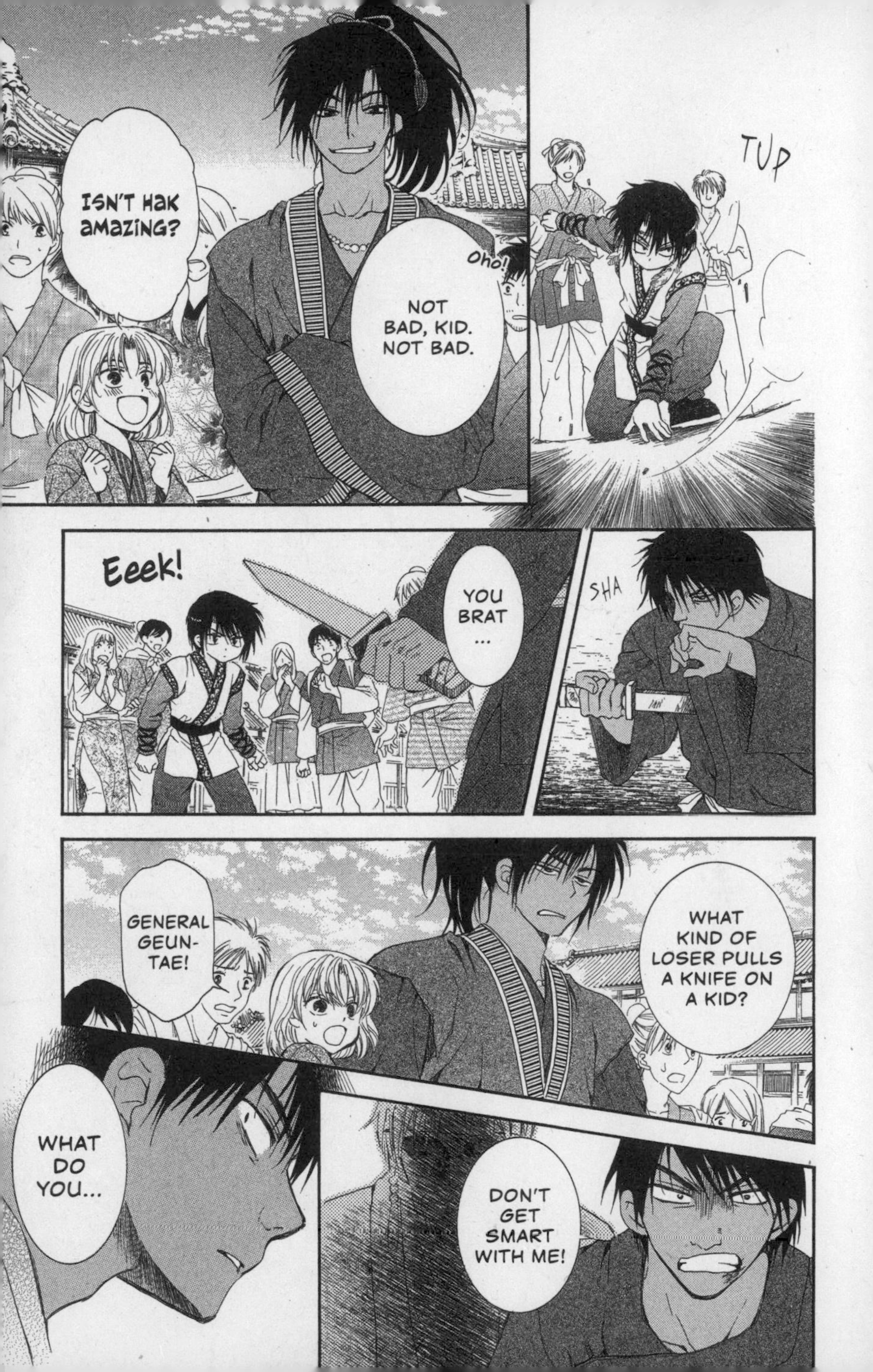
TUP
Oho!
NOT BAD, KID. NOT BAD.
ISN'T HAK AMAZING?
SHA
YOU BRAT ...
Eeek!
WHAT KIND OF LOSER PULLS A KNIFE ON A KID?
GENERAL GEUN-TAE!
DON'T GET SMART WITH ME!
WHAT DO YOU...

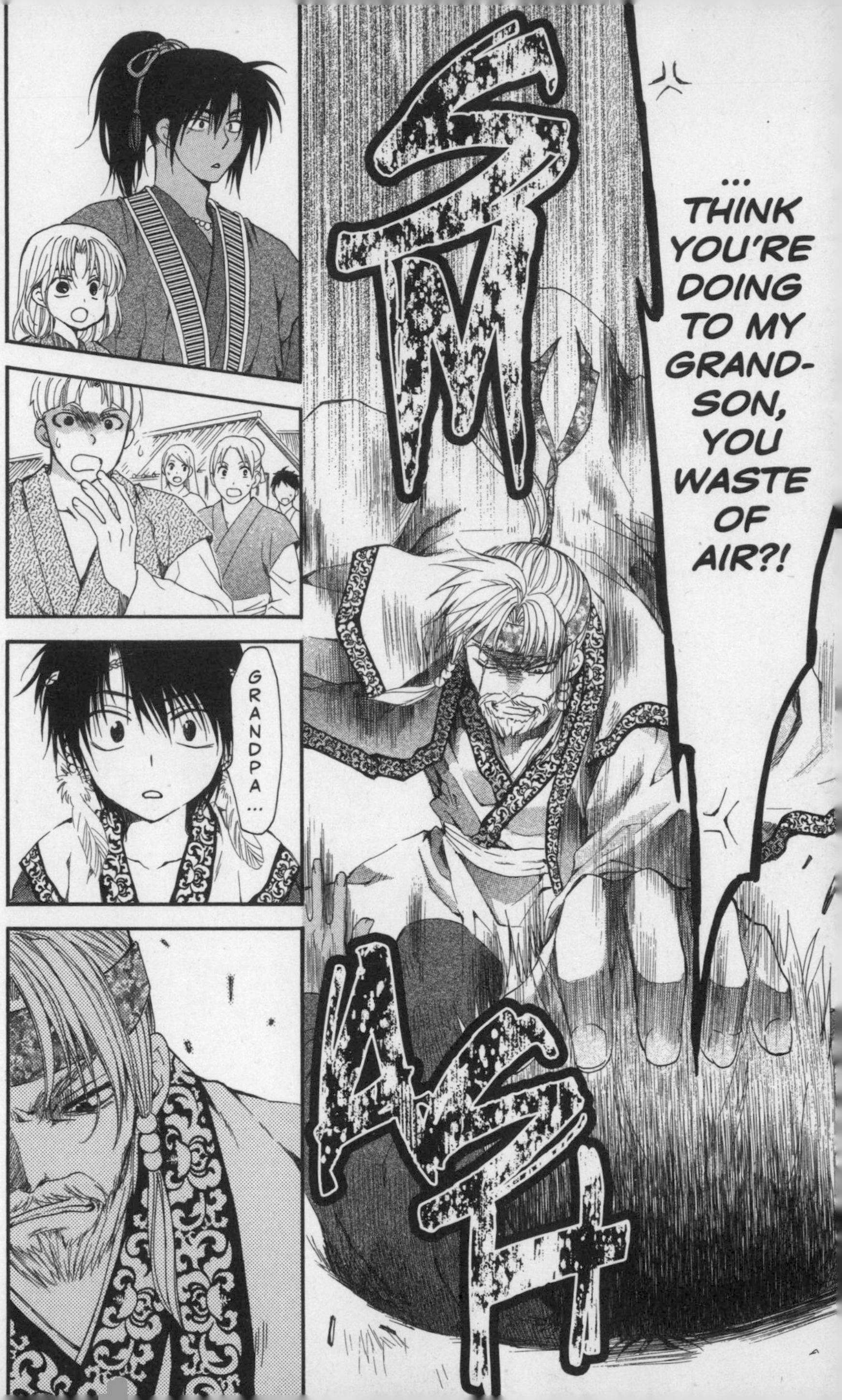
...THINK YOU'RE DOING TO MY GRANDSON, YOU WASTE OF AIR?!
GRANDPA...

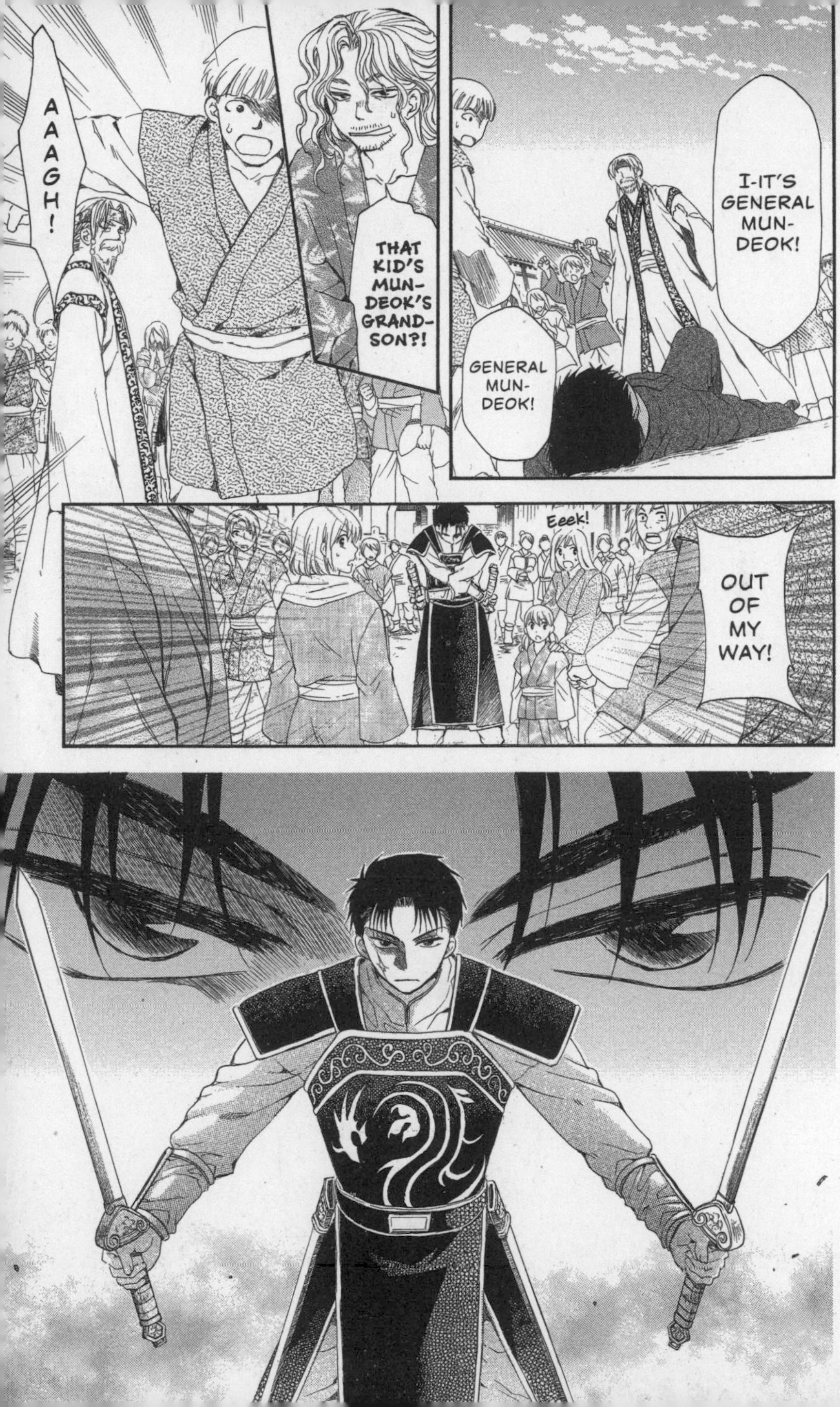
I-IT'S GENERAL MUN-DEOK!
GENERAL MUN-DEOK!
THAT KID'S MUN-DEOK'S GRAND-SON?!
AAAGH!
OUT OF MY WAY!
Eeek!

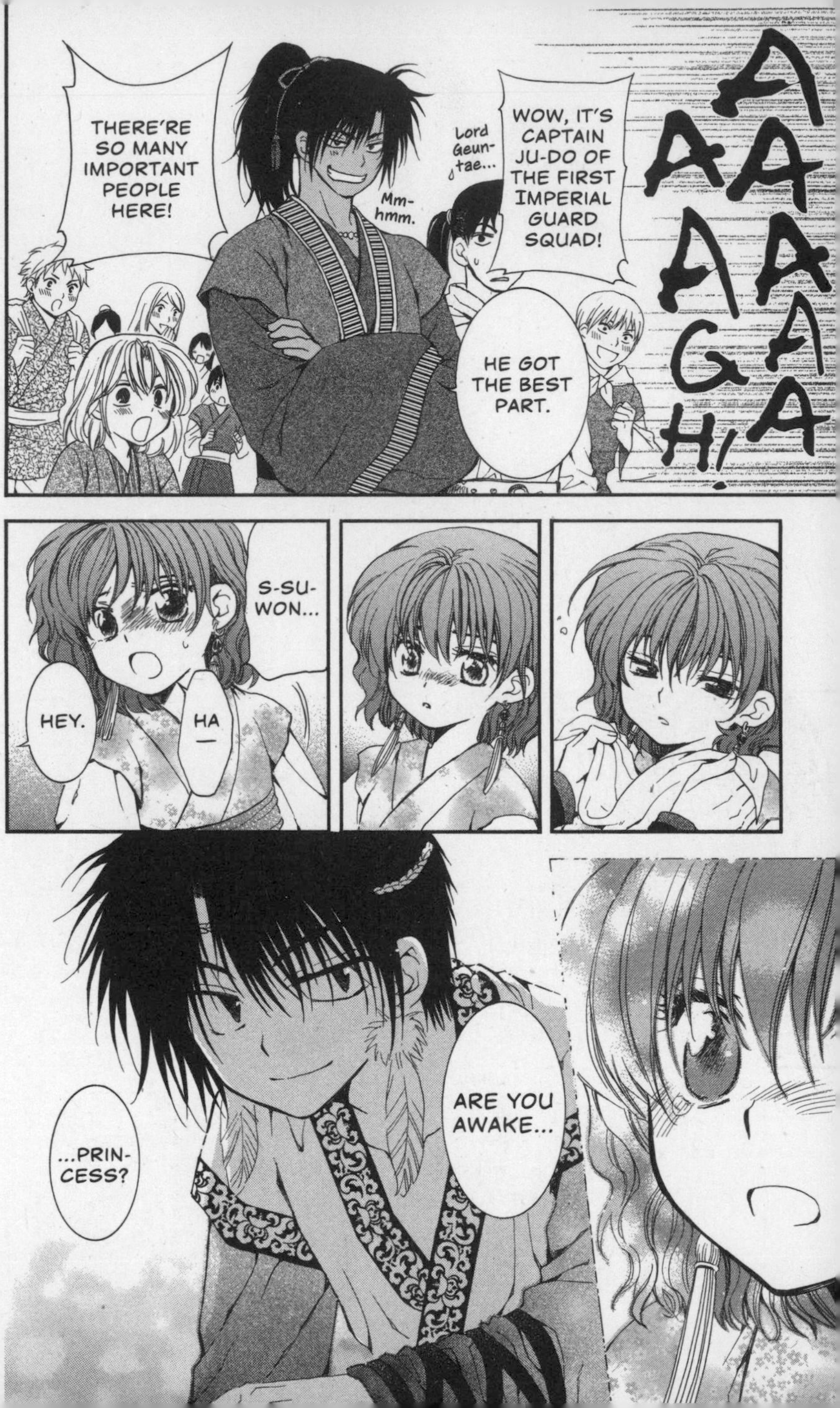
AAAAAAAGH!
WOW, IT'S CAPTAIN JU-DO OF THE FIRST IMPERIAL GUARD SQUAD!
Lord Geun-tae...
Mm-hmm.
THERE'RE SO MANY IMPORTANT PEOPLE HERE!
HE GOT THE BEST PART.
S-SU-WON...
HA—
HEY.
ARE YOU AWAKE...
...PRINCESS?

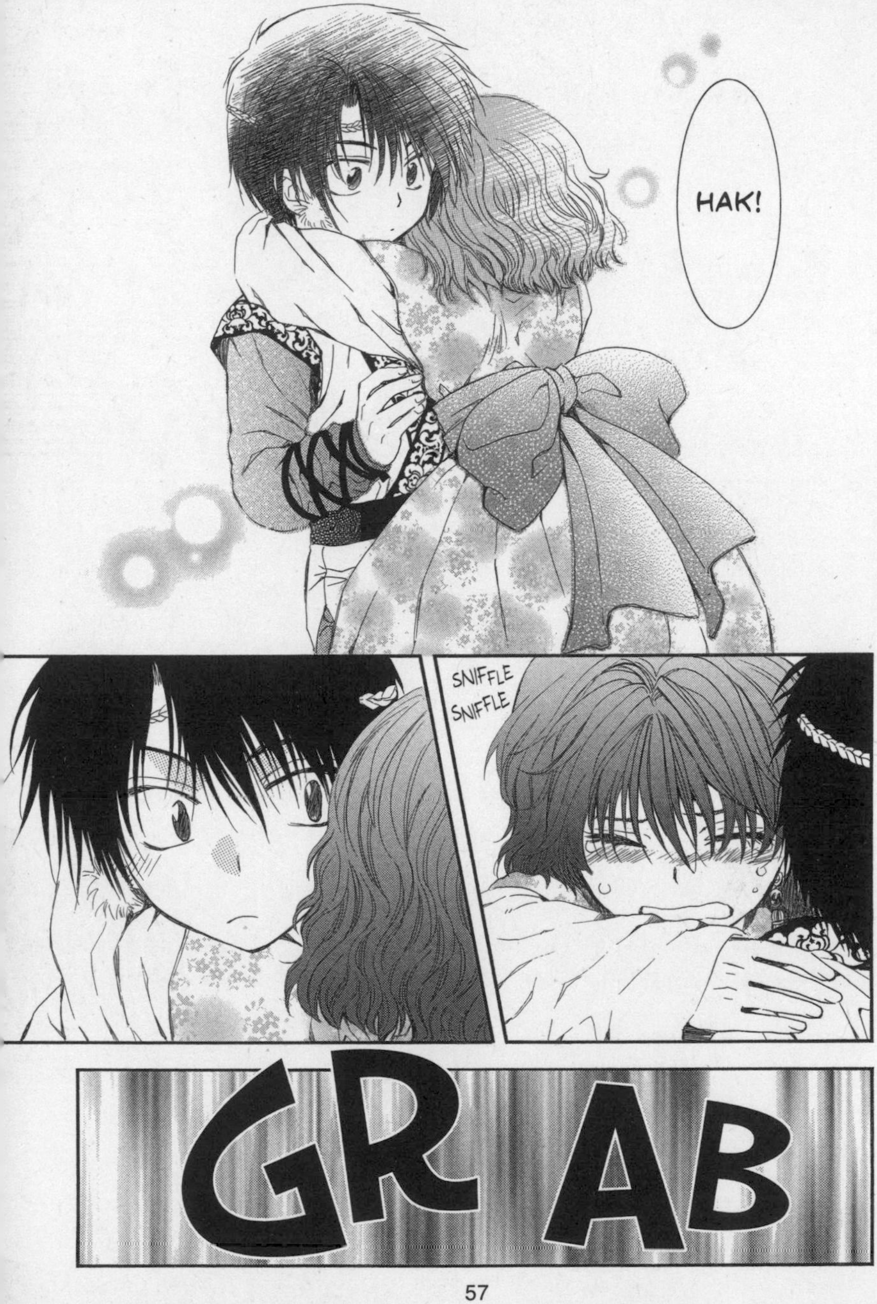
HAK!
SNIFFLE SNIFFLE
GRAB

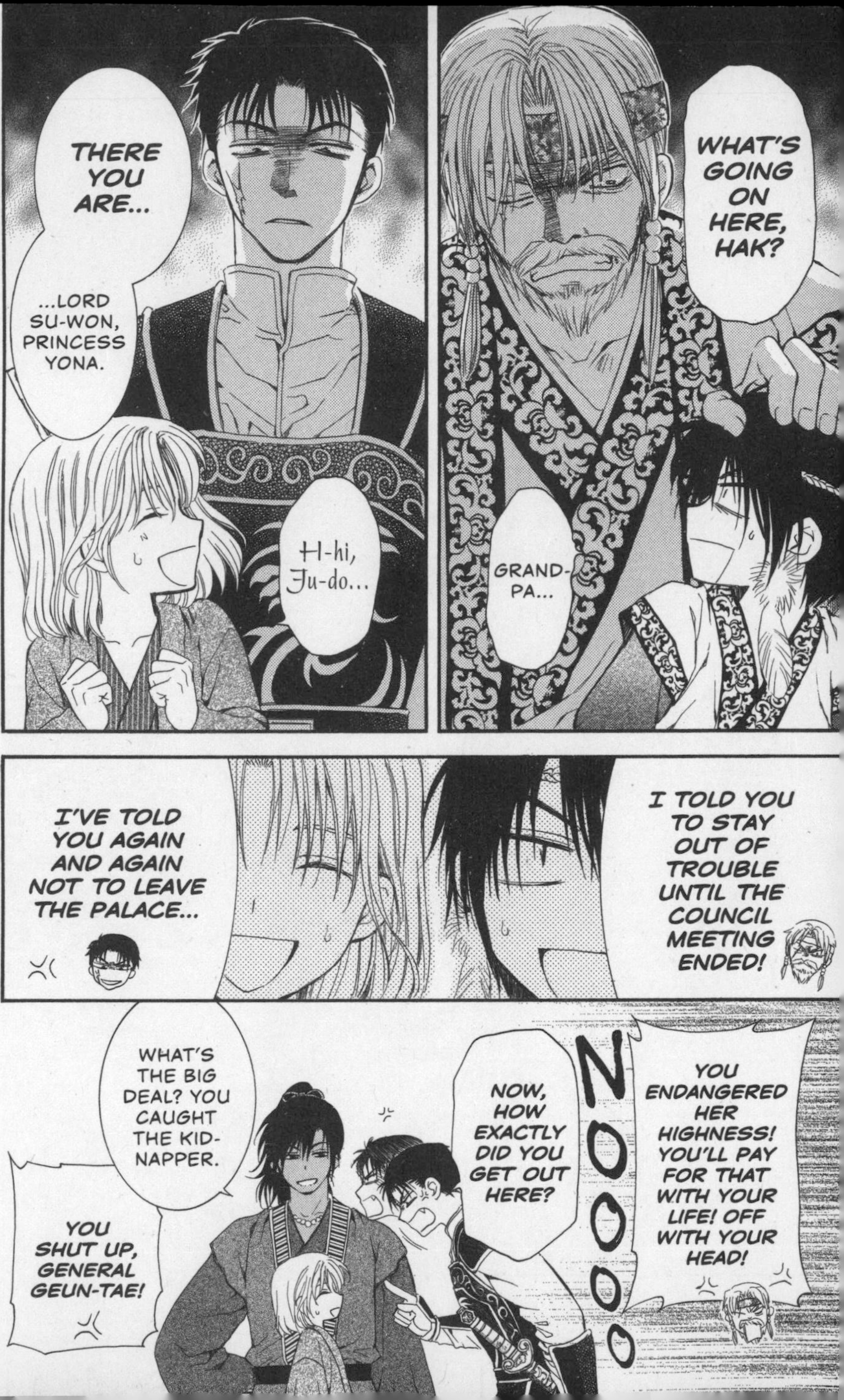
WHAT'S GOING ON HERE, HAK?
GRAND-PA...
THERE YOU ARE...
...LORD SU-WON, PRINCESS YONA.
H-hi, Ju-do...
I TOLD YOU TO STAY OUT OF TROUBLE UNTIL THE COUNCIL MEETING ENDED!
I'VE TOLD YOU AGAIN AND AGAIN NOT TO LEAVE THE PALACE...
YOU ENDANGERED HER HIGHNESS! YOU'LL PAY FOR THAT WITH YOUR LIFE! OFF WITH YOUR HEAD!
NOOO
NOW, HOW EXACTLY DID YOU GET OUT HERE?
WHAT'S THE BIG DEAL? YOU CAUGHT THE KID-NAPPER.
YOU SHUT UP, GENERAL GEUN-TAE!

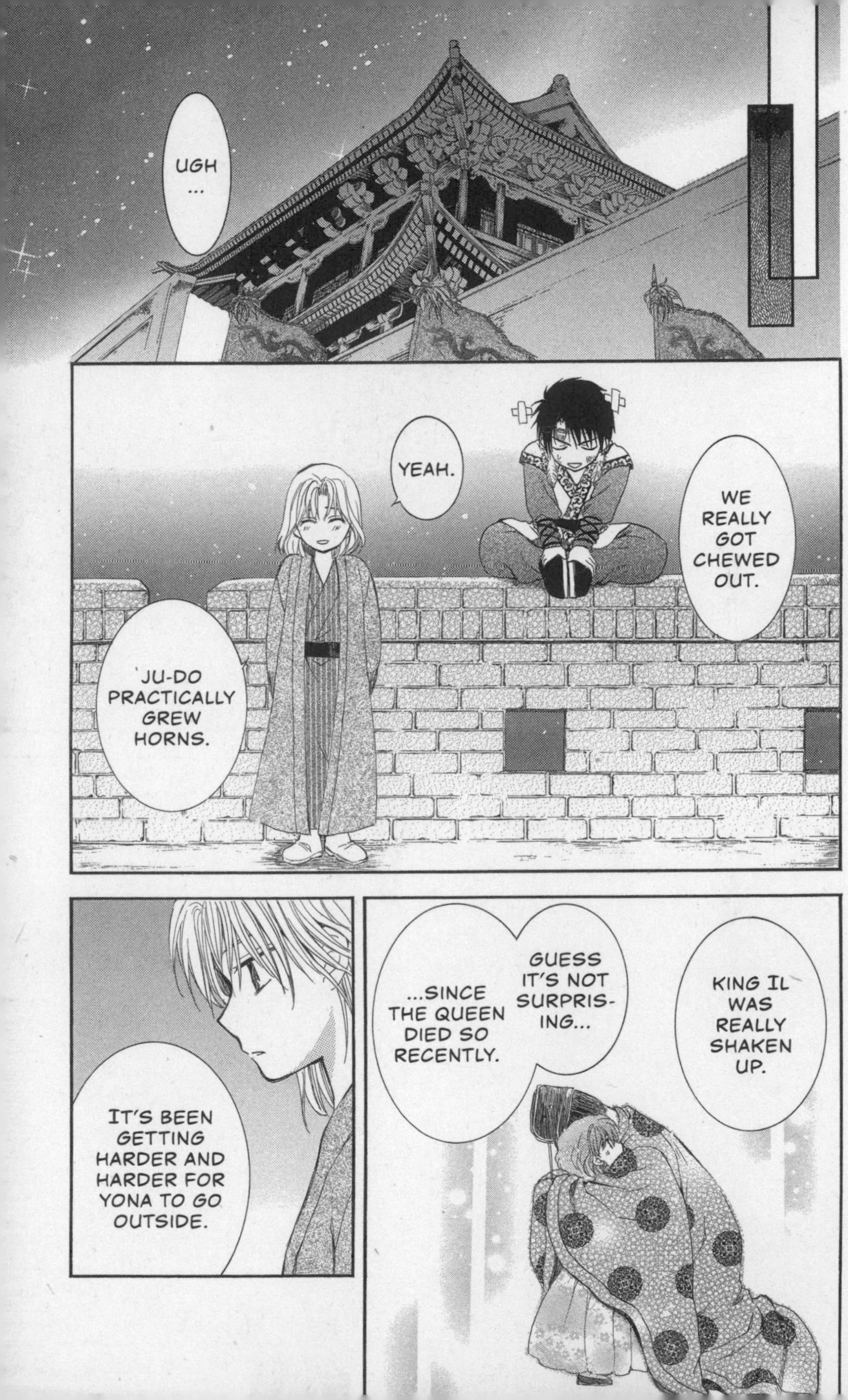
UGH ...
WE REALLY GOT CHEWED OUT.
YEAH.
JU-DO PRACTICALLY GREW HORNS.
KING IL WAS REALLY SHAKEN UP.
GUESS IT'S NOT SURPRISING...
...SINCE THE QUEEN DIED SO RECENTLY.
IT'S BEEN GETTING HARDER AND HARDER FOR YONA TO GO OUTSIDE.

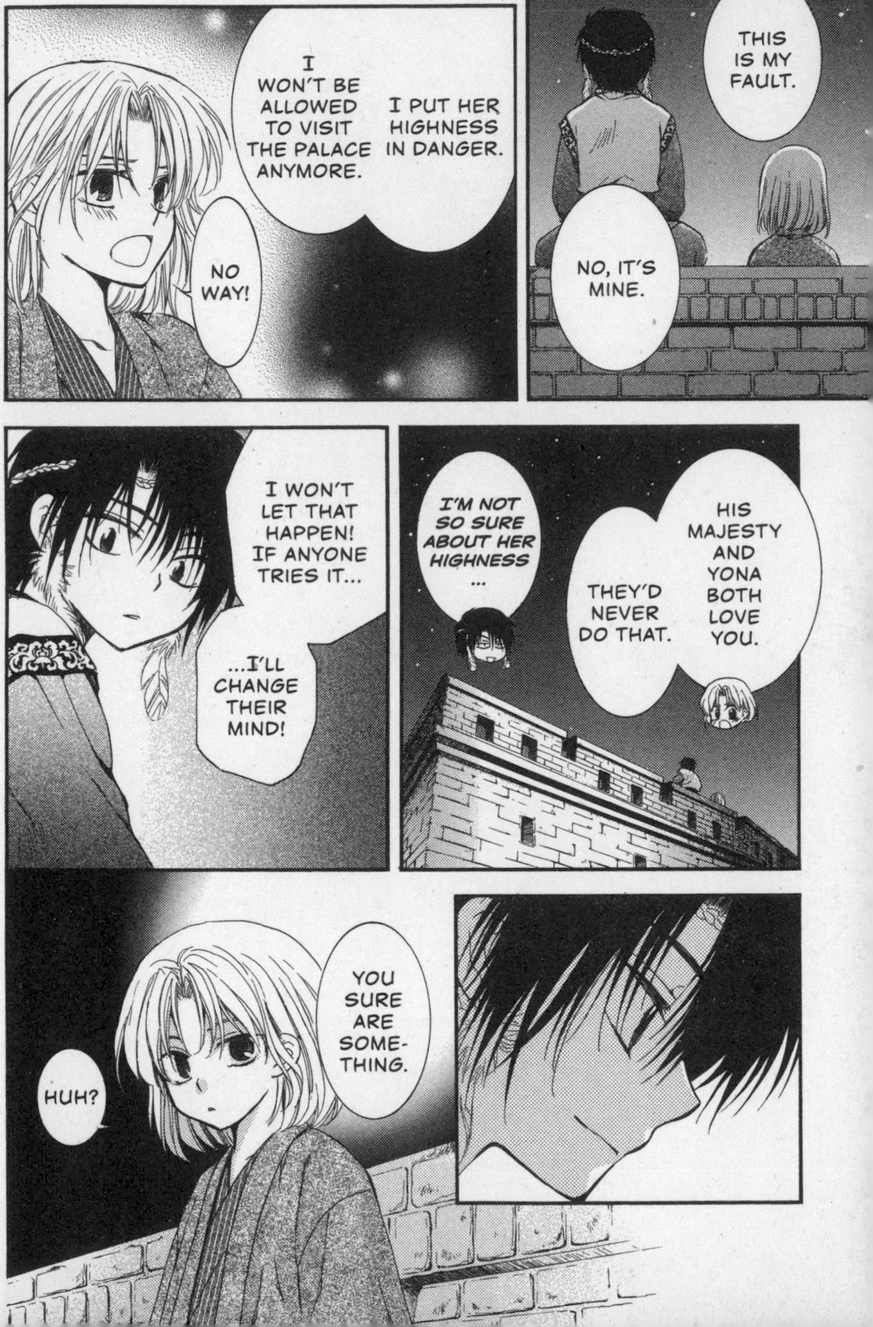
THIS IS MY FAULT.
NO, IT'S MINE.
I PUT HER HIGHNESS IN DANGER.
I WON'T BE ALLOWED TO VISIT THE PALACE ANYMORE.
NO WAY!
HIS MAJESTY AND YONA BOTH LOVE YOU.
THEY'D NEVER DO THAT.
I'M NOT SO SURE ABOUT HER HIGHNESS...
I WON'T LET THAT HAPPEN! IF ANYONE TRIES IT...
...I'LL CHANGE THEIR MIND!
YOU SURE ARE SOME-THING.
HUH?

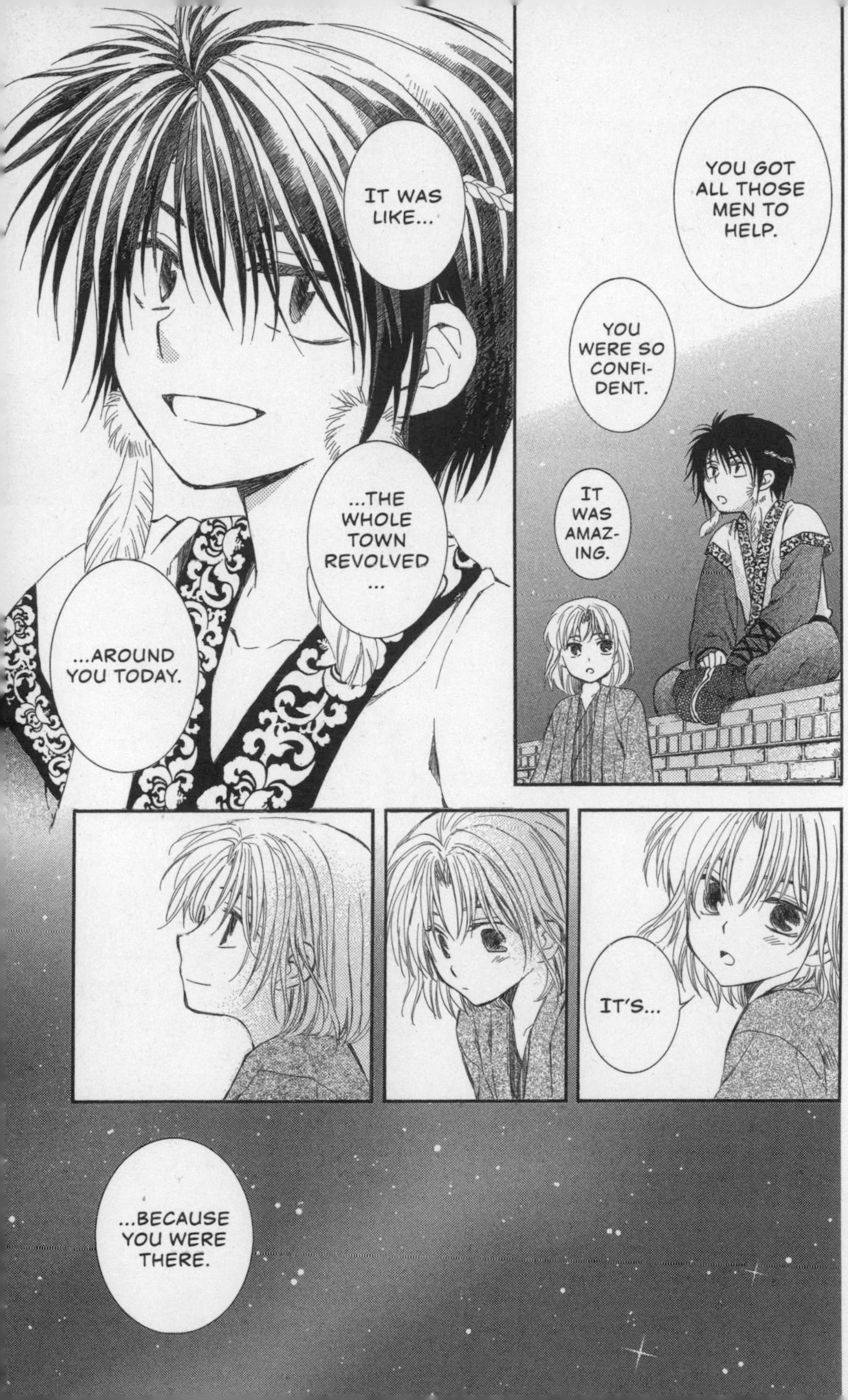
YOU GOT ALL THOSE MEN TO HELP.
YOU WERE SO CONFIDENT.
IT WAS AMAZING.
IT WAS LIKE...
...THE WHOLE TOWN REVOLVED...
...AROUND YOU TODAY.
IT'S...
...BECAUSE YOU WERE THERE.

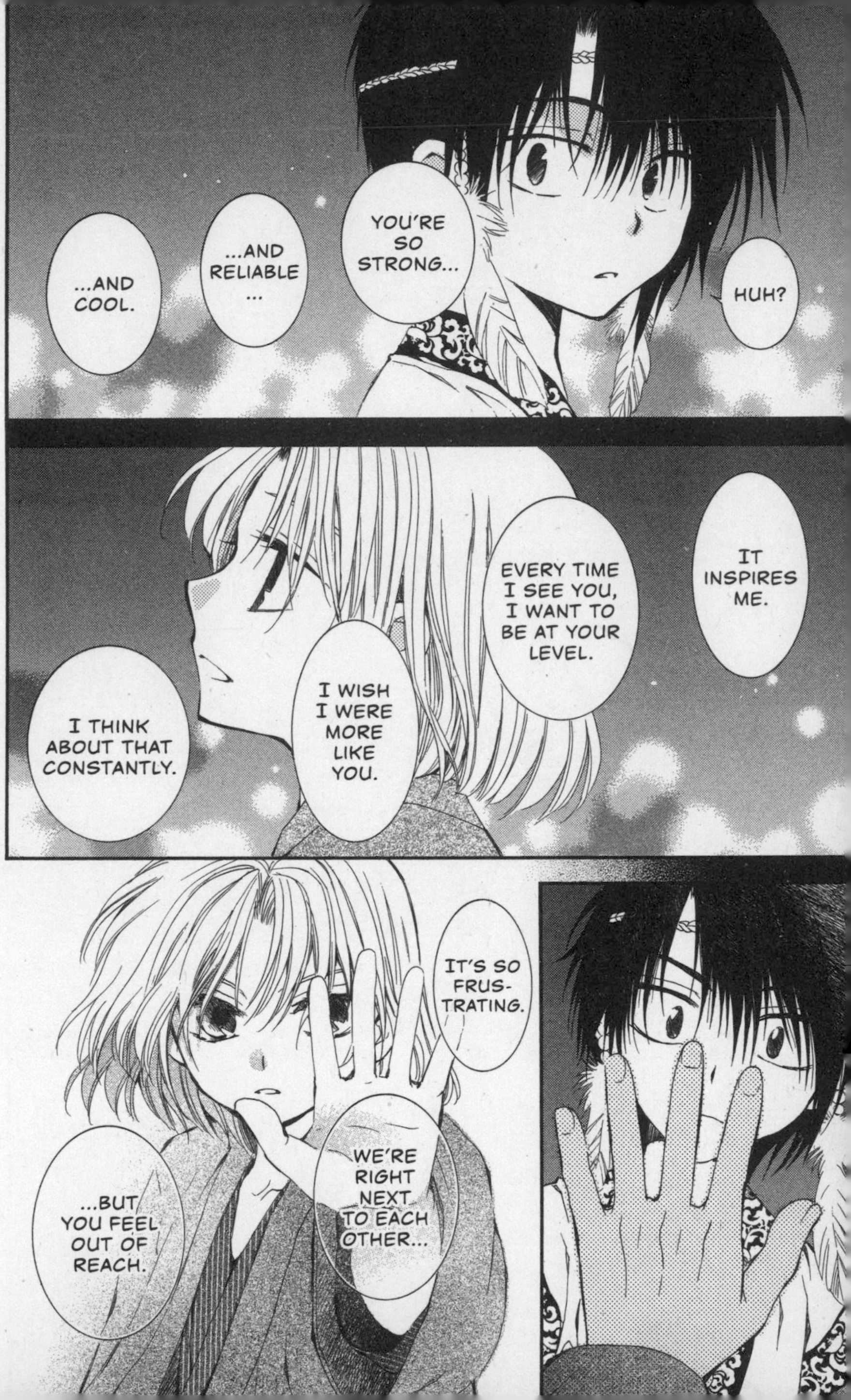
HUH?
YOU'RE SO STRONG...
...AND RELIABLE ...
...AND COOL.
IT INSPIRES ME.
EVERY TIME I SEE YOU, I WANT TO BE AT YOUR LEVEL.
I WISH I WERE MORE LIKE YOU.
I THINK ABOUT THAT CONSTANTLY.
IT'S SO FRUS-TRATING.
WE'RE RIGHT NEXT TO EACH OTHER...
...BUT YOU FEEL OUT OF REACH.

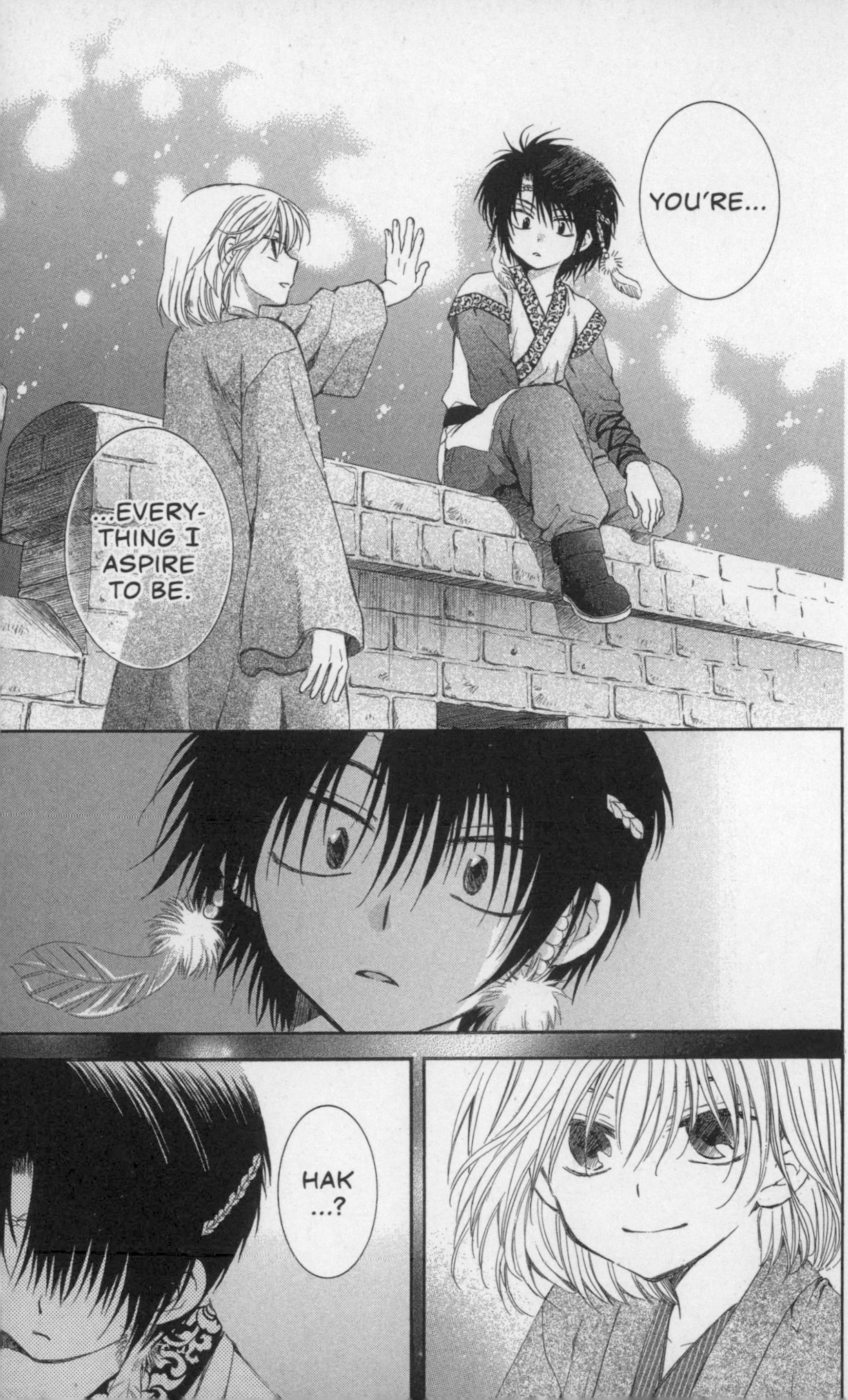
YOU'RE...
...EVERY-THING I ASPIRE TO BE.
HAK ...?

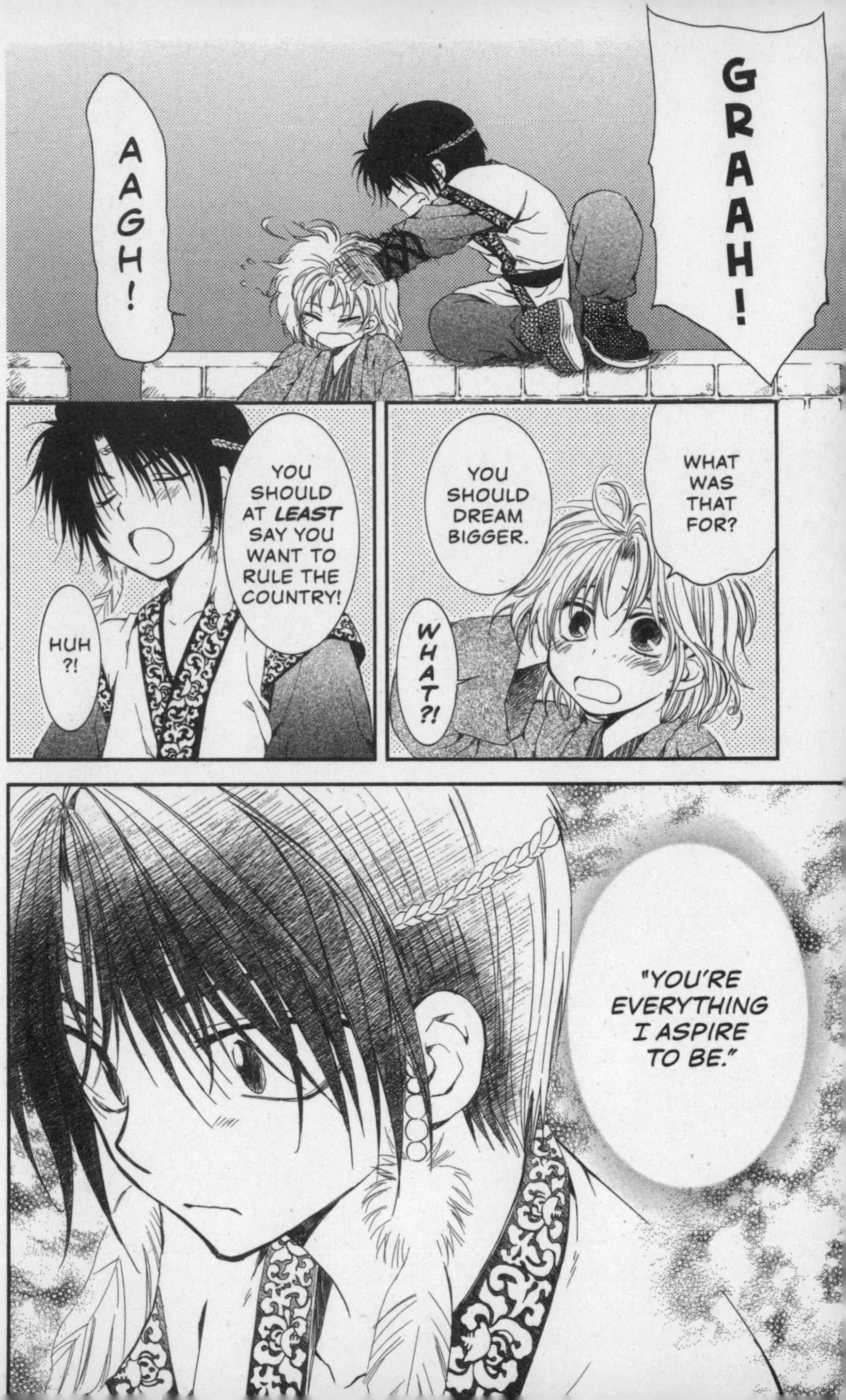
GRAAH!
AAGH!
WHAT WAS THAT FOR?
YOU SHOULD DREAM BIGGER.
WHAT?!
YOU SHOULD AT *LEAST* SAY YOU WANT TO RULE THE COUNTRY!
HUH?!
"YOU'RE EVERYTHING I ASPIRE TO BE."

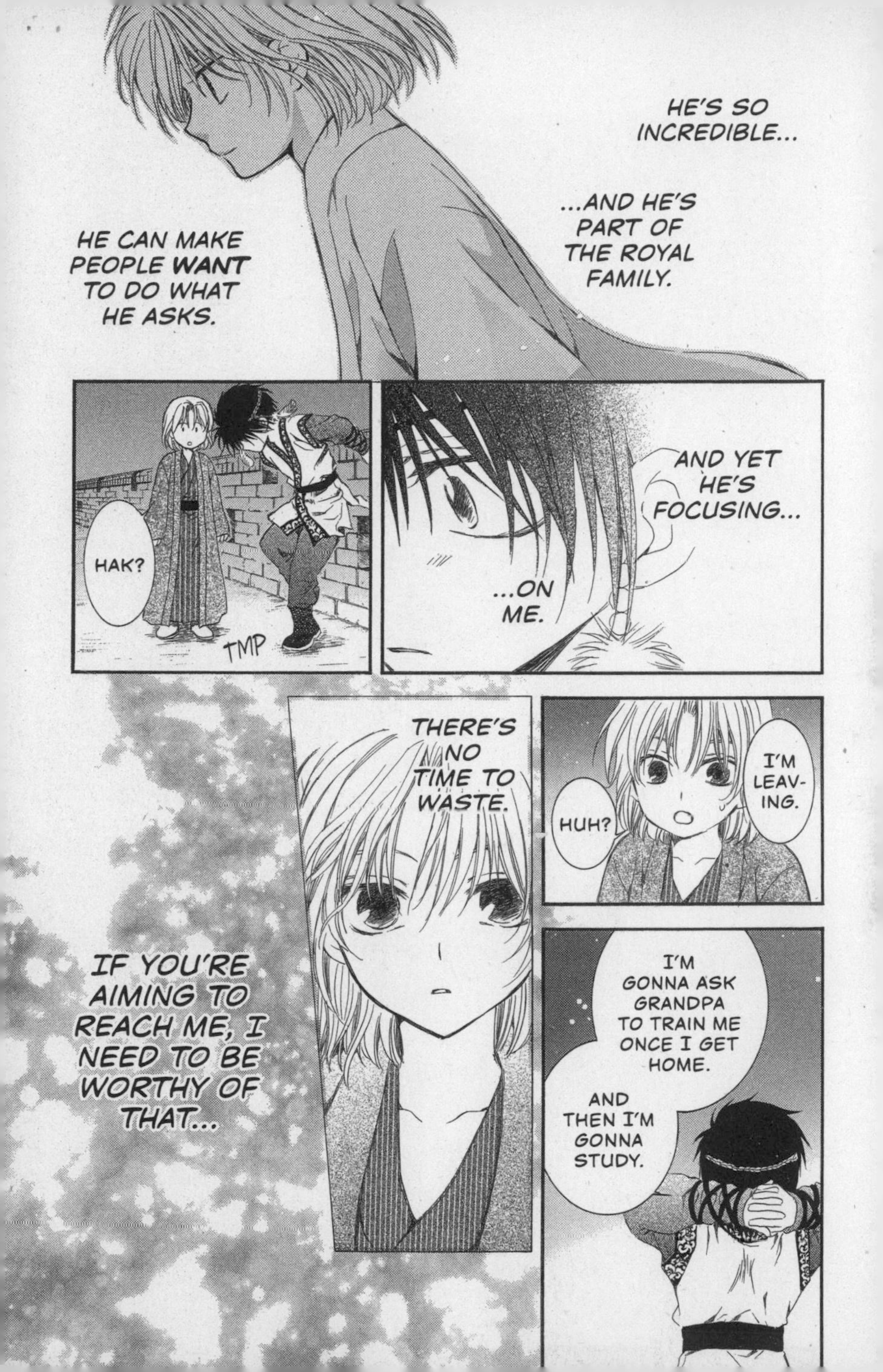
HE'S SO INCREDIBLE...
...AND HE'S PART OF THE ROYAL FAMILY.
HE CAN MAKE PEOPLE **WANT** TO DO WHAT HE ASKS.
AND YET HE'S FOCUSING...
...ON ME.
HAK?
TMP
I'M LEAV-ING.
HUH?
I'M GONNA ASK GRANDPA TO TRAIN ME ONCE I GET HOME.
AND THEN I'M GONNA STUDY.
THERE'S NO TIME TO WASTE.
IF YOU'RE AIMING TO REACH ME, I NEED TO BE WORTHY OF THAT...

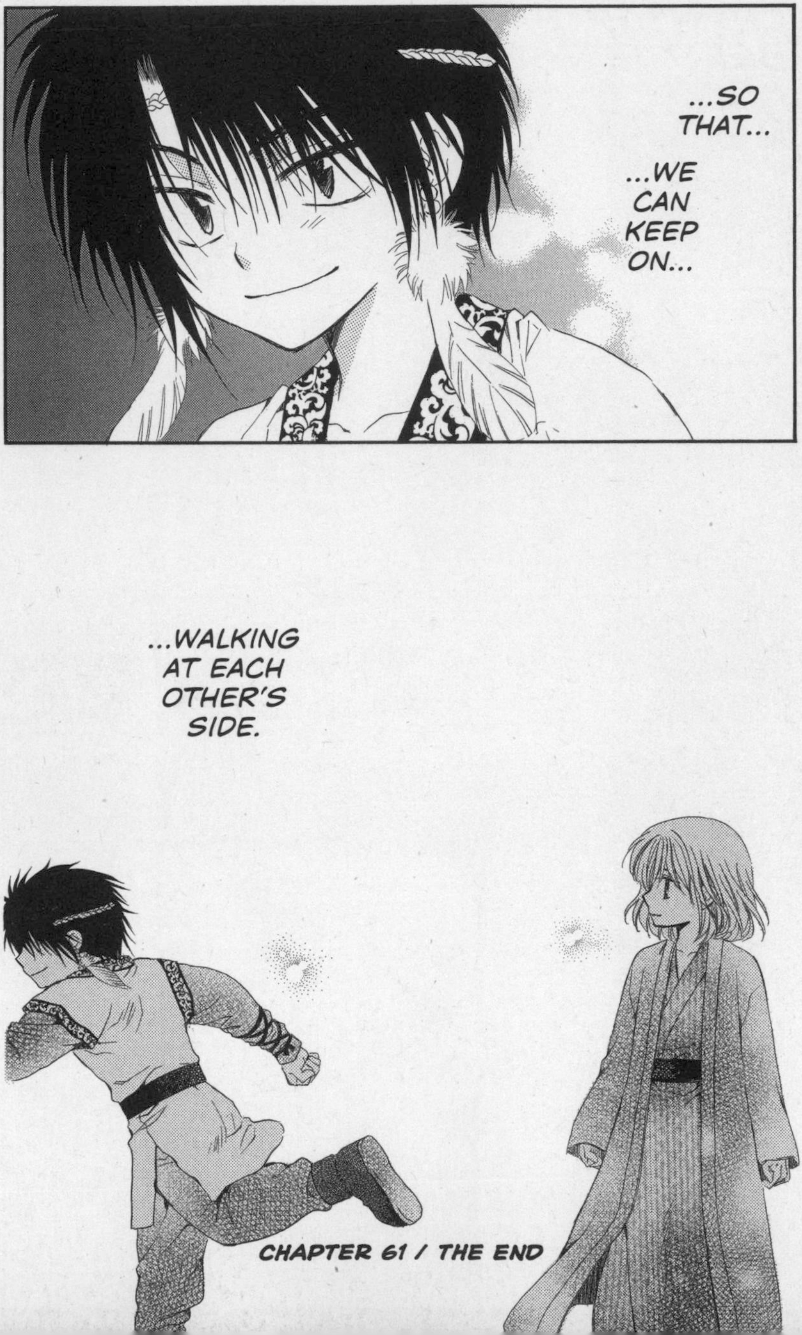
...SO THAT...
...WE CAN KEEP ON...
...WALKING AT EACH OTHER'S SIDE.
CHAPTER 61 / THE END

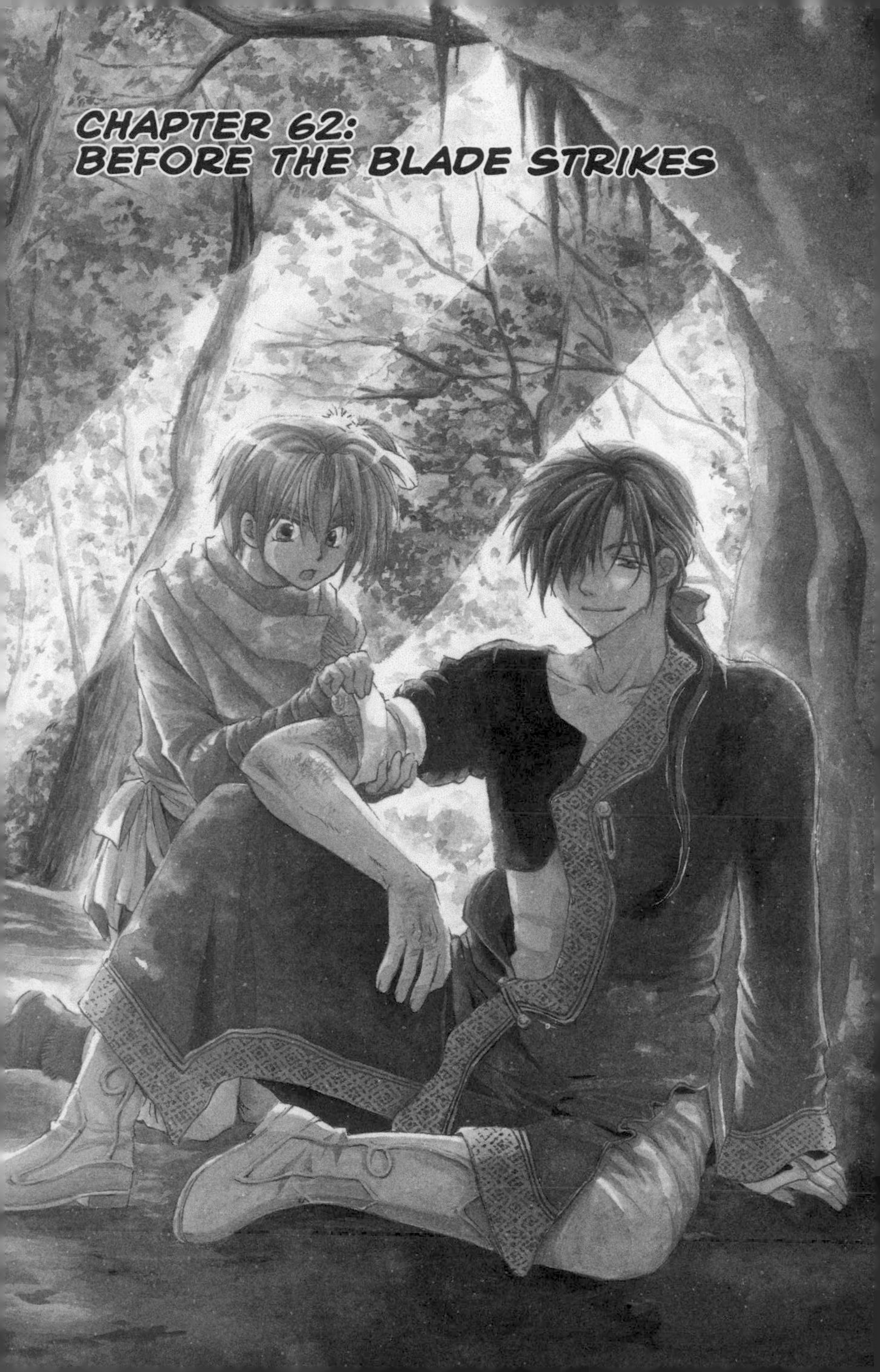
CHAPTER 62:
BEFORE THE BLADE STRIKES

General Geun-tae & Captain Ju-do

Ju-do is younger than Geun-tae. Geun-tae became general unusually young, and he's quite a bit more powerful than Ju-do. Ju-do is a hard worker, though, and after rigorous training, he now rivals Geun-tae.

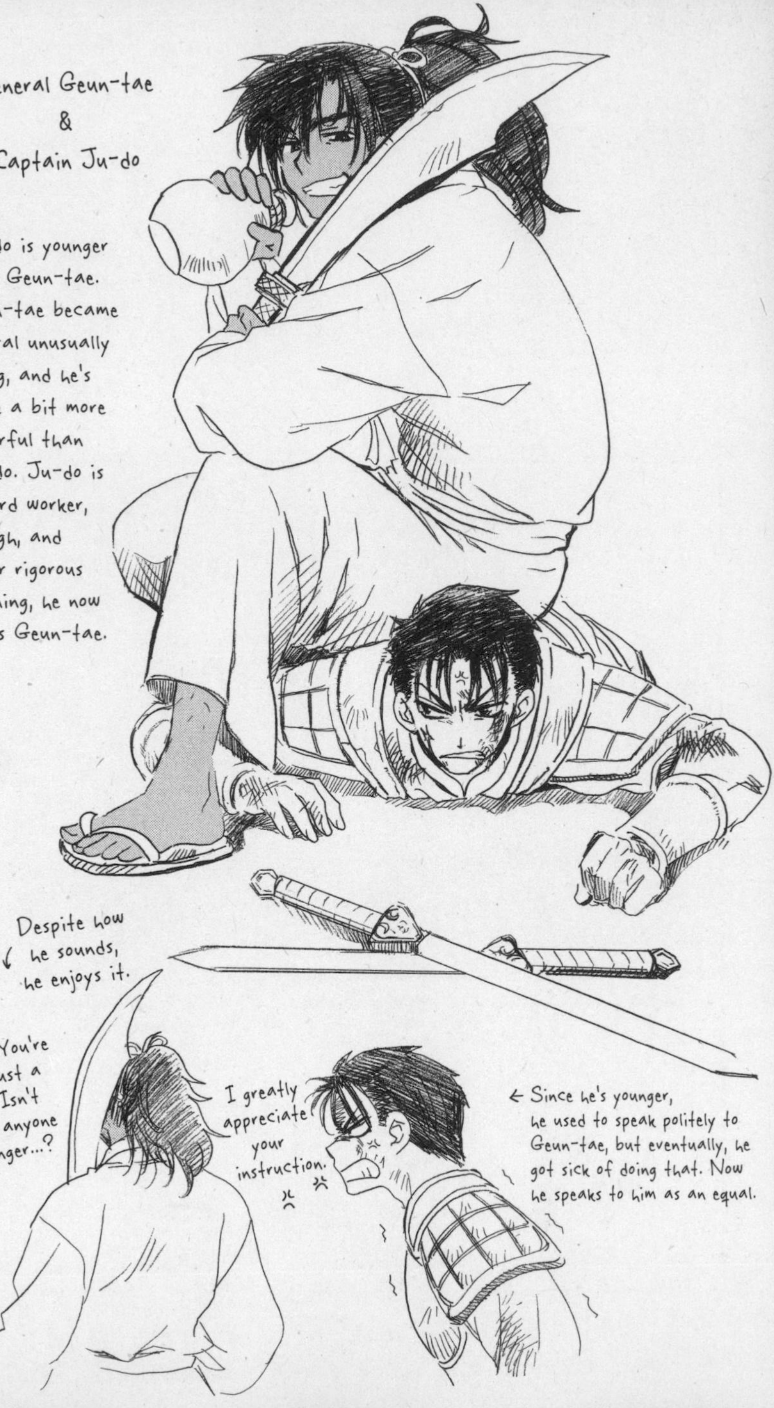

Despite how he sounds, he enjoys it.
Since he's younger, he used to speak politely to Geun-tae, but eventually, he got sick of doing that. Now he speaks to him as an equal.
I greatly appreciate your instruction.
Sigh... You're still just a kid. Isn't there anyone stronger...?

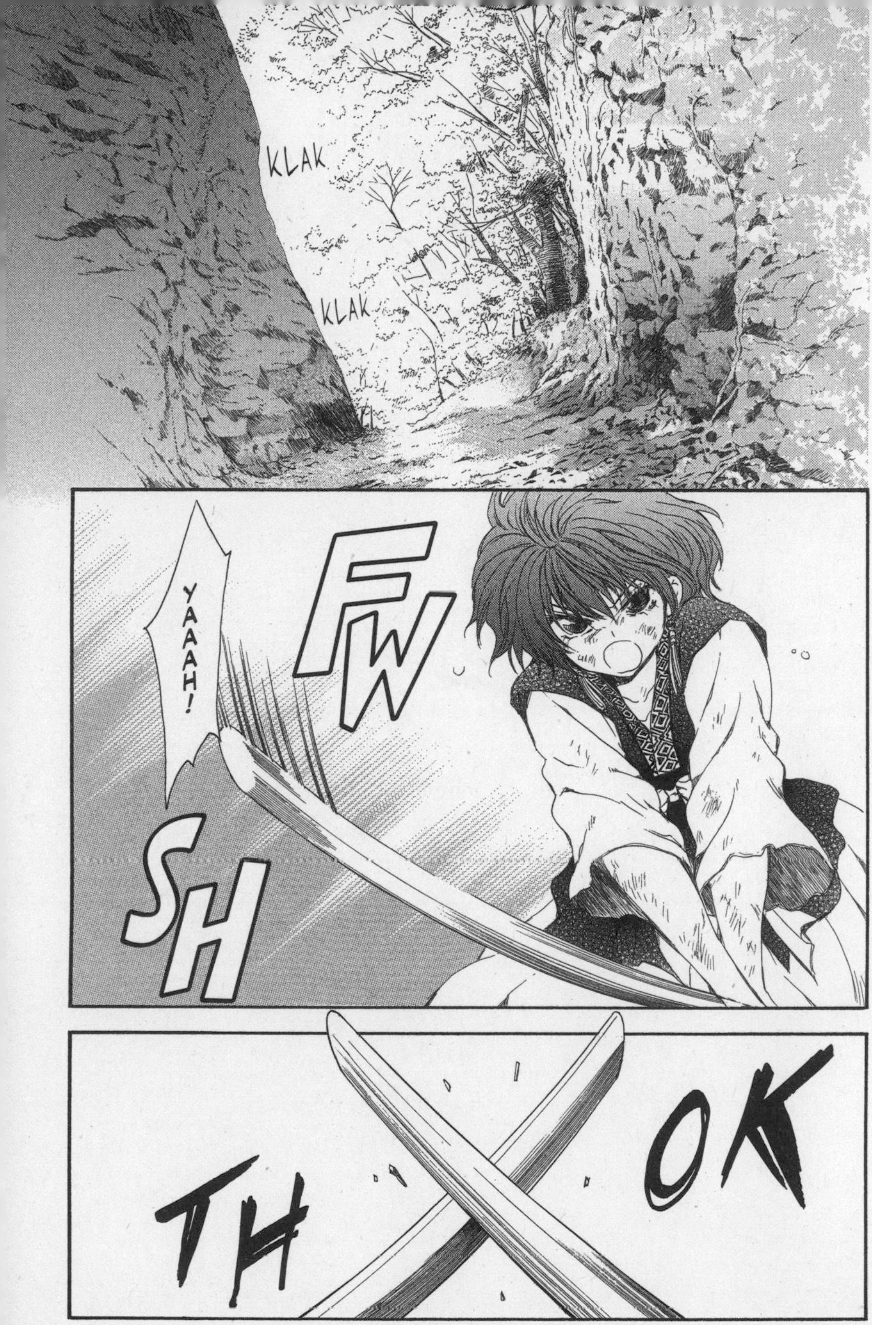
KLAK
KLAK
FW
YAAAH!
SH
TH
OK

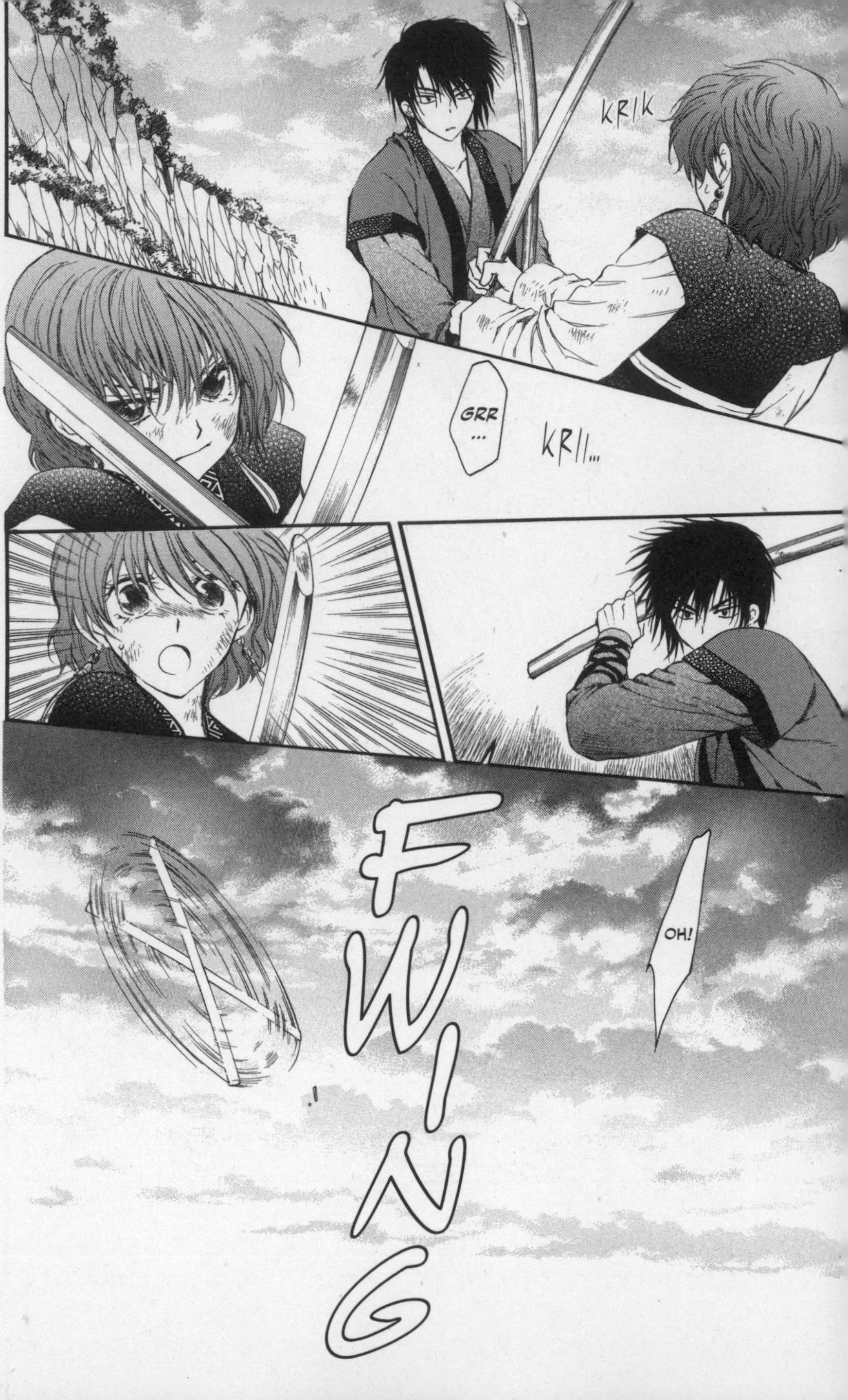
KRIK
KRII...
GRR ...
OH!
FWING

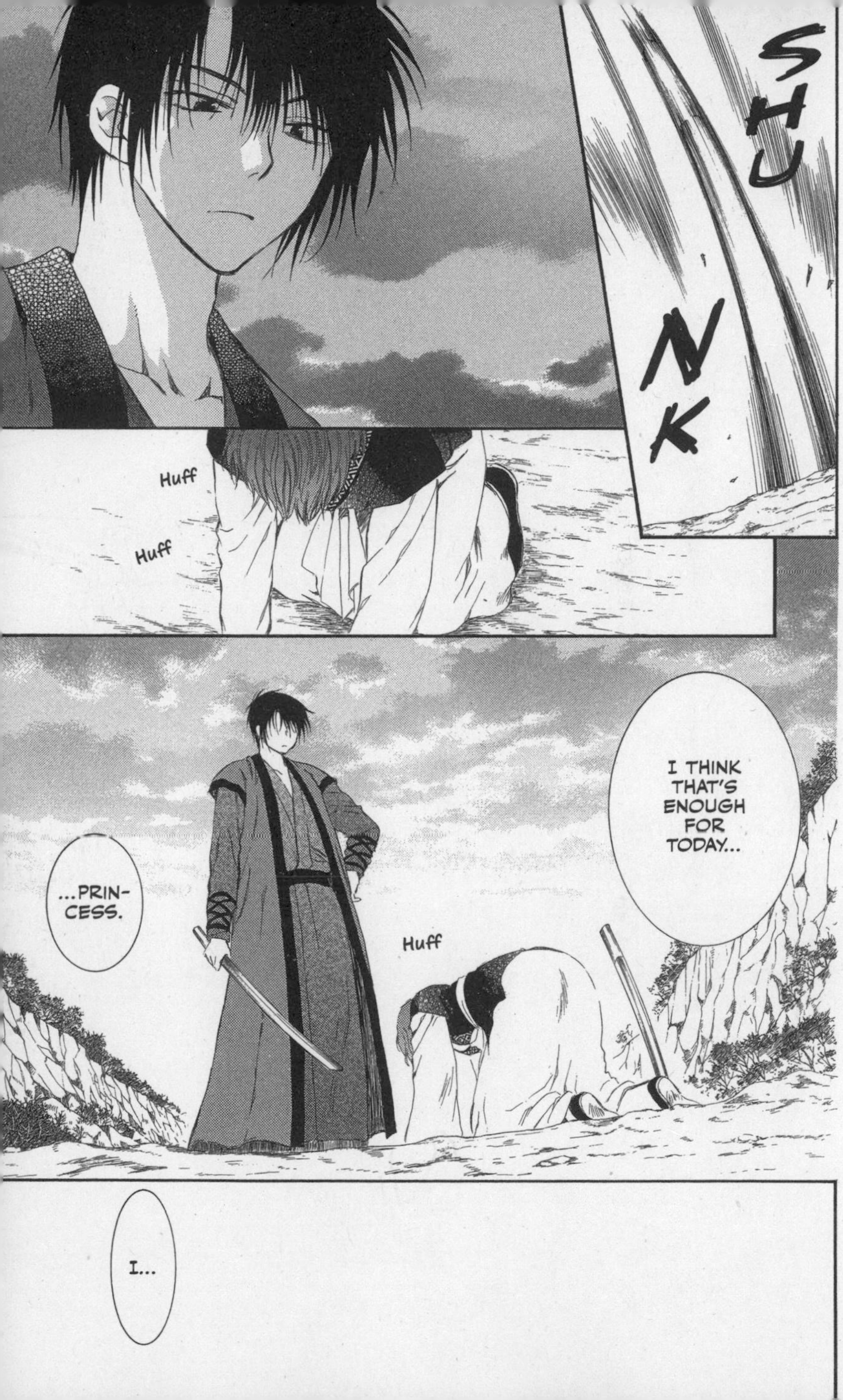
SHUNK
Huff
Huff
I THINK THAT'S ENOUGH FOR TODAY...
...PRIN-CESS.
Huff
I...

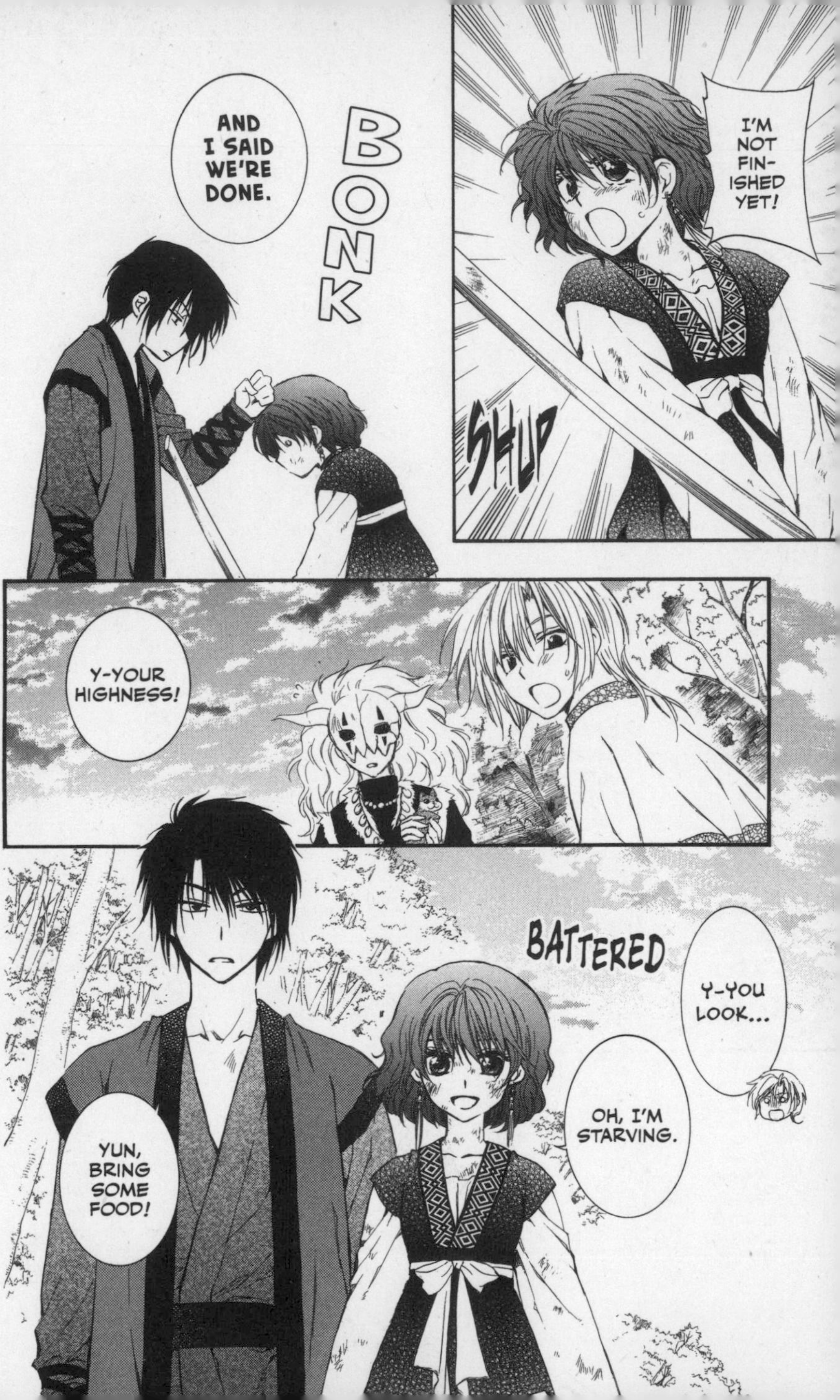
I'M NOT FIN-ISHED YET!
SHUP
BONK
AND I SAID WE'RE DONE.
Y-YOUR HIGHNESS!
Y-YOU LOOK...
BATTERED
OH, I'M STARVING.
YUN, BRING SOME FOOD!

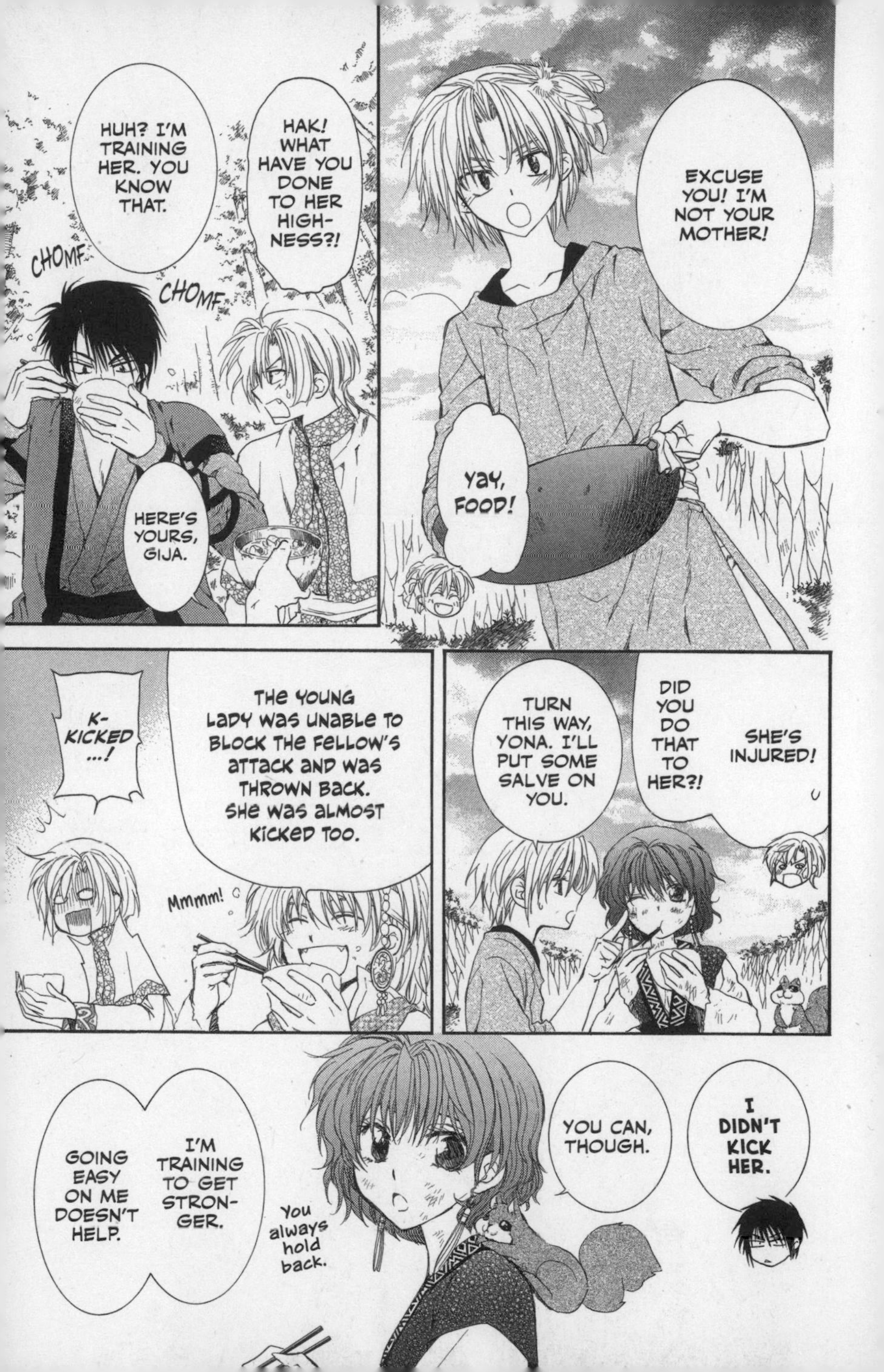

EXCUSE YOU! I'M NOT YOUR MOTHER!
Yay, FOOD!
HAK! WHAT HAVE YOU DONE TO HER HIGHNESS?!
HUH? I'M TRAINING HER. YOU KNOW THAT.
CHOMF
CHOMF
HERE'S YOURS, GIJA.
SHE'S INJURED!
DID YOU DO THAT TO HER?!
TURN THIS WAY, YONA. I'LL PUT SOME SALVE ON YOU.
The young lady was unable to block the fellow's attack and was thrown back. She was almost kicked too.
K-KICKED ...!
Mmmm!
I DIDN'T KICK HER.
YOU CAN, THOUGH.
You always hold back.
I'M TRAINING TO GET STRONGER.
GOING EASY ON ME DOESN'T HELP.

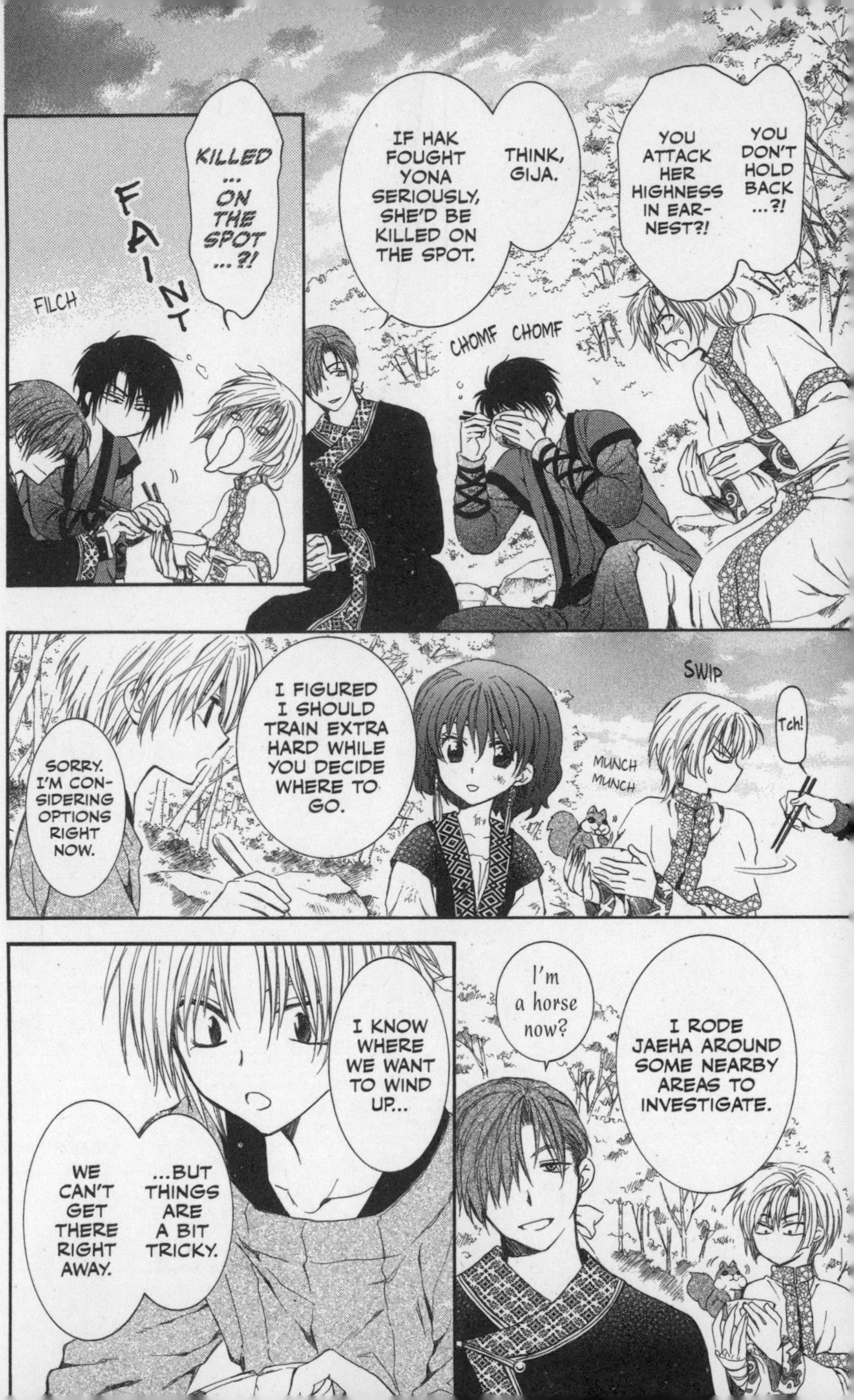
YOU DON'T HOLD BACK...?!
YOU ATTACK HER HIGHNESS IN EARNEST?!
THINK, GIJA.
IF HAK FOUGHT YONA SERIOUSLY, SHE'D BE KILLED ON THE SPOT.
CHOMF CHOMF
KILLED... ON THE SPOT...?!
FAINT
FILCH
SWIP
Tch!
MUNCH MUNCH
I FIGURED I SHOULD TRAIN EXTRA HARD WHILE YOU DECIDE WHERE TO GO.
SORRY. I'M CONSIDERING OPTIONS RIGHT NOW.
I RODE JAEHA AROUND SOME NEARBY AREAS TO INVESTIGATE.
I'm a horse now?
I KNOW WHERE WE WANT TO WIND UP...
...BUT THINGS ARE A BIT TRICKY.
WE CAN'T GET THERE RIGHT AWAY.

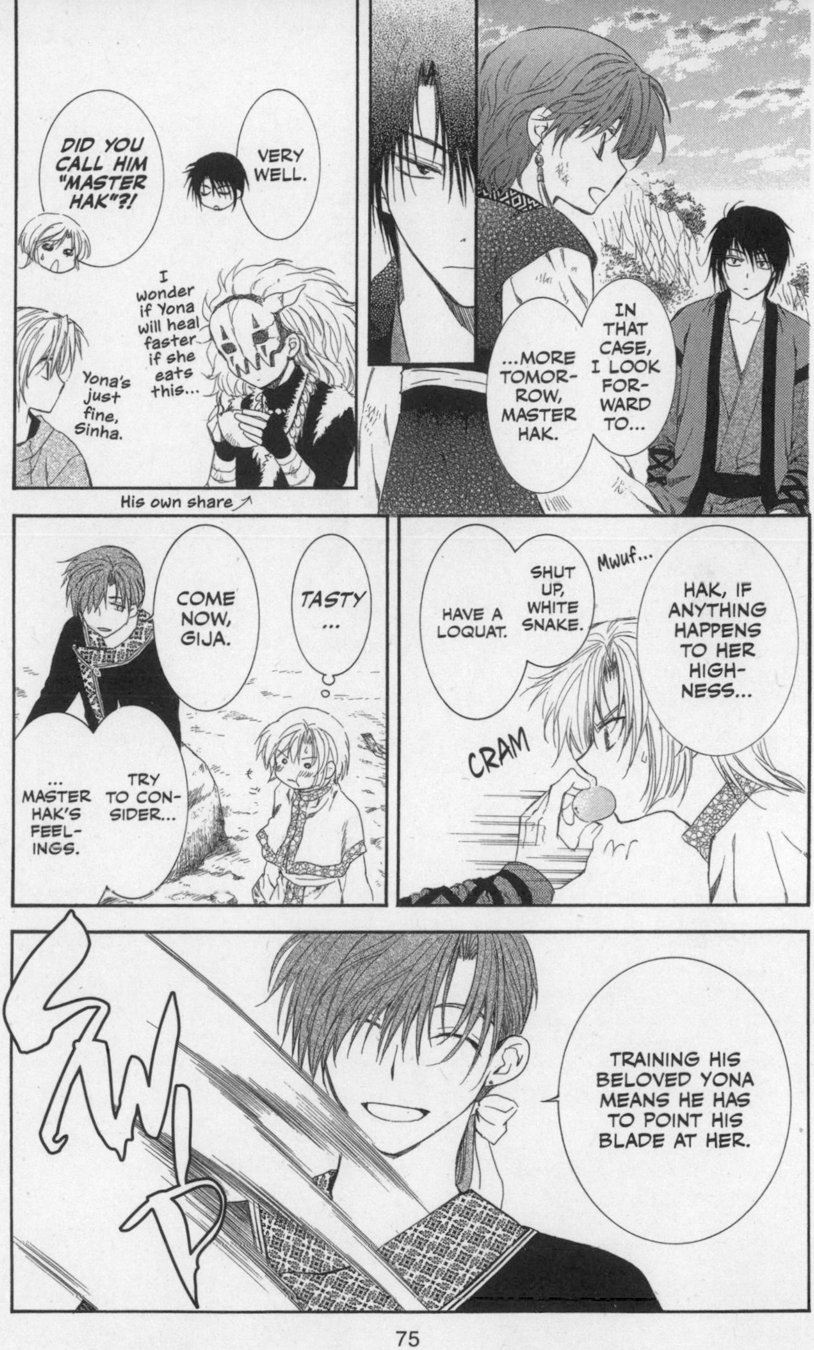
IN THAT CASE, I LOOK FORWARD TO...
...MORE TOMORROW, MASTER HAK.
VERY WELL.
DID YOU CALL HIM "MASTER HAK"?!
I wonder if Yona will heal faster if she eats this...
Yona's just fine, Sinha.
His own share
HAK, IF ANYTHING HAPPENS TO HER HIGHNESS...
Mwuf...
SHUT UP, WHITE SNAKE.
HAVE A LOQUAT.
CRAM
TASTY ...
COME NOW, GIJA.
TRY TO CONSIDER...
... MASTER HAK'S FEELINGS.
TRAINING HIS BELOVED YONA MEANS HE HAS TO POINT HIS BLADE AT HER.

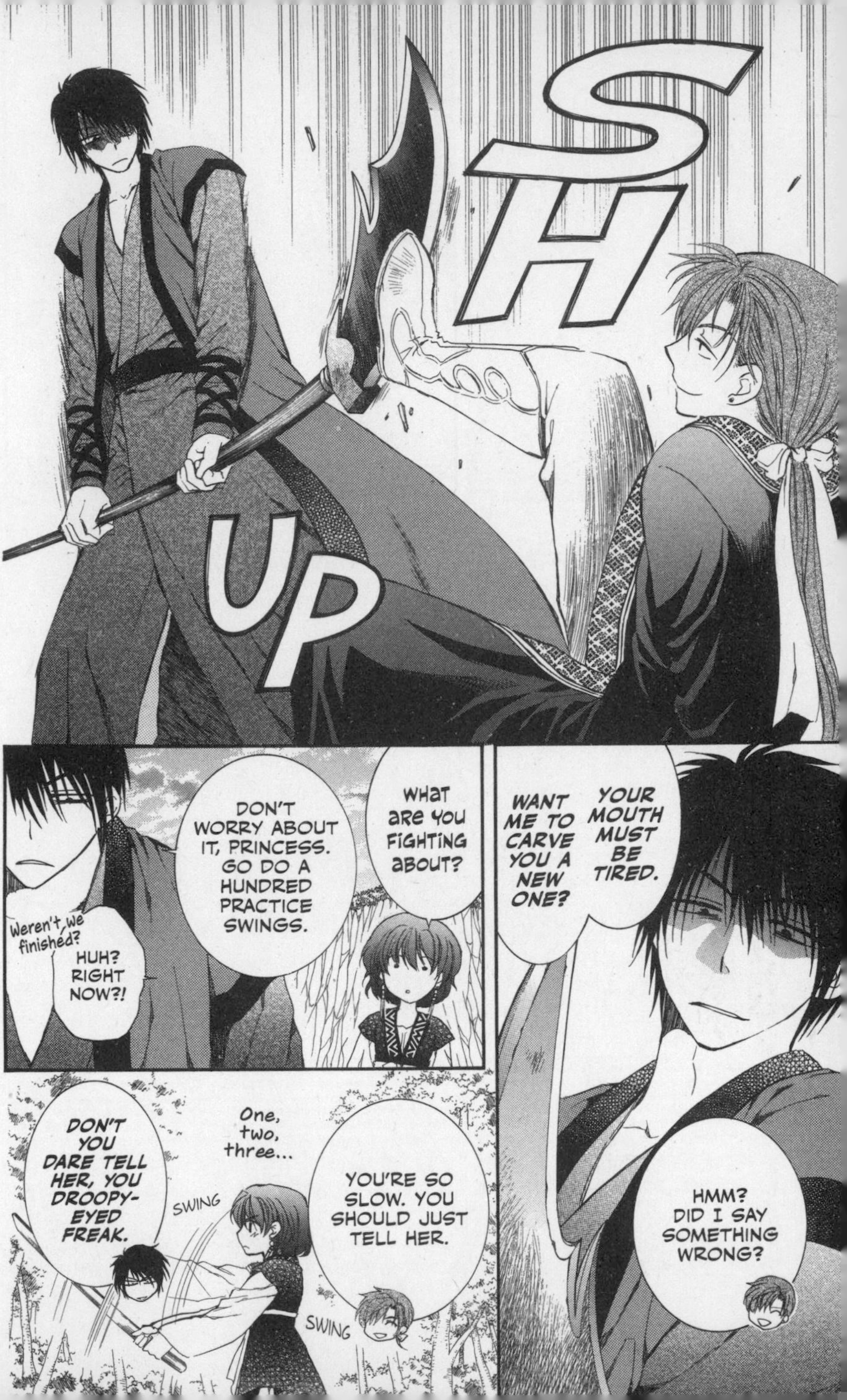
SH
UP
YOUR MOUTH MUST BE TIRED.
WANT ME TO CARVE YOU A NEW ONE?
HMM? DID I SAY SOMETHING WRONG?
WHAT are you FIGHTING about?
DON'T WORRY ABOUT IT, PRINCESS. GO DO A HUNDRED PRACTICE SWINGS.
HUH? RIGHT NOW?!
Weren't we finished?
YOU'RE SO SLOW. YOU SHOULD JUST TELL HER.
One, two, three...
SWING
SWING
DON'T YOU DARE TELL HER, YOU DROOPY-EYED FREAK.

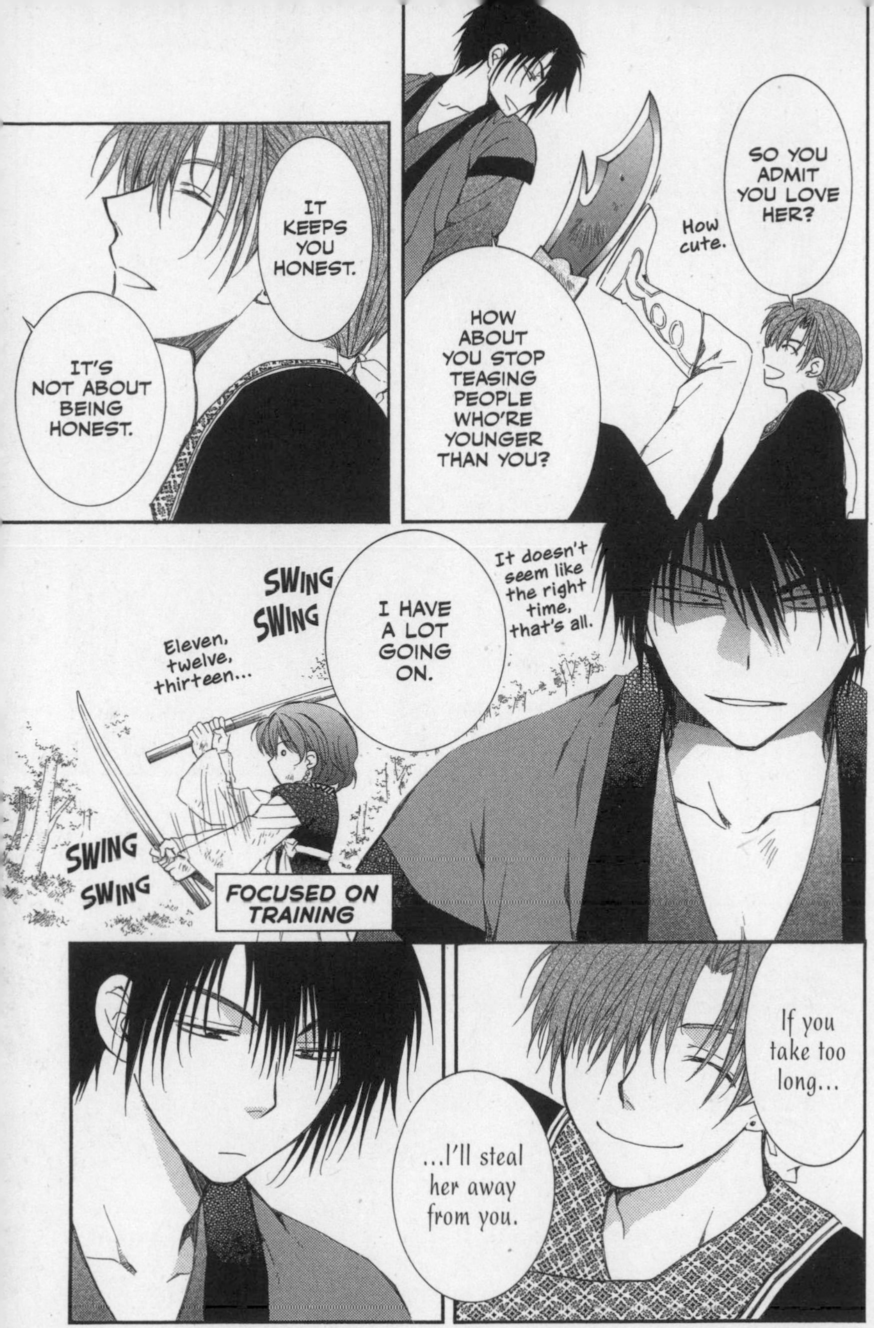
SO YOU ADMIT YOU LOVE HER?
How cute.
HOW ABOUT YOU STOP TEASING PEOPLE WHO'RE YOUNGER THAN YOU?
IT KEEPS YOU HONEST.
IT'S NOT ABOUT BEING HONEST.
It doesn't seem like the right time, that's all.
I HAVE A LOT GOING ON.
SWING SWING
Eleven, twelve, thirteen...
SWING SWING
FOCUSED ON TRAINING
If you take too long...
...I'll steal her away from you.

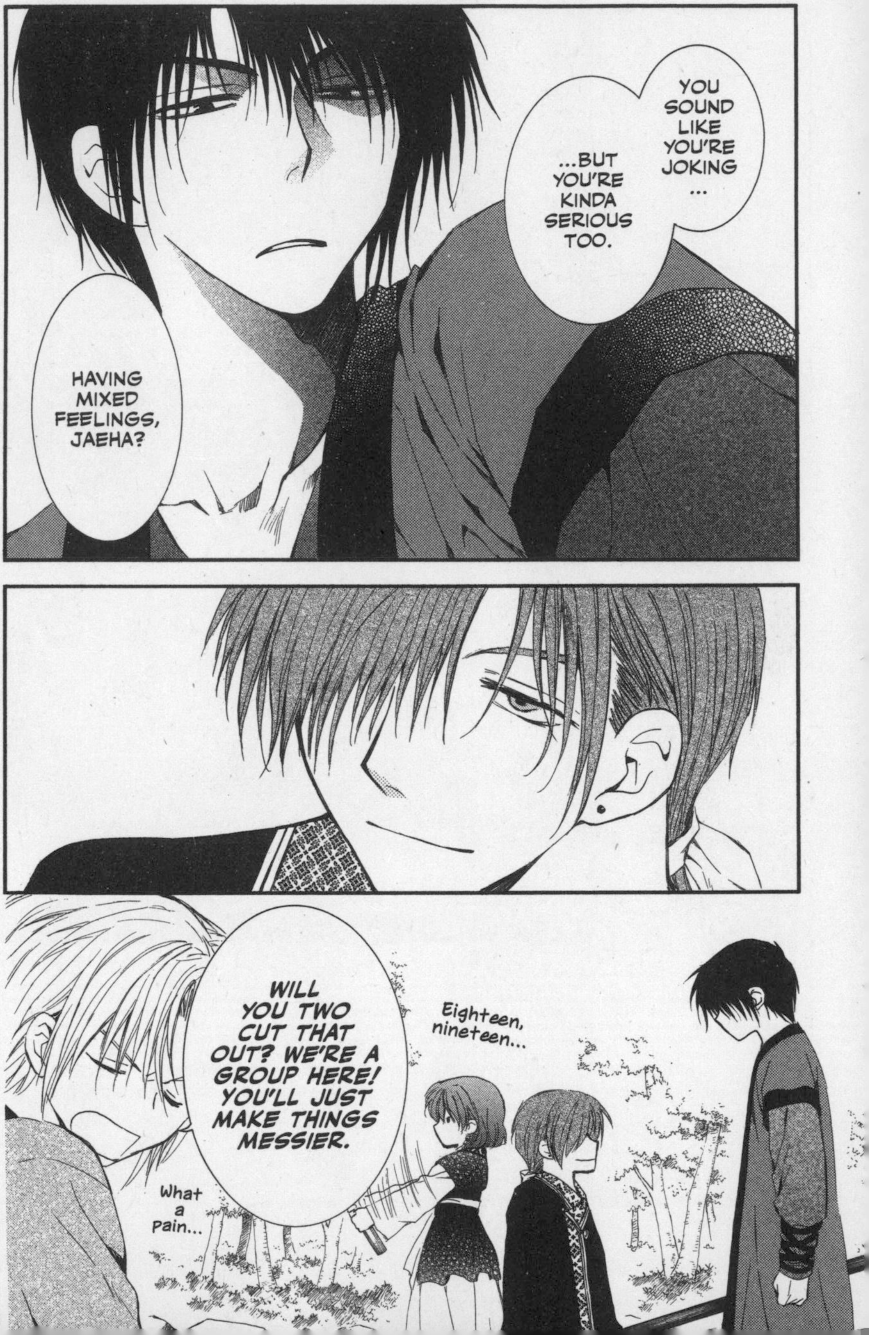
YOU SOUND LIKE YOU'RE JOKING...
...BUT YOU'RE KINDA SERIOUS TOO.
HAVING MIXED FEELINGS, JAEHA?
Eighteen, nineteen...
WILL YOU TWO CUT THAT OUT? WE'RE A GROUP HERE! YOU'LL JUST MAKE THINGS MESSIER.
What a pain...

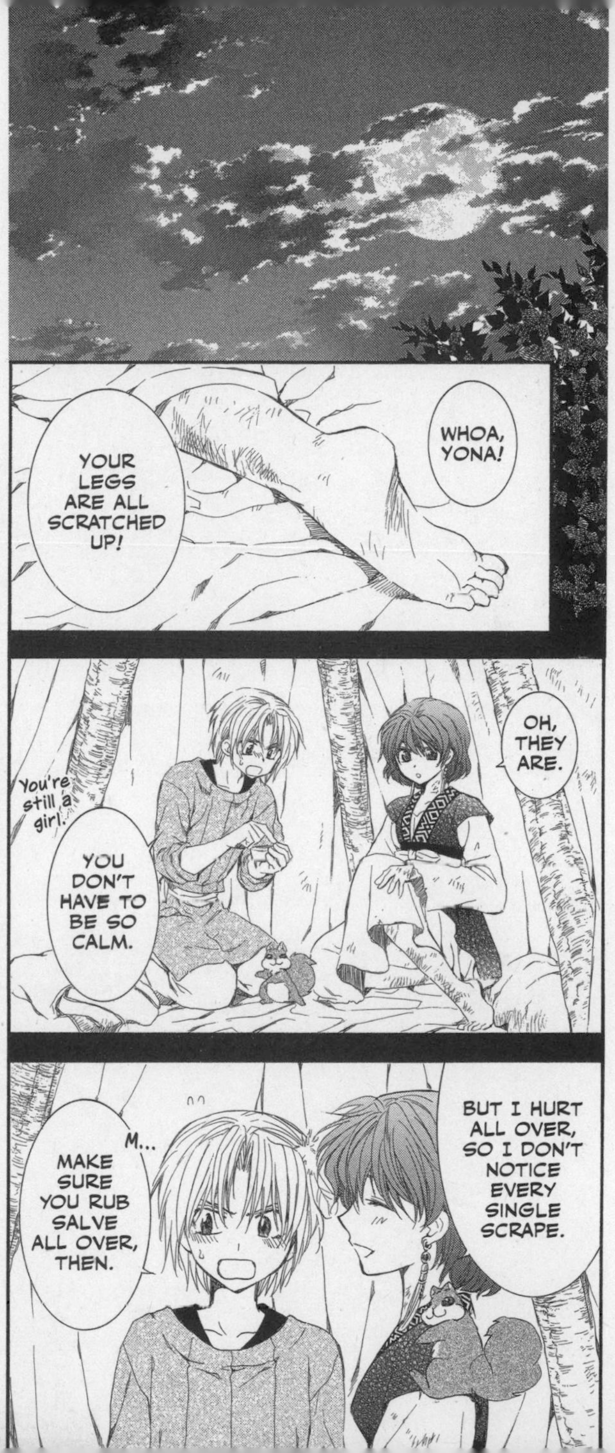
WHOA, YONA!
YOUR LEGS ARE ALL SCRATCHED UP!
OH, THEY ARE.
YOU DON'T HAVE TO BE SO CALM.
You're still a girl.
BUT I HURT ALL OVER, SO I DON'T NOTICE EVERY SINGLE SCRAPE.
M...
MAKE SURE YOU RUB SALVE ALL OVER, THEN.

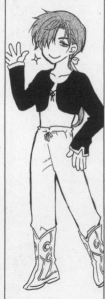

This is what Jaeha looks like under his coat.

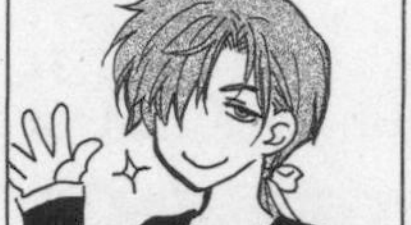

He has strange clothes.

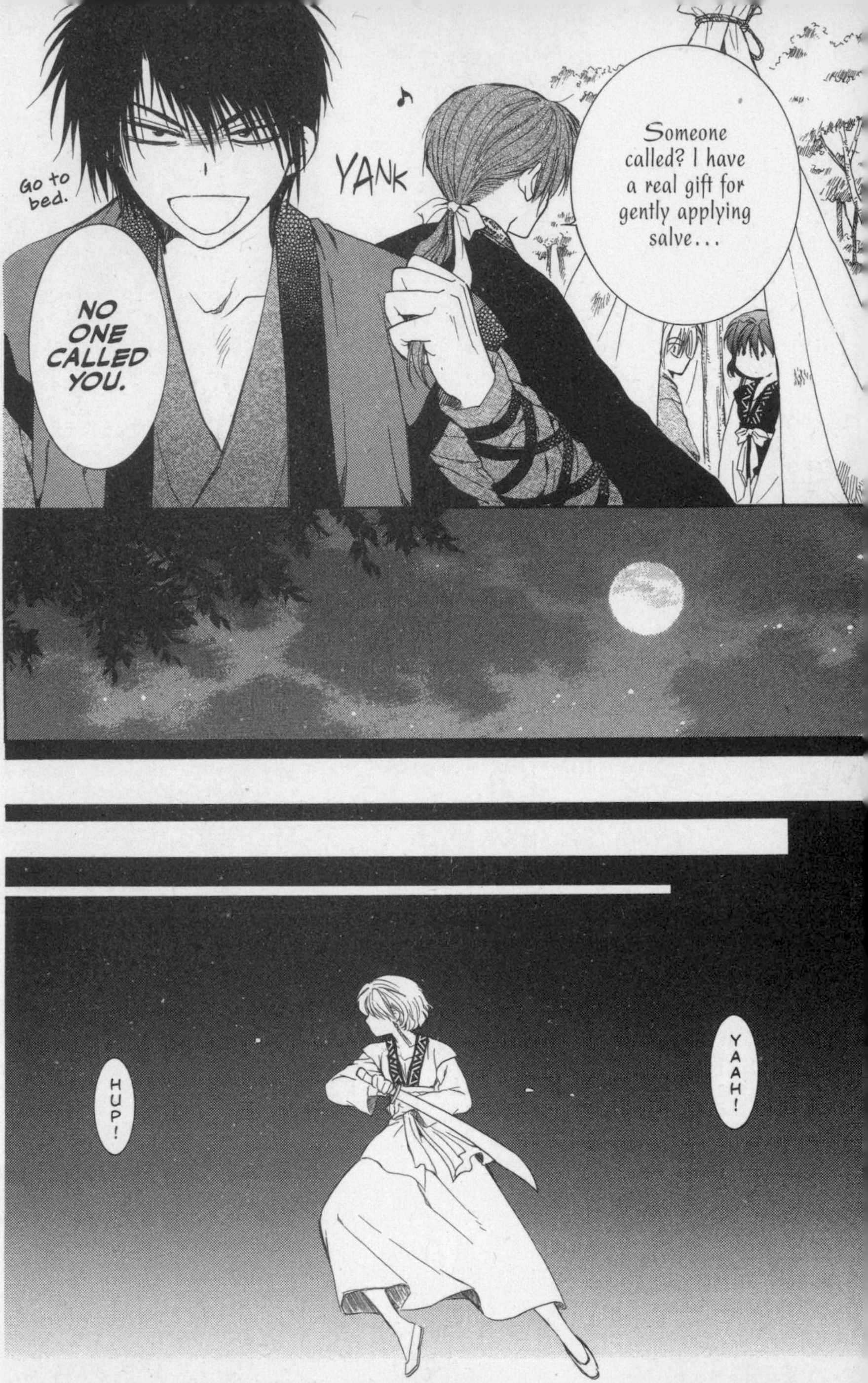
Someone called? I have a real gift for gently applying salve...
YANK
Go to bed.
NO ONE CALLED YOU.
YAAH!
HUP!

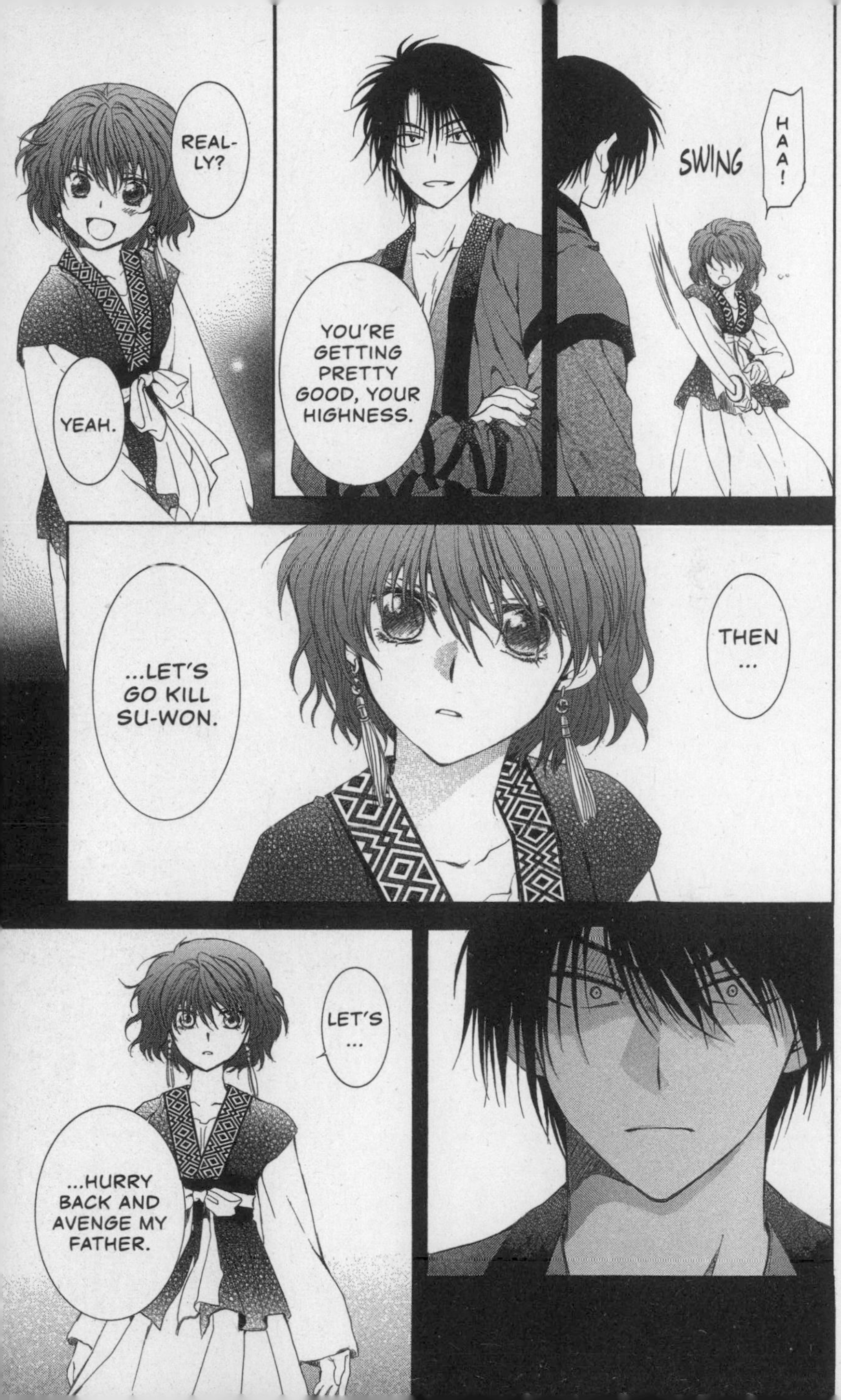
HAA!
SWING
YOU'RE GETTING PRETTY GOOD, YOUR HIGHNESS.
REAL-LY?
YEAH.
THEN...
...LET'S GO KILL SU-WON.
LET'S...
...HURRY BACK AND AVENGE MY FATHER.

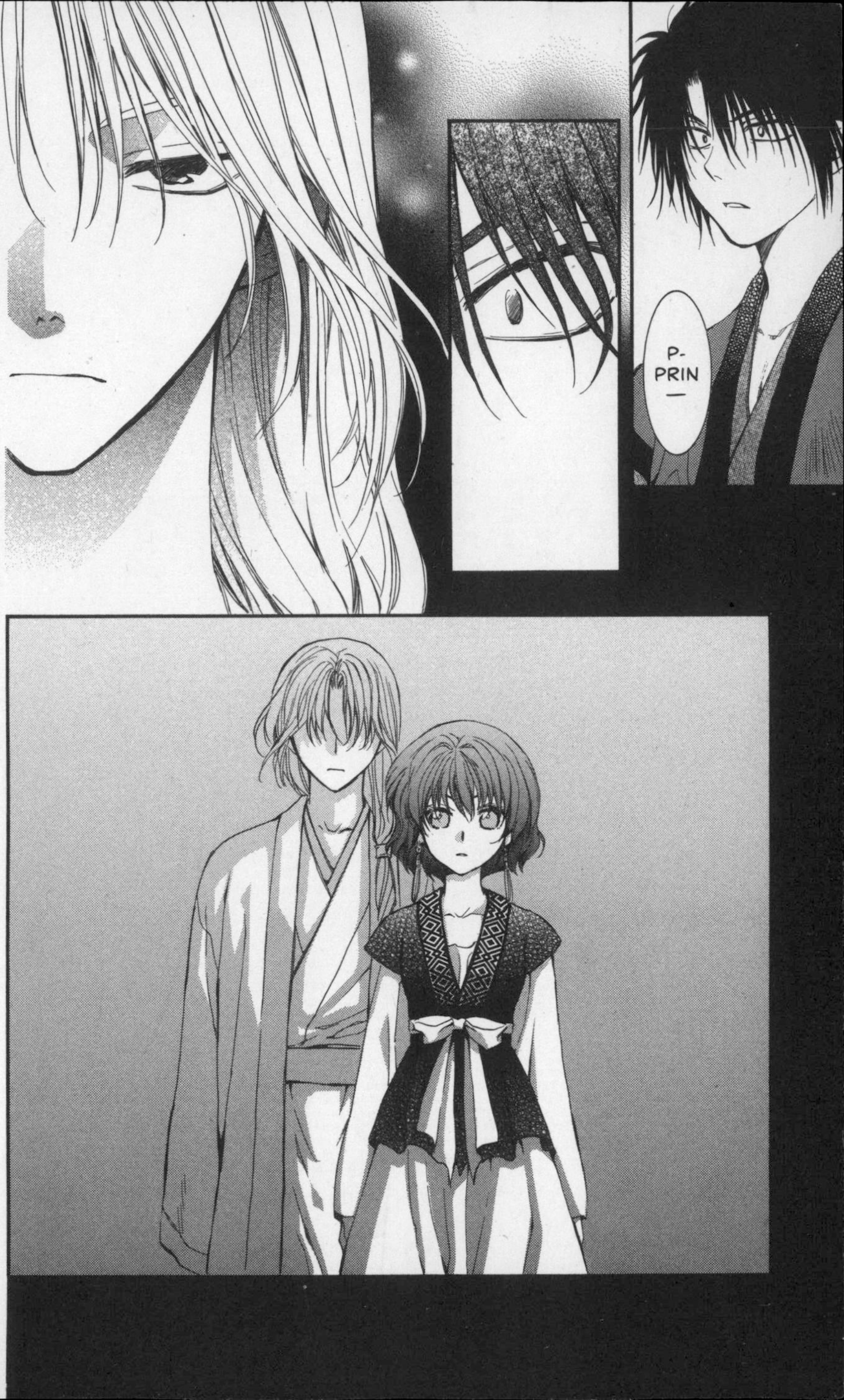
P-PRIN—

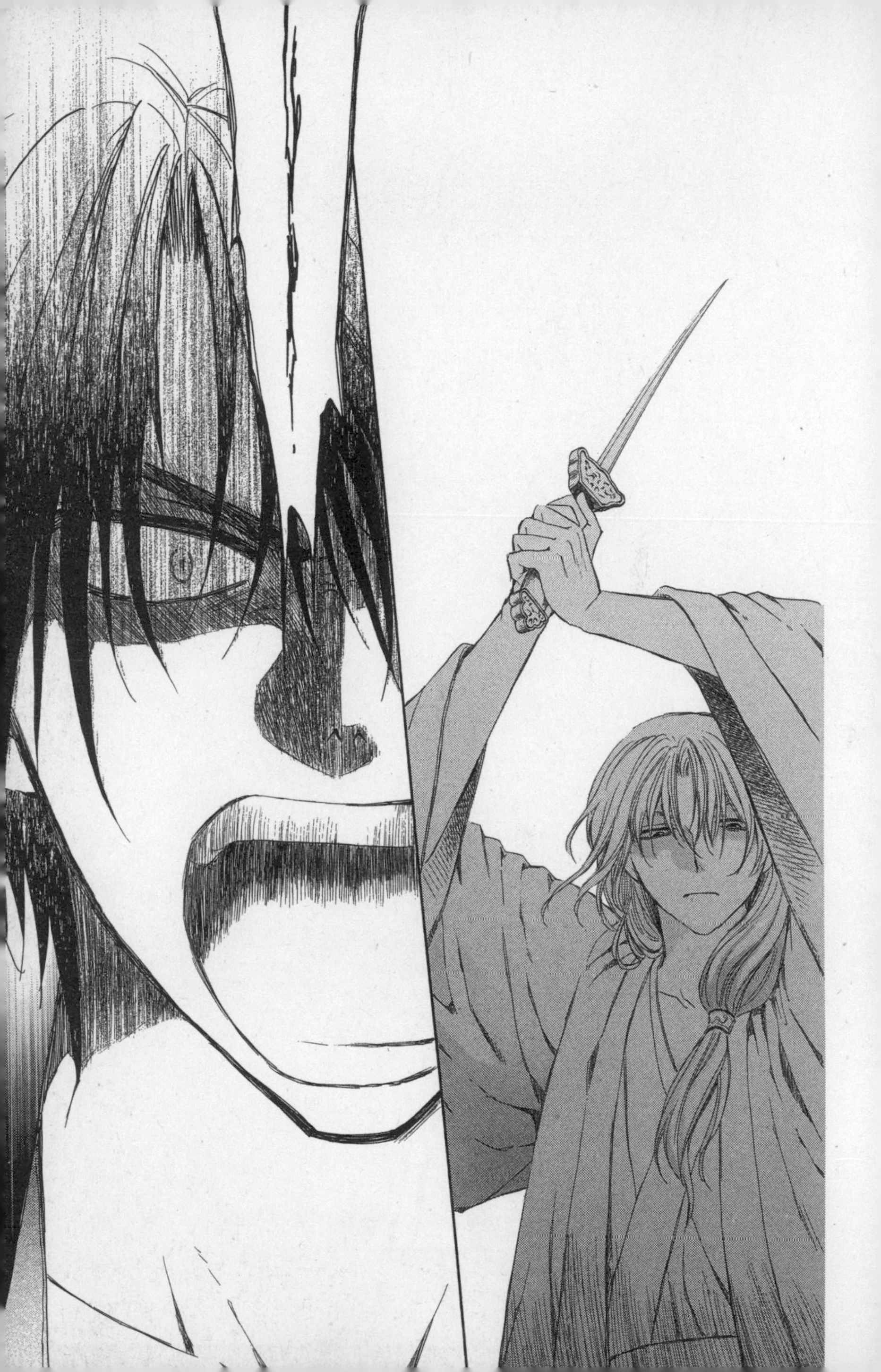

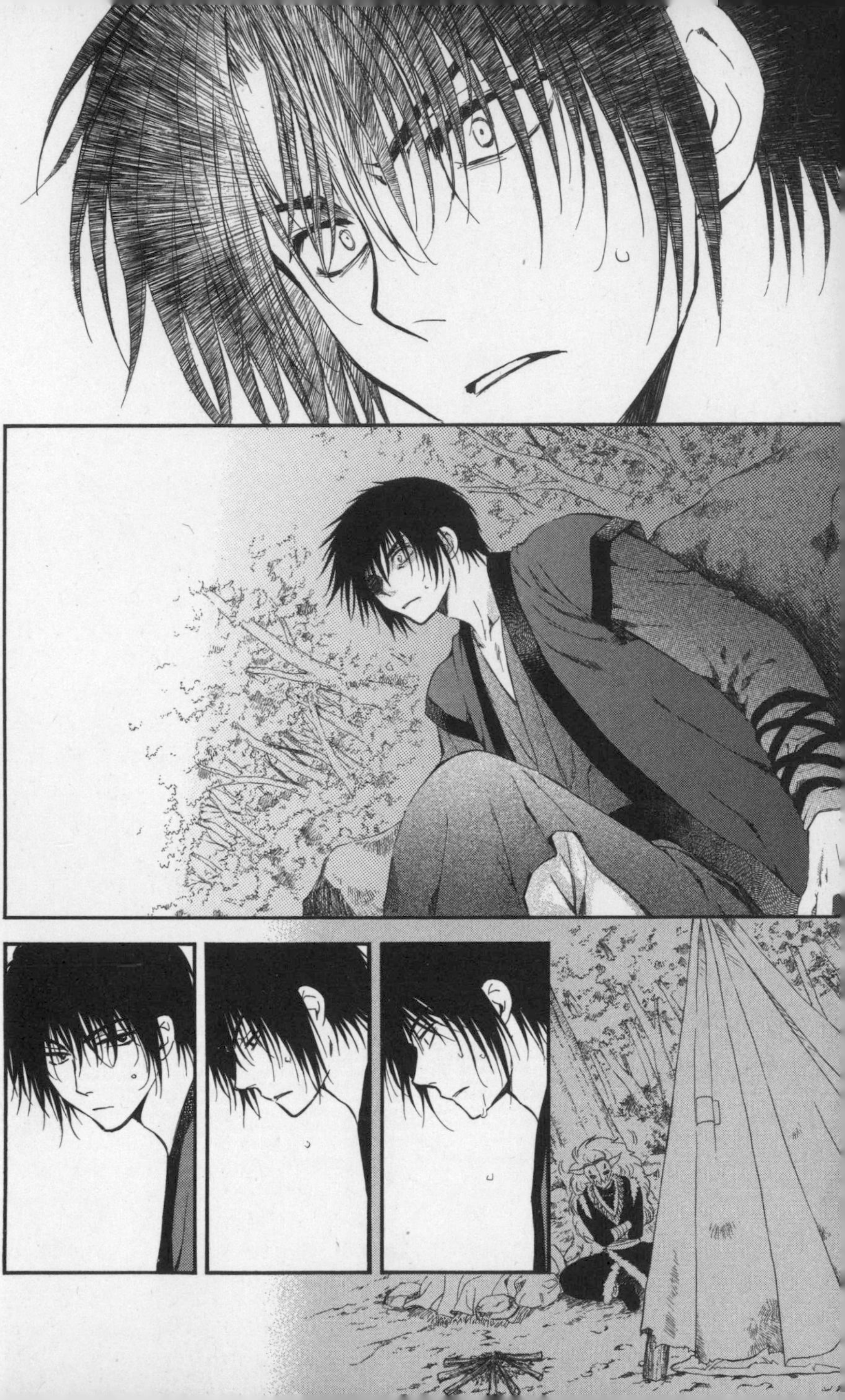

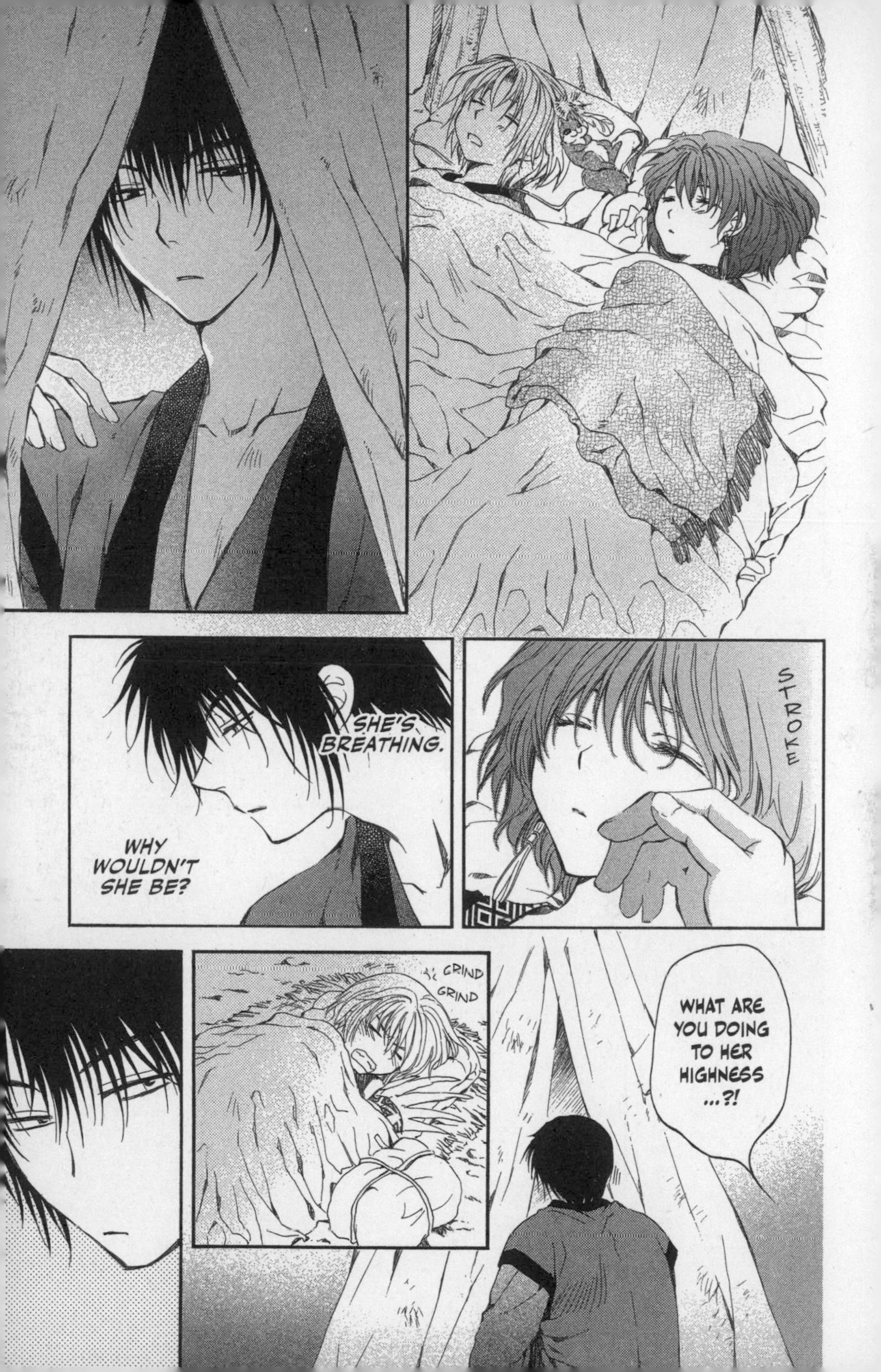
STROKE
SHE'S BREATHING.
WHY WOULDN'T SHE BE?
WHAT ARE YOU DOING TO HER HIGHNESS ...?!
GRIND GRIND

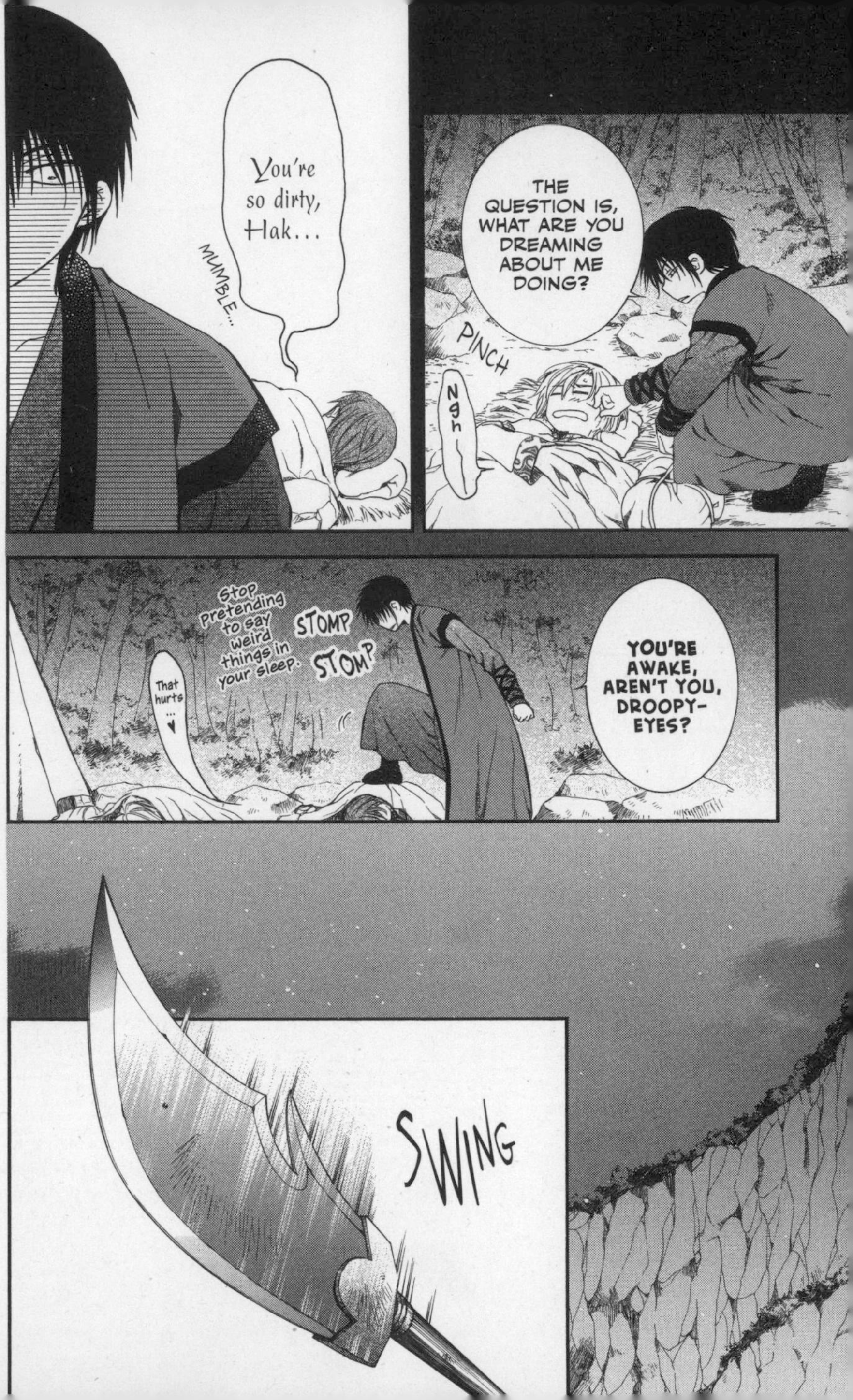
THE QUESTION IS, WHAT ARE YOU DREAMING ABOUT ME DOING?
PINCH
Ngh
You're so dirty, Hak...
MUMBLE...
YOU'RE AWAKE, AREN'T YOU, DROOPY-EYES?
STOMP
STOMP
Stop pretending to say weird things in your sleep.
That hurts... ♥
SWING

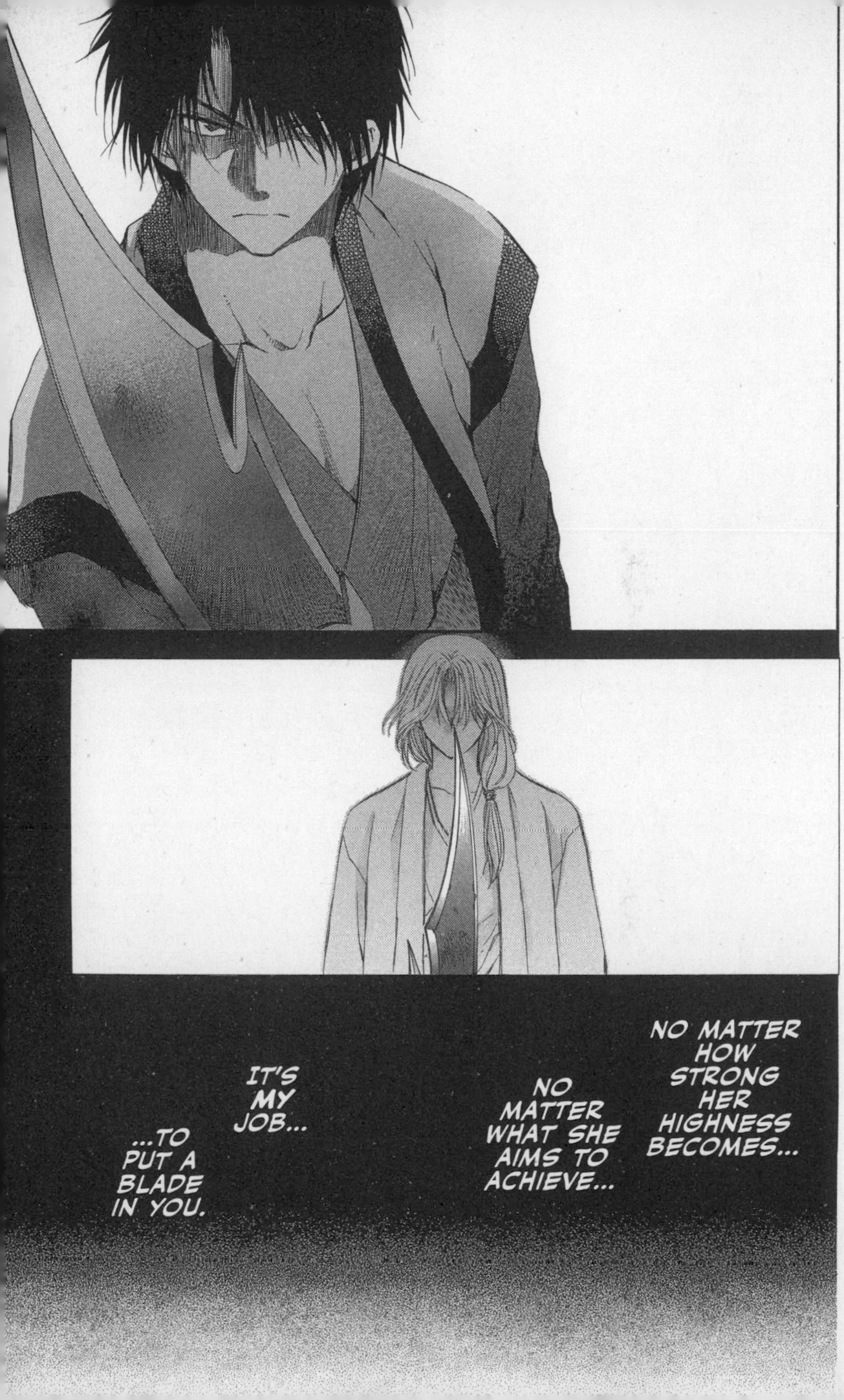
NO MATTER HOW STRONG HER HIGHNESS BECOMES...
NO MATTER WHAT SHE AIMS TO ACHIEVE...
IT'S MY JOB...
...TO PUT A BLADE IN YOU.

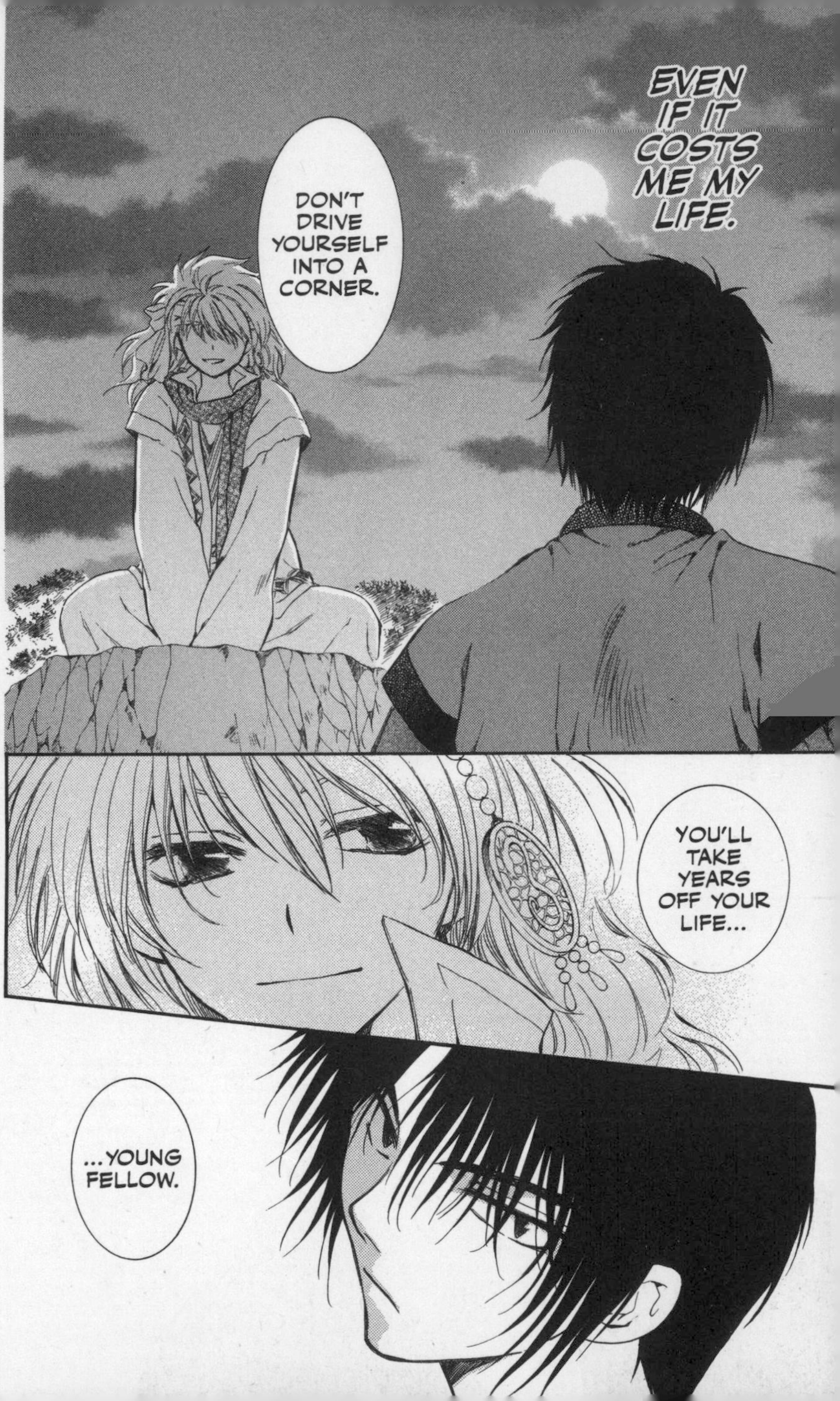
EVEN IF IT COSTS ME MY LIFE.
DON'T DRIVE YOURSELF INTO A CORNER.
YOU'LL TAKE YEARS OFF YOUR LIFE...
...YOUNG FELLOW.

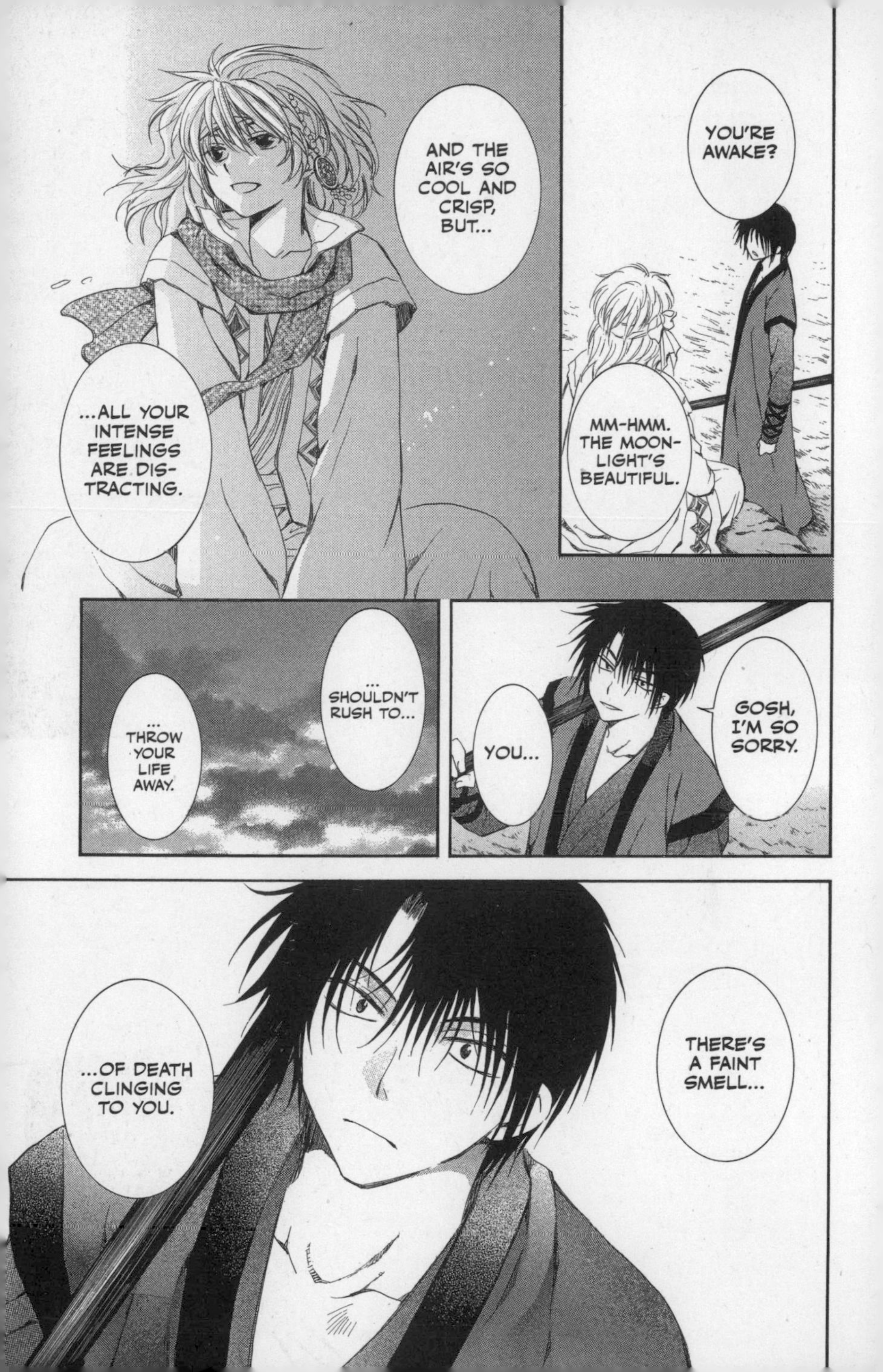
YOU'RE AWAKE?
MM-HMM. THE MOON-LIGHT'S BEAUTIFUL.
AND THE AIR'S SO COOL AND CRISP, BUT...
...ALL YOUR INTENSE FEELINGS ARE DIS-TRACTING.
GOSH, I'M SO SORRY.
YOU...
...SHOULDN'T RUSH TO...
...THROW YOUR LIFE AWAY.
THERE'S A FAINT SMELL...
...OF DEATH CLINGING TO YOU.

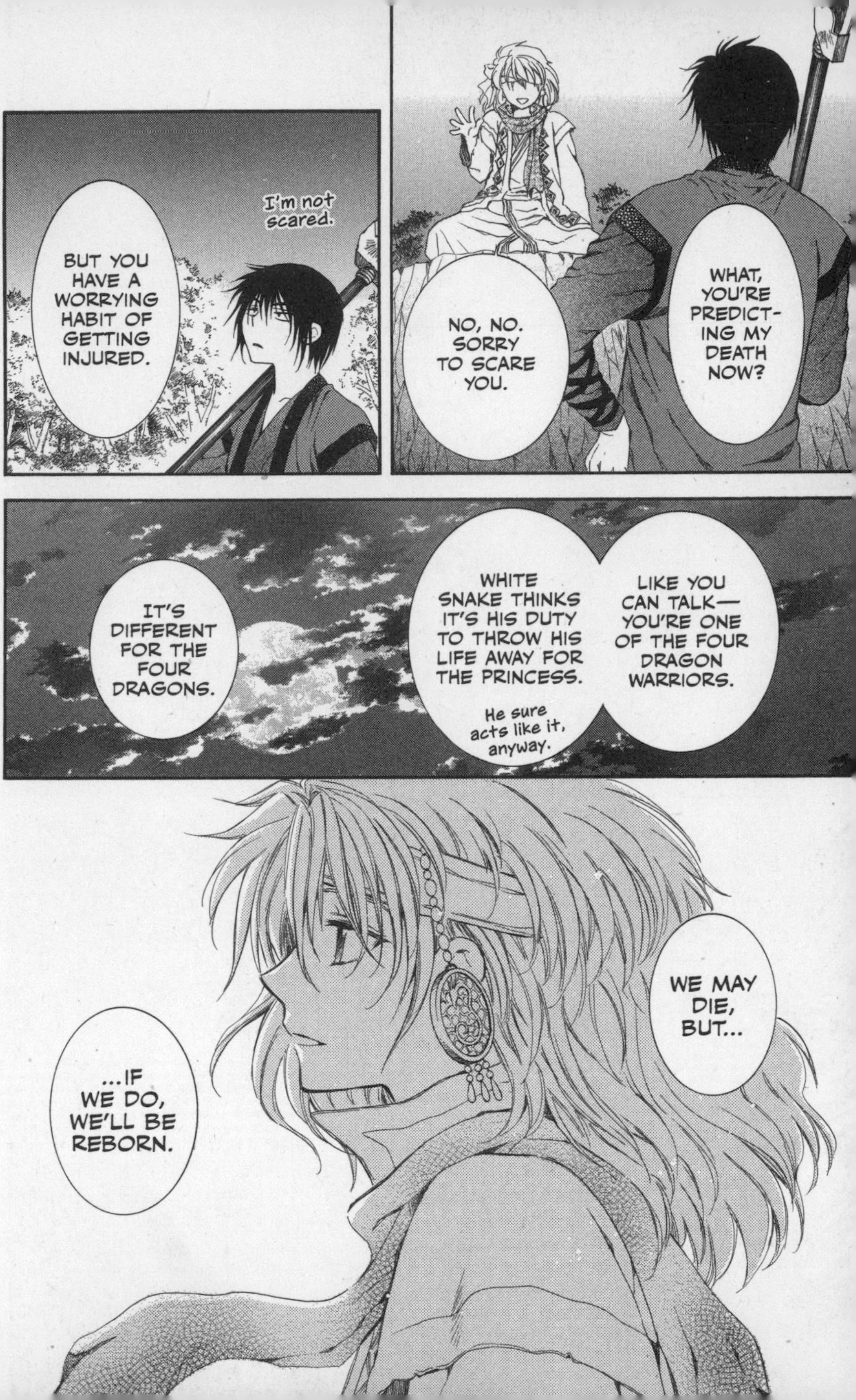
WHAT, YOU'RE PREDICTING MY DEATH NOW?
NO, NO. SORRY TO SCARE YOU.
I'm not scared.
BUT YOU HAVE A WORRYING HABIT OF GETTING INJURED.
LIKE YOU CAN TALK—YOU'RE ONE OF THE FOUR DRAGON WARRIORS.
WHITE SNAKE THINKS IT'S HIS DUTY TO THROW HIS LIFE AWAY FOR THE PRINCESS.
He sure acts like it, anyway.
IT'S DIFFERENT FOR THE FOUR DRAGONS.
WE MAY DIE, BUT...
...IF WE DO, WE'LL BE REBORN.

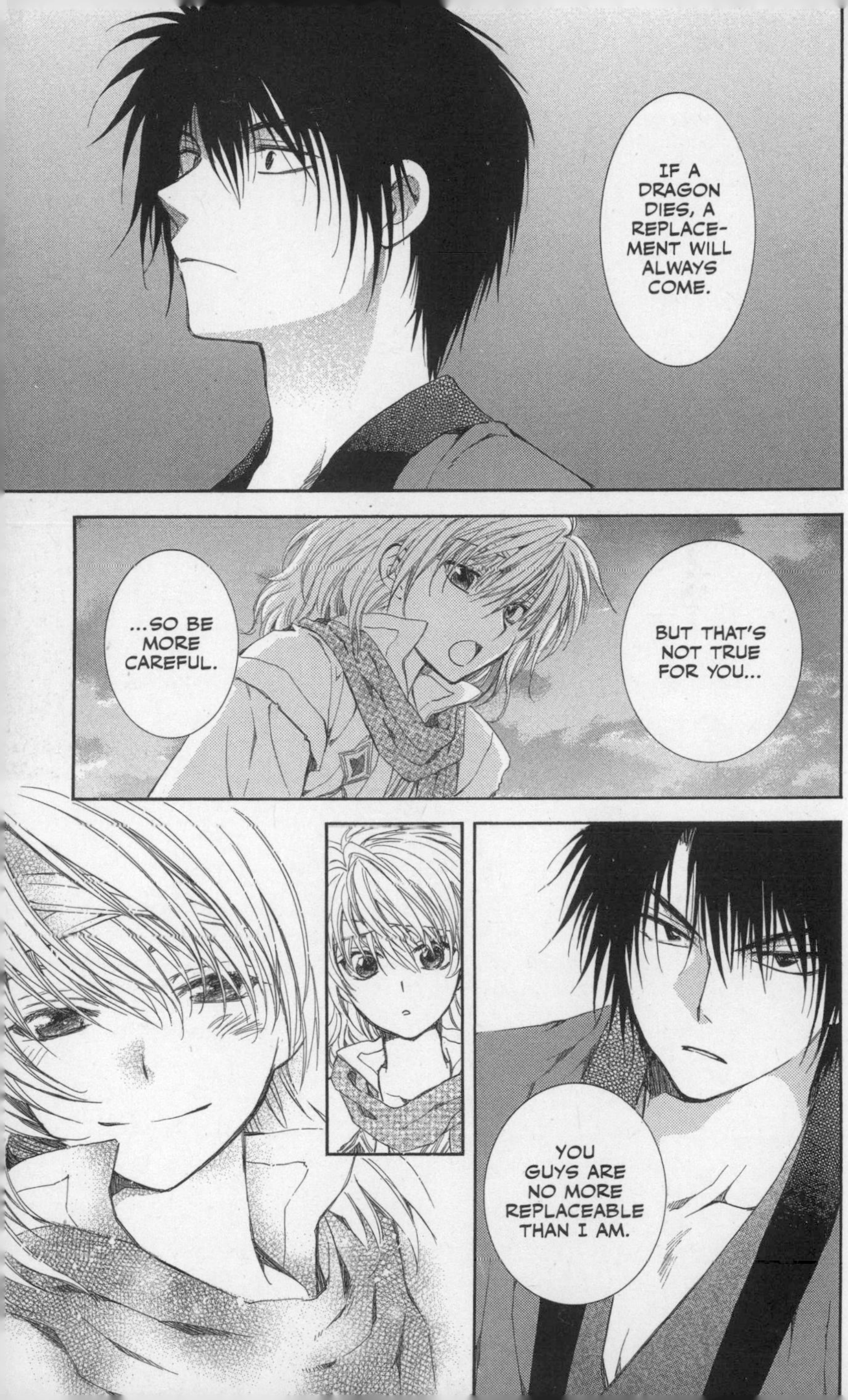
IF A DRAGON DIES, A REPLACEMENT WILL ALWAYS COME.
BUT THAT'S NOT TRUE FOR YOU...
...SO BE MORE CAREFUL.
YOU GUYS ARE NO MORE REPLACEABLE THAN I AM.

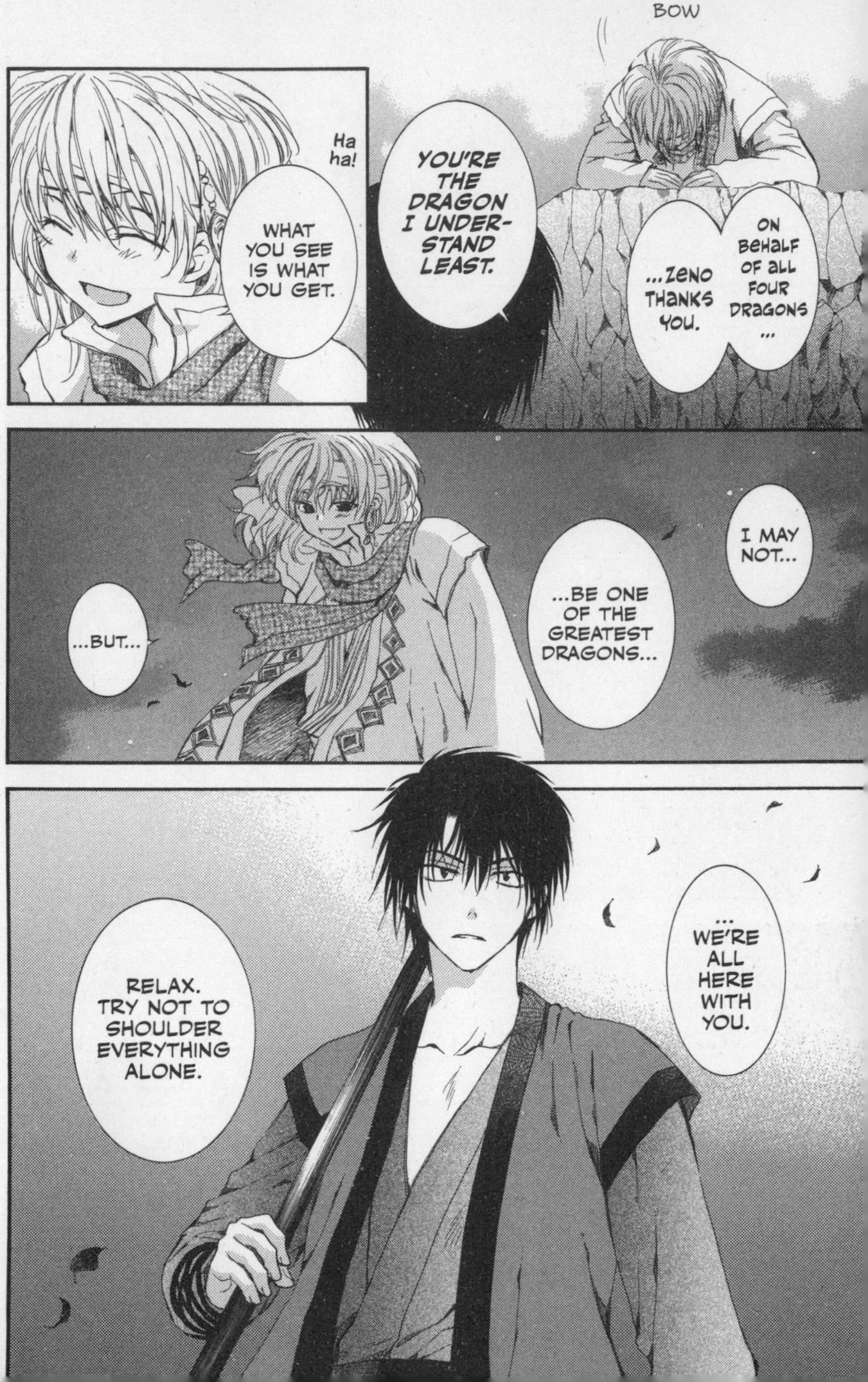
BOW
ON BEHALF OF ALL FOUR DRAGONS...
...ZENO THANKS YOU.
YOU'RE THE DRAGON I UNDER-STAND LEAST.
Ha ha!
WHAT YOU SEE IS WHAT YOU GET.
I MAY NOT...
...BE ONE OF THE GREATEST DRAGONS...
...BUT...
...WE'RE ALL HERE WITH YOU.
RELAX. TRY NOT TO SHOULDER EVERYTHING ALONE.

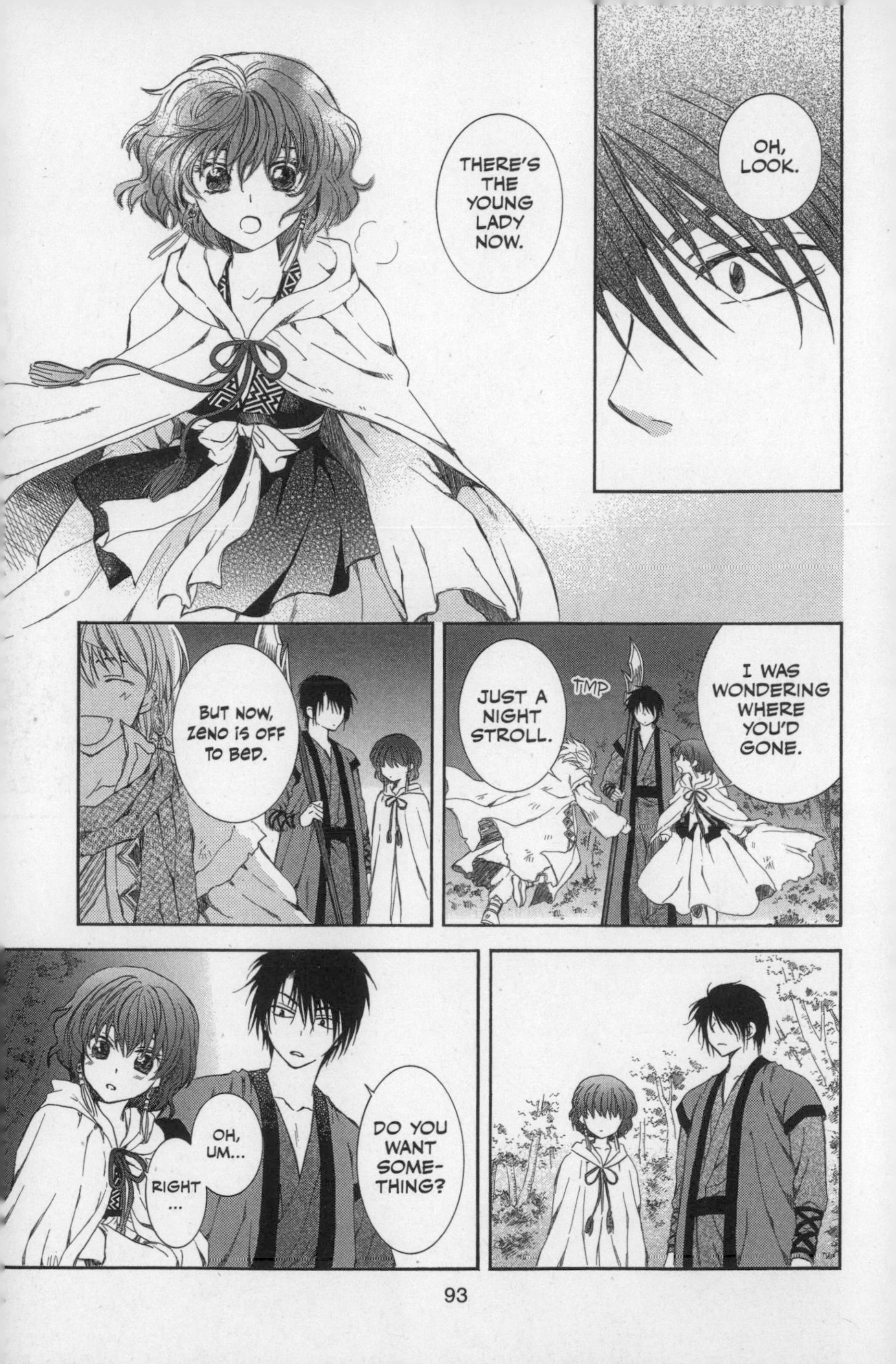
OH, LOOK.
THERE'S THE YOUNG LADY NOW.
I WAS WONDERING WHERE YOU'D GONE.
TMP
JUST A NIGHT STROLL.
BUT NOW, ZENO IS OFF TO BED.
DO YOU WANT SOME-THING?
OH, UM...
RIGHT...

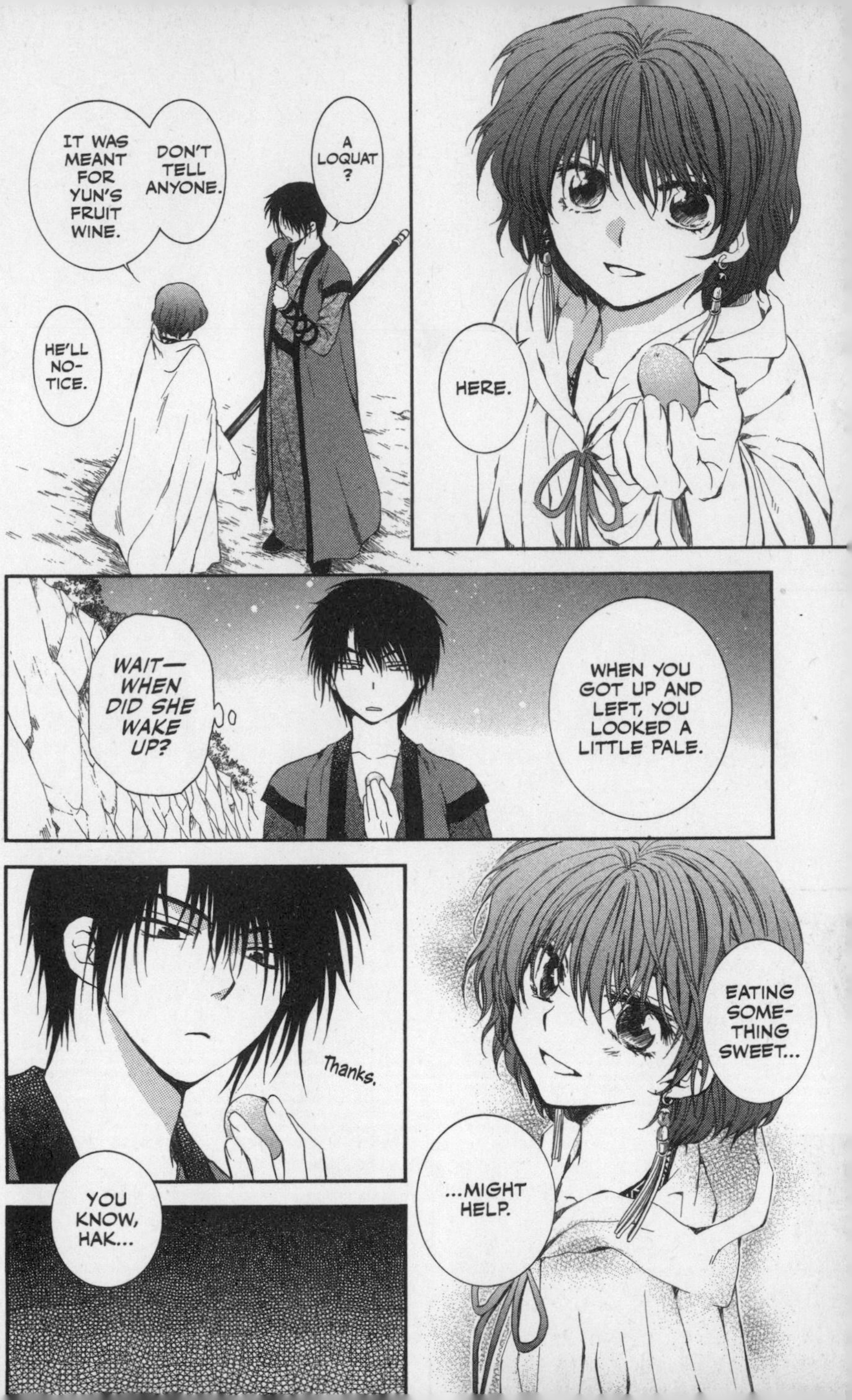
HERE.
A LOQUAT?
DON'T TELL ANYONE.
IT WAS MEANT FOR YUN'S FRUIT WINE.
HE'LL NO-TICE.
WHEN YOU GOT UP AND LEFT, YOU LOOKED A LITTLE PALE.
WAIT— WHEN DID SHE WAKE UP?
EATING SOME-THING SWEET...
...MIGHT HELP.
Thanks.
YOU KNOW, HAK...

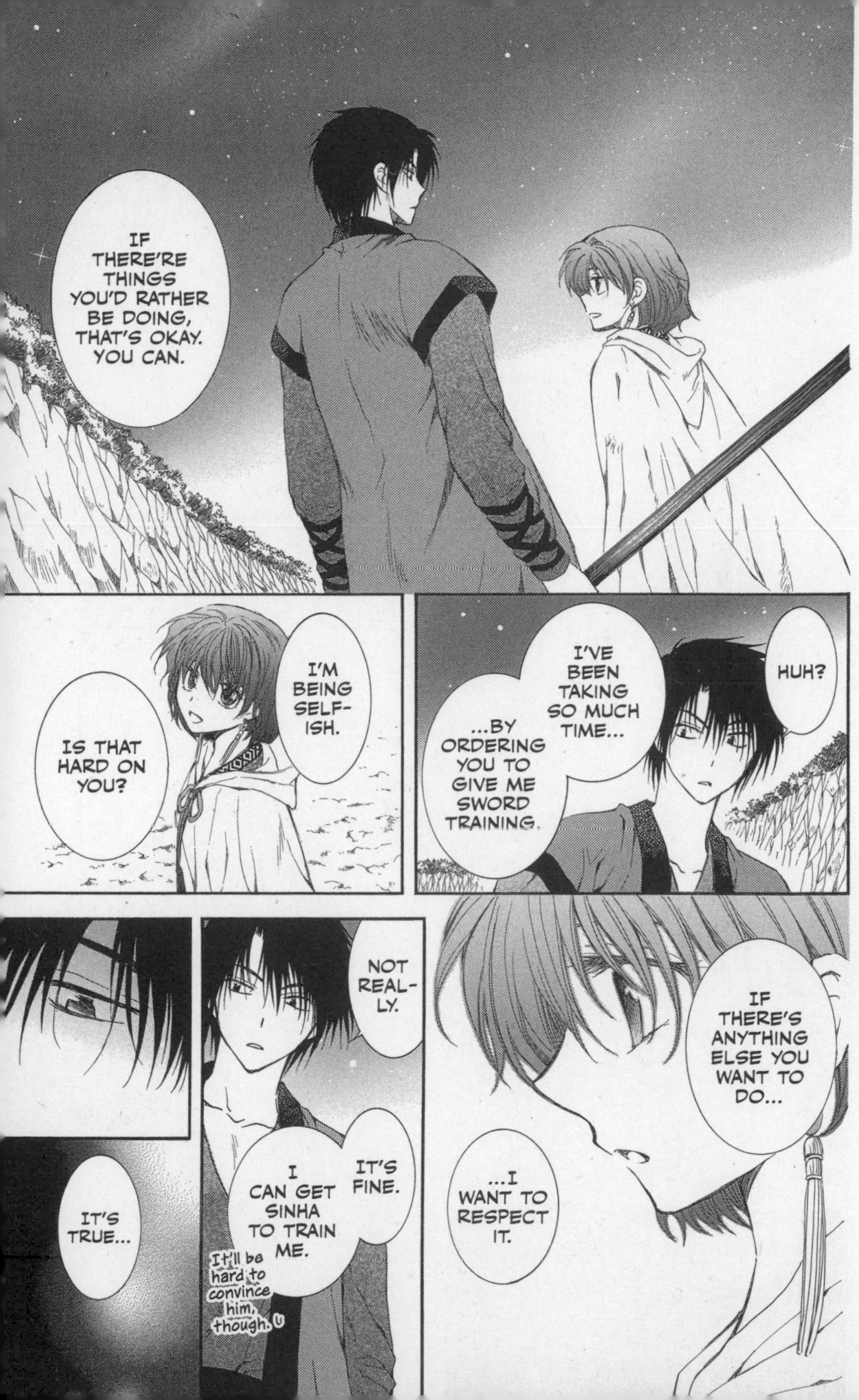
IF THERE'RE THINGS YOU'D RATHER BE DOING, THAT'S OKAY. YOU CAN.
HUH?
I'VE BEEN TAKING SO MUCH TIME...
...BY ORDERING YOU TO GIVE ME SWORD TRAINING.
I'M BEING SELF-ISH.
IS THAT HARD ON YOU?
IF THERE'S ANYTHING ELSE YOU WANT TO DO...
...I WANT TO RESPECT IT.
NOT REAL-LY.
IT'S FINE.
I CAN GET SINHA TO TRAIN ME.
It'll be hard to convince him, though.
IT'S TRUE...

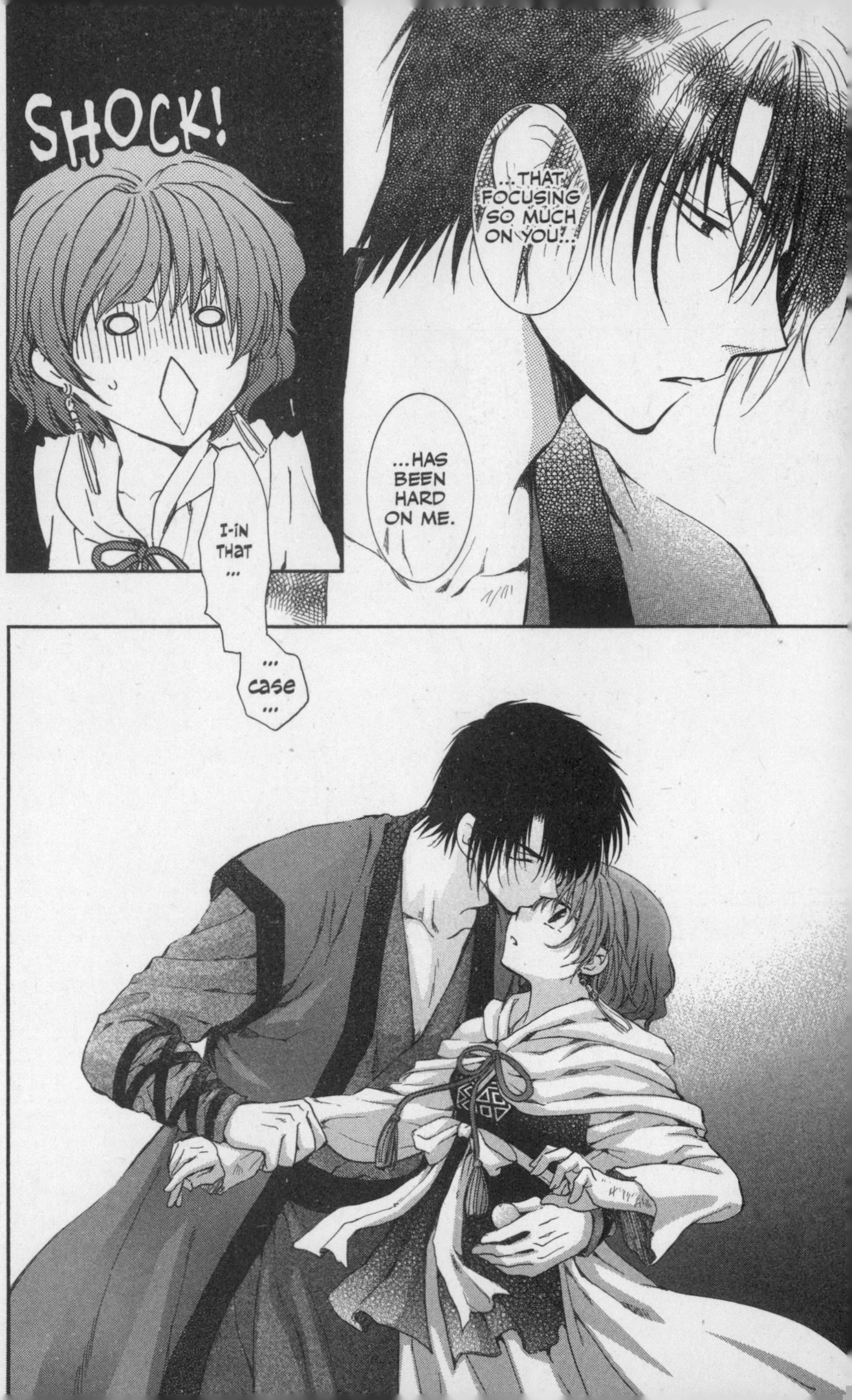
...THAT FOCUSING SO MUCH ON YOU...
...HAS BEEN HARD ON ME.
SHOCK!
I-IN THAT ...
... case ...

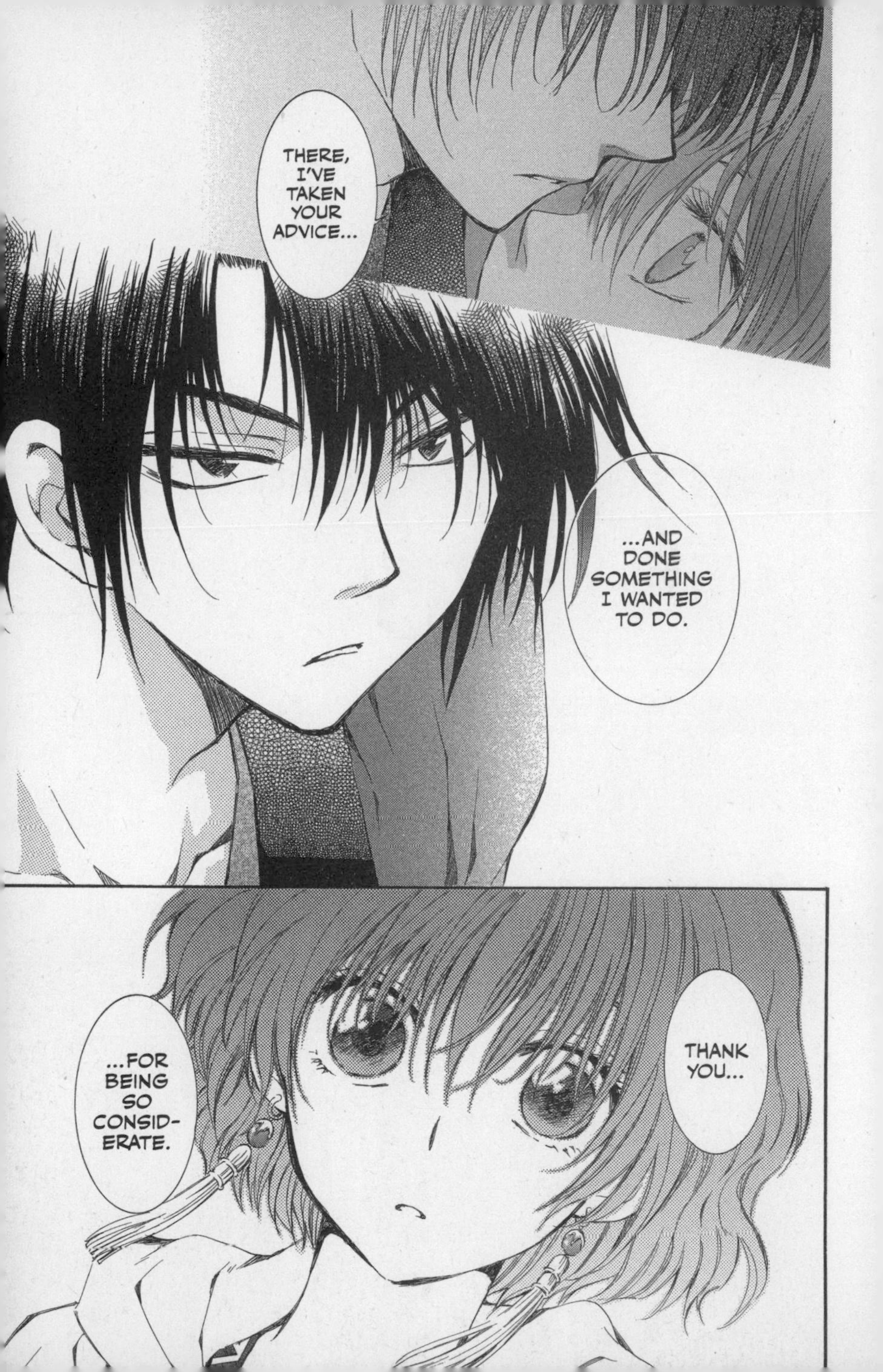
THERE, I'VE TAKEN YOUR ADVICE...
...AND DONE SOMETHING I WANTED TO DO.
THANK YOU...
...FOR BEING SO CONSID-ERATE.

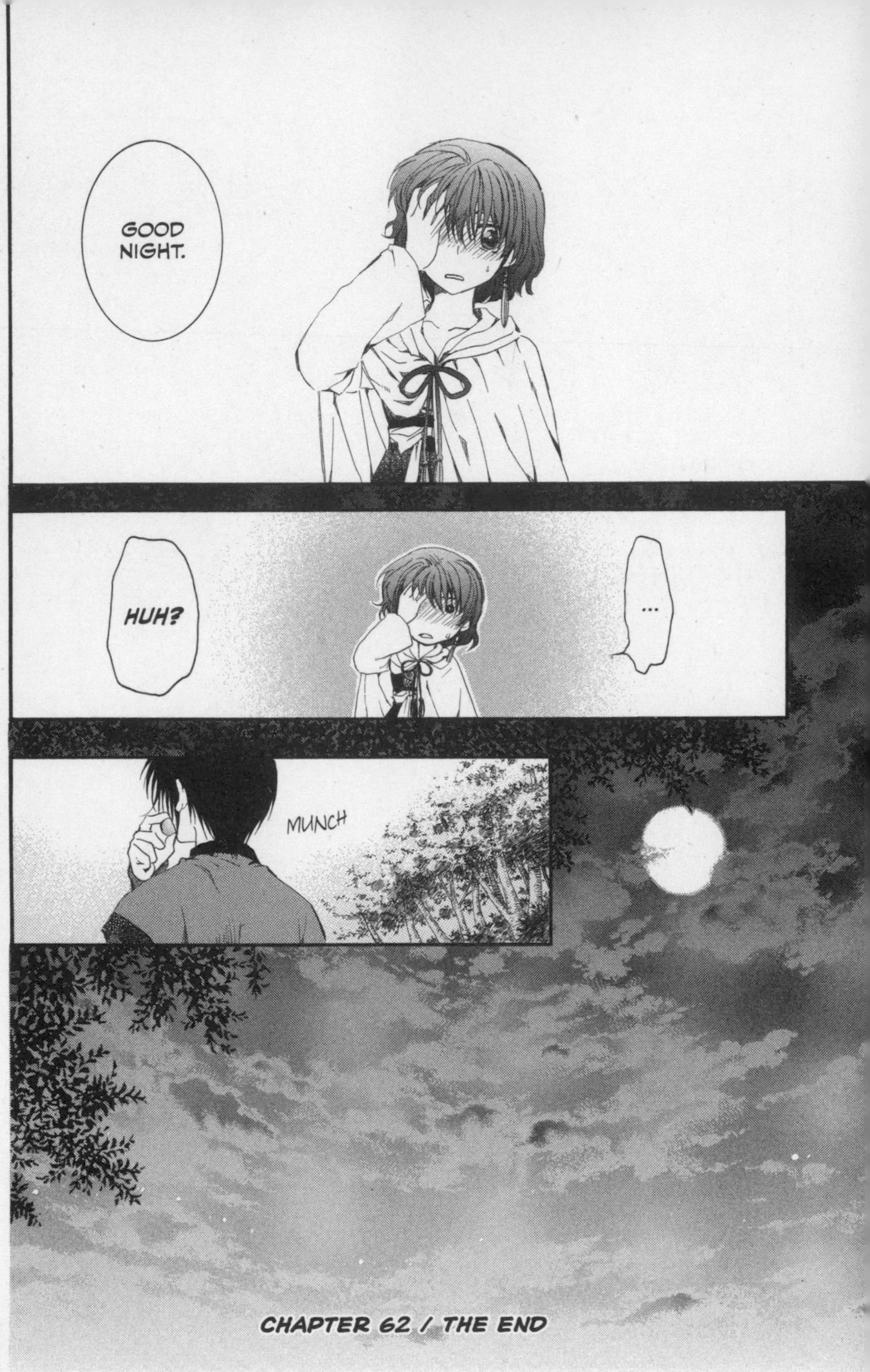
GOOD NIGHT.
...
HUH?
MUNCH
CHAPTER 62 / THE END

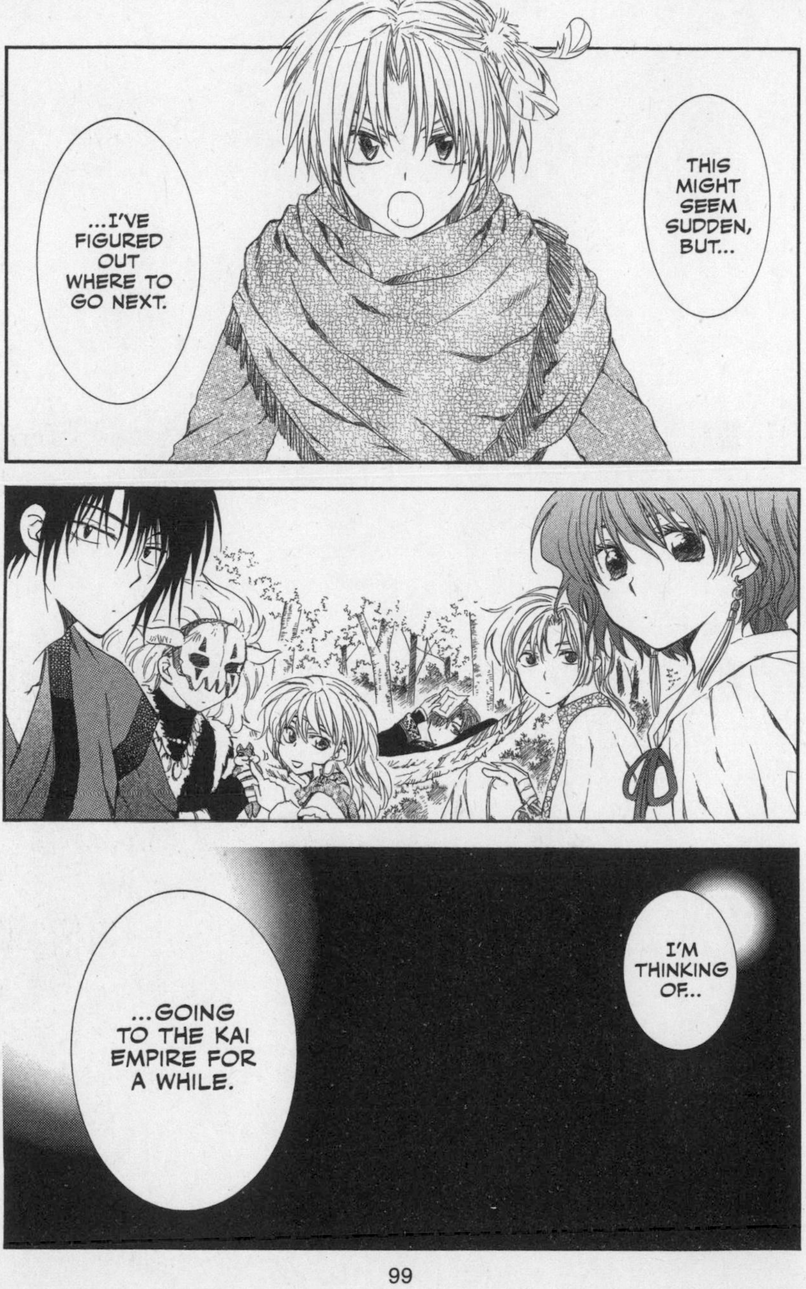
THIS MIGHT SEEM SUDDEN, BUT...
...I'VE FIGURED OUT WHERE TO GO NEXT.
I'M THINKING OF...
...GOING TO THE KAI EMPIRE FOR A WHILE.

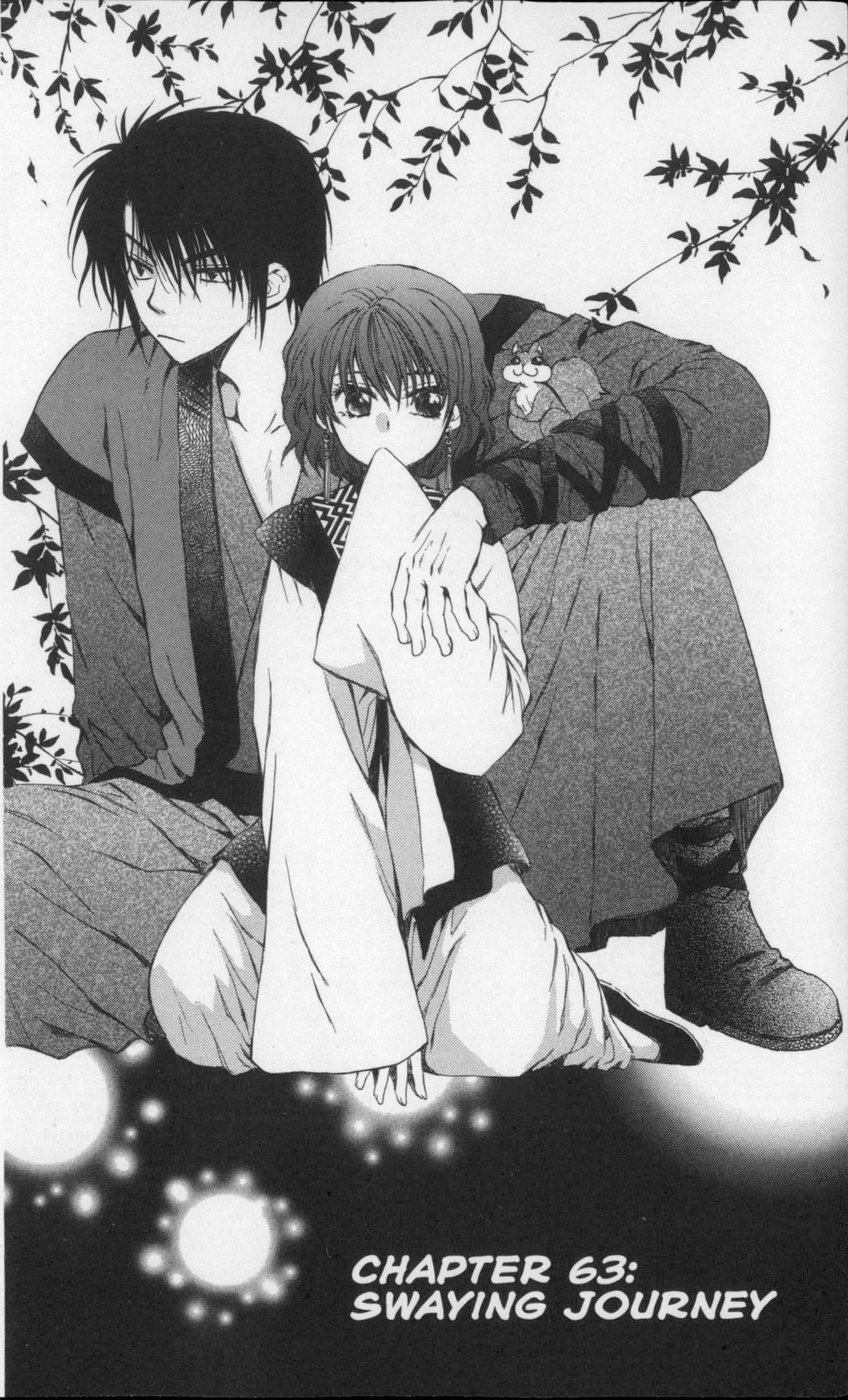
CHAPTER 63:
SWAYING JOURNEY

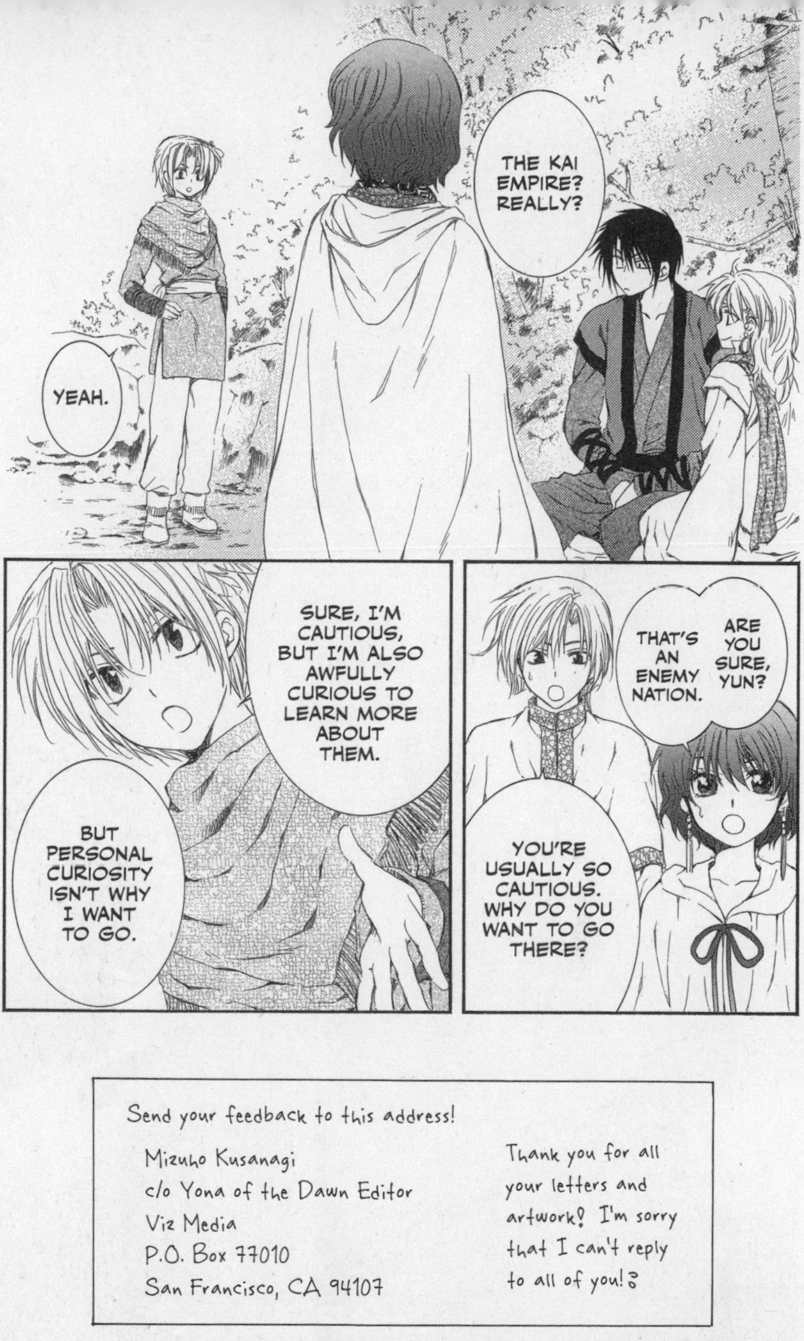
THE KAI EMPIRE? REALLY?
YEAH.
ARE YOU SURE, YUN?
THAT'S AN ENEMY NATION.
YOU'RE USUALLY SO CAUTIOUS. WHY DO YOU WANT TO GO THERE?
SURE, I'M CAUTIOUS, BUT I'M ALSO AWFULLY CURIOUS TO LEARN MORE ABOUT THEM.
BUT PERSONAL CURIOSITY ISN'T WHY I WANT TO GO.

Send your feedback to this address!

Mizuho Kusanagi
c/o Yona of the Dawn Editor
Viz Media
P.O. Box 77010
San Francisco, CA 94107

Thank you for all your letters and artwork! I'm sorry that I can't reply to all of you!

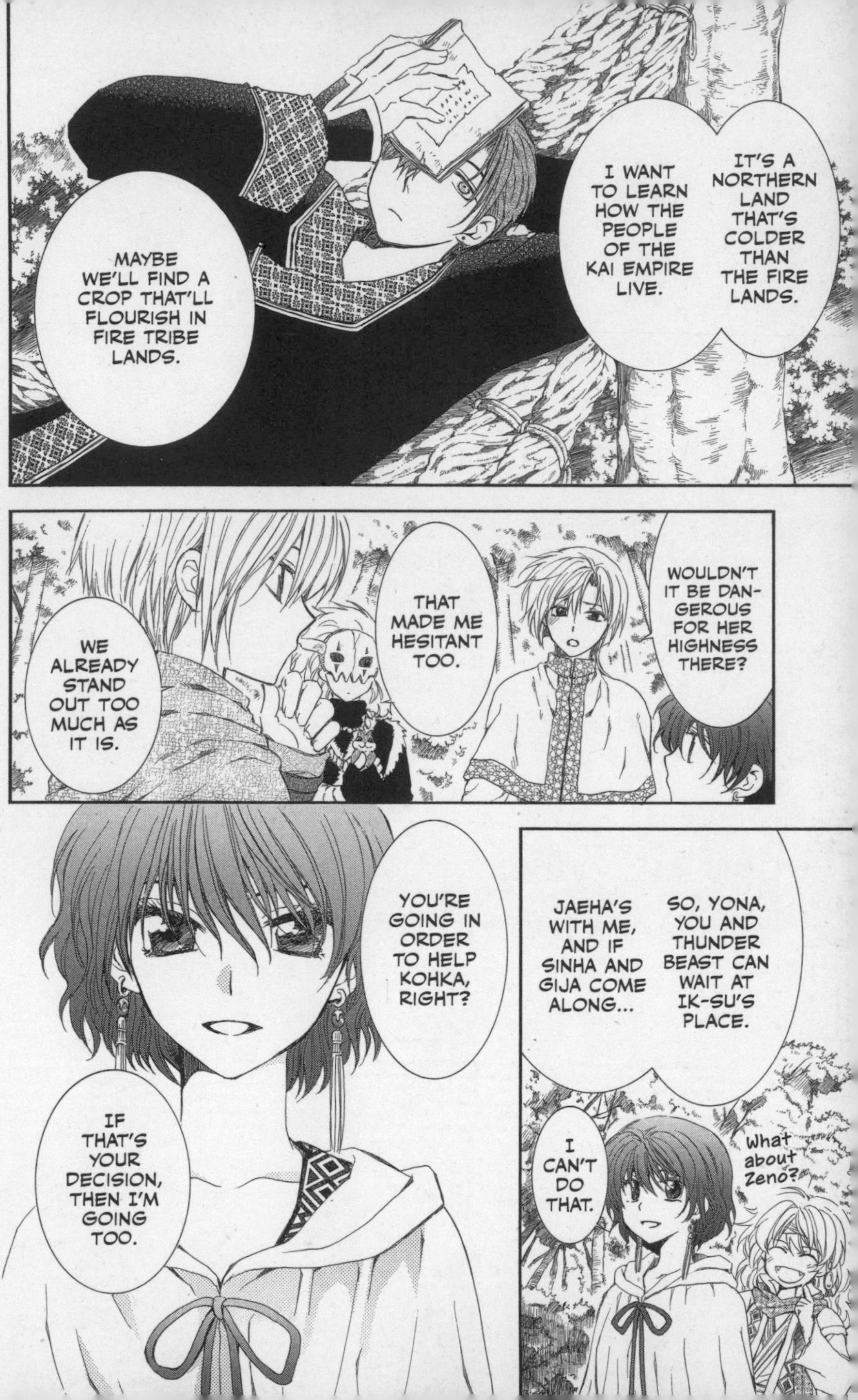
IT'S A NORTHERN LAND THAT'S COLDER THAN THE FIRE LANDS.
I WANT TO LEARN HOW THE PEOPLE OF THE KAI EMPIRE LIVE.
MAYBE WE'LL FIND A CROP THAT'LL FLOURISH IN FIRE TRIBE LANDS.
WOULDN'T IT BE DAN-GEROUS FOR HER HIGHNESS THERE?
THAT MADE ME HESITANT TOO.
WE ALREADY STAND OUT TOO MUCH AS IT IS.
SO, YONA, YOU AND THUNDER BEAST CAN WAIT AT IK-SU'S PLACE.
JAEHA'S WITH ME, AND IF SINHA AND GIJA COME ALONG...
What about Zeno?
I CAN'T DO THAT.
YOU'RE GOING IN ORDER TO HELP KOHKA, RIGHT?
IF THAT'S YOUR DECISION, THEN I'M GOING TOO.

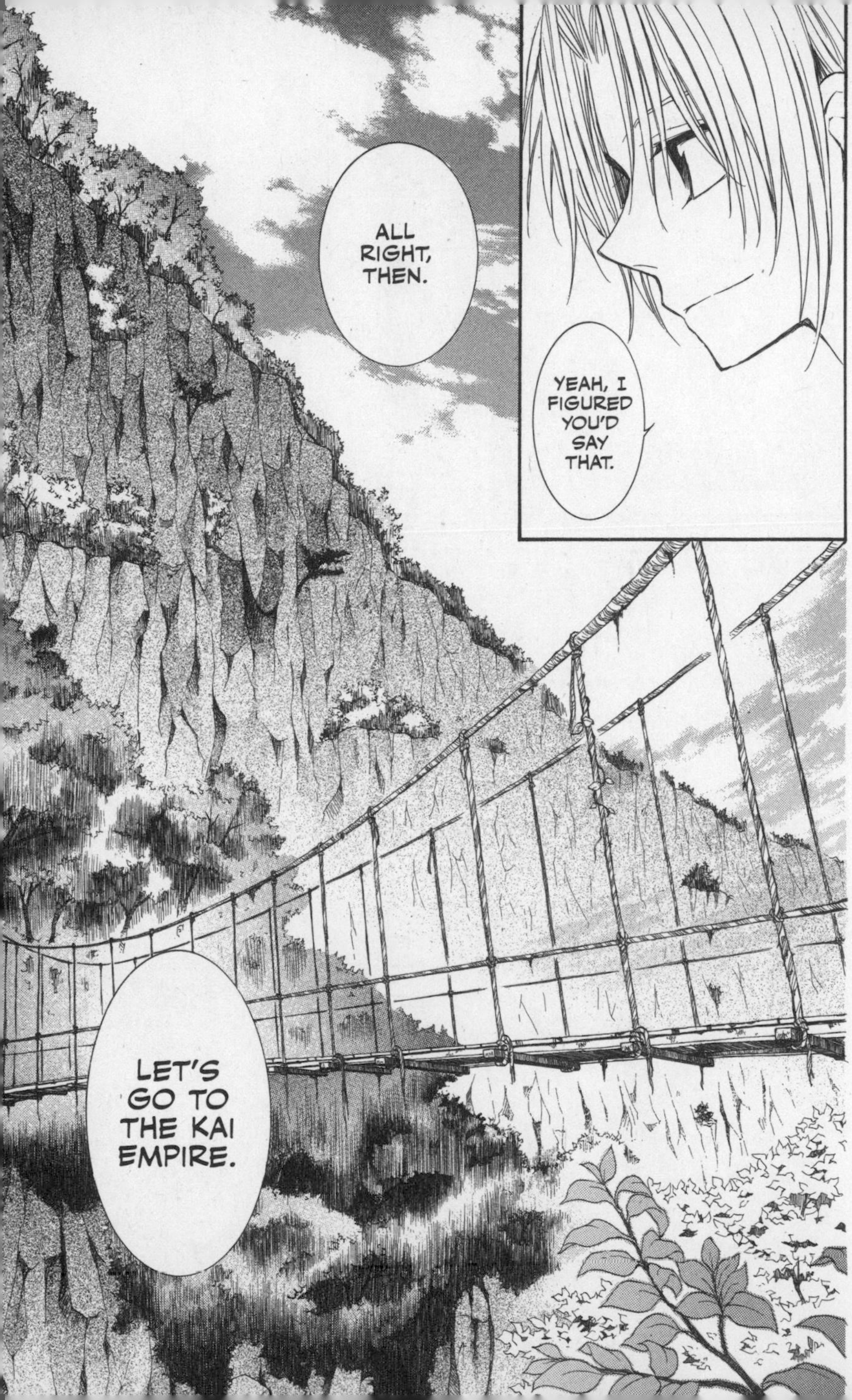
YEAH, I FIGURED YOU'D SAY THAT.
ALL RIGHT, THEN.
LET'S GO TO THE KAI EMPIRE.

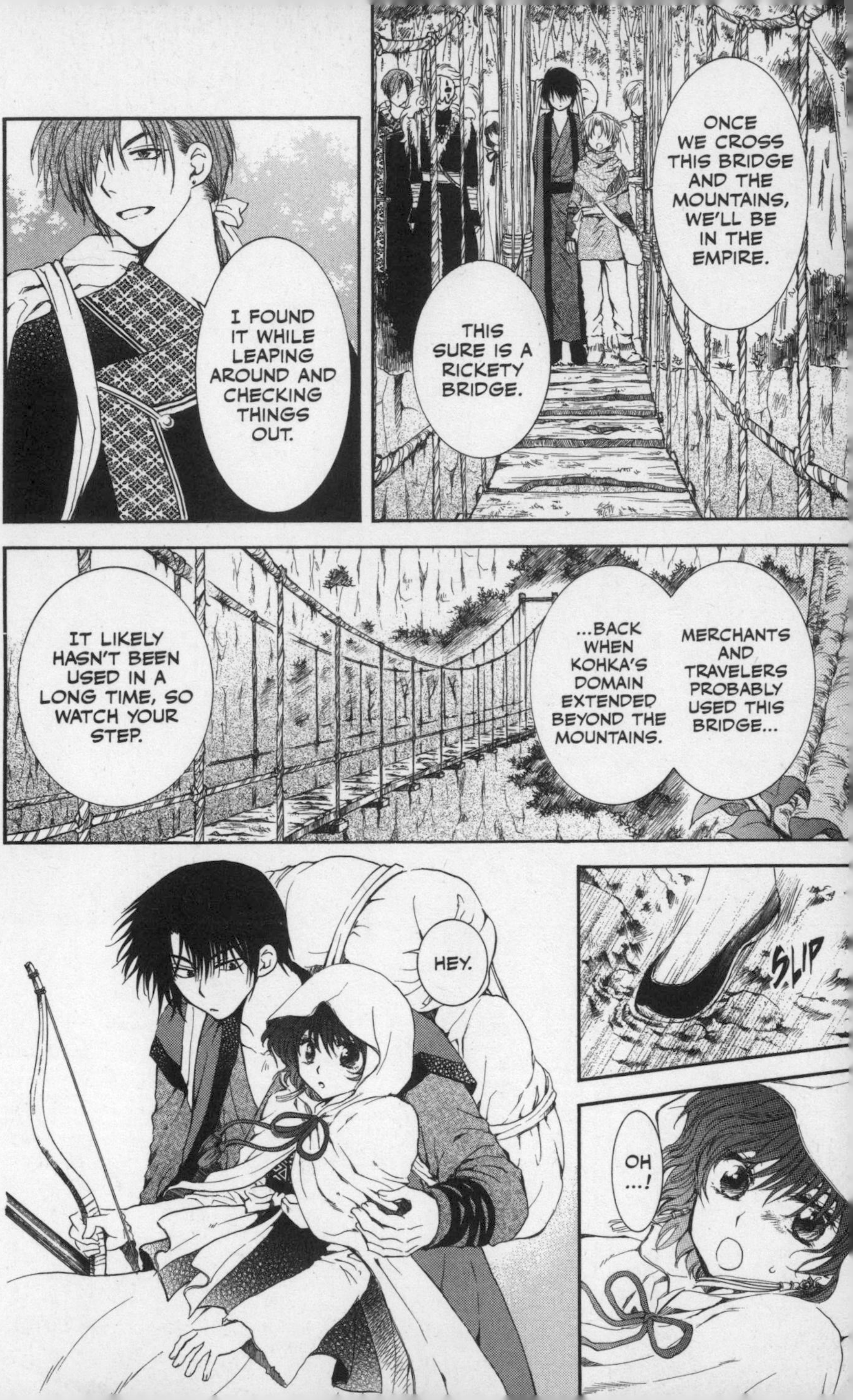
ONCE WE CROSS THIS BRIDGE AND THE MOUNTAINS, WE'LL BE IN THE EMPIRE.
THIS SURE IS A RICKETY BRIDGE.
I FOUND IT WHILE LEAPING AROUND AND CHECKING THINGS OUT.
MERCHANTS AND TRAVELERS PROBABLY USED THIS BRIDGE...
...BACK WHEN KOHKA'S DOMAIN EXTENDED BEYOND THE MOUNTAINS.
IT LIKELY HASN'T BEEN USED IN A LONG TIME, SO WATCH YOUR STEP.
SLIP
OH ...!
HEY.

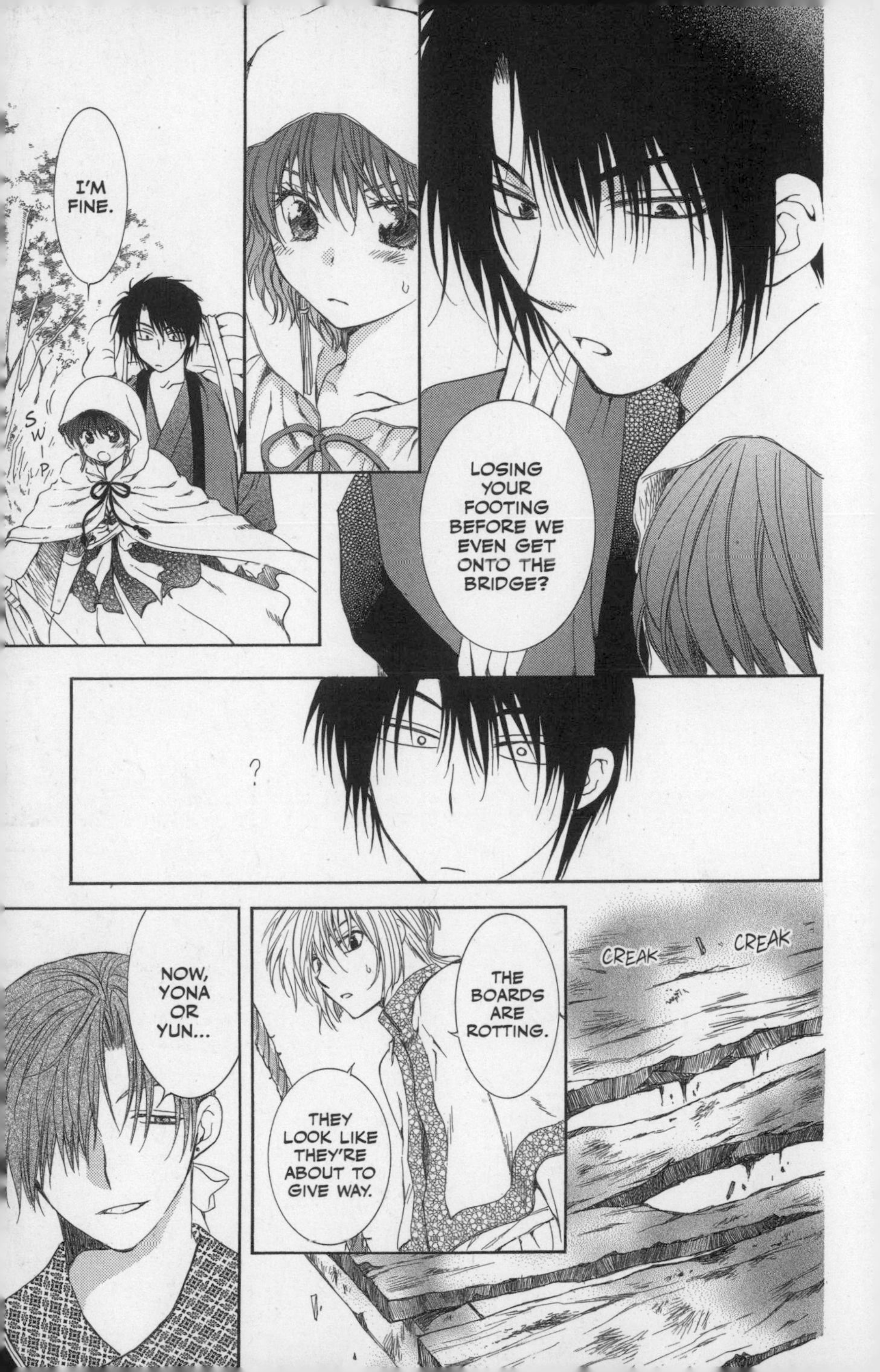
LOSING YOUR FOOTING BEFORE WE EVEN GET ONTO THE BRIDGE?
SWIP
I'M FINE.
?
CREAK
CREAK
THE BOARDS ARE ROTTING.
THEY LOOK LIKE THEY'RE ABOUT TO GIVE WAY.
NOW, YONA OR YUN...

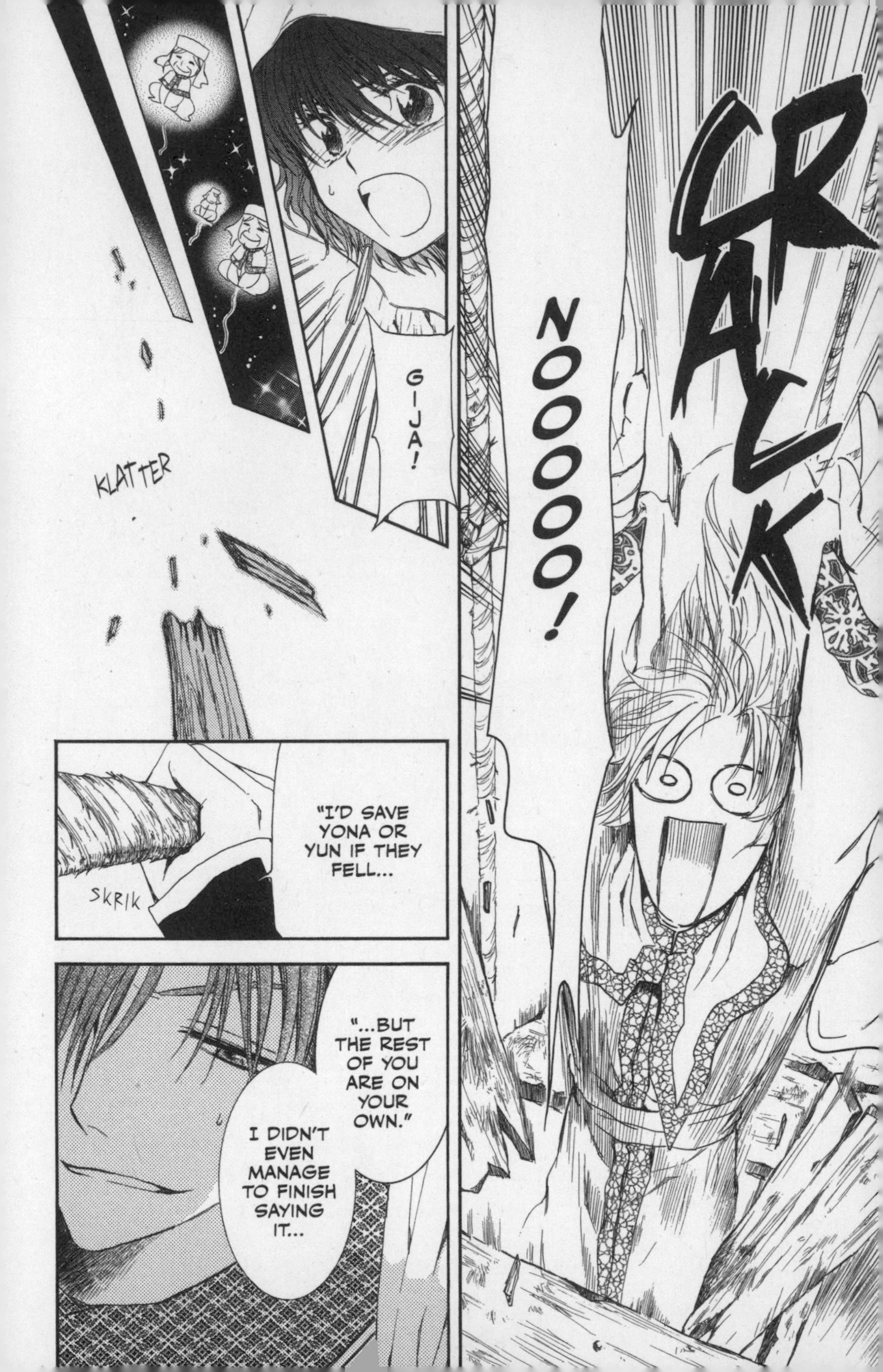
CRACK
NOOOOOO!
GIJA!
KLATTER
"I'D SAVE YONA OR YUN IF THEY FELL...
SKRIK
"...BUT THE REST OF YOU ARE ON YOUR OWN."
I DIDN'T EVEN MANAGE TO FINISH SAYING IT...

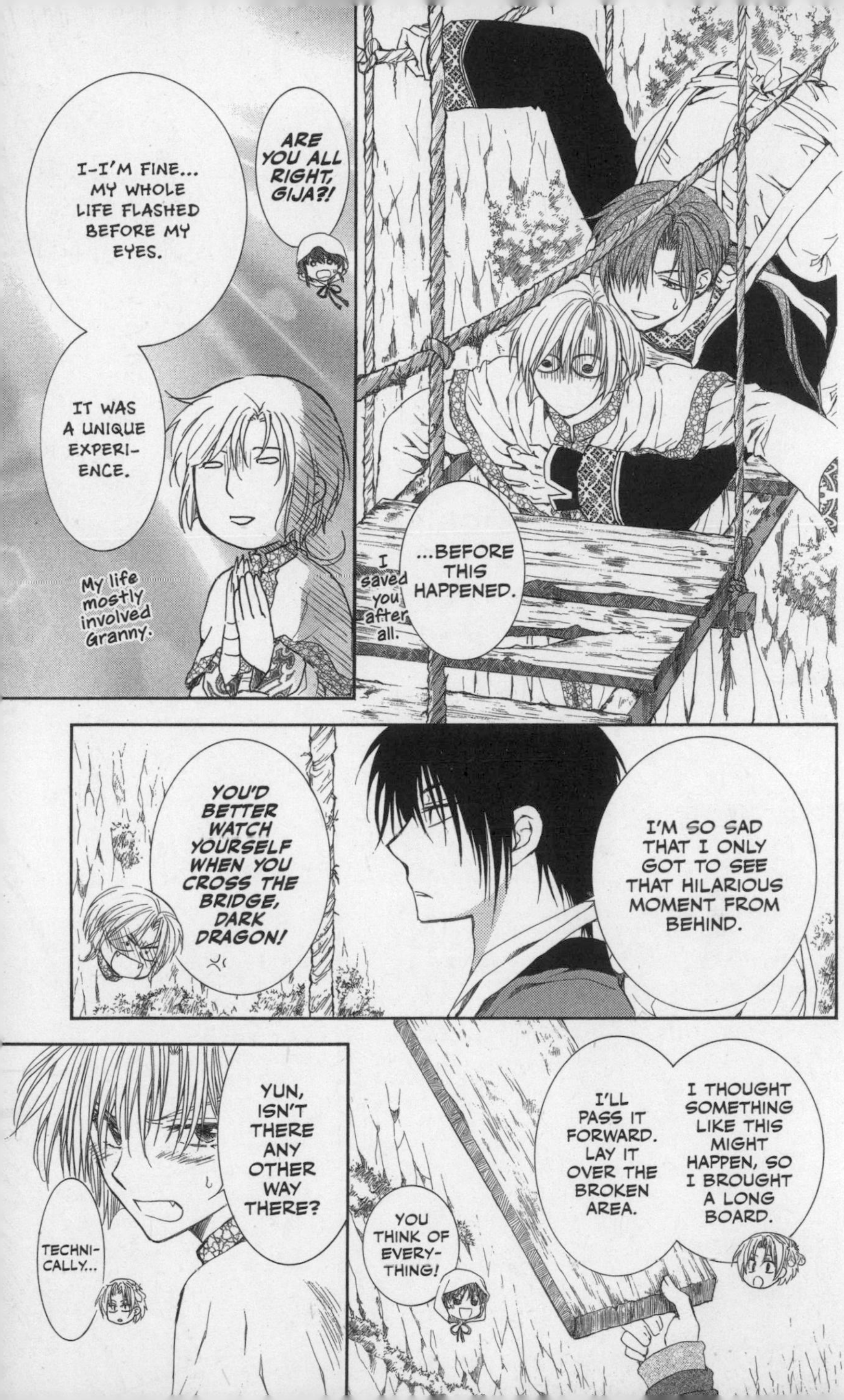
...BEFORE THIS HAPPENED.
I saved you after all.
ARE YOU ALL RIGHT, GIJA?!
I-I'M FINE... MY WHOLE LIFE FLASHED BEFORE MY EYES.
IT WAS A UNIQUE EXPERI-ENCE.
My life mostly involved Granny.
I'M SO SAD THAT I ONLY GOT TO SEE THAT HILARIOUS MOMENT FROM BEHIND.
YOU'D BETTER WATCH YOURSELF WHEN YOU CROSS THE BRIDGE, DARK DRAGON!
I THOUGHT SOMETHING LIKE THIS MIGHT HAPPEN, SO I BROUGHT A LONG BOARD.
I'LL PASS IT FORWARD. LAY IT OVER THE BROKEN AREA.
YOU THINK OF EVERY-THING!
YUN, ISN'T THERE ANY OTHER WAY THERE?
TECHNI-CALLY...

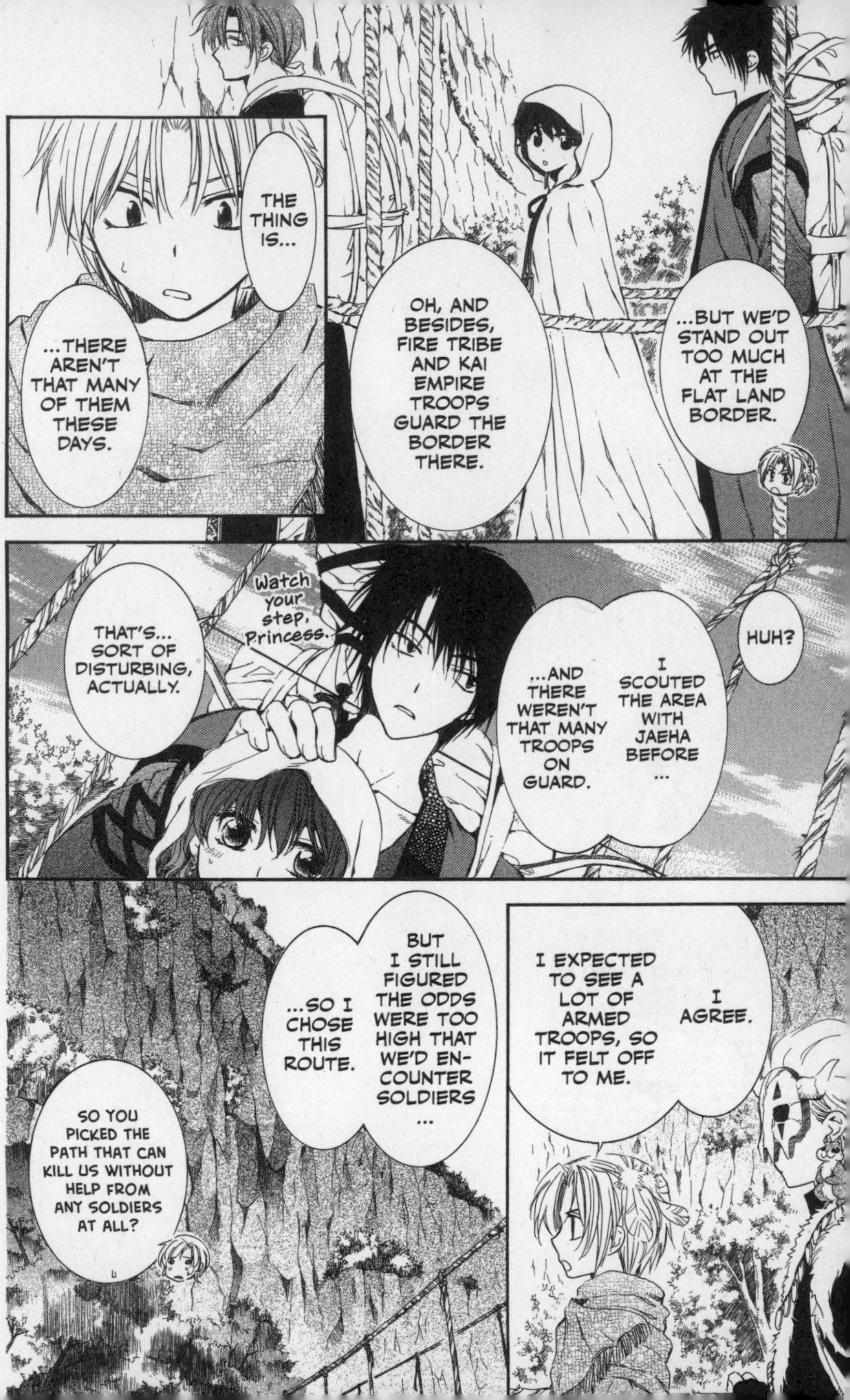
...BUT WE'D STAND OUT TOO MUCH AT THE FLAT LAND BORDER.
OH, AND BESIDES, FIRE TRIBE AND KAI EMPIRE TROOPS GUARD THE BORDER THERE.
THE THING IS...
...THERE AREN'T THAT MANY OF THEM THESE DAYS.
HUH?
I SCOUTED THE AREA WITH JAEHA BEFORE...
...AND THERE WEREN'T THAT MANY TROOPS ON GUARD.
Watch your step, Princess.
THAT'S... SORT OF DISTURBING, ACTUALLY.
I AGREE.
I EXPECTED TO SEE A LOT OF ARMED TROOPS, SO IT FELT OFF TO ME.
BUT I STILL FIGURED THE ODDS WERE TOO HIGH THAT WE'D EN-COUNTER SOLDIERS...
...SO I CHOSE THIS ROUTE.
SO YOU PICKED THE PATH THAT CAN KILL US WITHOUT HELP FROM ANY SOLDIERS AT ALL?

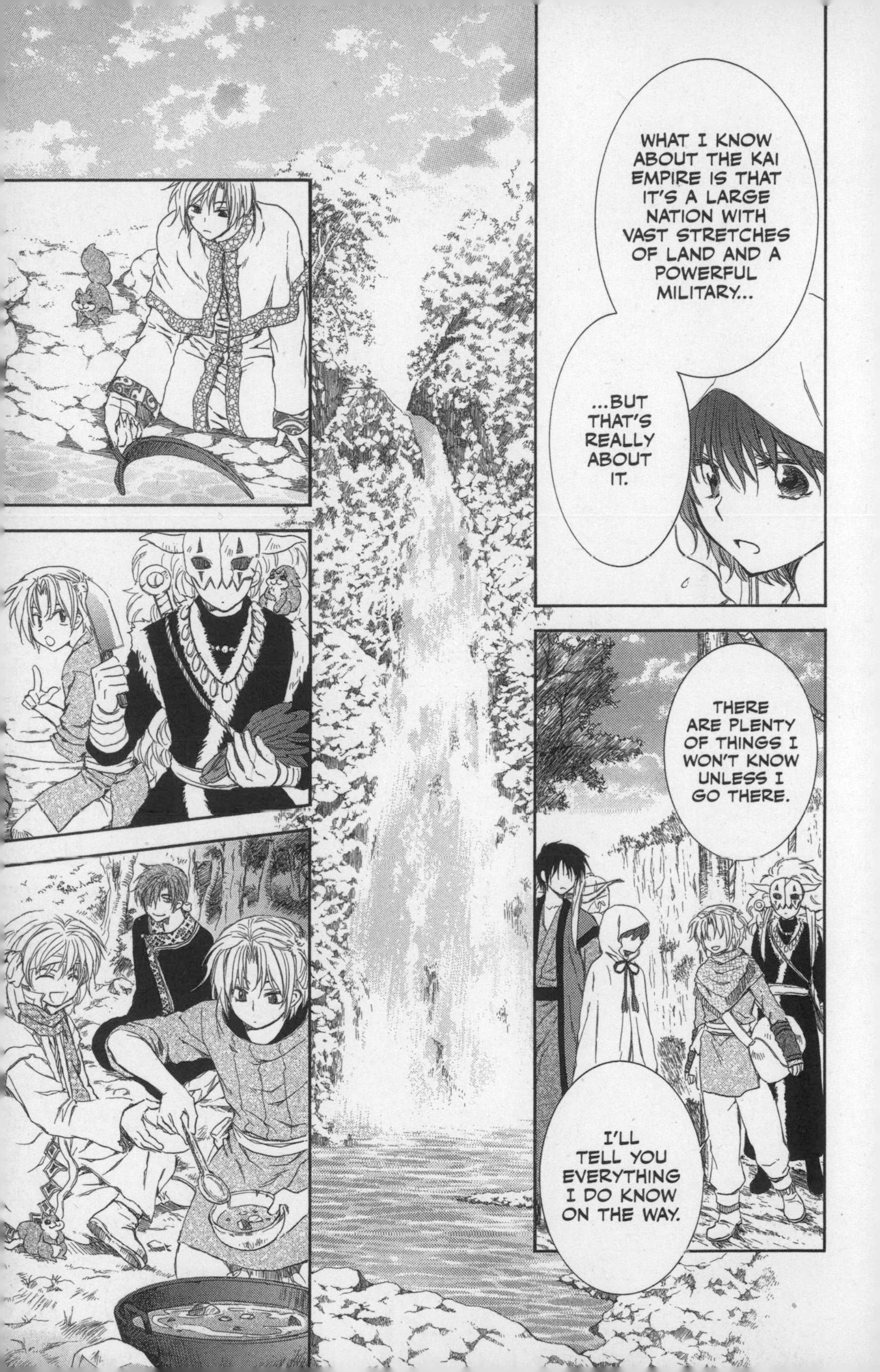
WHAT I KNOW ABOUT THE KAI EMPIRE IS THAT IT'S A LARGE NATION WITH VAST STRETCHES OF LAND AND A POWERFUL MILITARY...
...BUT THAT'S REALLY ABOUT IT.
THERE ARE PLENTY OF THINGS I WON'T KNOW UNLESS I GO THERE.
I'LL TELL YOU EVERYTHING I DO KNOW ON THE WAY.

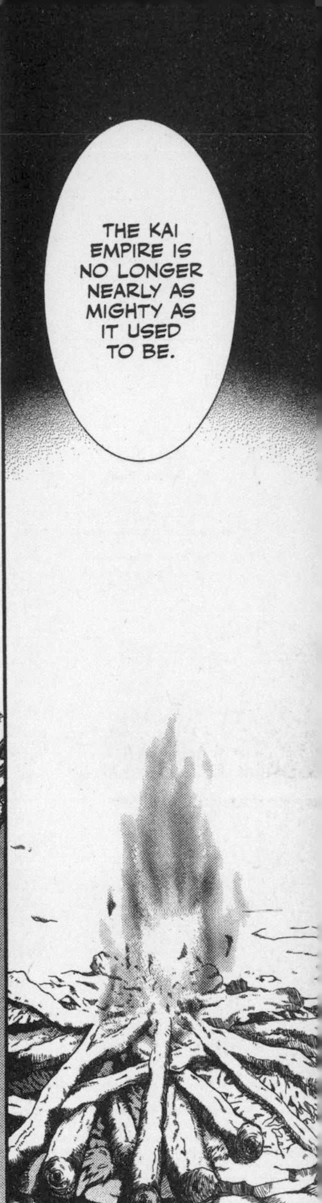
THE KAI EMPIRE IS NO LONGER NEARLY AS MIGHTY AS IT USED TO BE.
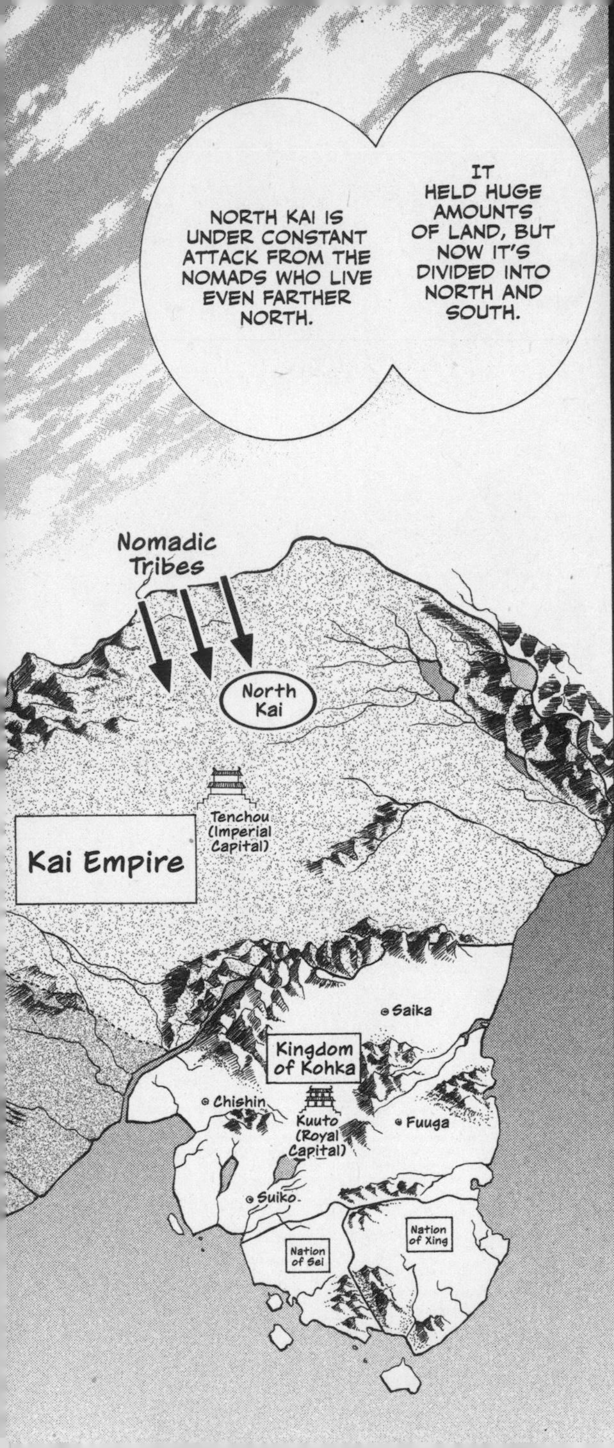
IT HELD HUGE AMOUNTS OF LAND, BUT NOW IT'S DIVIDED INTO NORTH AND SOUTH.
NORTH KAI IS UNDER CONSTANT ATTACK FROM THE NOMADS WHO LIVE EVEN FARTHER NORTH.
Nomadic Tribes
North Kai
Tenchou (Imperial Capital)
Kai Empire
Saika
Kingdom of Kohka
Chishin
Kuuto (Royal Capital)
Fuuga
Suiko
Nation of Xing
Nation of Sei

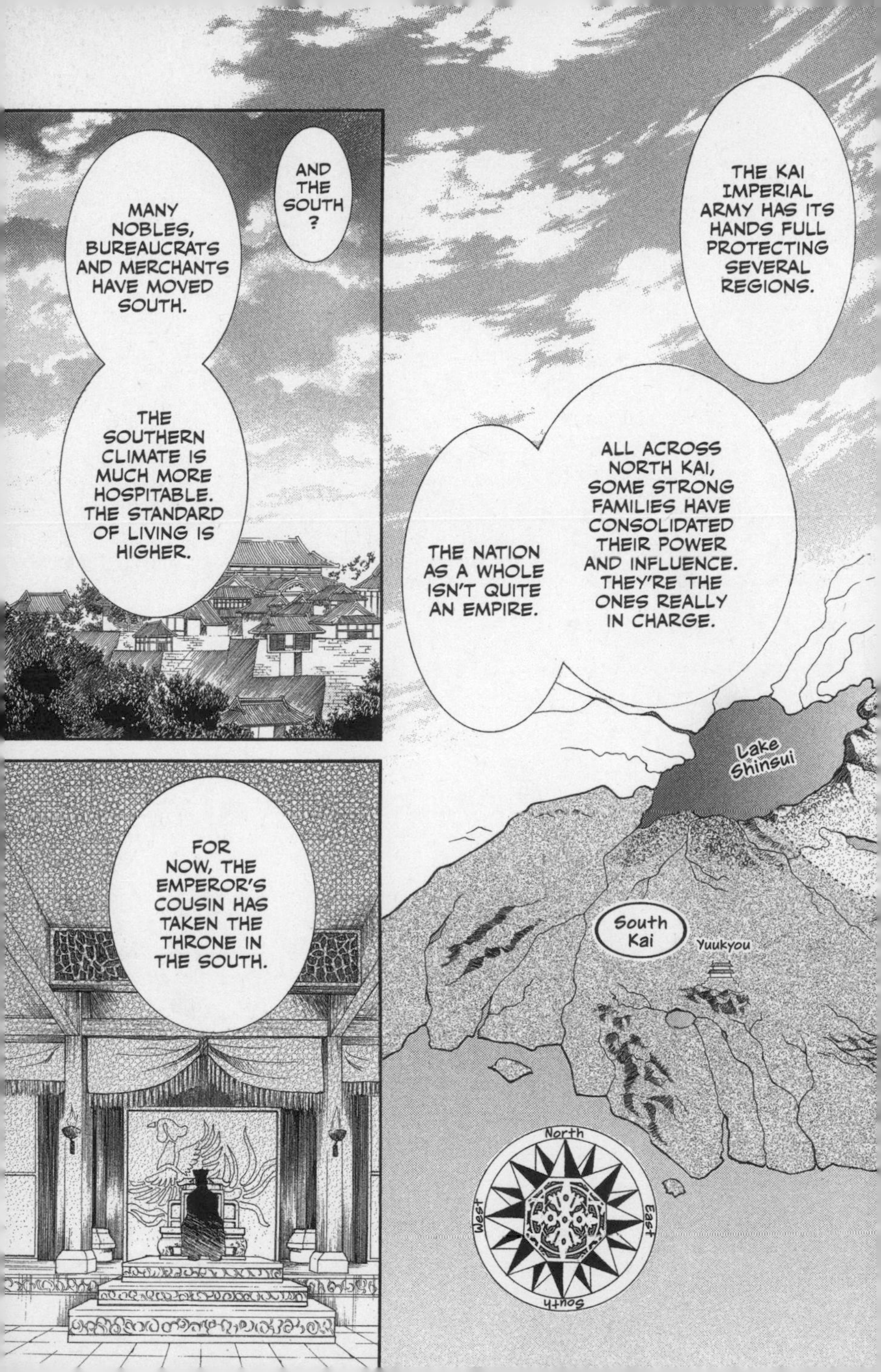
THE KAI IMPERIAL ARMY HAS ITS HANDS FULL PROTECTING SEVERAL REGIONS.
ALL ACROSS NORTH KAI, SOME STRONG FAMILIES HAVE CONSOLIDATED THEIR POWER AND INFLUENCE. THEY'RE THE ONES REALLY IN CHARGE.
THE NATION AS A WHOLE ISN'T QUITE AN EMPIRE.
Lake Shinsui
South Kai
Yuukyou
North
East
South
West
AND THE SOUTH?
MANY NOBLES, BUREAUCRATS AND MERCHANTS HAVE MOVED SOUTH.
THE SOUTHERN CLIMATE IS MUCH MORE HOSPITABLE. THE STANDARD OF LIVING IS HIGHER.
FOR NOW, THE EMPEROR'S COUSIN HAS TAKEN THE THRONE IN THE SOUTH.

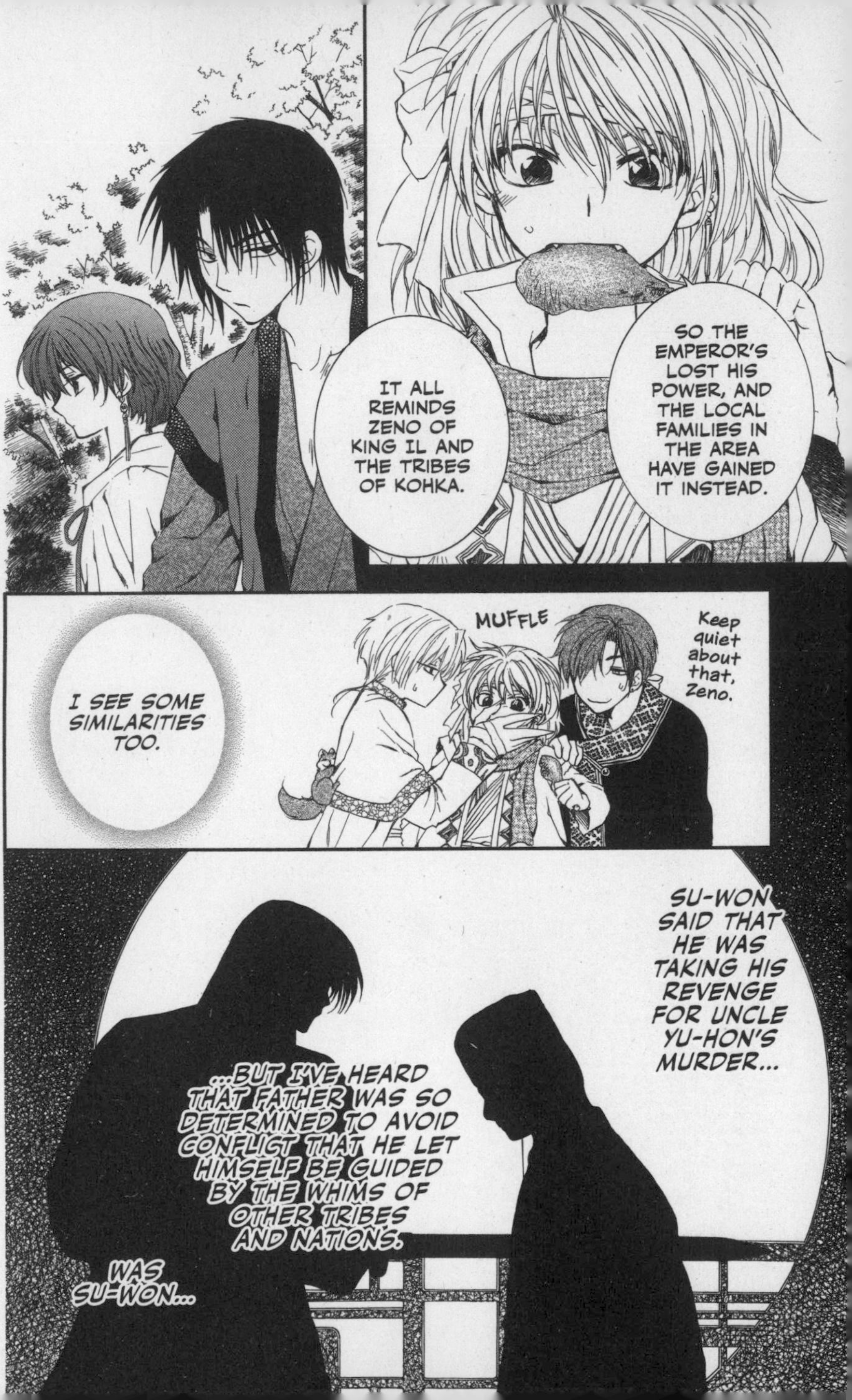
SO THE EMPEROR'S LOST HIS POWER, AND THE LOCAL FAMILIES IN THE AREA HAVE GAINED IT INSTEAD.
IT ALL REMINDS ZENO OF KING IL AND THE TRIBES OF KOHKA.
Keep quiet about that, Zeno.
MUFFLE
I SEE SOME SIMILARITIES TOO.
SU-WON SAID THAT HE WAS TAKING HIS REVENGE FOR UNCLE YU-HON'S MURDER...
...BUT I'VE HEARD THAT FATHER WAS SO DETERMINED TO AVOID CONFLICT THAT HE LET HIMSELF BE GUIDED BY THE WHIMS OF OTHER TRIBES AND NATIONS.
WAS SU-WON...

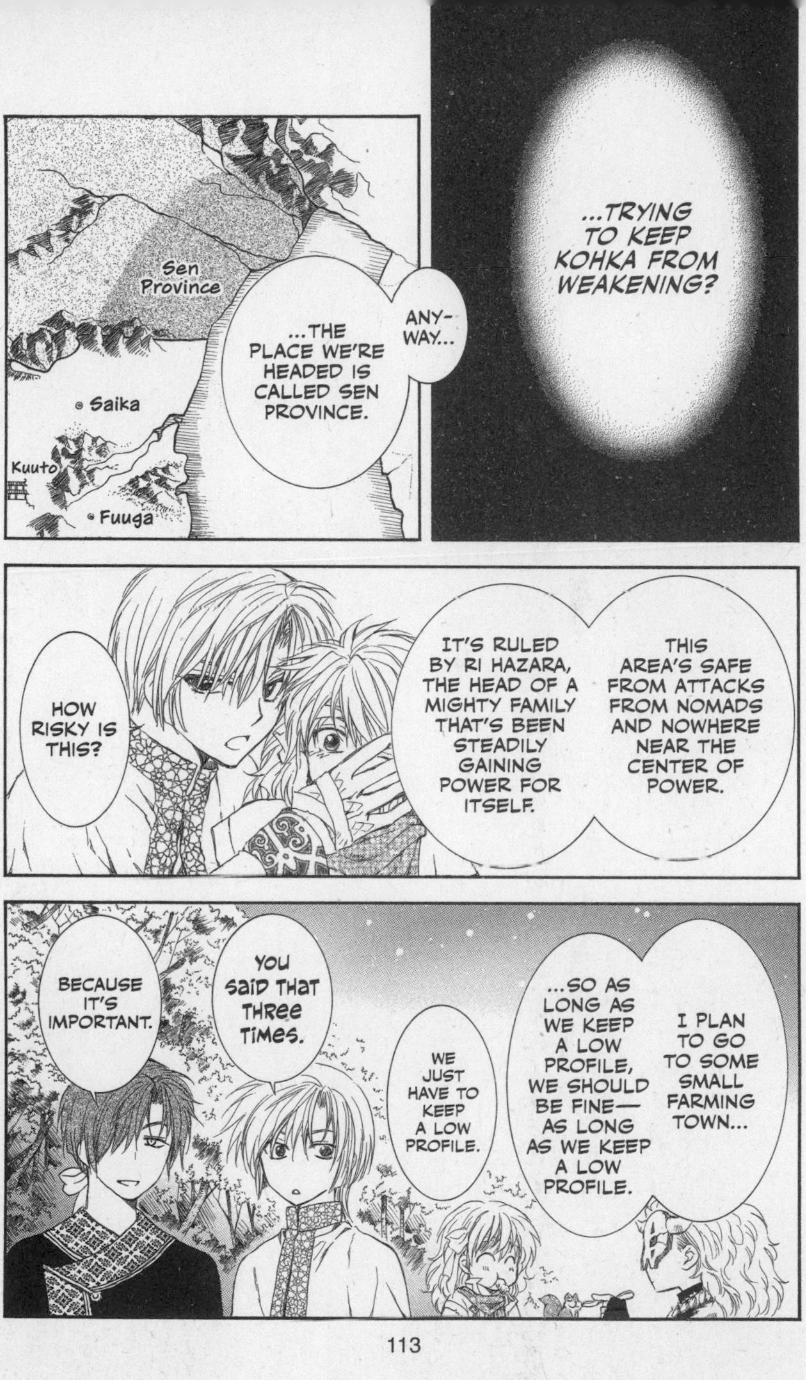
...TRYING TO KEEP KOHKA FROM WEAKENING?
ANY-WAY...
...THE PLACE WE'RE HEADED IS CALLED SEN PROVINCE.
Sen Province
Saika
Kuuto
Fuuga
THIS AREA'S SAFE FROM ATTACKS FROM NOMADS AND NOWHERE NEAR THE CENTER OF POWER.
IT'S RULED BY RI HAZARA, THE HEAD OF A MIGHTY FAMILY THAT'S BEEN STEADILY GAINING POWER FOR ITSELF.
HOW RISKY IS THIS?
I PLAN TO GO TO SOME SMALL FARMING TOWN...
...SO AS LONG AS WE KEEP A LOW PROFILE, WE SHOULD BE FINE—AS LONG AS WE KEEP A LOW PROFILE.
WE JUST HAVE TO KEEP A LOW PROFILE.
YOU SAID THAT THREE TIMES.
BECAUSE IT'S IMPORTANT.

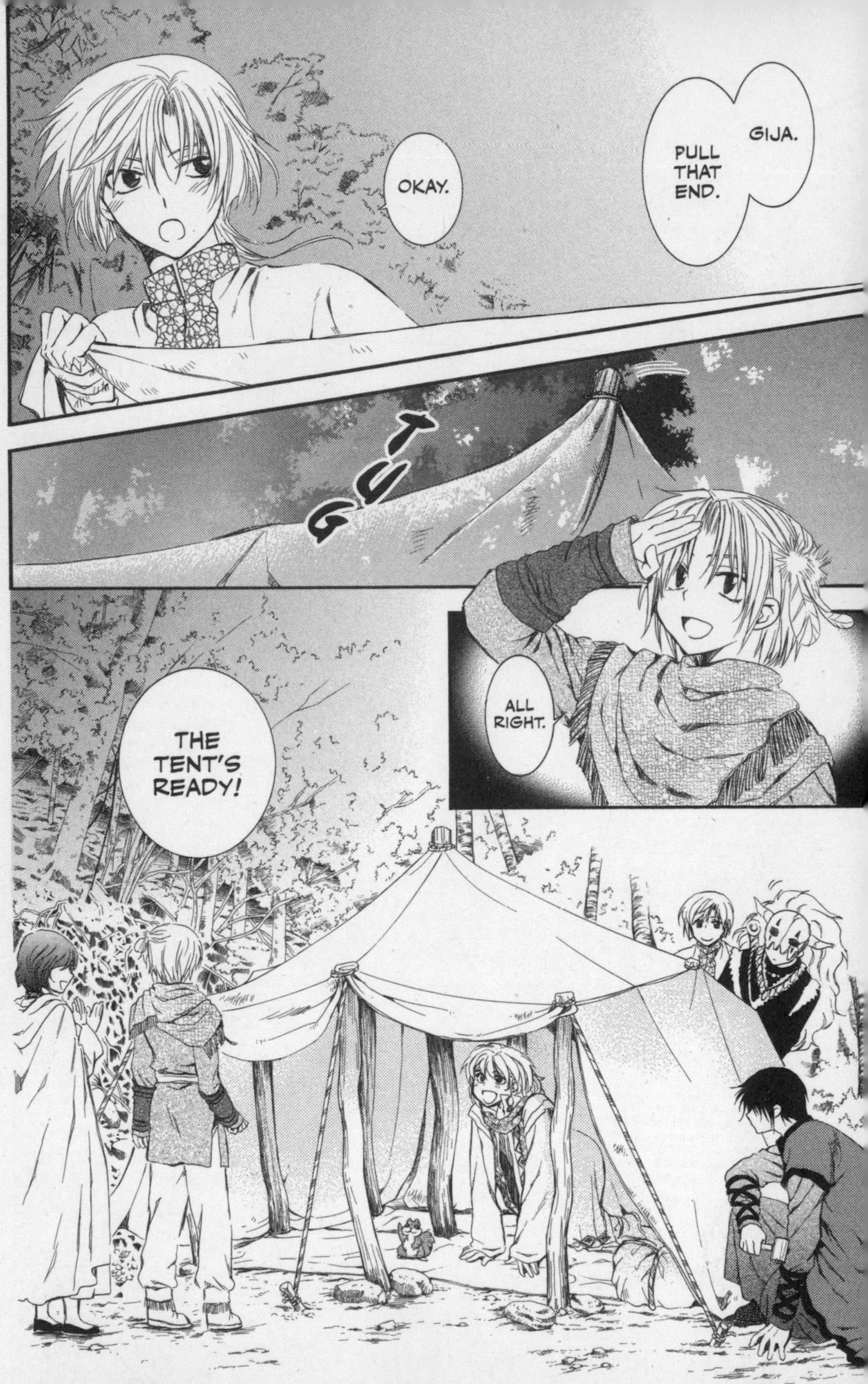
GIJA. PULL THAT END.
OKAY.
TUG
ALL RIGHT.
THE TENT'S READY!

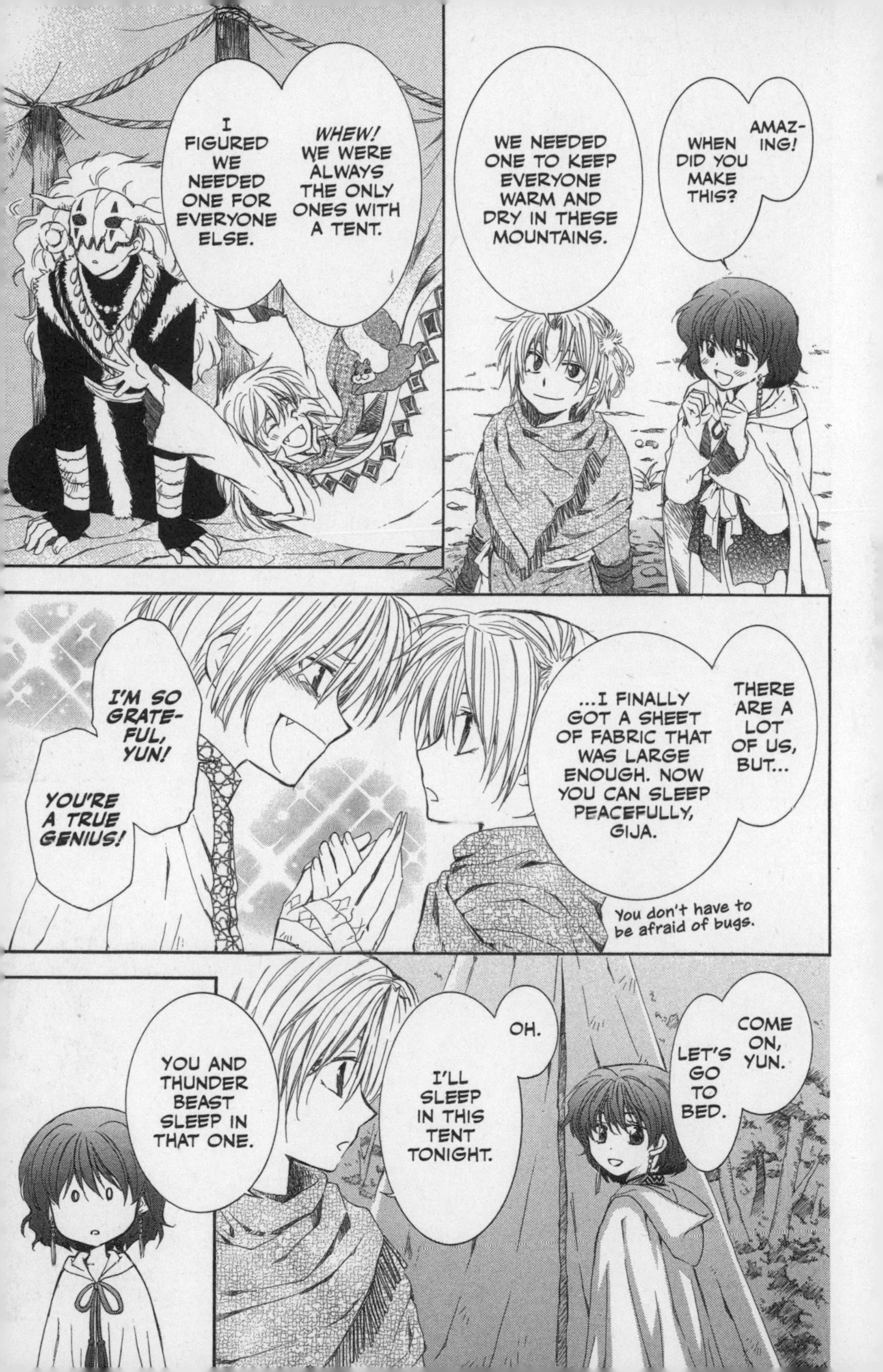

AMAZING! WHEN DID YOU MAKE THIS?
WE NEEDED ONE TO KEEP EVERYONE WARM AND DRY IN THESE MOUNTAINS.
WHEW! WE WERE ALWAYS THE ONLY ONES WITH A TENT.
I FIGURED WE NEEDED ONE FOR EVERYONE ELSE.
THERE ARE A LOT OF US, BUT...
...I FINALLY GOT A SHEET OF FABRIC THAT WAS LARGE ENOUGH. NOW YOU CAN SLEEP PEACEFULLY, GIJA.
You don't have to be afraid of bugs.
I'M SO GRATEFUL, YUN!
YOU'RE A TRUE GENIUS!
COME ON, YUN.
LET'S GO TO BED.
OH.
I'LL SLEEP IN THIS TENT TONIGHT.
YOU AND THUNDER BEAST SLEEP IN THAT ONE.

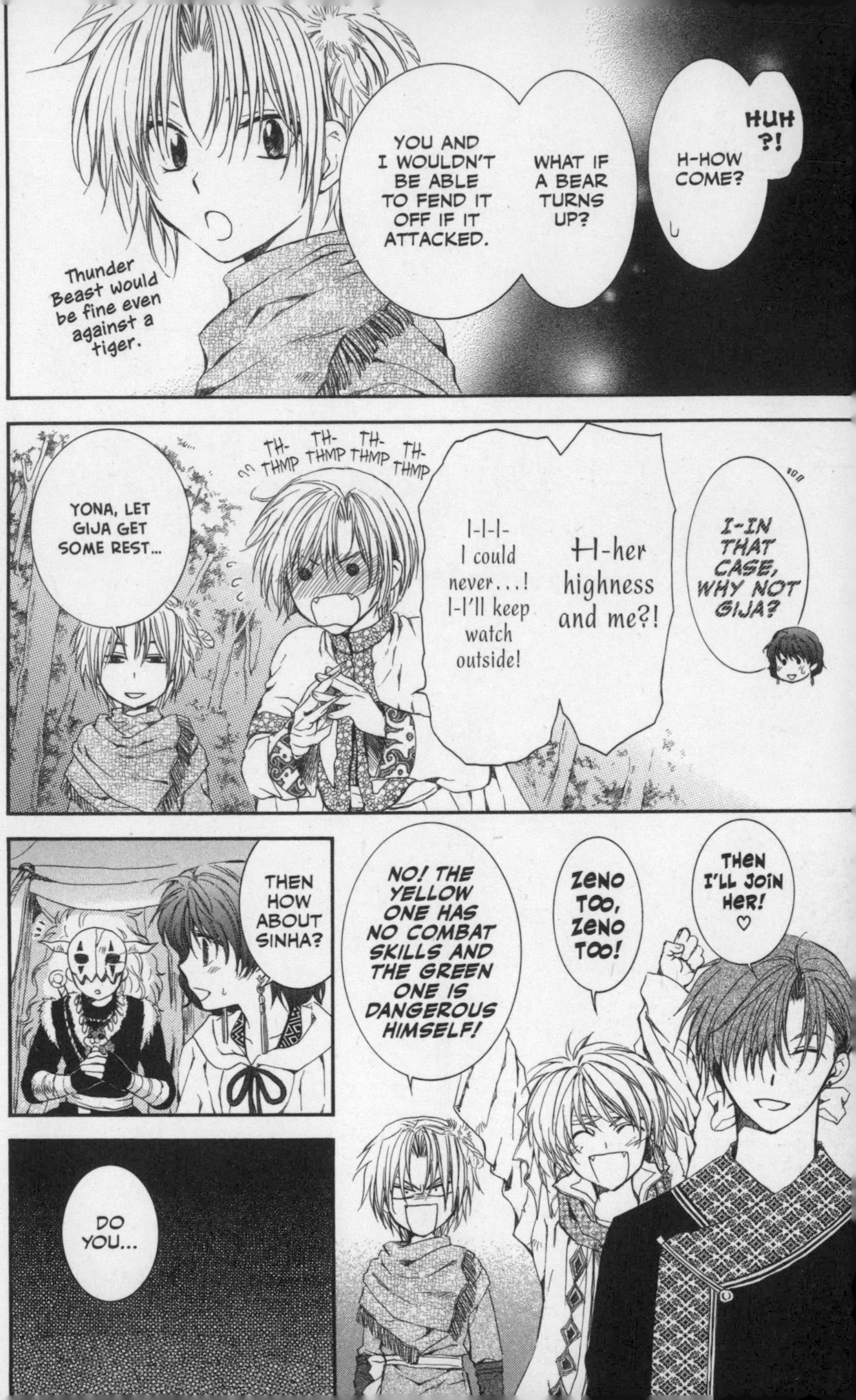
HUH ?!
H-HOW COME?
WHAT IF A BEAR TURNS UP?
YOU AND I WOULDN'T BE ABLE TO FEND IT OFF IF IT ATTACKED.
Thunder Beast would be fine even against a tiger.
I-IN THAT CASE, WHY NOT GIJA?
H-her highness and me?!
I-I-I- I could never...! I-I'll keep watch outside!
TH-THMP TH-THMP TH-THMP TH-THMP
YONA, LET GIJA GET SOME REST...
THEN I'LL JOIN HER! ♡
ZENO TOO, ZENO TOO!
NO! THE YELLOW ONE HAS NO COMBAT SKILLS AND THE GREEN ONE IS DANGEROUS HIMSELF!
THEN HOW ABOUT SINHA?
DO YOU...

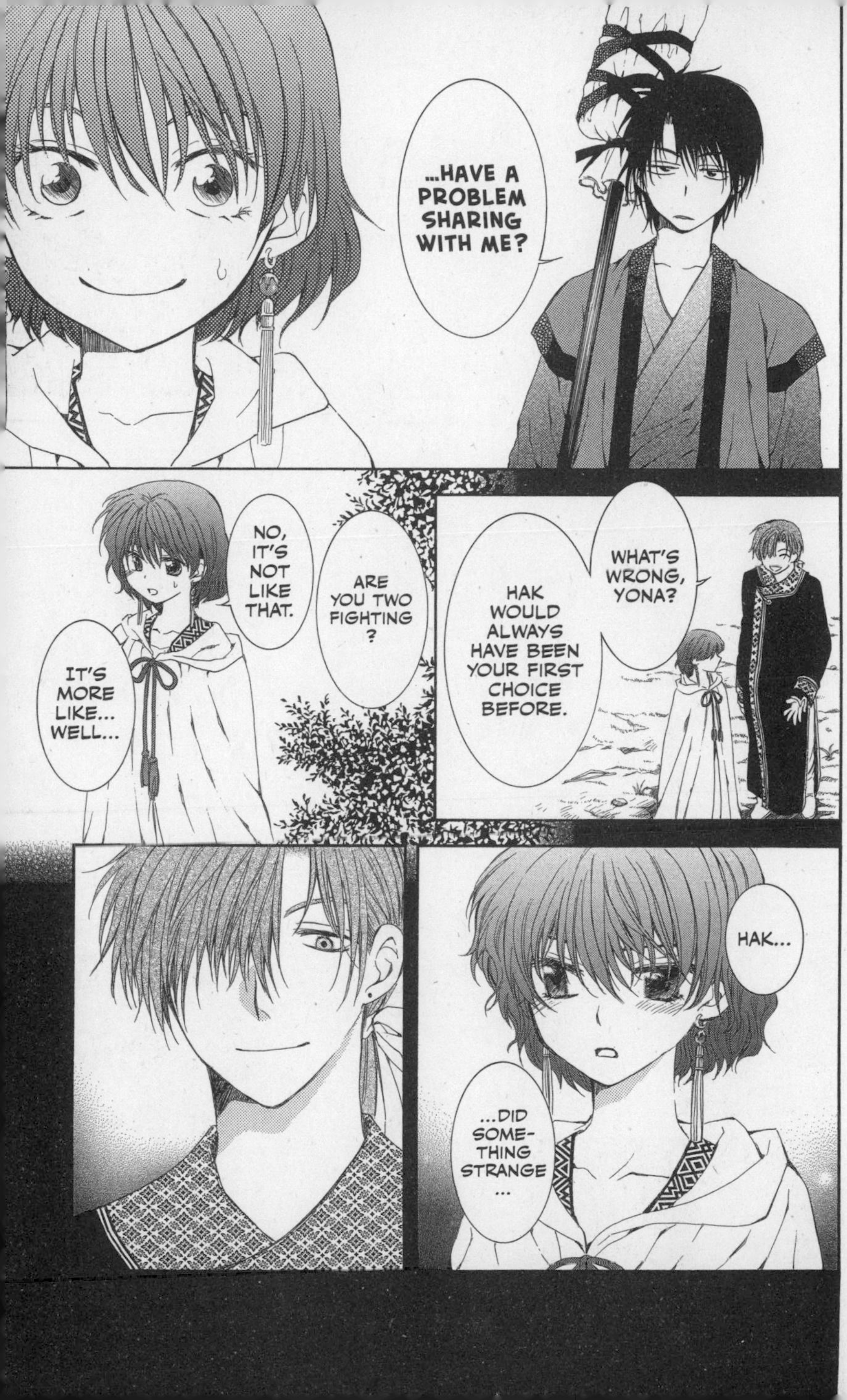
...HAVE A PROBLEM SHARING WITH ME?
WHAT'S WRONG, YONA?
HAK WOULD ALWAYS HAVE BEEN YOUR FIRST CHOICE BEFORE.
ARE YOU TWO FIGHTING?
NO, IT'S NOT LIKE THAT.
IT'S MORE LIKE... WELL...
HAK...
...DID SOME-THING STRANGE...

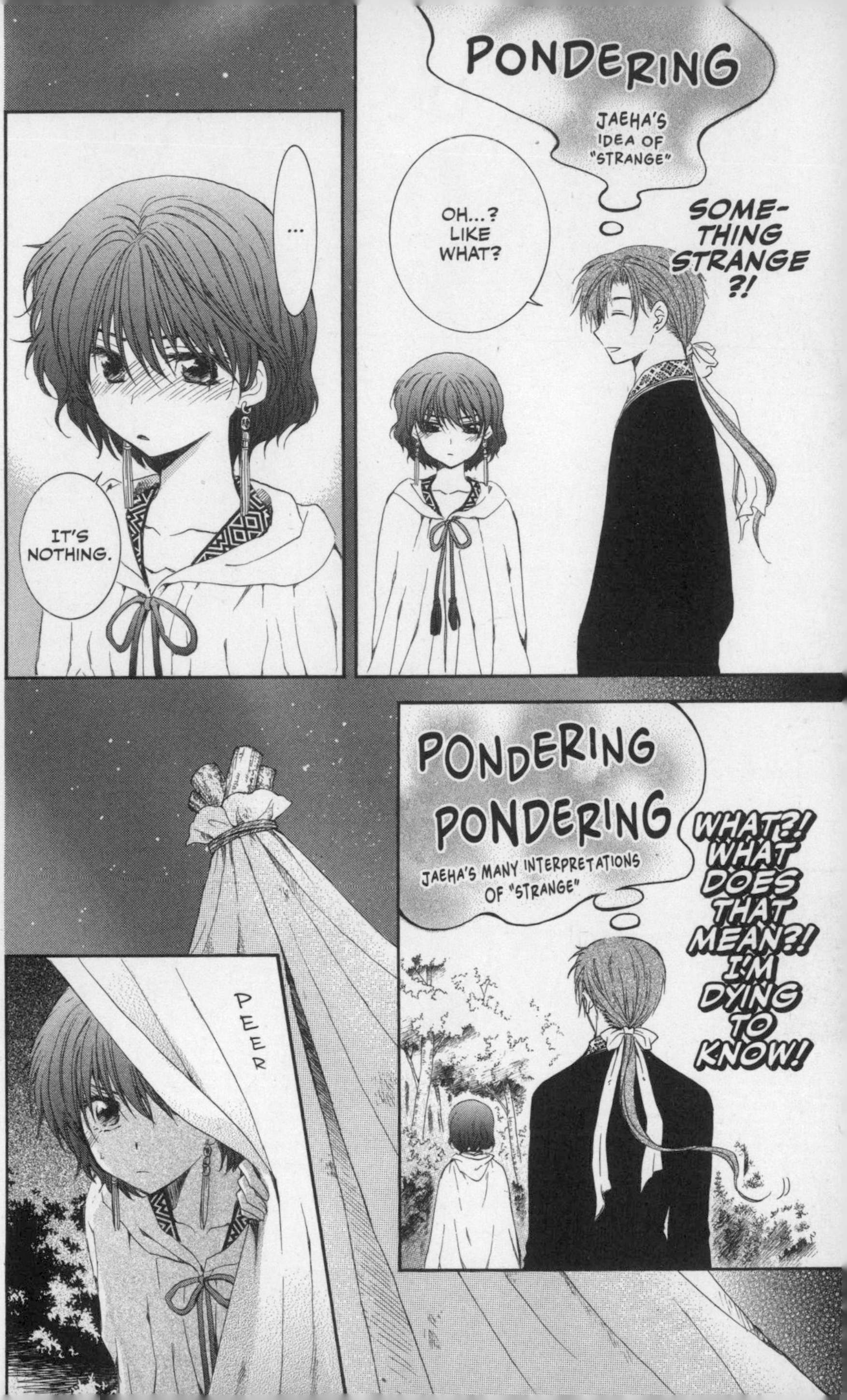
SOME-THING STRANGE?!
PONDERING
JAEHA'S IDEA OF "STRANGE"
OH...? LIKE WHAT?
...
IT'S NOTHING.
WHAT?! WHAT DOES THAT MEAN?! I'M DYING TO KNOW!
PONDERING PONDERING
JAEHA'S MANY INTERPRETATIONS OF "STRANGE"
PEER

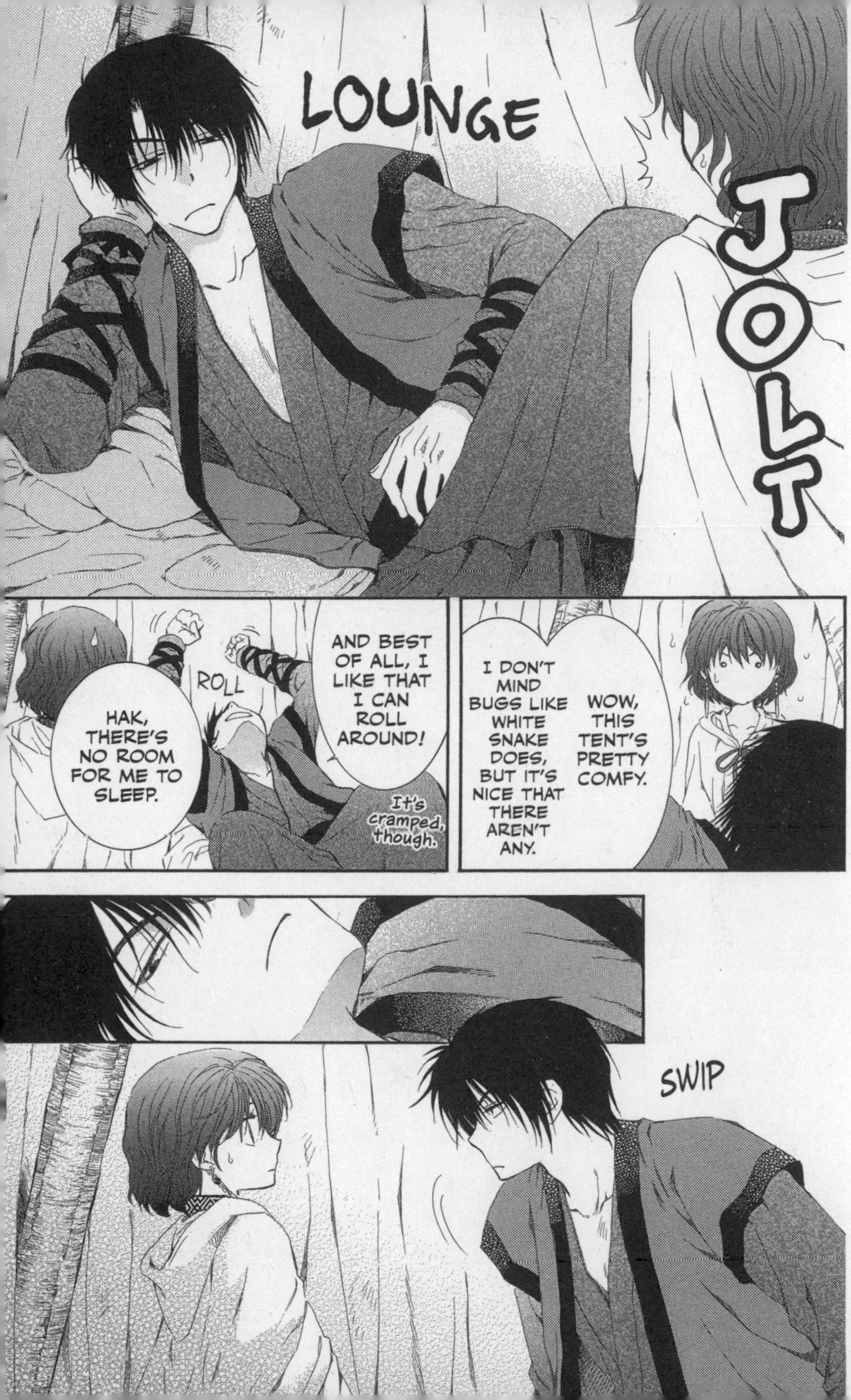
LOUNGE
JOLT
WOW, THIS TENT'S PRETTY COMFY.
I DON'T MIND BUGS LIKE WHITE SNAKE DOES, BUT IT'S NICE THAT THERE AREN'T ANY.
AND BEST OF ALL, I LIKE THAT I CAN ROLL AROUND!
It's cramped, though.
ROLL
HAK, THERE'S NO ROOM FOR ME TO SLEEP.
SWIP

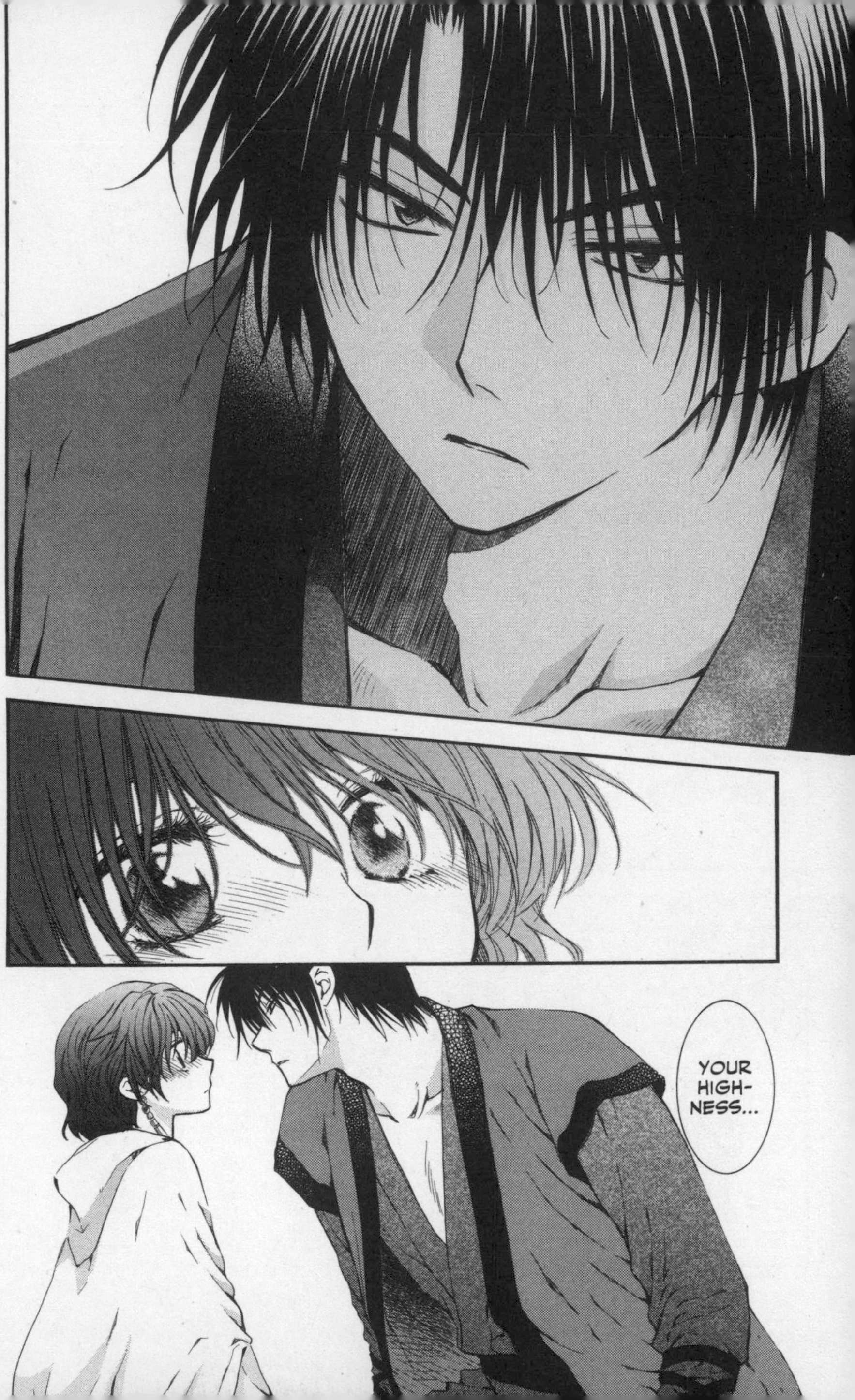
YOUR HIGH-NESS...

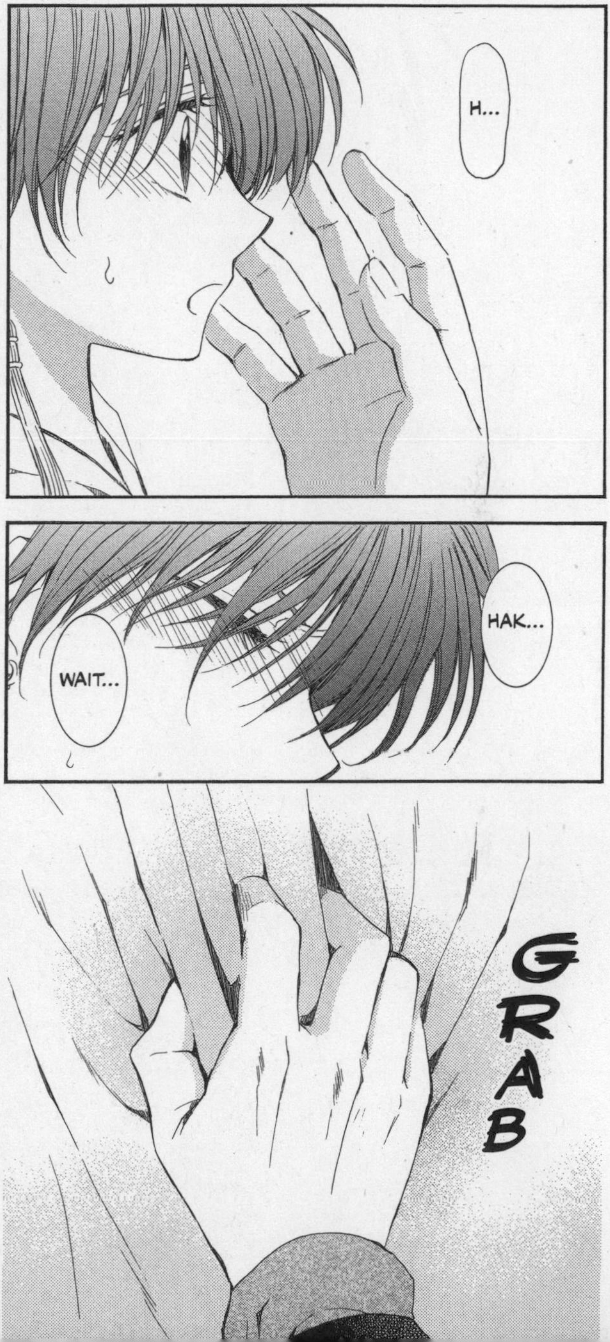
H...
HAK...
WAIT...
GRAB

Screentone is one of the many things I use to make manga. It's like stickers with various patterns that I place on characters or backgrounds. My sister created a reference chart for my assistants to show which tone to use. It looks like this:

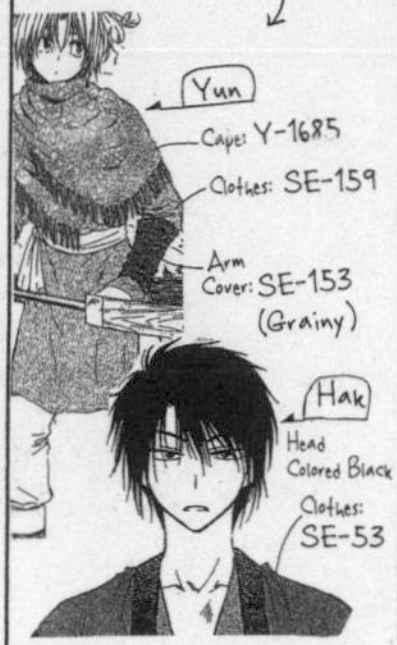
Yun
Cape: Y-1685
Clothes: SE-159
Arm Cover: SE-153 (Grainy)
Hak
Head Colored Black
Clothes: SE-53

For some reason...

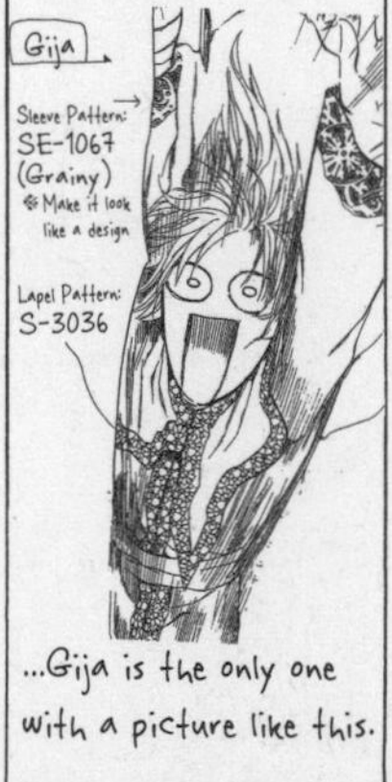
Gija
Sleeve Pattern: SE-1067 (Grainy)
※ Make it look like a design
Lapel Pattern: S-3036

...Gija is the only one with a picture like this.

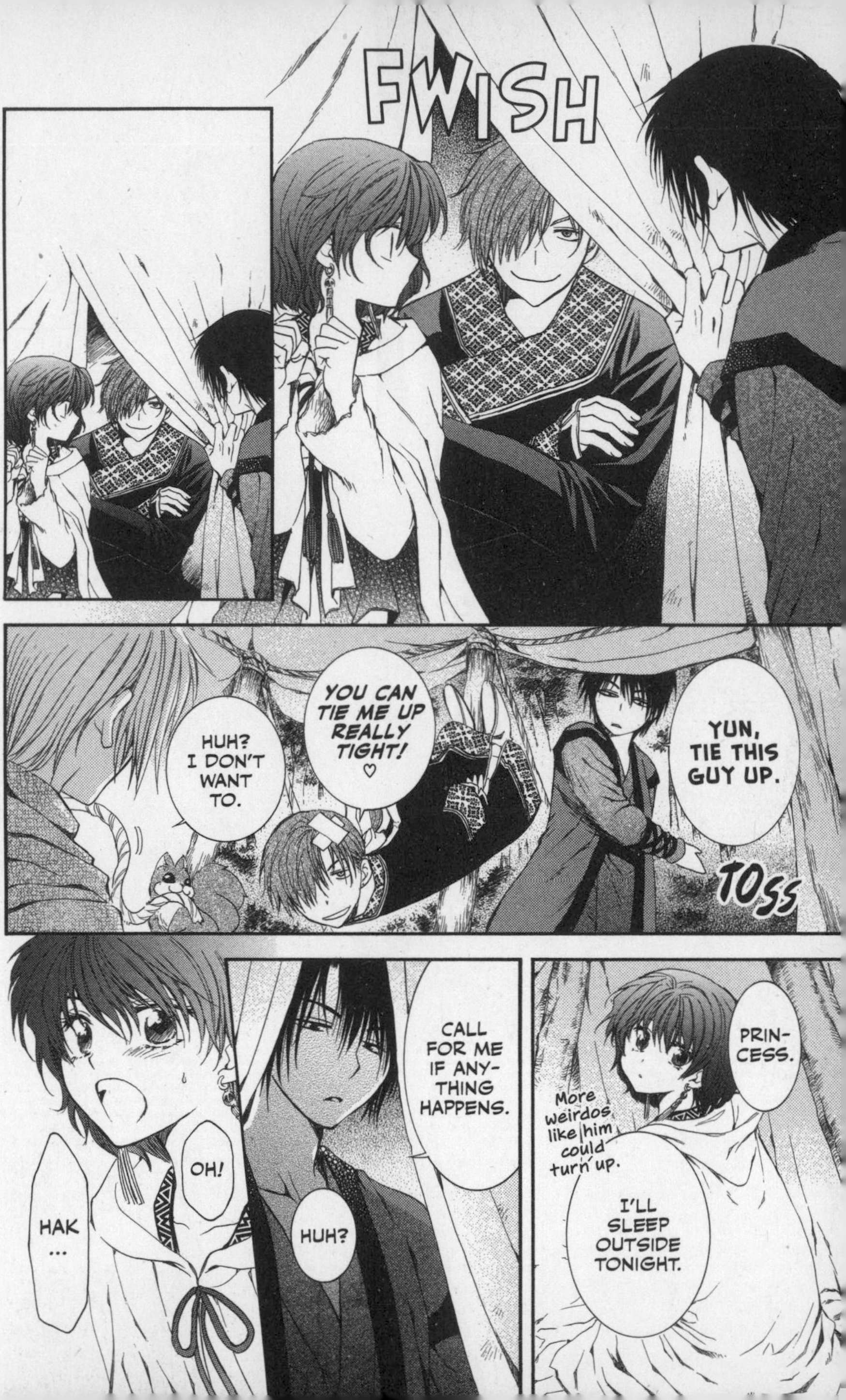
FWISH
YUN, TIE THIS GUY UP.
TOSS
YOU CAN TIE ME UP REALLY TIGHT! ♡
HUH? I DON'T WANT TO.
PRINCESS.
More weirdos like him could turn up.
I'LL SLEEP OUTSIDE TONIGHT.
CALL FOR ME IF ANYTHING HAPPENS.
HUH?
OH!
HAK ...

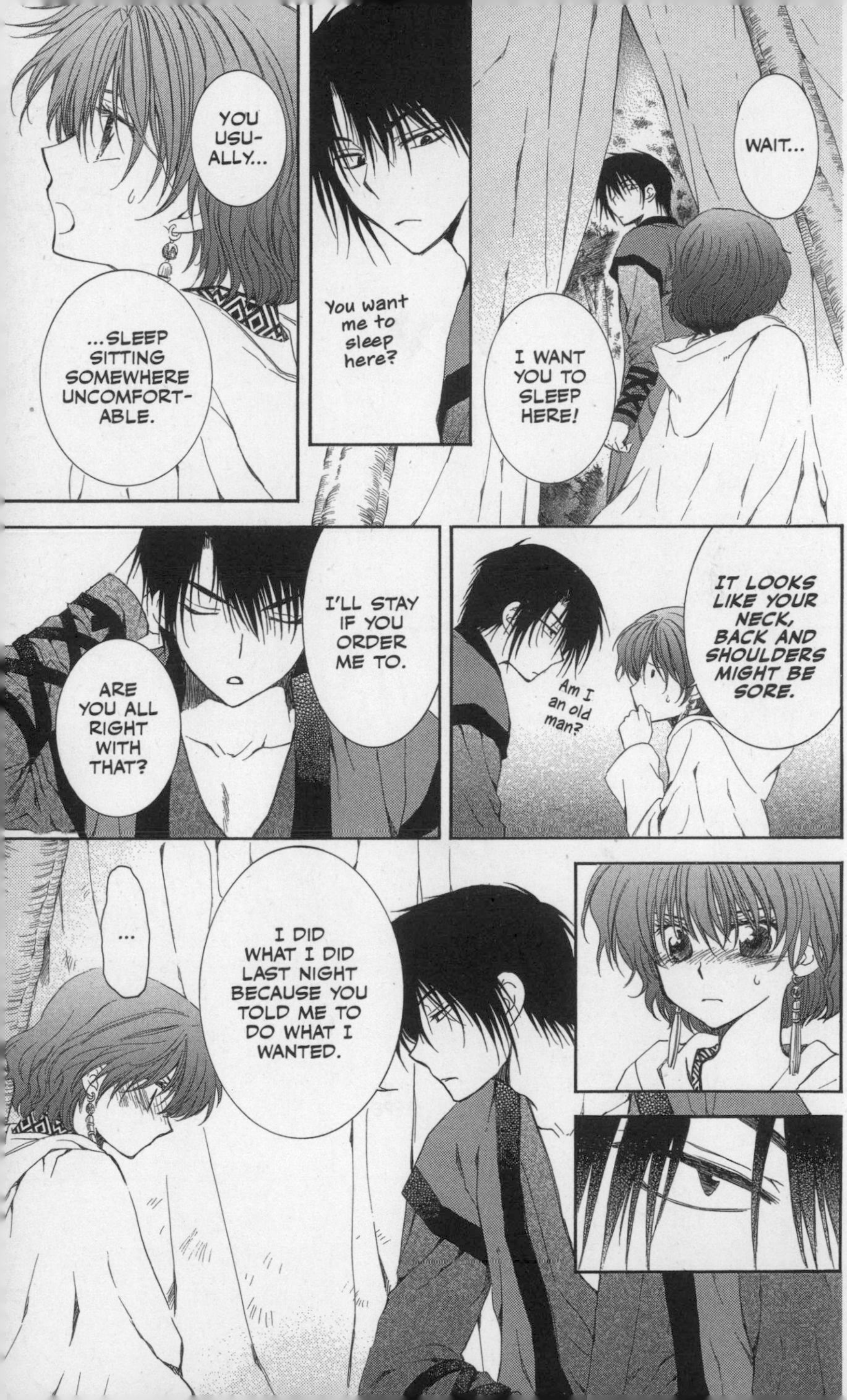
WAIT...
I WANT YOU TO SLEEP HERE!
You want me to sleep here?
YOU USUALLY...
...SLEEP SITTING SOMEWHERE UNCOMFORTABLE.
IT LOOKS LIKE YOUR NECK, BACK AND SHOULDERS MIGHT BE SORE.
Am I an old man?
I'LL STAY IF YOU ORDER ME TO.
ARE YOU ALL RIGHT WITH THAT?
I DID WHAT I DID LAST NIGHT BECAUSE YOU TOLD ME TO DO WHAT I WANTED.
...

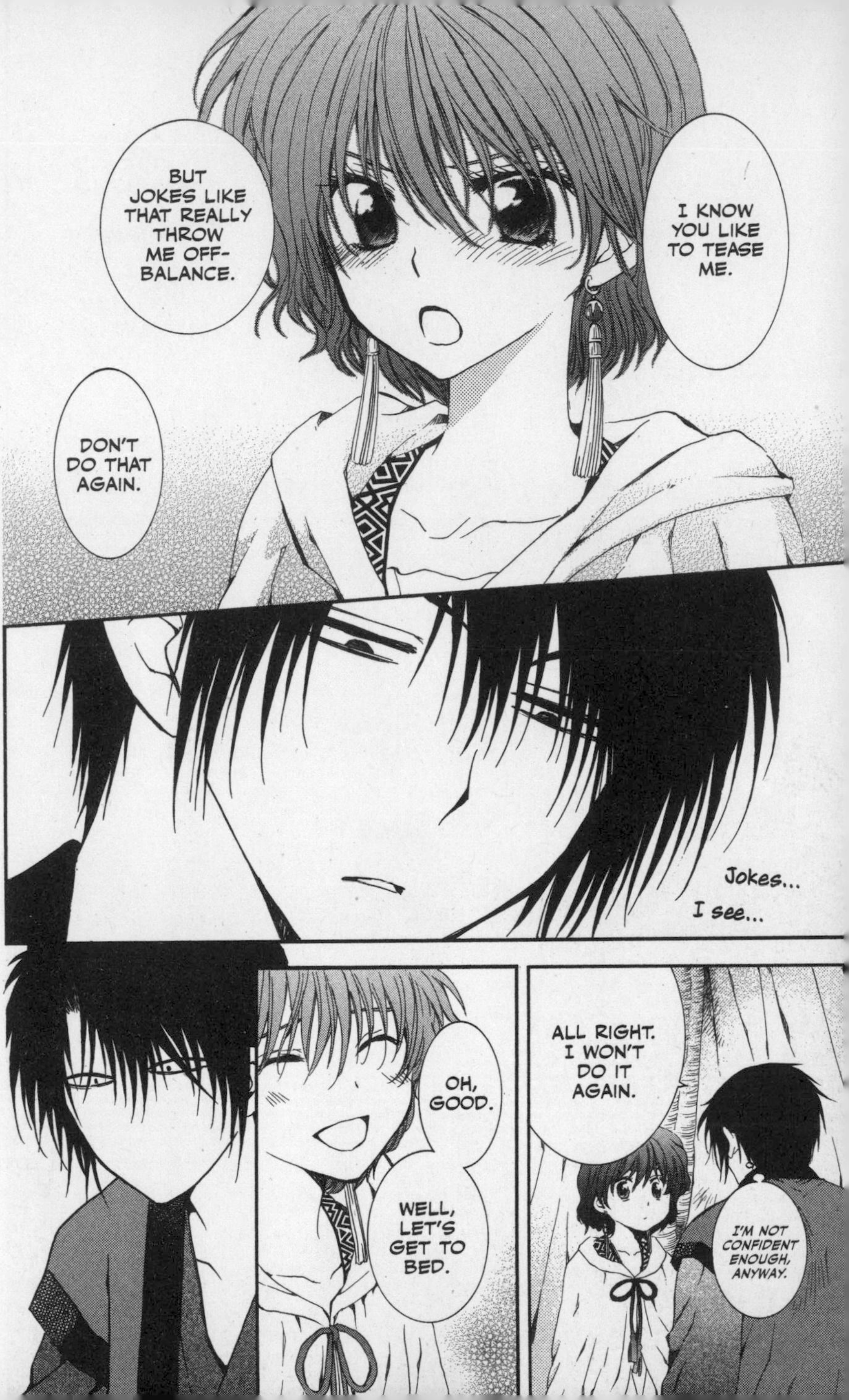
I KNOW YOU LIKE TO TEASE ME.
BUT JOKES LIKE THAT REALLY THROW ME OFF-BALANCE.
DON'T DO THAT AGAIN.
Jokes...
I see...
ALL RIGHT. I WON'T DO IT AGAIN.
I'M NOT CONFIDENT ENOUGH, ANYWAY.
OH, GOOD.
WELL, LET'S GET TO BED.

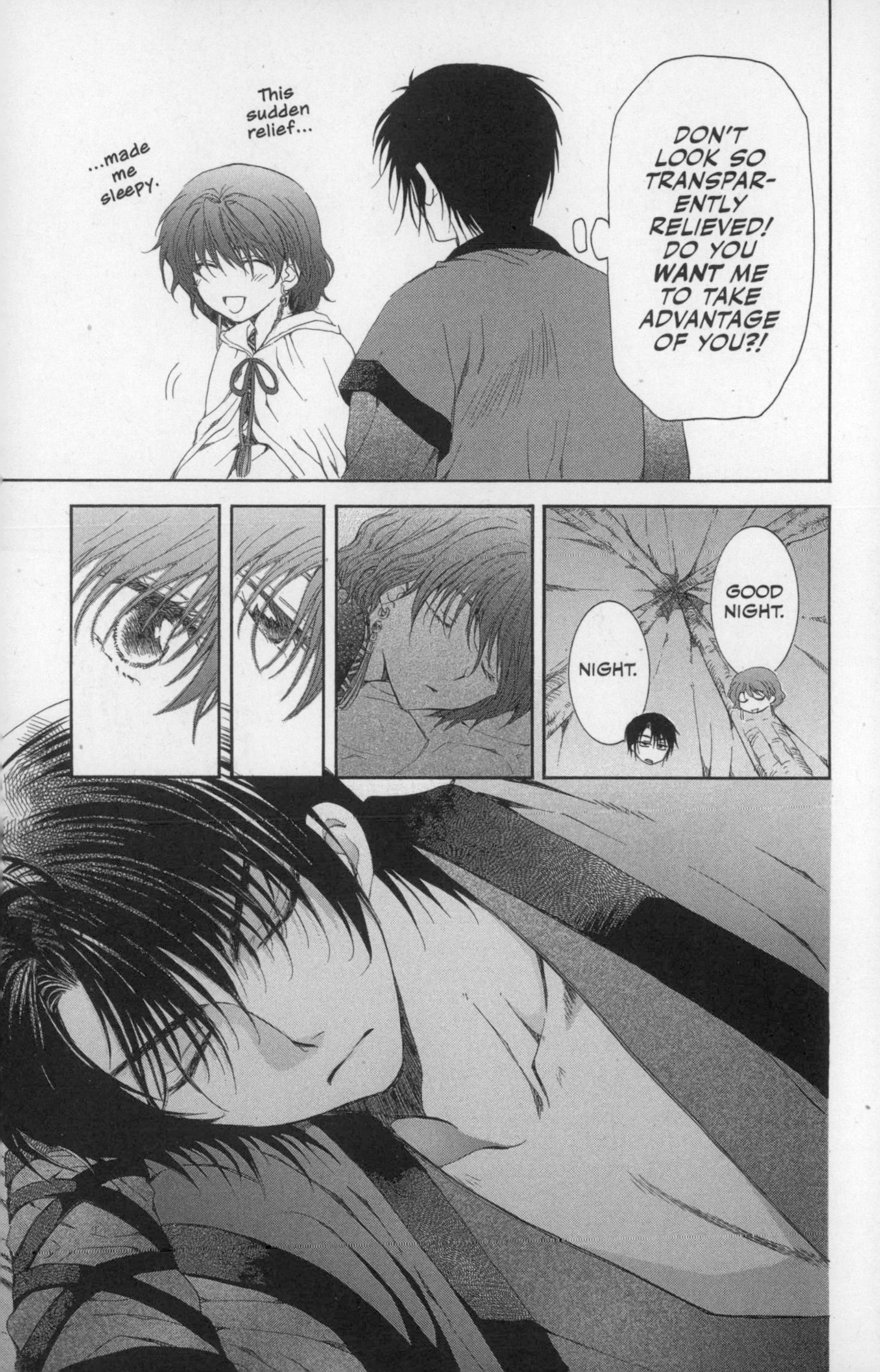
DON'T LOOK SO TRANSPARENTLY RELIEVED! DO YOU WANT ME TO TAKE ADVANTAGE OF YOU?!
This sudden relief...
...made me sleepy.
GOOD NIGHT.
NIGHT.

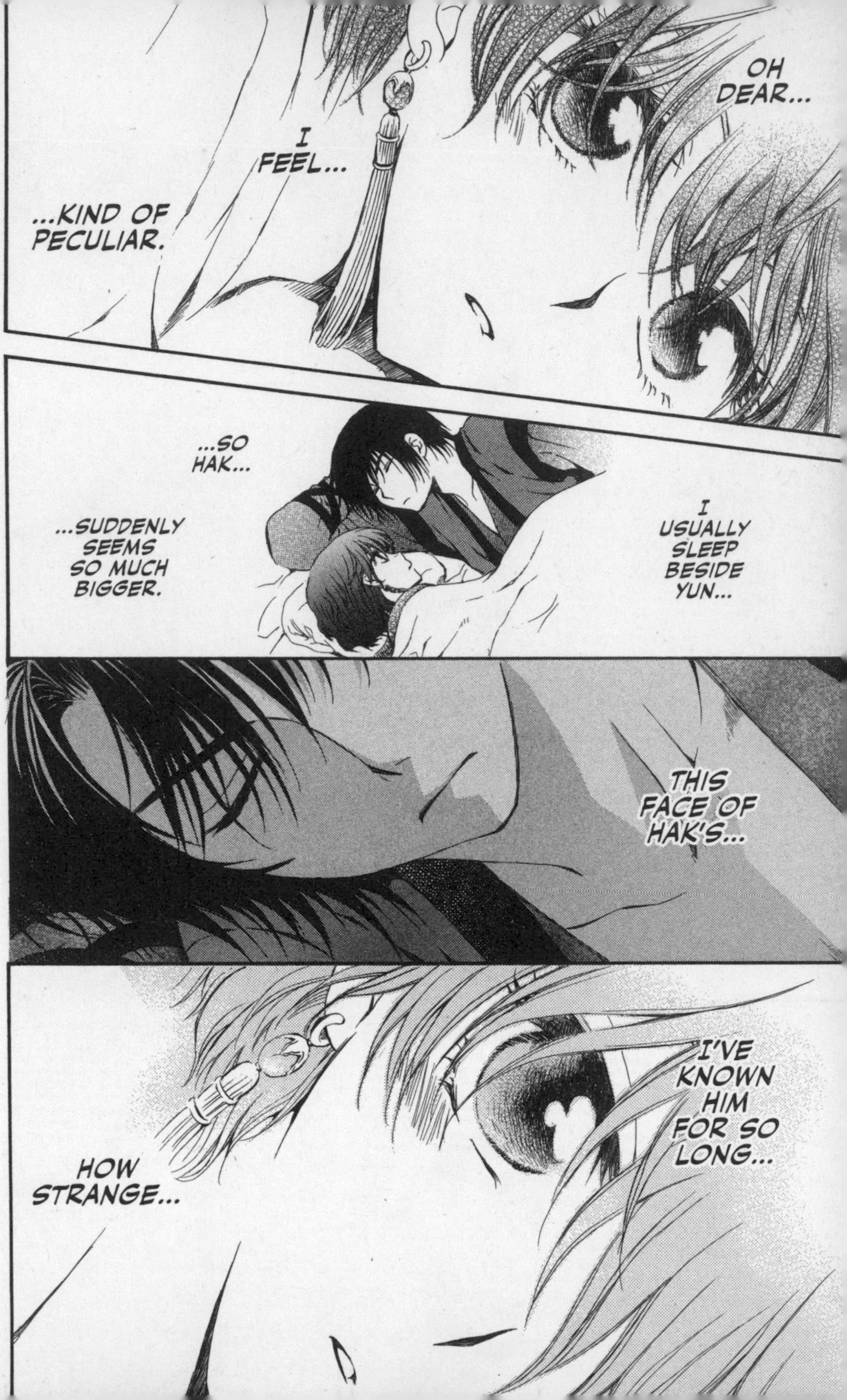
OH DEAR...
I FEEL...
...KIND OF PECULIAR.
I USUALLY SLEEP BESIDE YUN...
...SO HAK...
...SUDDENLY SEEMS SO MUCH BIGGER.
THIS FACE OF HAK'S...
I'VE KNOWN HIM FOR SO LONG...
HOW STRANGE...

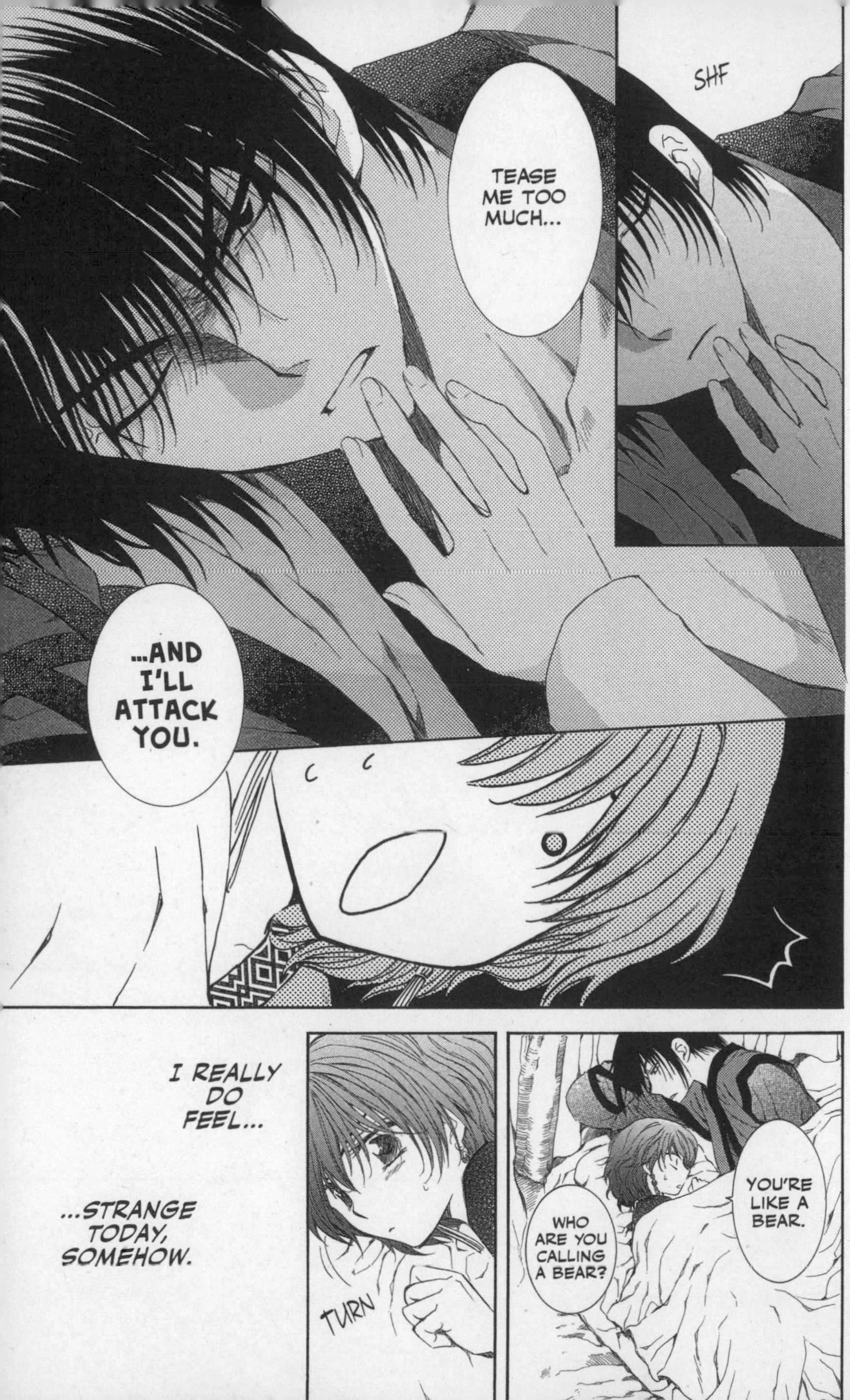
SHF
TEASE ME TOO MUCH...
...AND I'LL ATTACK YOU.
YOU'RE LIKE A BEAR.
WHO ARE YOU CALLING A BEAR?
I REALLY DO FEEL...
...STRANGE TODAY, SOMEHOW.
TURN

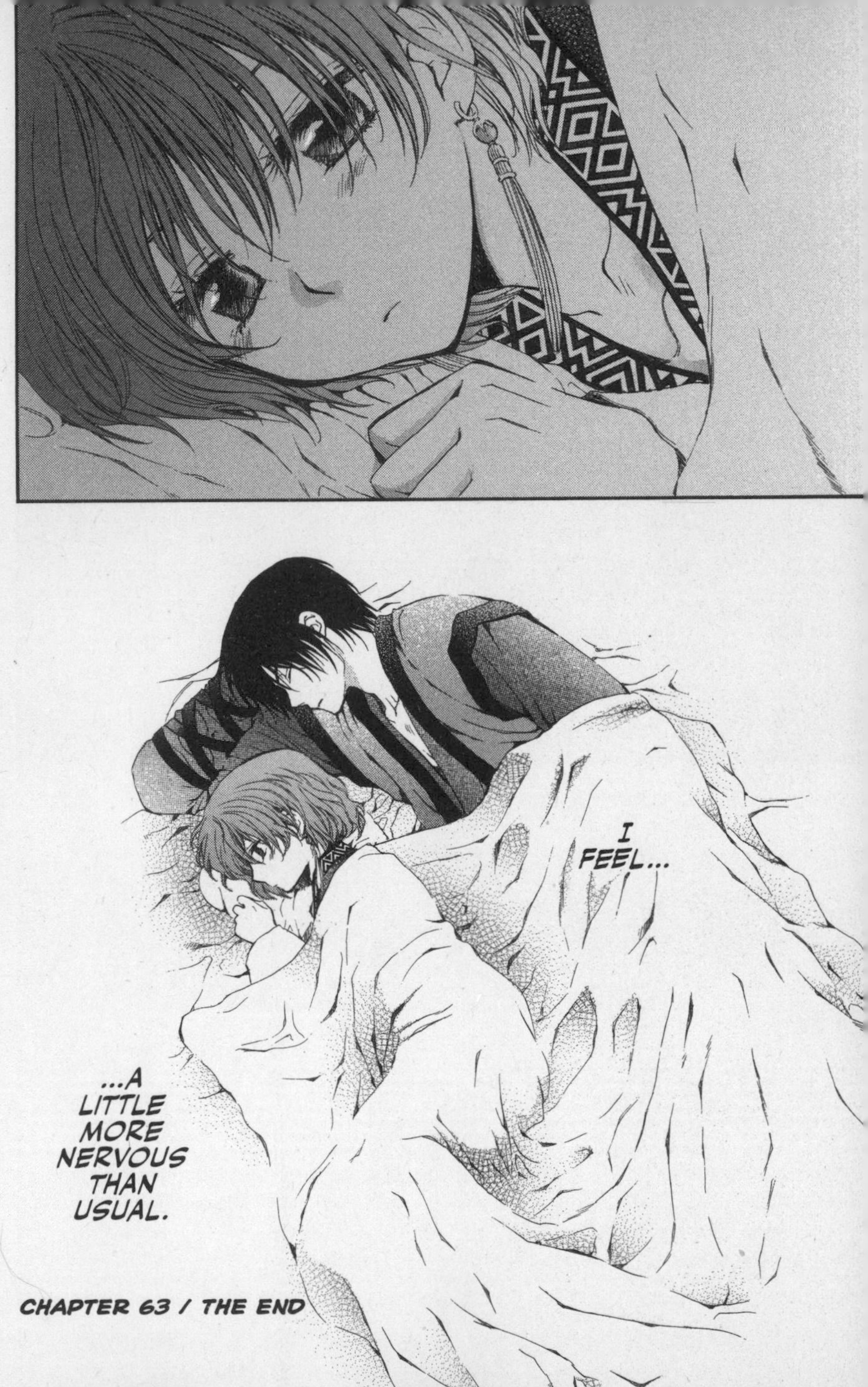
I FEEL...
...A LITTLE MORE NERVOUS THAN USUAL.

CHAPTER 63 / THE END

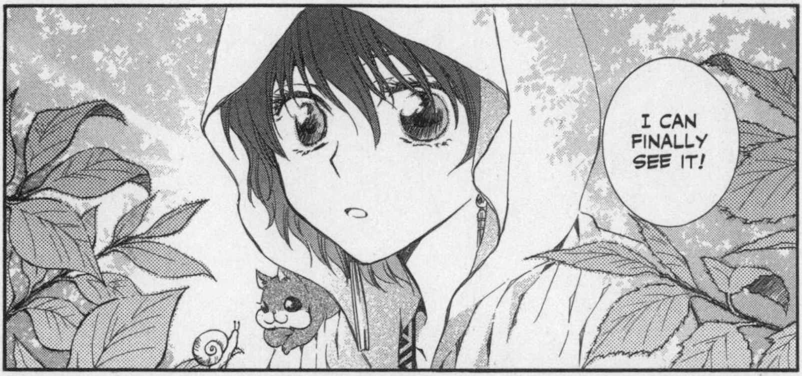
I CAN FINALLY SEE IT!

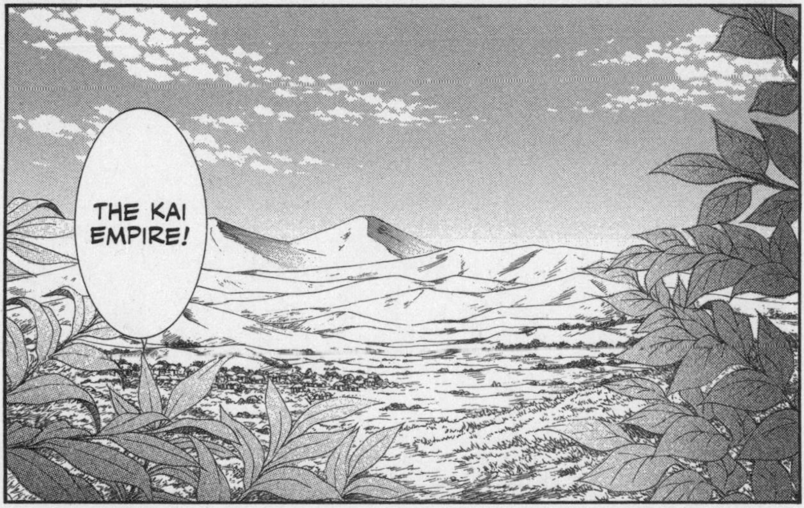
THE KAI EMPIRE!

Special thanks to everyone who helped create *Yona of the Dawn!*
My assistants → Mikorun, Kyoko, Oka, Ryo, C.F., Awafuji and my little sister...
My editor Ishihara, my previous editors and the *Hana to Yume* editorial office...
Everyone who's helped me create and sell this manga...
Family, friends and readers who've supported me...!

I'm so grateful to you all for letting me enjoy drawing manga.
I'll do my best for manga. I'll do my best for *Yona!*

CHAPTER 64: SENRI VILLAGE, SEN PROVINCE, KAI EMPIRE

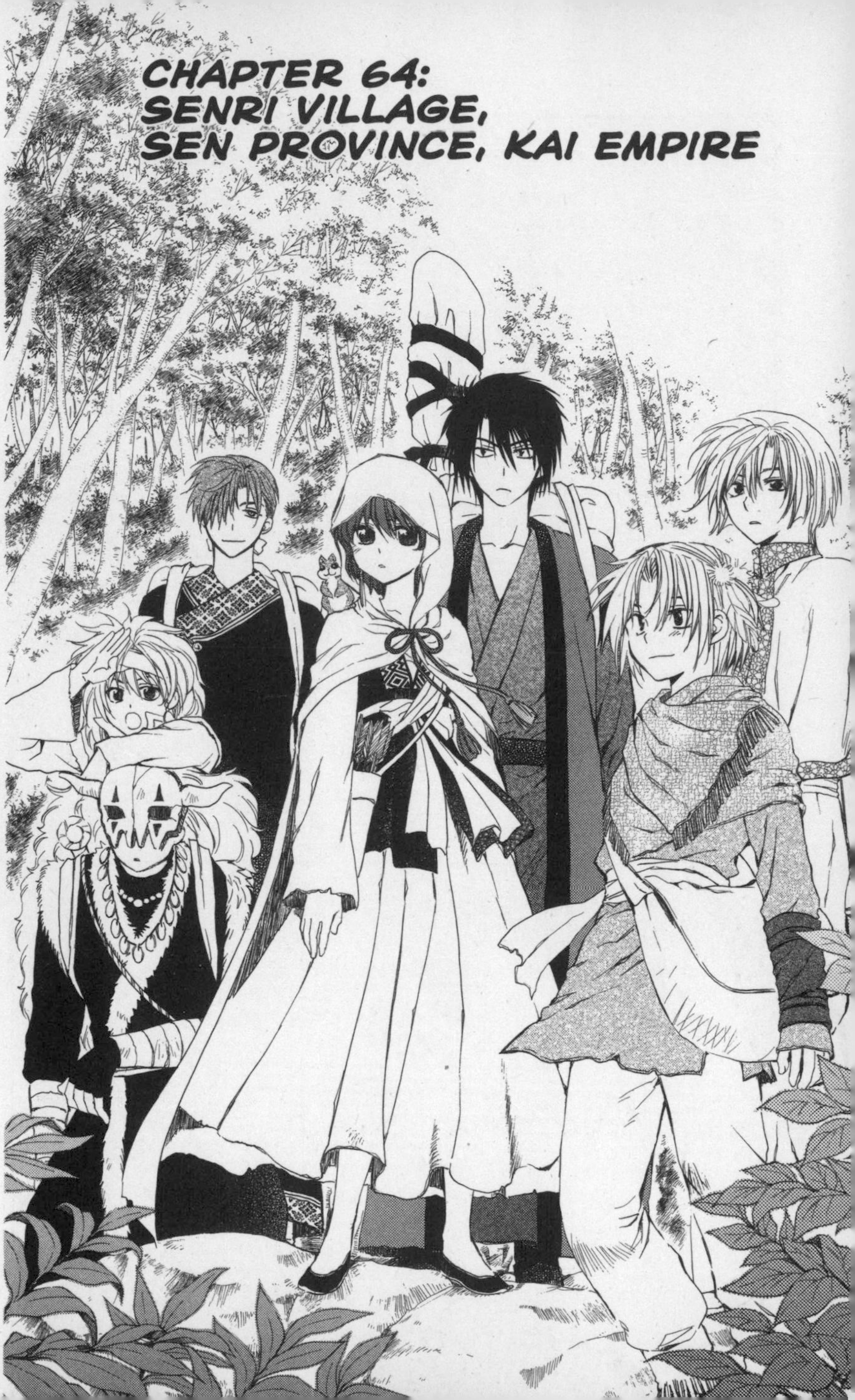

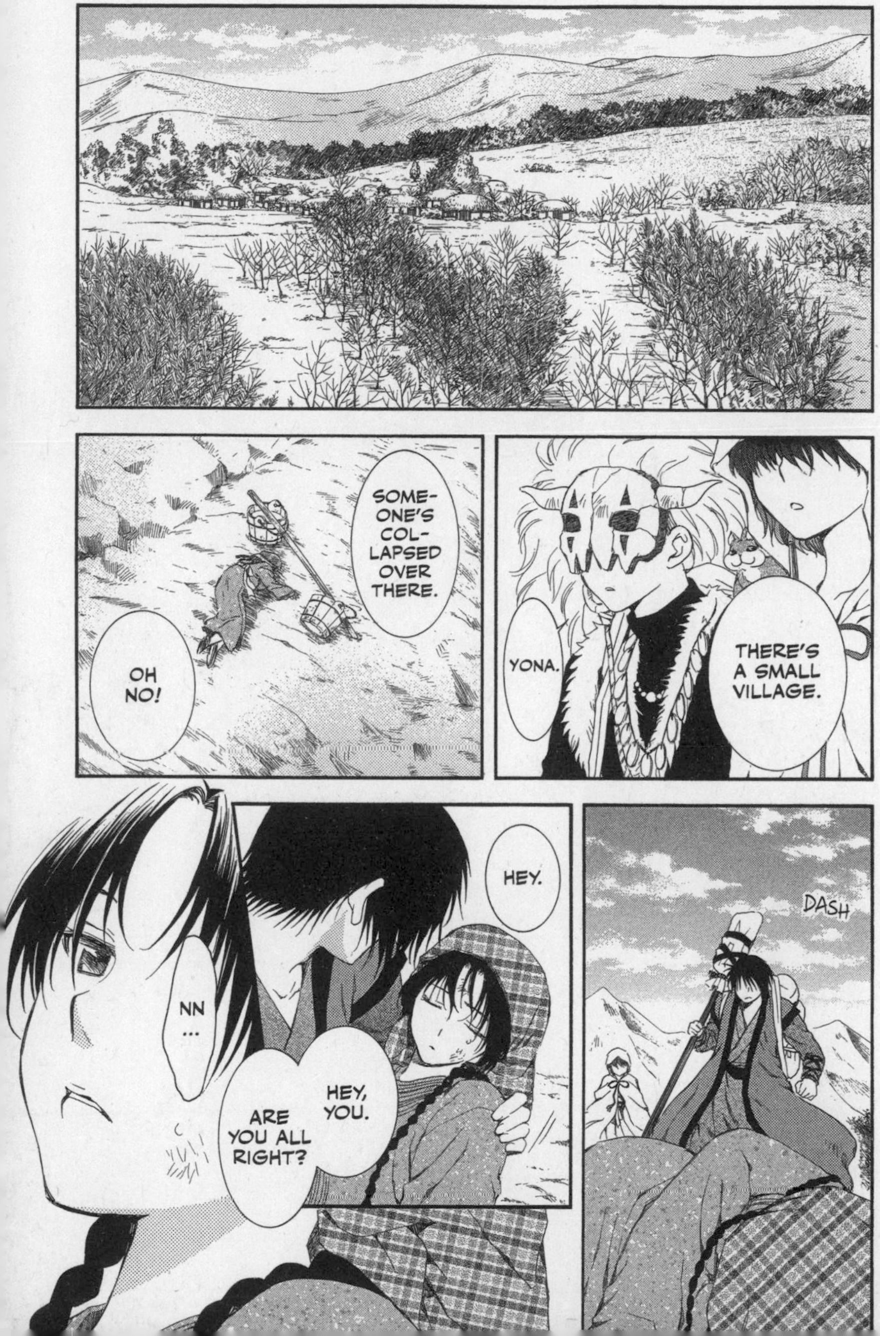
THERE'S A SMALL VILLAGE.
YONA.
SOME-ONE'S COL-LAPSED OVER THERE.
OH NO!
DASH
HEY.
NN ...
HEY, YOU. ARE YOU ALL RIGHT?

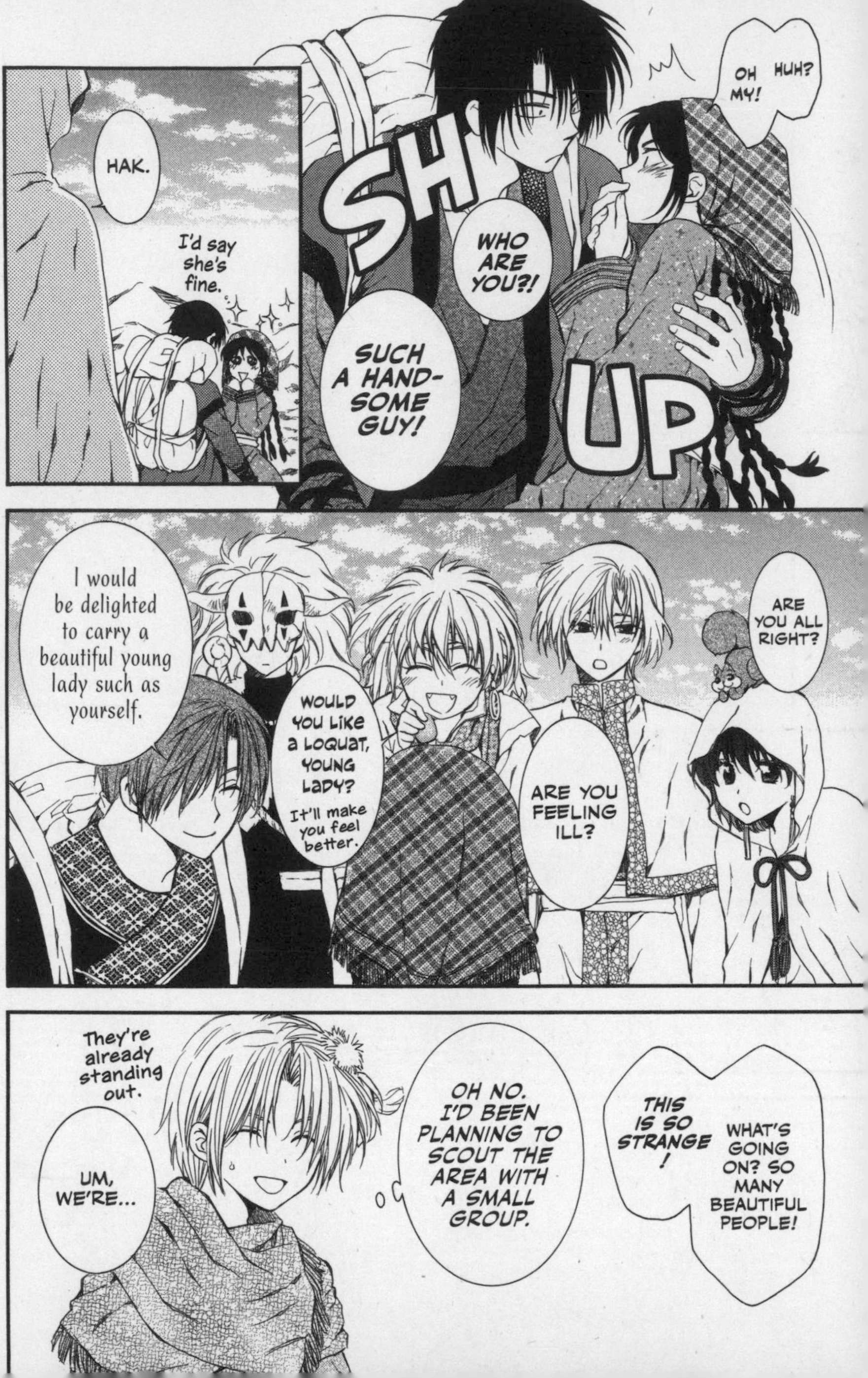
HUH? OH MY!
SHUP
WHO ARE YOU?!
SUCH A HANDSOME GUY!
HAK.
I'd say she's fine.
ARE YOU ALL RIGHT?
ARE YOU FEELING ILL?
WOULD YOU LIKE A LOQUAT, YOUNG LADY?
It'll make you feel better.
I would be delighted to carry a beautiful young lady such as yourself.
THIS IS SO STRANGE!
WHAT'S GOING ON? SO MANY BEAUTIFUL PEOPLE!
OH NO. I'D BEEN PLANNING TO SCOUT THE AREA WITH A SMALL GROUP.
They're already standing out.
UM, WE'RE...

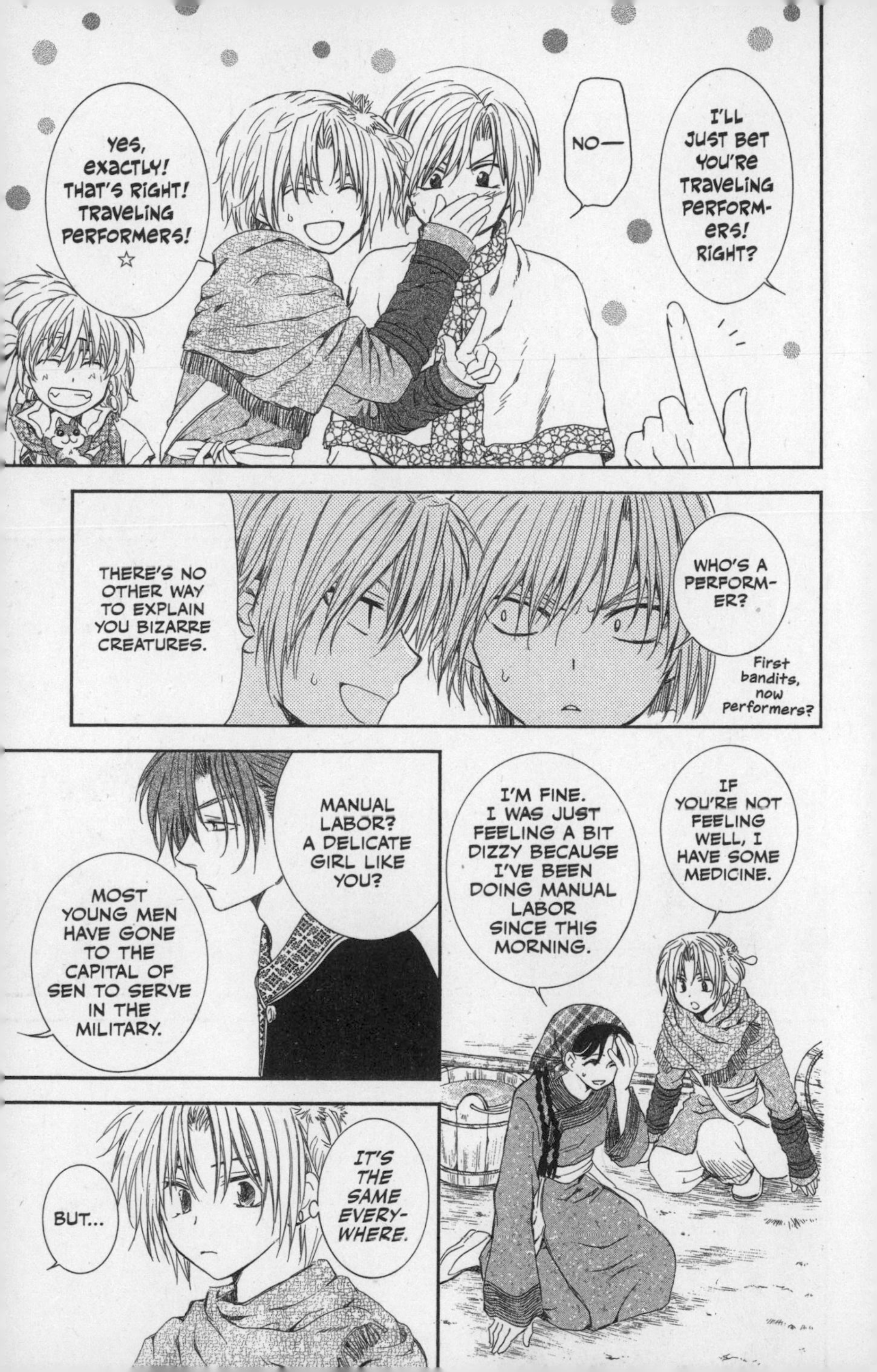
I'LL JUST BET YOU'RE TRAVELING PERFORMERS! RIGHT?
NO—
YES, EXACTLY! THAT'S RIGHT! TRAVELING PERFORMERS! ☆
WHO'S A PERFORMER?
First bandits, now performers?
THERE'S NO OTHER WAY TO EXPLAIN YOU BIZARRE CREATURES.
IF YOU'RE NOT FEELING WELL, I HAVE SOME MEDICINE.
I'M FINE. I WAS JUST FEELING A BIT DIZZY BECAUSE I'VE BEEN DOING MANUAL LABOR SINCE THIS MORNING.
MANUAL LABOR? A DELICATE GIRL LIKE YOU?
MOST YOUNG MEN HAVE GONE TO THE CAPITAL OF SEN TO SERVE IN THE MILITARY.
IT'S THE SAME EVERYWHERE.
BUT...

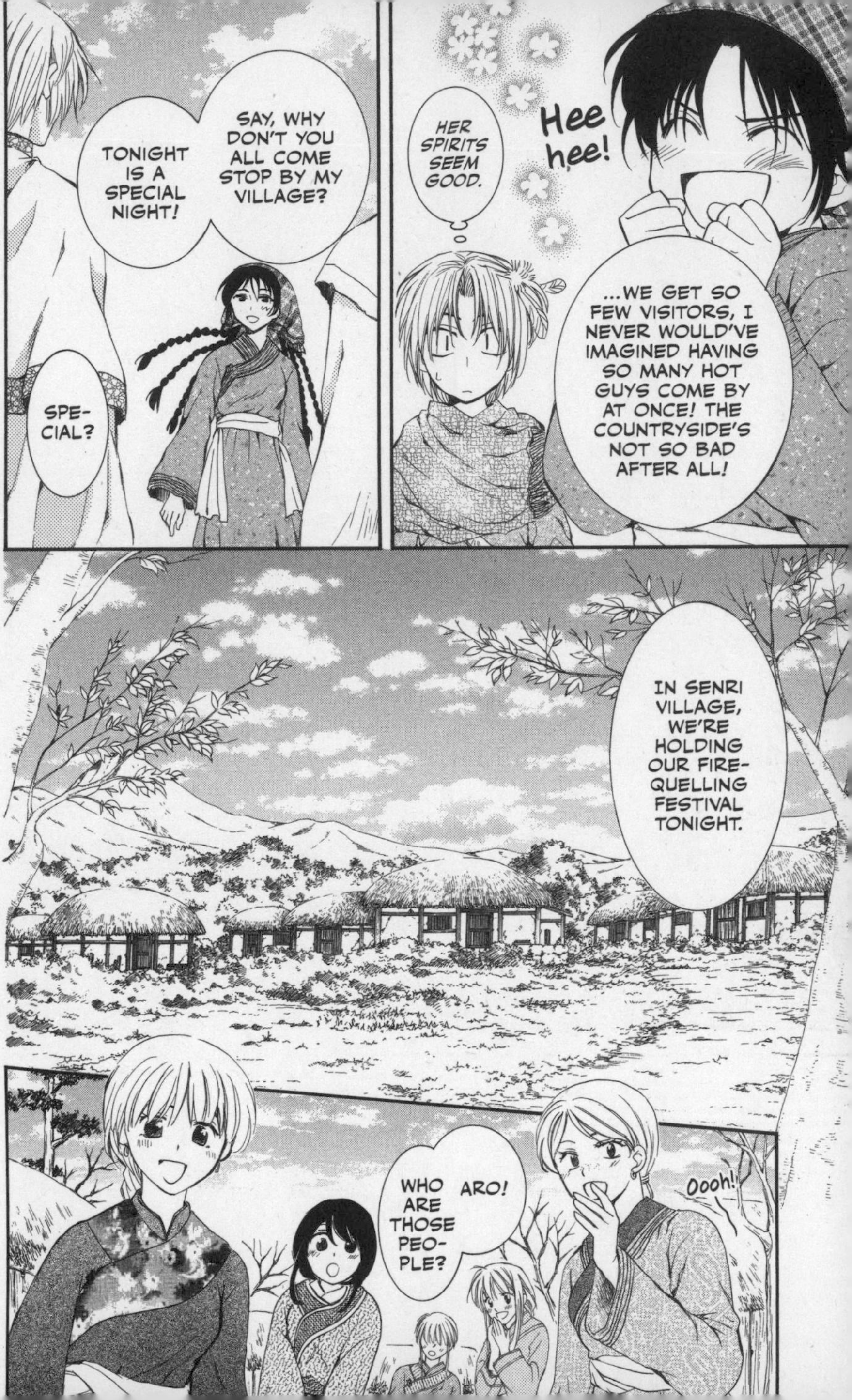
Hee hee!
HER SPIRITS SEEM GOOD.
...WE GET SO FEW VISITORS, I NEVER WOULD'VE IMAGINED HAVING SO MANY HOT GUYS COME BY AT ONCE! THE COUNTRYSIDE'S NOT SO BAD AFTER ALL!
SAY, WHY DON'T YOU ALL COME STOP BY MY VILLAGE?
TONIGHT IS A SPECIAL NIGHT!
SPE-CIAL?
IN SENRI VILLAGE, WE'RE HOLDING OUR FIRE-QUELLING FESTIVAL TONIGHT.
Oooh!
ARO!
WHO ARE THOSE PEO-PLE?

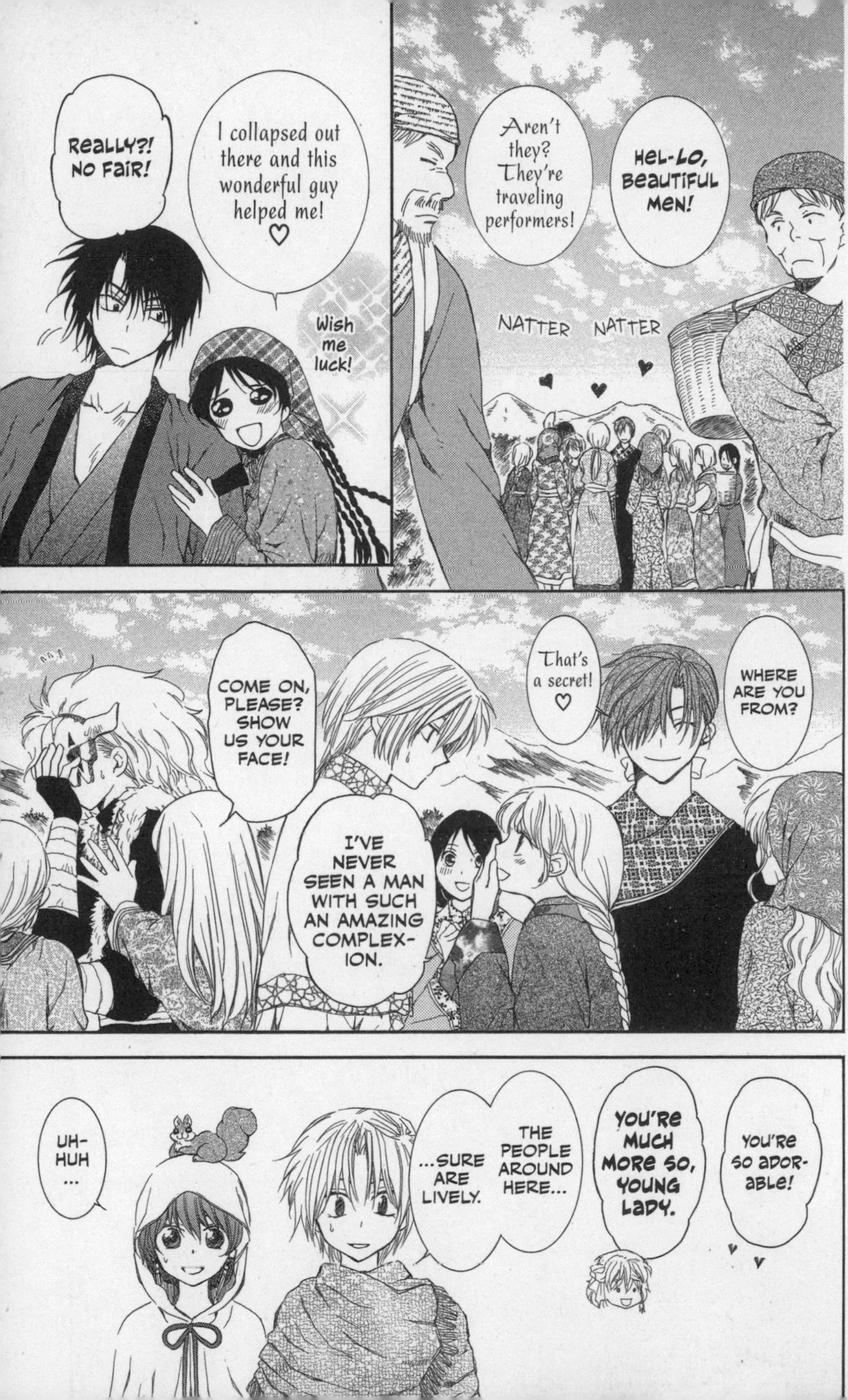
HEL-LO, BEAUTIFUL MEN!
Aren't they? They're traveling performers!
NATTER NATTER
I collapsed out there and this wonderful guy helped me! ♡
REALLY?! NO FAIR!
Wish me luck!
WHERE ARE YOU FROM?
That's a secret! ♡
COME ON, PLEASE? SHOW US YOUR FACE!
I'VE NEVER SEEN A MAN WITH SUCH AN AMAZING COMPLEX-ION.
YOU'RE SO ADOR-ABLE!
YOU'RE MUCH MORE SO, YOUNG LADY.
THE PEOPLE AROUND HERE...
...SURE ARE LIVELY.
UH-HUH ...

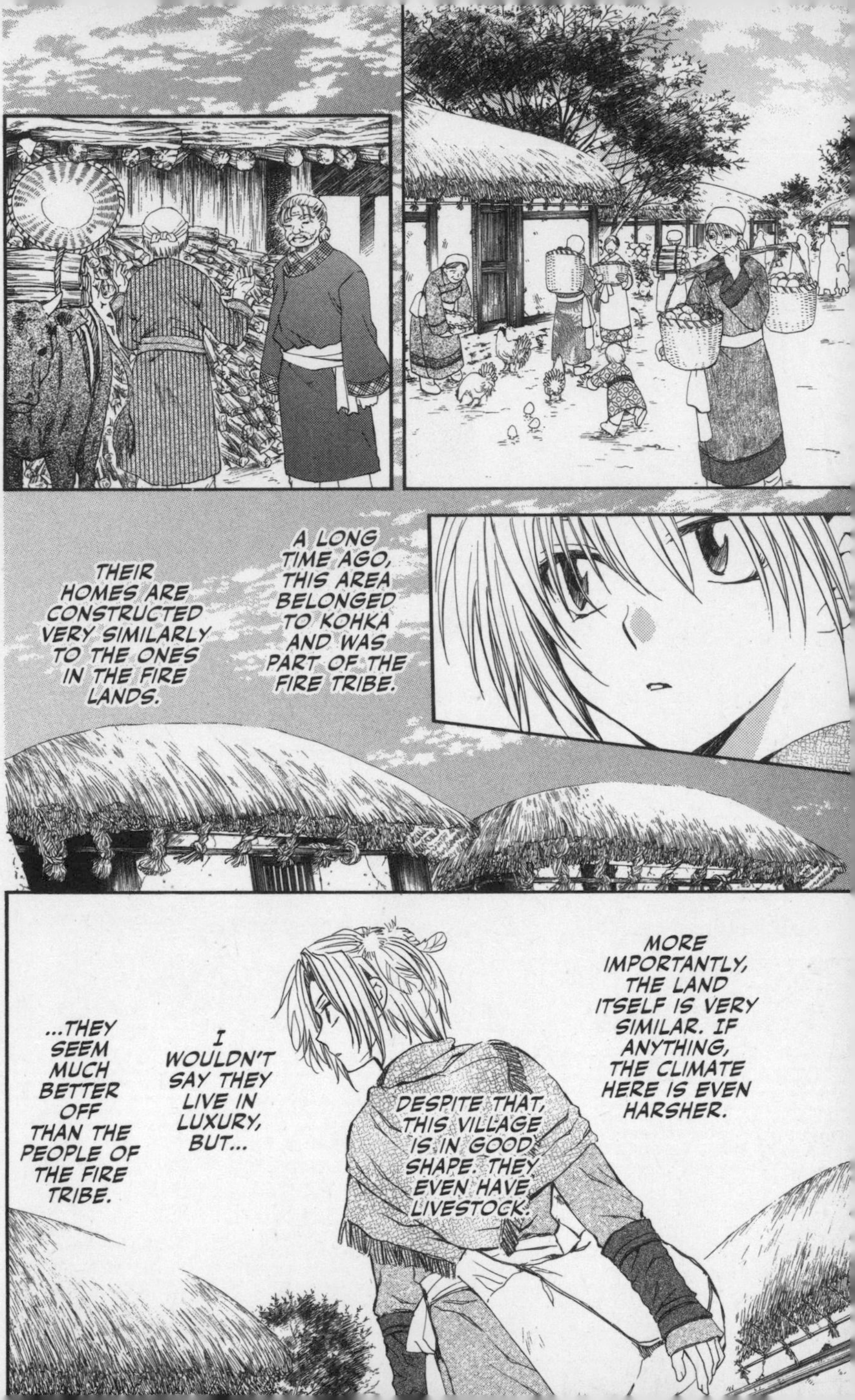
A LONG TIME AGO, THIS AREA BELONGED TO KOHKA AND WAS PART OF THE FIRE TRIBE.
THEIR HOMES ARE CONSTRUCTED VERY SIMILARLY TO THE ONES IN THE FIRE LANDS.
MORE IMPORTANTLY, THE LAND ITSELF IS VERY SIMILAR. IF ANYTHING, THE CLIMATE HERE IS EVEN HARSHER.
DESPITE THAT, THIS VILLAGE IS IN GOOD SHAPE. THEY EVEN HAVE LIVESTOCK.
I WOULDN'T SAY THEY LIVE IN LUXURY, BUT...
...THEY SEEM MUCH BETTER OFF THAN THE PEOPLE OF THE FIRE TRIBE.

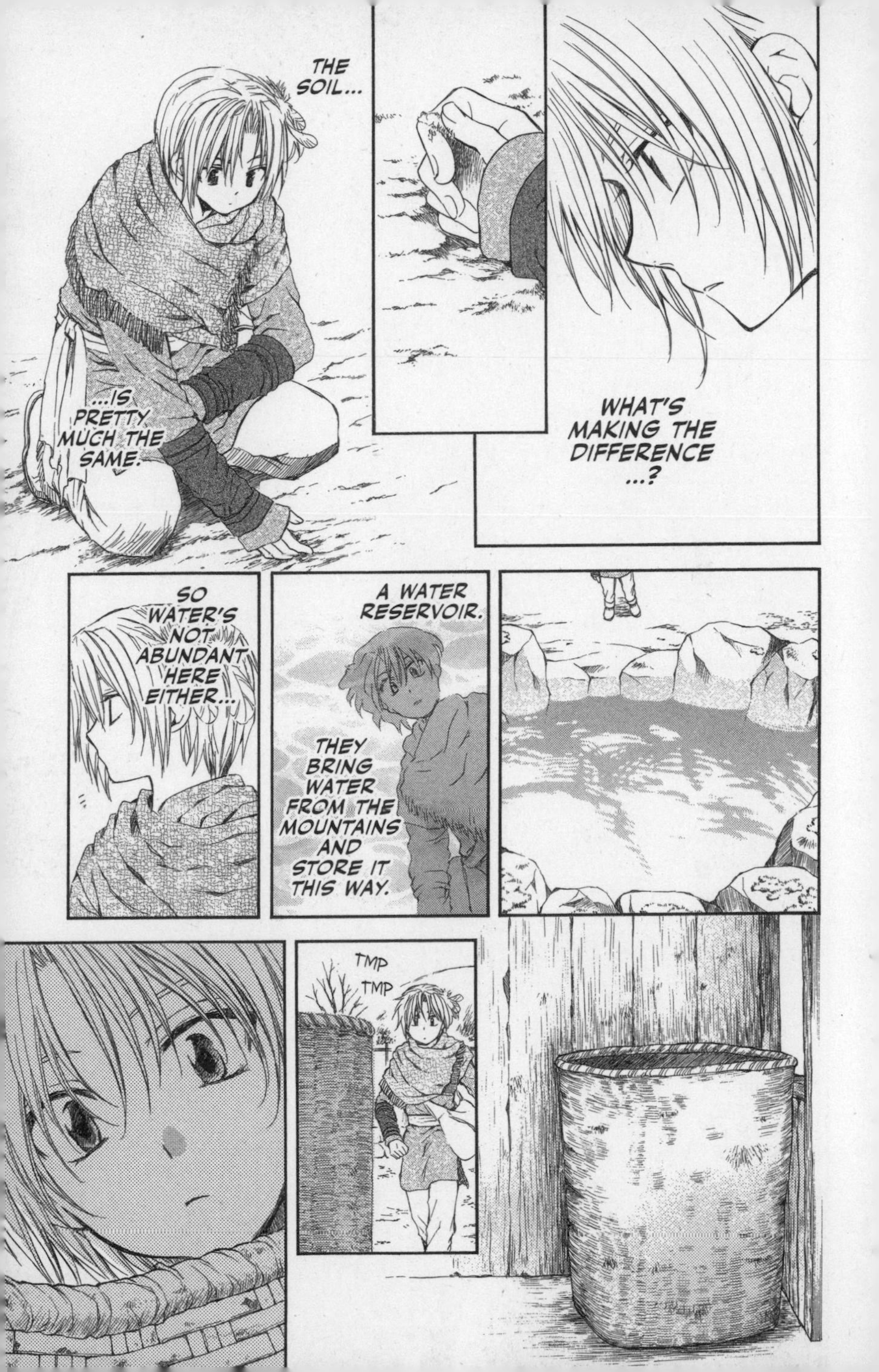
WHAT'S MAKING THE DIFFERENCE ...?
THE SOIL...
...IS PRETTY MUCH THE SAME.
A WATER RESERVOIR.
THEY BRING WATER FROM THE MOUNTAINS AND STORE IT THIS WAY.
SO WATER'S NOT ABUNDANT HERE EITHER...
TMP
TMP

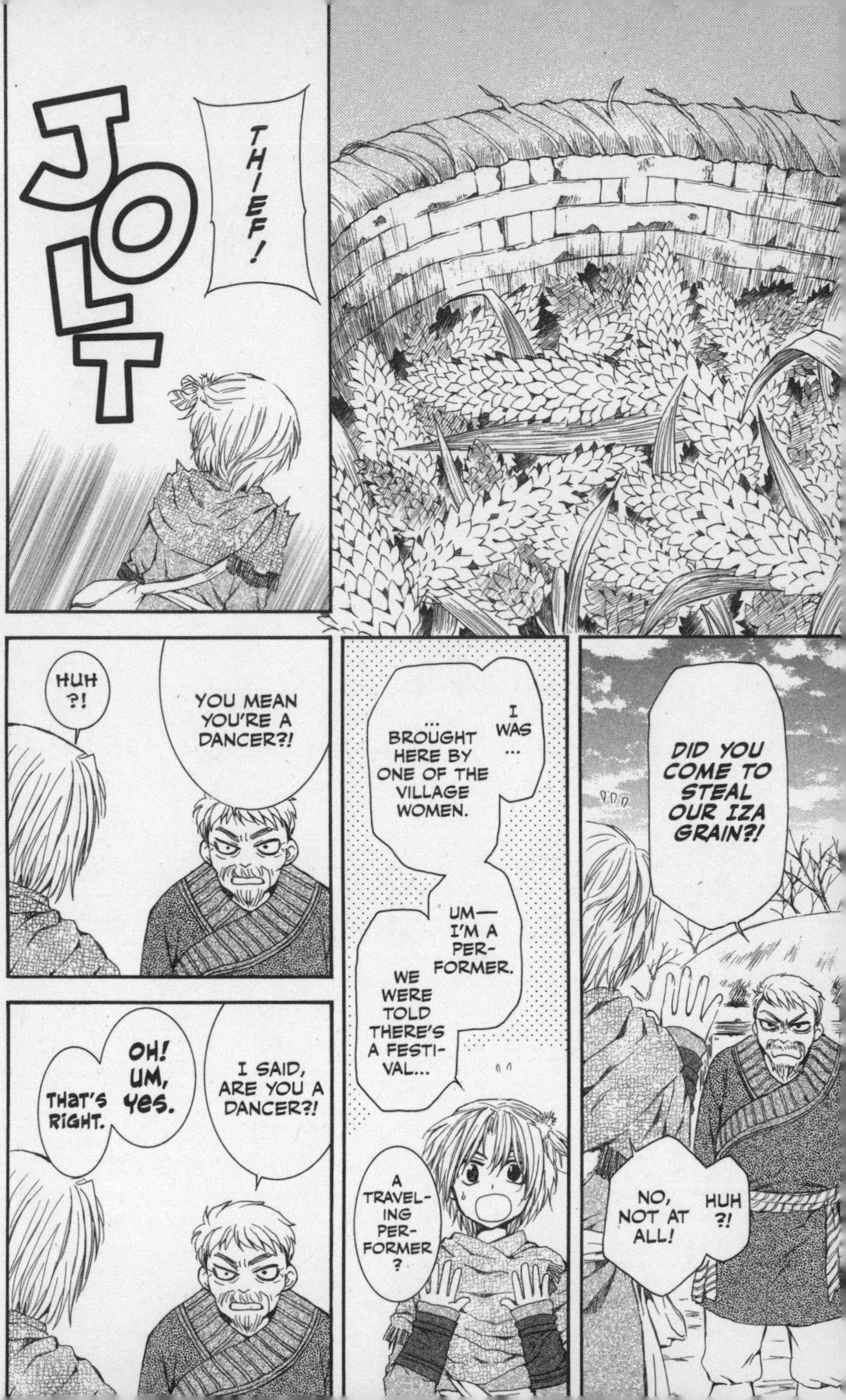
THIEF!
JOLT
DID YOU COME TO STEAL OUR IZA GRAIN?!
HUH ?!
NO, NOT AT ALL!
I WAS ... ... BROUGHT HERE BY ONE OF THE VILLAGE WOMEN.
UM— I'M A PERFORMER.
WE WERE TOLD THERE'S A FESTIVAL...
A TRAVELING PERFORMER?
YOU MEAN YOU'RE A DANCER?!
HUH ?!
I SAID, ARE YOU A DANCER?!
OH! UM, YES.
THAT'S RIGHT.

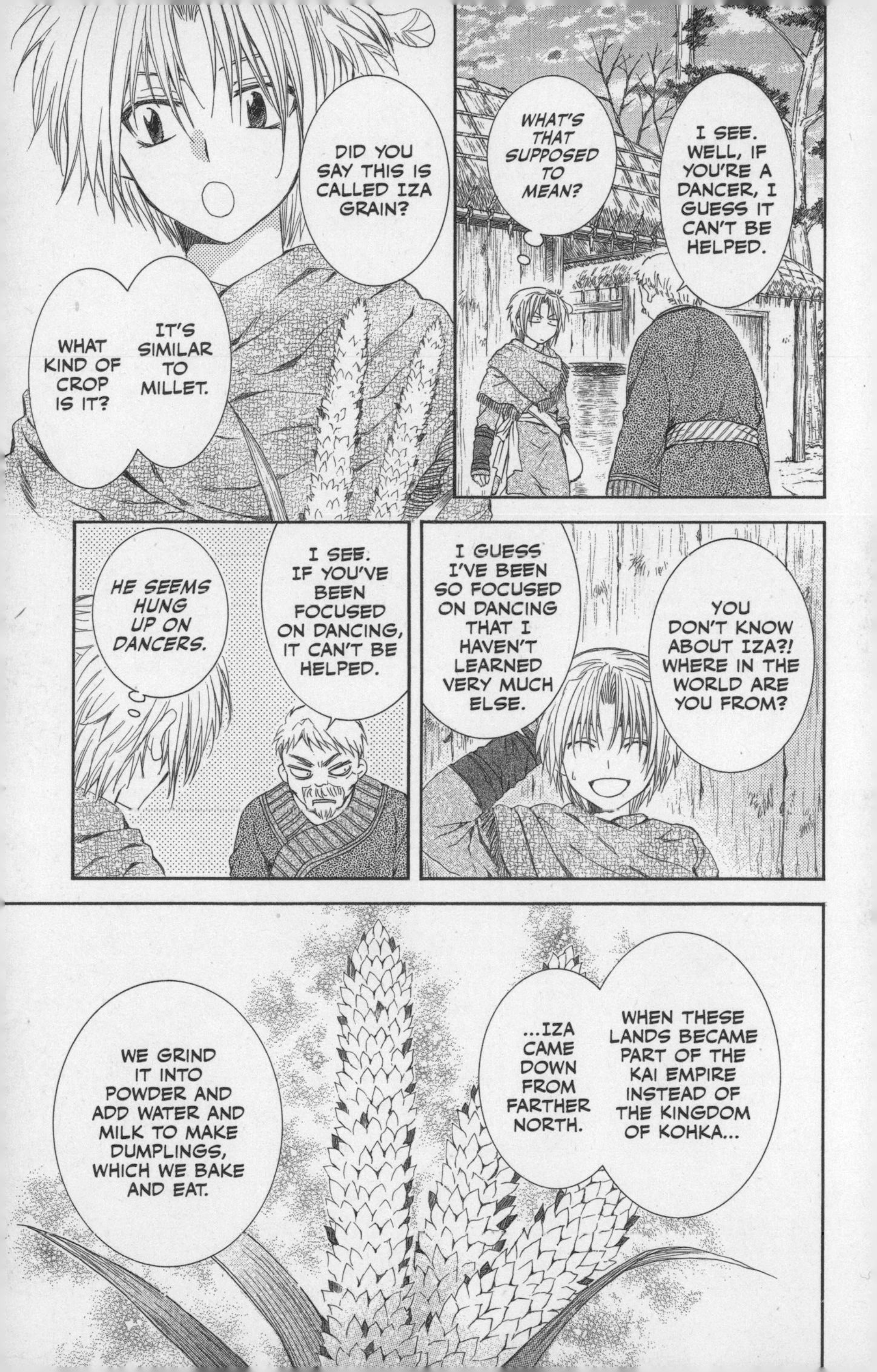
I SEE. WELL, IF YOU'RE A DANCER, I GUESS IT CAN'T BE HELPED.
WHAT'S THAT SUPPOSED TO MEAN?
DID YOU SAY THIS IS CALLED IZA GRAIN?
IT'S SIMILAR TO MILLET.
WHAT KIND OF CROP IS IT?
YOU DON'T KNOW ABOUT IZA?! WHERE IN THE WORLD ARE YOU FROM?
I GUESS I'VE BEEN SO FOCUSED ON DANCING THAT I HAVEN'T LEARNED VERY MUCH ELSE.
I SEE. IF YOU'VE BEEN FOCUSED ON DANCING, IT CAN'T BE HELPED.
HE SEEMS HUNG UP ON DANCERS.
WHEN THESE LANDS BECAME PART OF THE KAI EMPIRE INSTEAD OF THE KINGDOM OF KOHKA...
...IZA CAME DOWN FROM FARTHER NORTH.
WE GRIND IT INTO POWDER AND ADD WATER AND MILK TO MAKE DUMPLINGS, WHICH WE BAKE AND EAT.

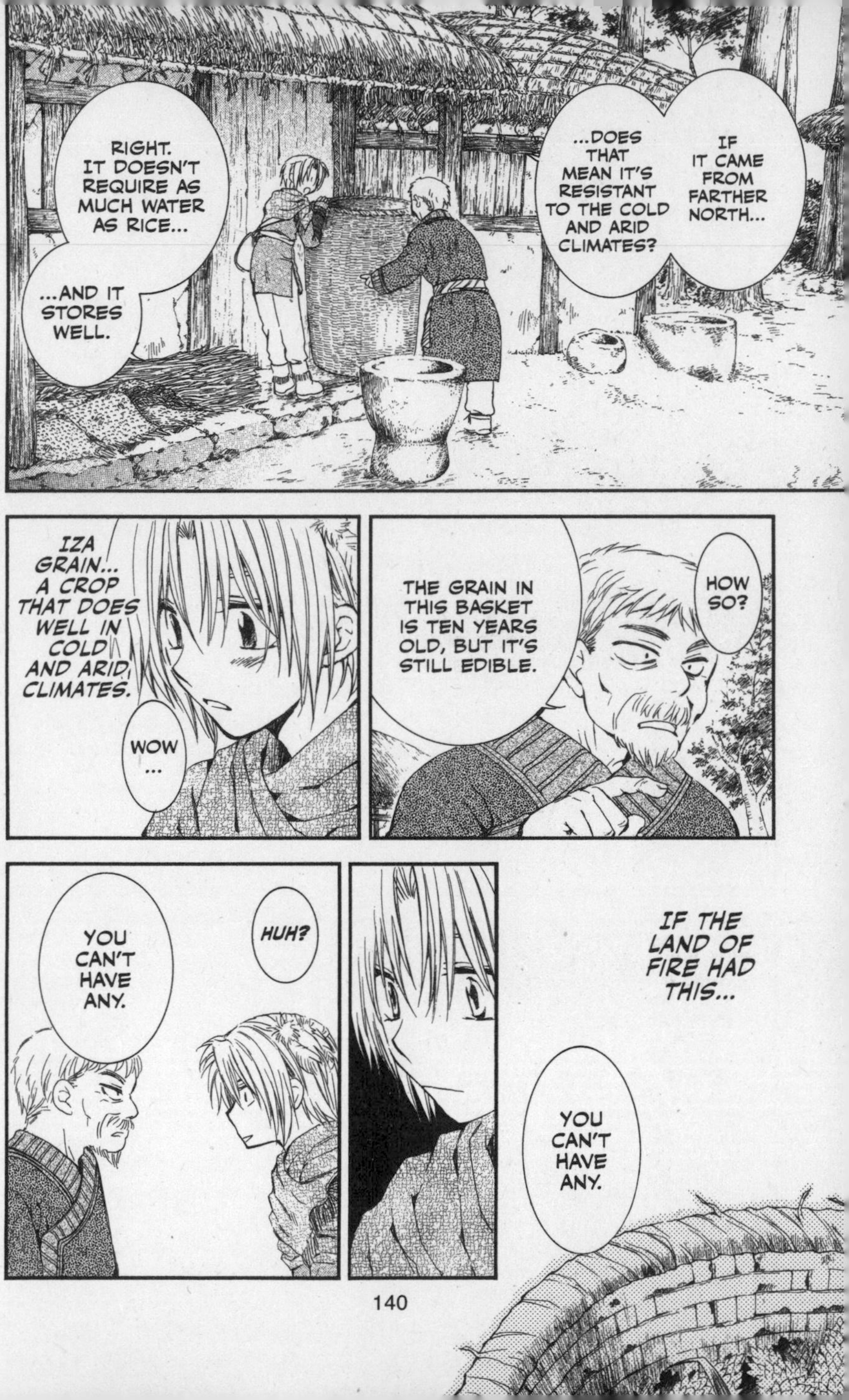
IF IT CAME FROM FARTHER NORTH...
...DOES THAT MEAN IT'S RESISTANT TO THE COLD AND ARID CLIMATES?
RIGHT. IT DOESN'T REQUIRE AS MUCH WATER AS RICE...
...AND IT STORES WELL.
HOW SO?
THE GRAIN IN THIS BASKET IS TEN YEARS OLD, BUT IT'S STILL EDIBLE.
IZA GRAIN... A CROP THAT DOES WELL IN COLD AND ARID CLIMATES.
WOW...
IF THE LAND OF FIRE HAD THIS...
YOU CAN'T HAVE ANY.
HUH?
YOU CAN'T HAVE ANY.

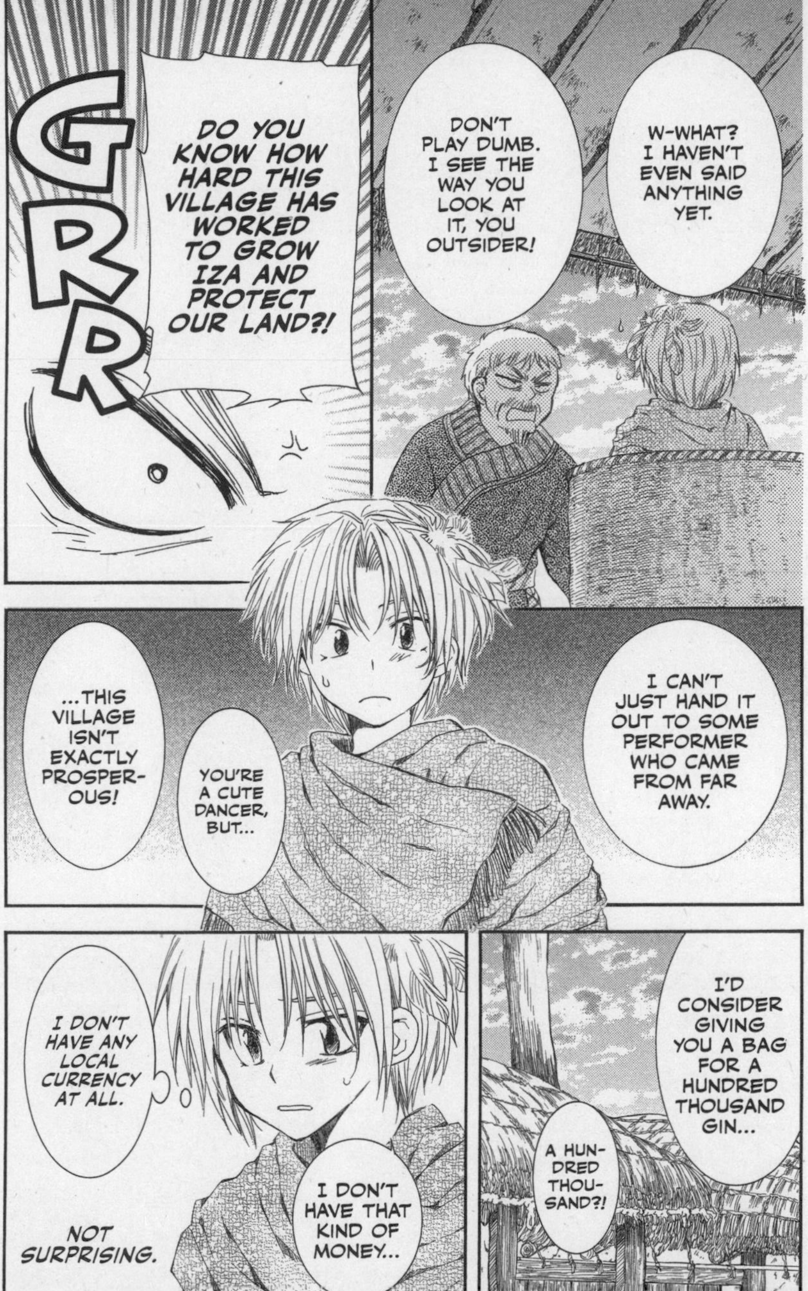
W-WHAT? I HAVEN'T EVEN SAID ANYTHING YET.
DON'T PLAY DUMB. I SEE THE WAY YOU LOOK AT IT, YOU OUTSIDER!
GRR
DO YOU KNOW HOW HARD THIS VILLAGE HAS WORKED TO GROW IZA AND PROTECT OUR LAND?!
I CAN'T JUST HAND IT OUT TO SOME PERFORMER WHO CAME FROM FAR AWAY.
YOU'RE A CUTE DANCER, BUT...
...THIS VILLAGE ISN'T EXACTLY PROSPER-OUS!
I'D CONSIDER GIVING YOU A BAG FOR A HUNDRED THOUSAND GIN...
A HUN-DRED THOU-SAND?!
I DON'T HAVE THAT KIND OF MONEY...
I DON'T HAVE ANY LOCAL CURRENCY AT ALL.
NOT SURPRISING.

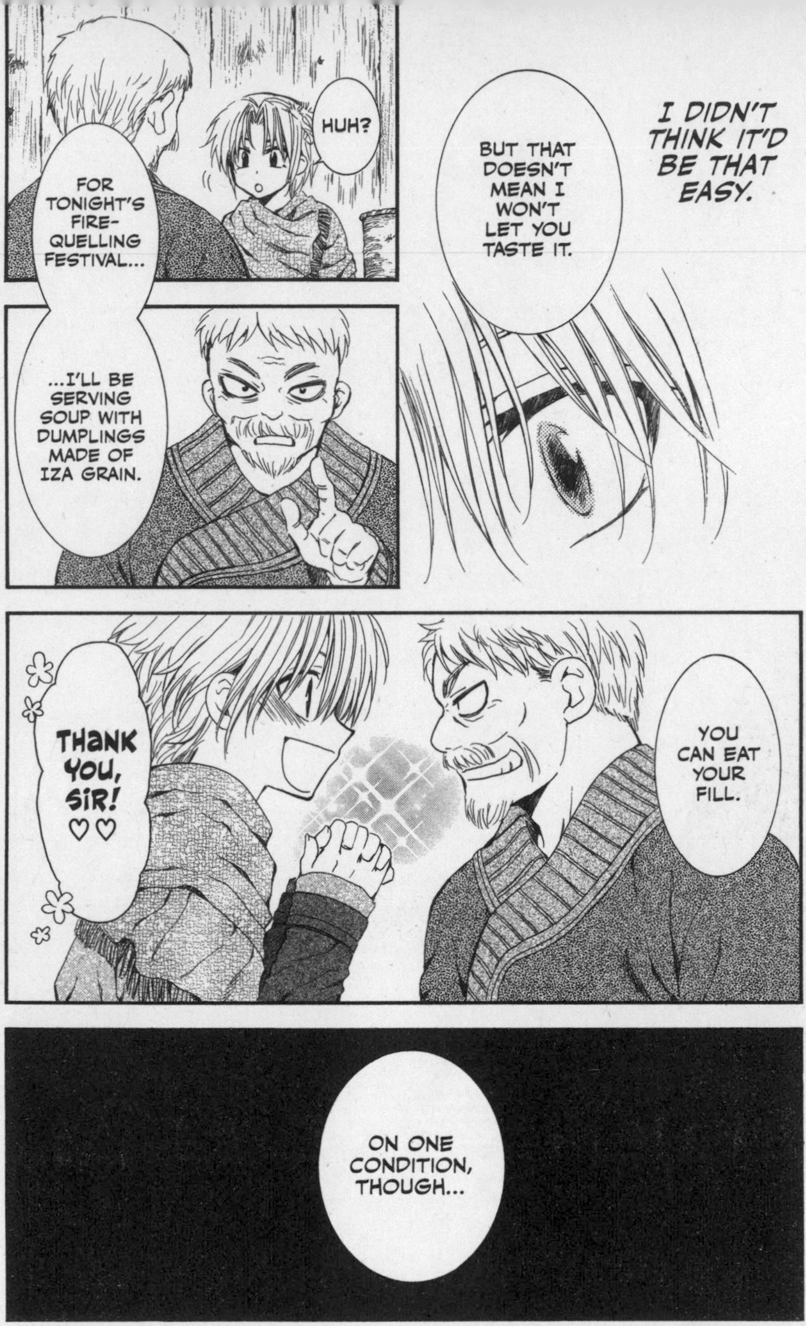
I DIDN'T THINK IT'D BE THAT EASY.
BUT THAT DOESN'T MEAN I WON'T LET YOU TASTE IT.
HUH?
FOR TONIGHT'S FIRE-QUELLING FESTIVAL...
...I'LL BE SERVING SOUP WITH DUMPLINGS MADE OF IZA GRAIN.
YOU CAN EAT YOUR FILL.
THANK YOU, SIR! ♡♡
ON ONE CONDITION, THOUGH...

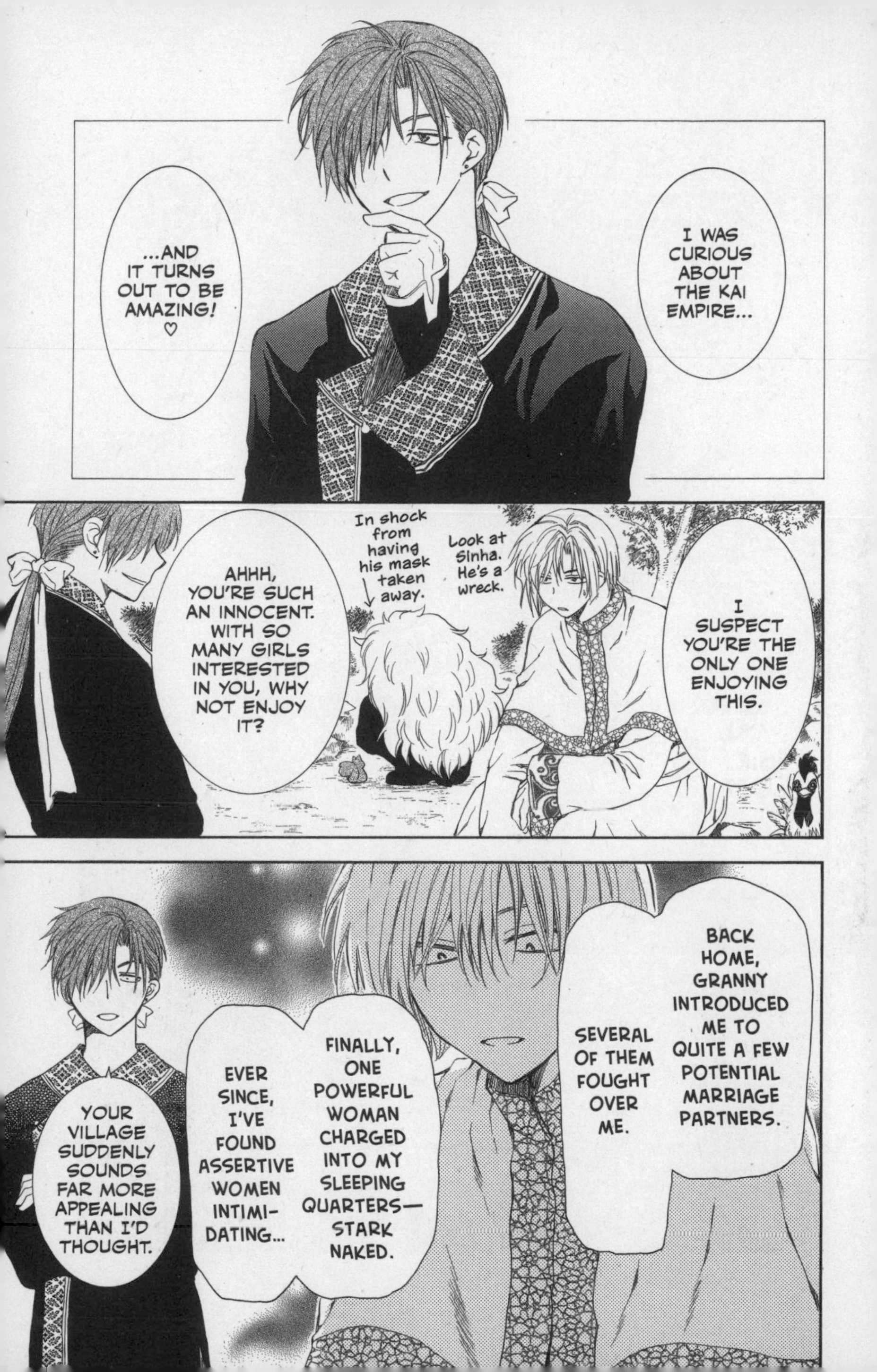
I WAS CURIOUS ABOUT THE KAI EMPIRE...
...AND IT TURNS OUT TO BE AMAZING! ♡
I SUSPECT YOU'RE THE ONLY ONE ENJOYING THIS.
Look at Sinha. He's a wreck.
In shock from having his mask taken away.
AHHH, YOU'RE SUCH AN INNOCENT. WITH SO MANY GIRLS INTERESTED IN YOU, WHY NOT ENJOY IT?
BACK HOME, GRANNY INTRODUCED ME TO QUITE A FEW POTENTIAL MARRIAGE PARTNERS.
SEVERAL OF THEM FOUGHT OVER ME.
FINALLY, ONE POWERFUL WOMAN CHARGED INTO MY SLEEPING QUARTERS—STARK NAKED.
EVER SINCE, I'VE FOUND ASSERTIVE WOMEN INTIMIDATING...
YOUR VILLAGE SUDDENLY SOUNDS FAR MORE APPEALING THAN I'D THOUGHT.

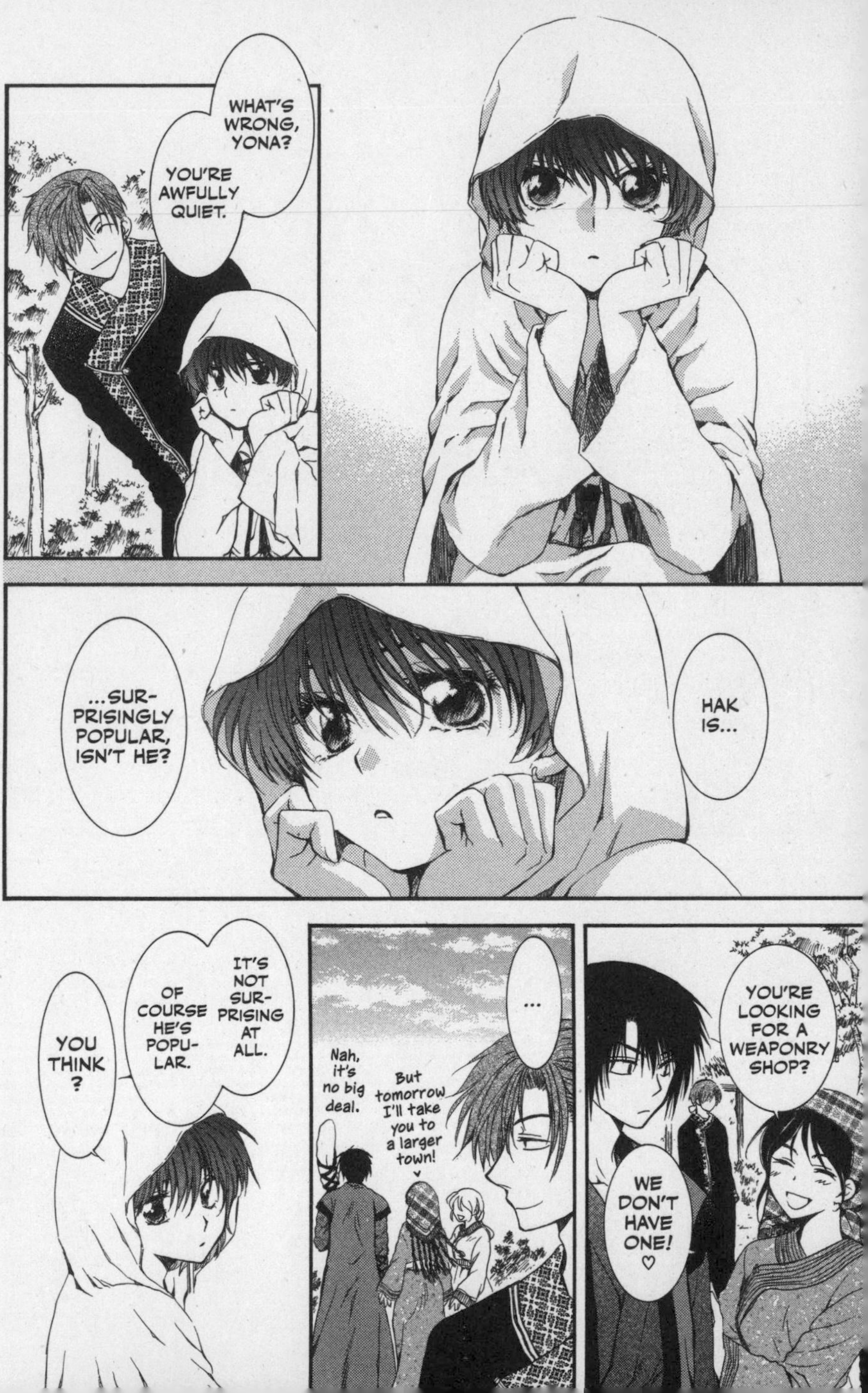
WHAT'S WRONG, YONA?
YOU'RE AWFULLY QUIET.
HAK IS...
...SURPRISINGLY POPULAR, ISN'T HE?
YOU'RE LOOKING FOR A WEAPONRY SHOP?
WE DON'T HAVE ONE! ♡
...
But tomorrow I'll take you to a larger town! ♥
Nah, it's no big deal.
IT'S NOT SURPRISING AT ALL.
OF COURSE HE'S POPULAR.
YOU THINK?

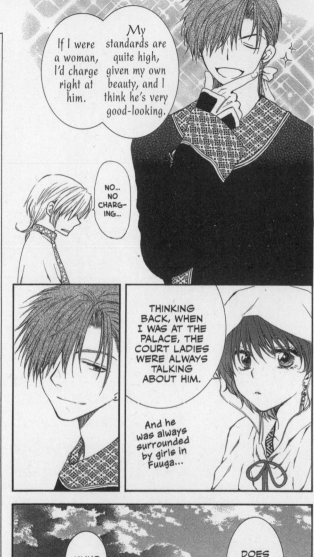

My standards are quite high, given my own beauty, and I think he's very good-looking.
If I were a woman, I'd charge right at him.
NO... NO CHARGING...
THINKING BACK, WHEN I WAS AT THE PALACE, THE COURT LADIES WERE ALWAYS TALKING ABOUT HIM.
And he was always surrounded by girls in Fuuga...
DOES THAT BOTHER YOU?
HUH?

In commemoration of volume 10, my assistants threw me a surprise celebration! They got me a card and a cake with Yona on it! I was surprised that one of my friends (an assistant), who moved to Fukuoka when she married, was able to make it!

They all help me so much. I'm deeply grateful to everyone.

I got congratulatory messages from readers too. Readers are the ones who make it possible for me to keep drawing Yona!

Oh! And I hadn't realized it, but when I counted back, I noticed it's also been ten years since I debuted as a manga creator. I almost missed my ten-year anniversary!

I hope you'll all continue to support me.

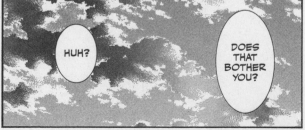

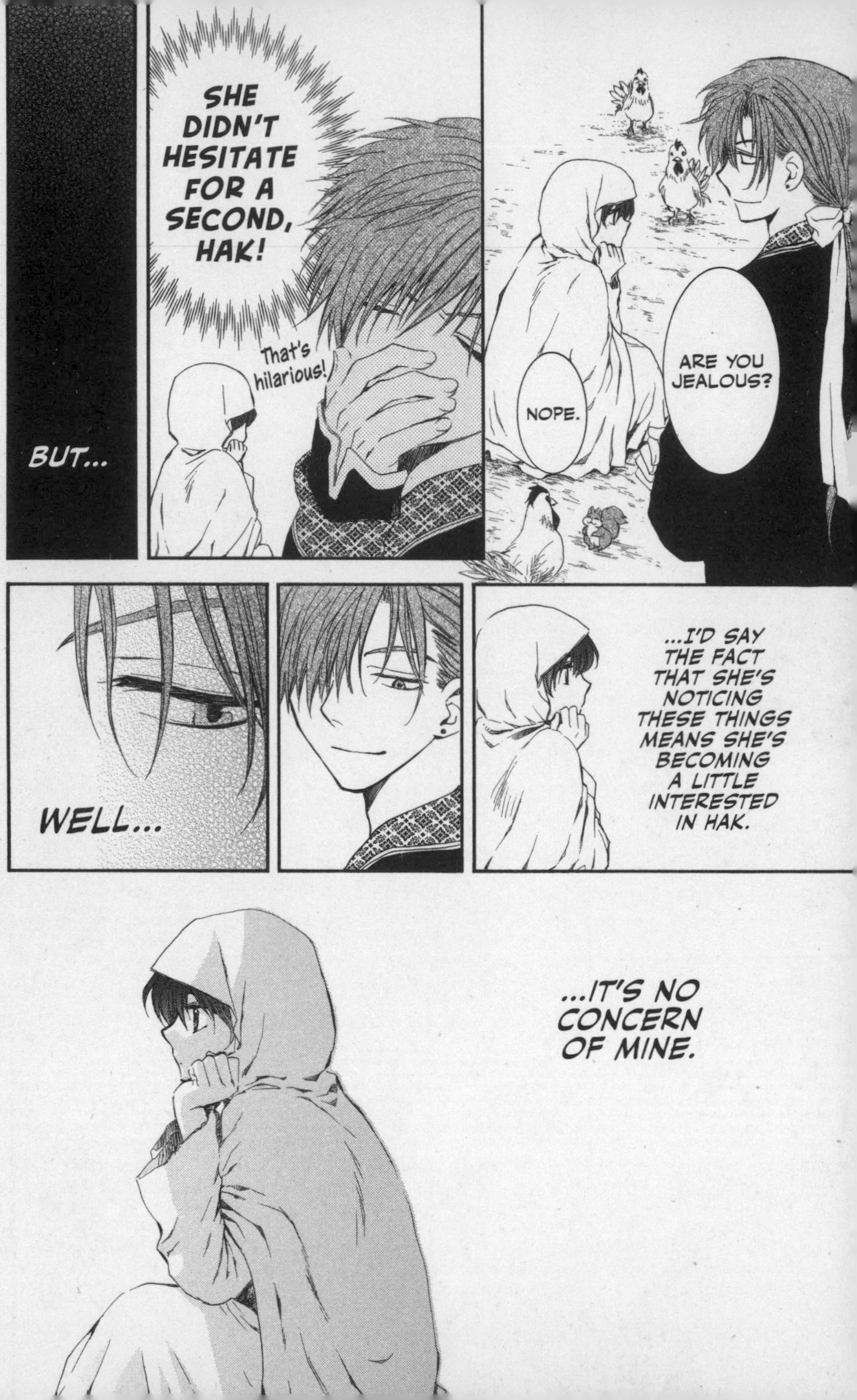
ARE YOU JEALOUS?
NOPE.
SHE DIDN'T HESITATE FOR A SECOND, HAK!
That's hilarious!
BUT...
...I'D SAY THE FACT THAT SHE'S NOTICING THESE THINGS MEANS SHE'S BECOMING A LITTLE INTERESTED IN HAK.
WELL...
...IT'S NO CONCERN OF MINE.

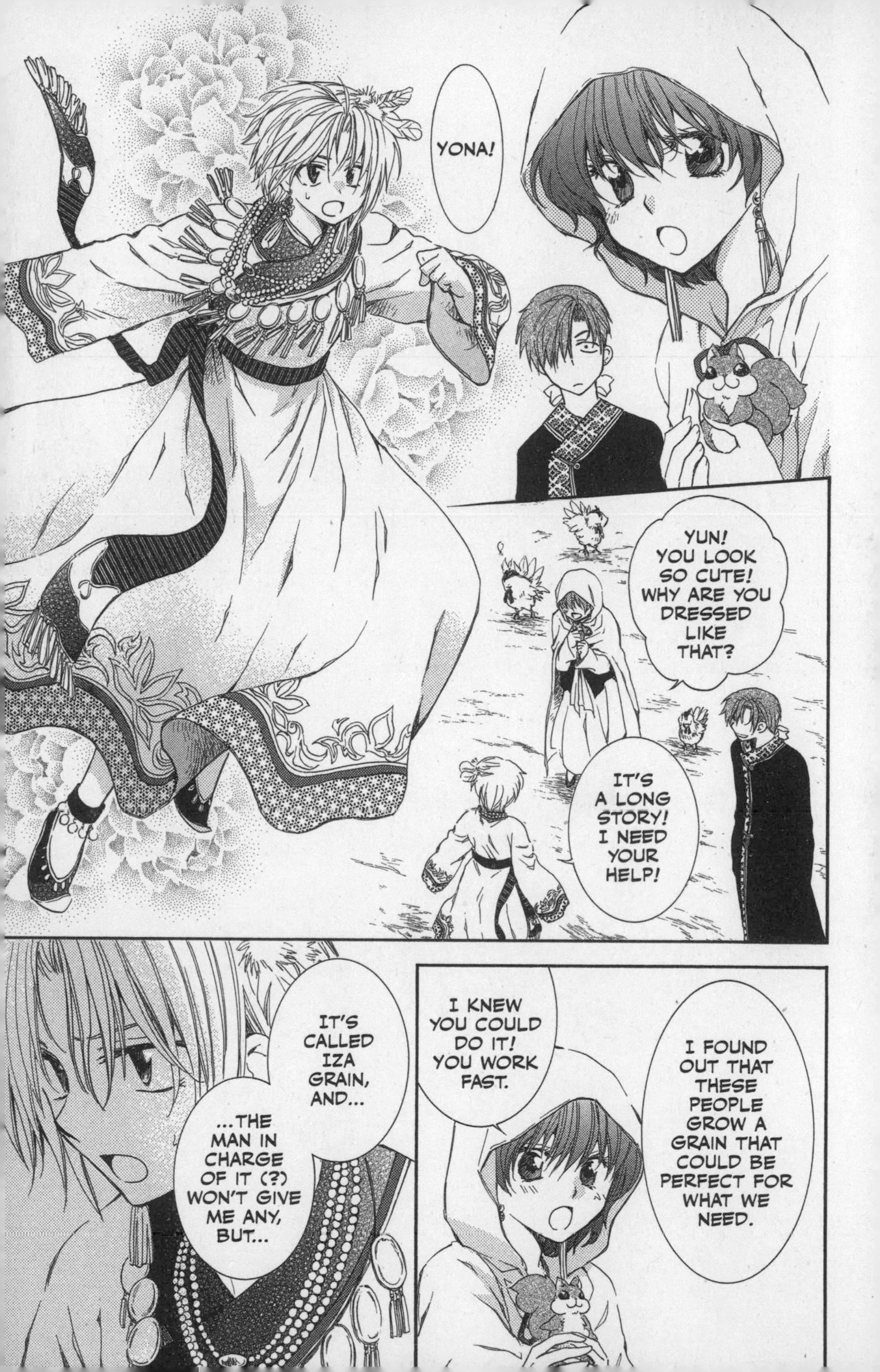
YONA!
YUN! YOU LOOK SO CUTE! WHY ARE YOU DRESSED LIKE THAT?
IT'S A LONG STORY! I NEED YOUR HELP!
I FOUND OUT THAT THESE PEOPLE GROW A GRAIN THAT COULD BE PERFECT FOR WHAT WE NEED.
I KNEW YOU COULD DO IT! YOU WORK FAST.
IT'S CALLED IZA GRAIN, AND...
...THE MAN IN CHARGE OF IT (?) WON'T GIVE ME ANY, BUT...

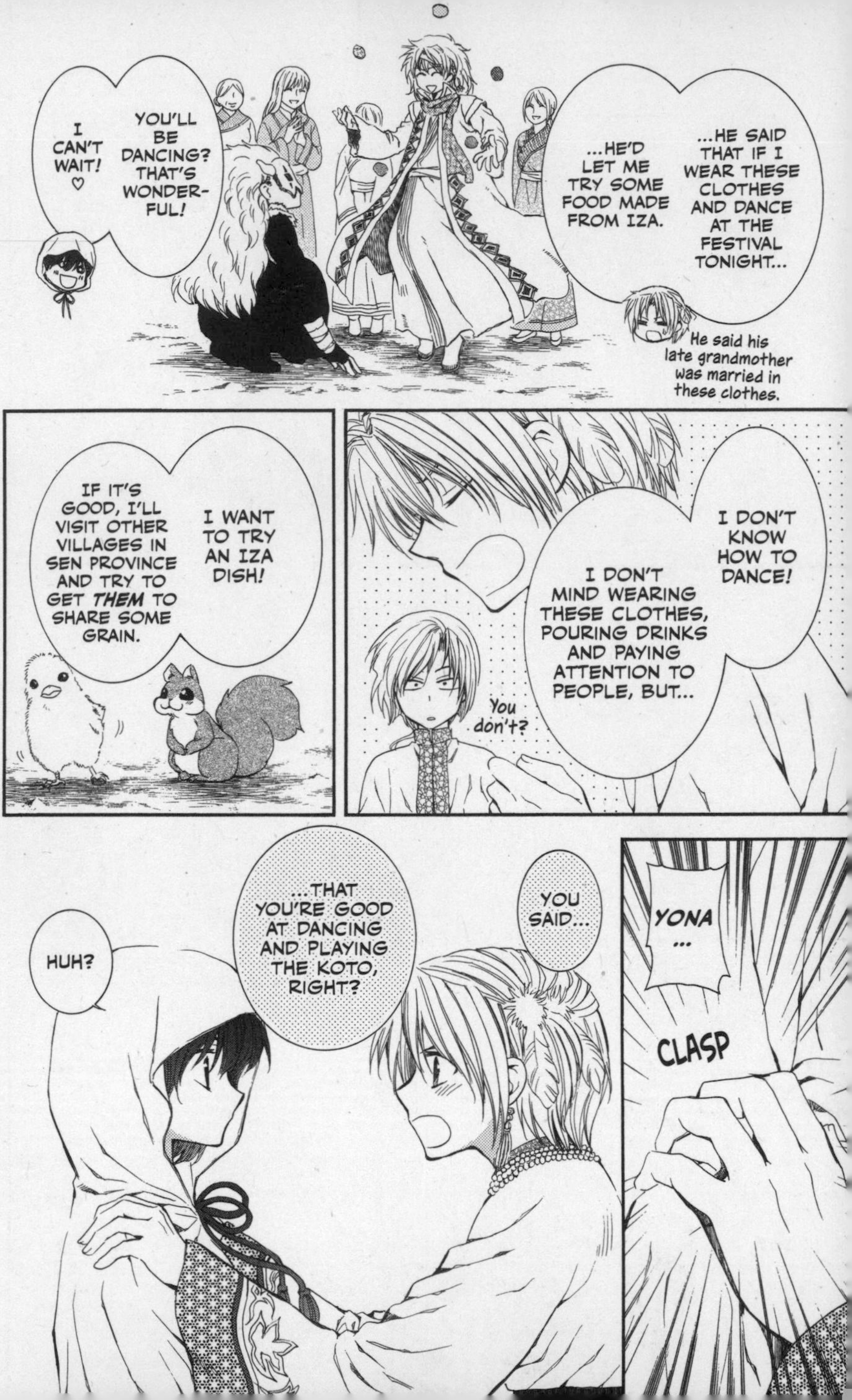
...HE SAID THAT IF I WEAR THESE CLOTHES AND DANCE AT THE FESTIVAL TONIGHT...
...HE'D LET ME TRY SOME FOOD MADE FROM IZA.
He said his late grandmother was married in these clothes.
YOU'LL BE DANCING? THAT'S WONDERFUL!
I CAN'T WAIT! ♡
I DON'T KNOW HOW TO DANCE!
I DON'T MIND WEARING THESE CLOTHES, POURING DRINKS AND PAYING ATTENTION TO PEOPLE, BUT...
You don't?
I WANT TO TRY AN IZA DISH!
IF IT'S GOOD, I'LL VISIT OTHER VILLAGES IN SEN PROVINCE AND TRY TO GET *THEM* TO SHARE SOME GRAIN.
YONA...
CLASP
YOU SAID...
...THAT YOU'RE GOOD AT DANCING AND PLAYING THE KOTO, RIGHT?
HUH?

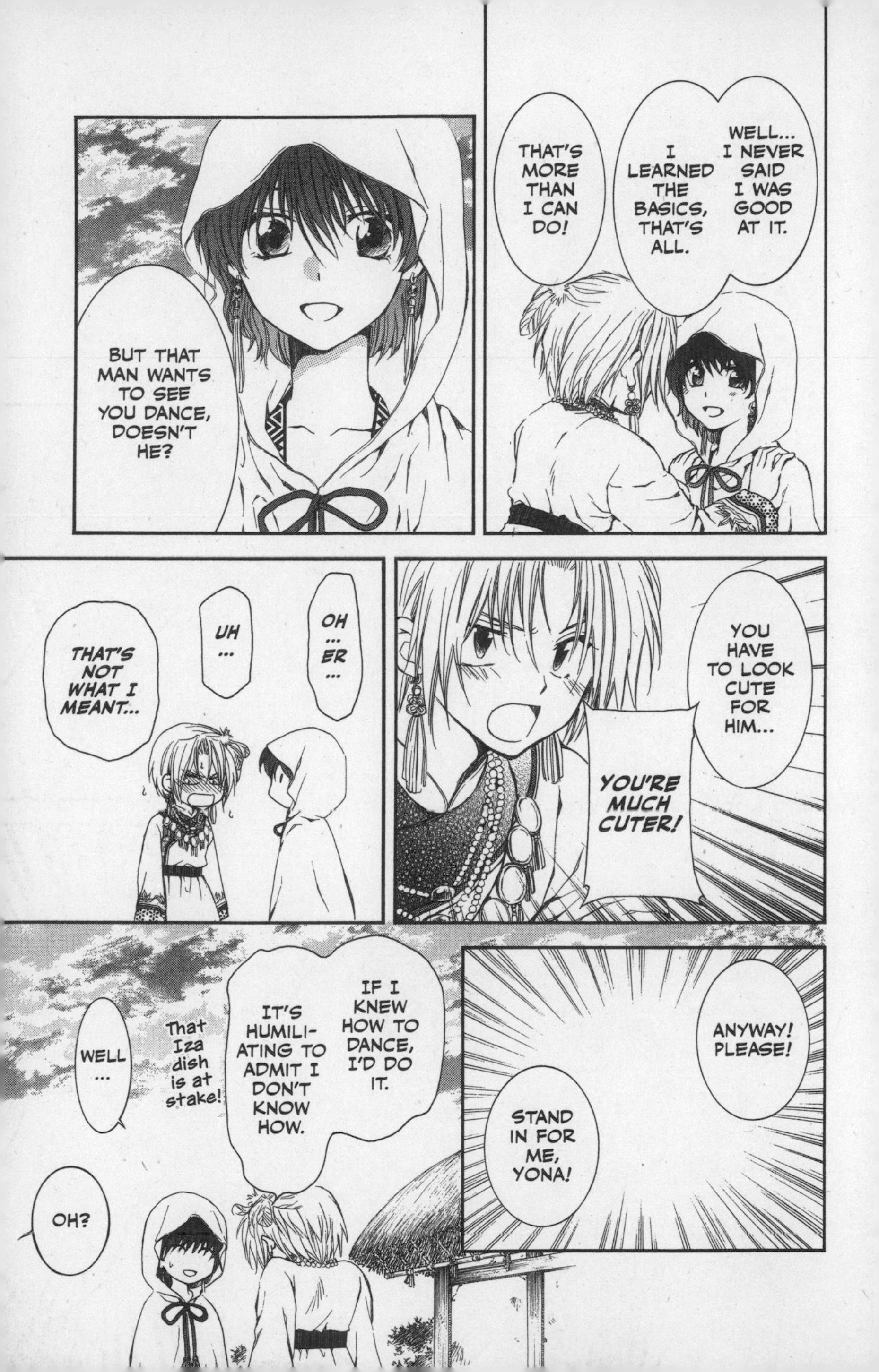
WELL... I NEVER SAID I WAS GOOD AT IT.
I LEARNED THE BASICS, THAT'S ALL.
THAT'S MORE THAN I CAN DO!
BUT THAT MAN WANTS TO SEE YOU DANCE, DOESN'T HE?
YOU HAVE TO LOOK CUTE FOR HIM...
YOU'RE MUCH CUTER!
OH ... ER ...
UH ...
THAT'S NOT WHAT I MEANT...
ANYWAY! PLEASE!
STAND IN FOR ME, YONA!
IF I KNEW HOW TO DANCE, I'D DO IT.
IT'S HUMILI-ATING TO ADMIT I DON'T KNOW HOW.
That Iza dish is at stake!
WELL ...
OH?

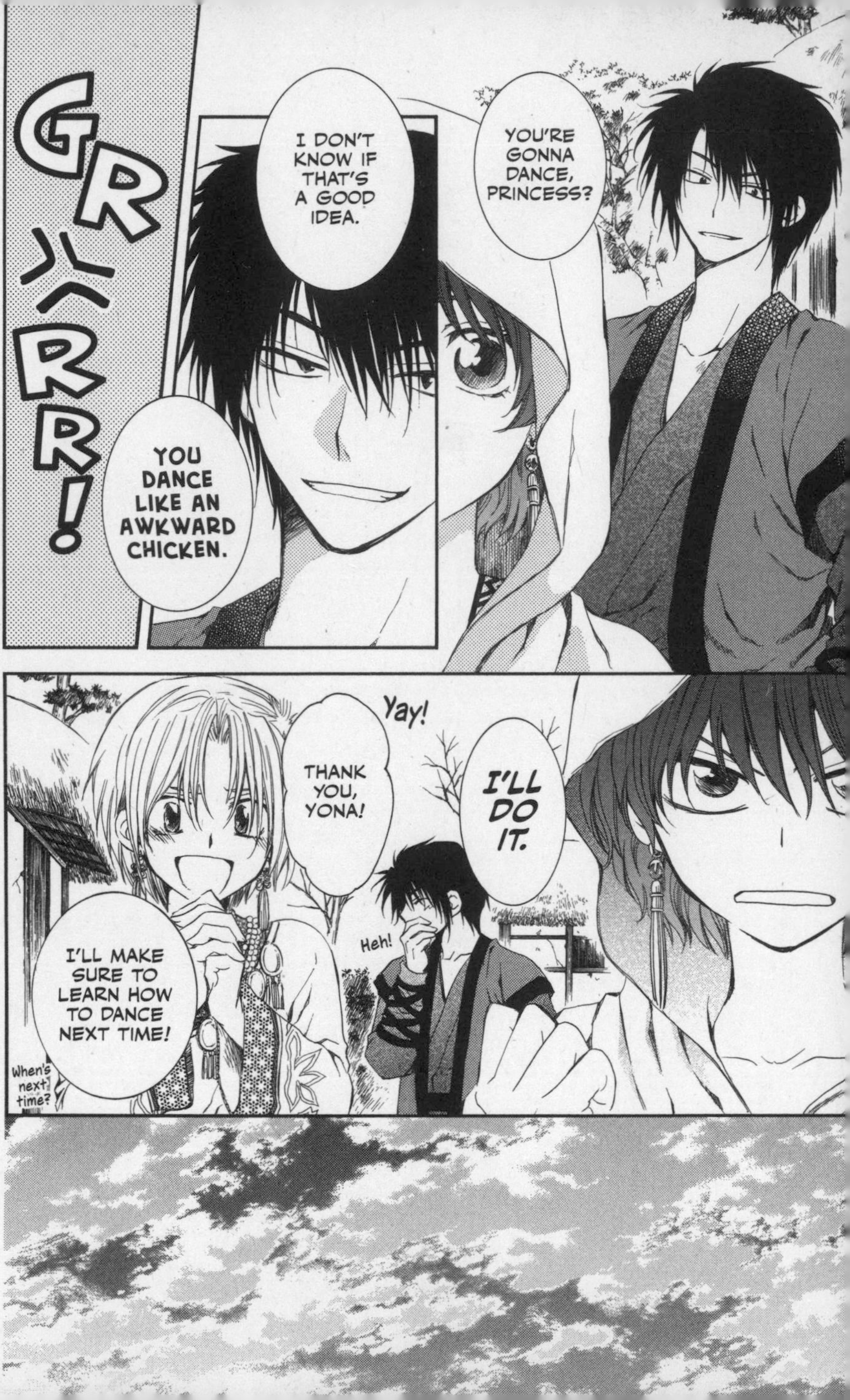
YOU'RE GONNA DANCE, PRINCESS?
I DON'T KNOW IF THAT'S A GOOD IDEA.
YOU DANCE LIKE AN AWKWARD CHICKEN.
GRRR!
I'LL DO IT.
Yay!
THANK YOU, YONA!
Heh!
I'LL MAKE SURE TO LEARN HOW TO DANCE NEXT TIME!
When's next time?

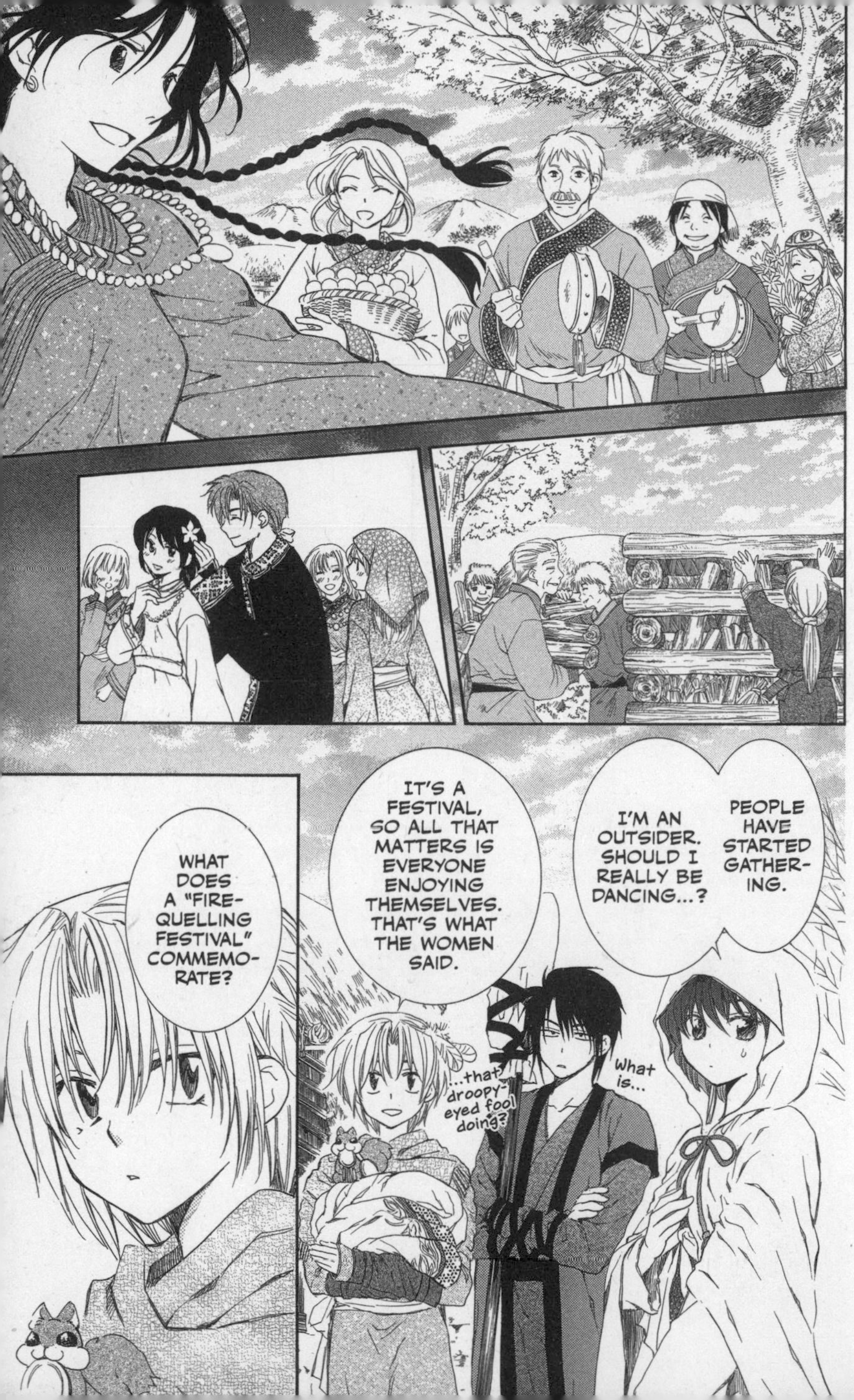
PEOPLE HAVE STARTED GATHER-ING.
I'M AN OUTSIDER. SHOULD I REALLY BE DANCING...?
IT'S A FESTIVAL, SO ALL THAT MATTERS IS EVERYONE ENJOYING THEMSELVES. THAT'S WHAT THE WOMEN SAID.
What is...
...that droopy-eyed fool doing?
WHAT DOES A "FIRE-QUELLING FESTIVAL" COMMEMO-RATE?

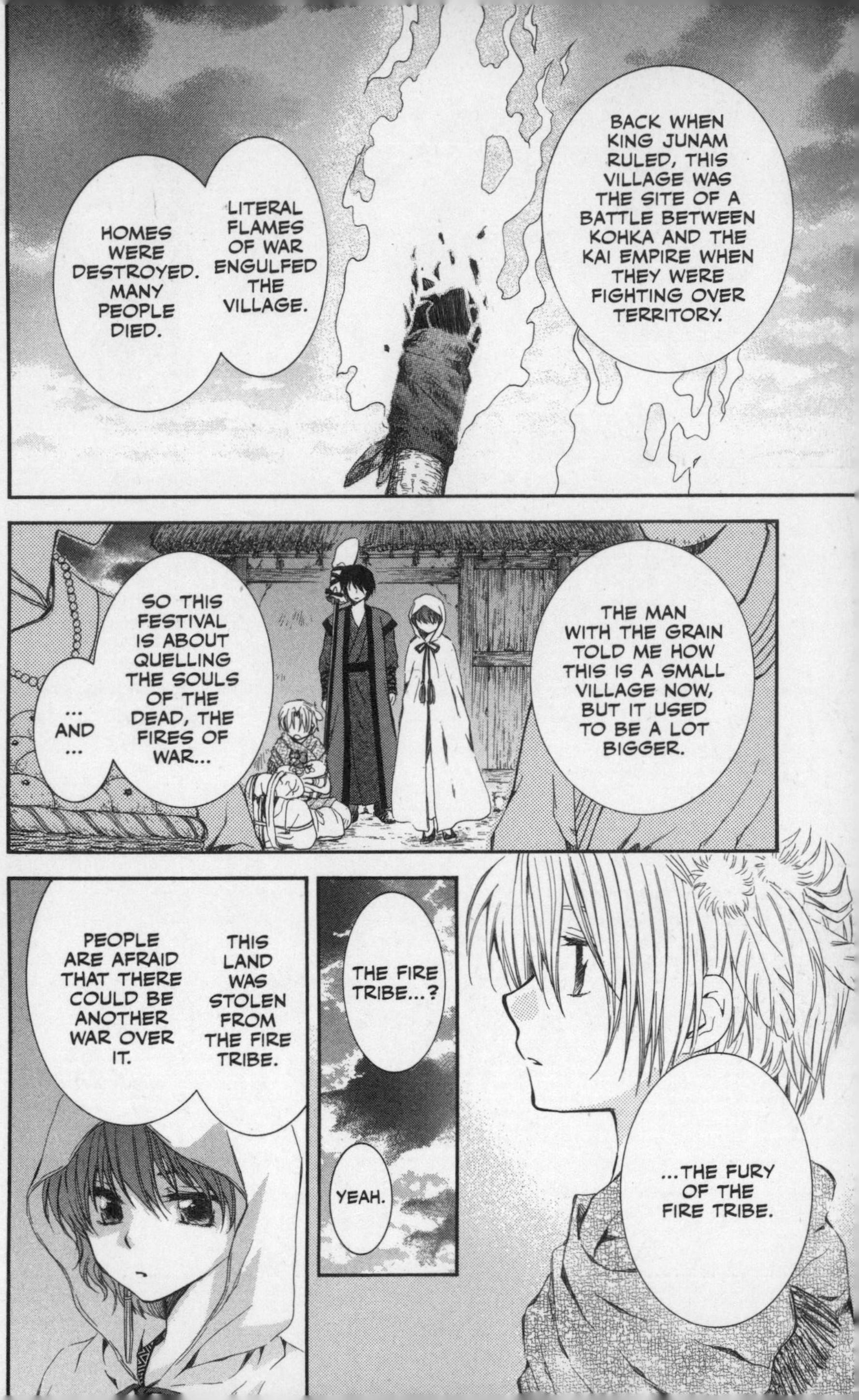
BACK WHEN KING JUNAM RULED, THIS VILLAGE WAS THE SITE OF A BATTLE BETWEEN KOHKA AND THE KAI EMPIRE WHEN THEY WERE FIGHTING OVER TERRITORY.
LITERAL FLAMES OF WAR ENGULFED THE VILLAGE.
HOMES WERE DESTROYED. MANY PEOPLE DIED.
THE MAN WITH THE GRAIN TOLD ME HOW THIS IS A SMALL VILLAGE NOW, BUT IT USED TO BE A LOT BIGGER.
SO THIS FESTIVAL IS ABOUT QUELLING THE SOULS OF THE DEAD, THE FIRES OF WAR...
... AND ...
...THE FURY OF THE FIRE TRIBE.
THE FIRE TRIBE...?
YEAH.
THIS LAND WAS STOLEN FROM THE FIRE TRIBE.
PEOPLE ARE AFRAID THAT THERE COULD BE ANOTHER WAR OVER IT.

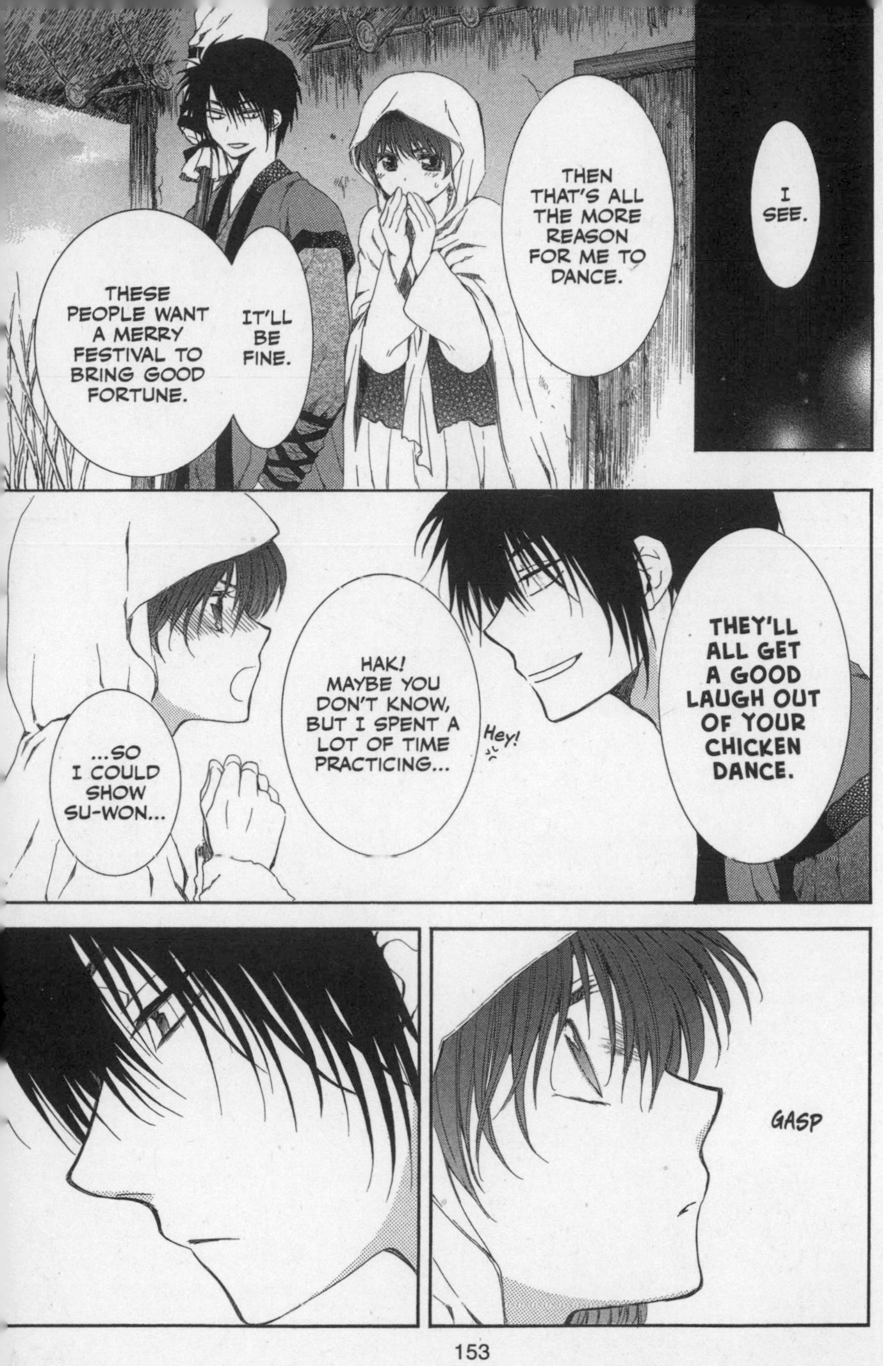
I SEE.
THEN THAT'S ALL THE MORE REASON FOR ME TO DANCE.
IT'LL BE FINE.
THESE PEOPLE WANT A MERRY FESTIVAL TO BRING GOOD FORTUNE.
THEY'LL ALL GET A GOOD LAUGH OUT OF YOUR CHICKEN DANCE.
Hey!
HAK! MAYBE YOU DON'T KNOW, BUT I SPENT A LOT OF TIME PRACTICING...
...SO I COULD SHOW SU-WON...
GASP

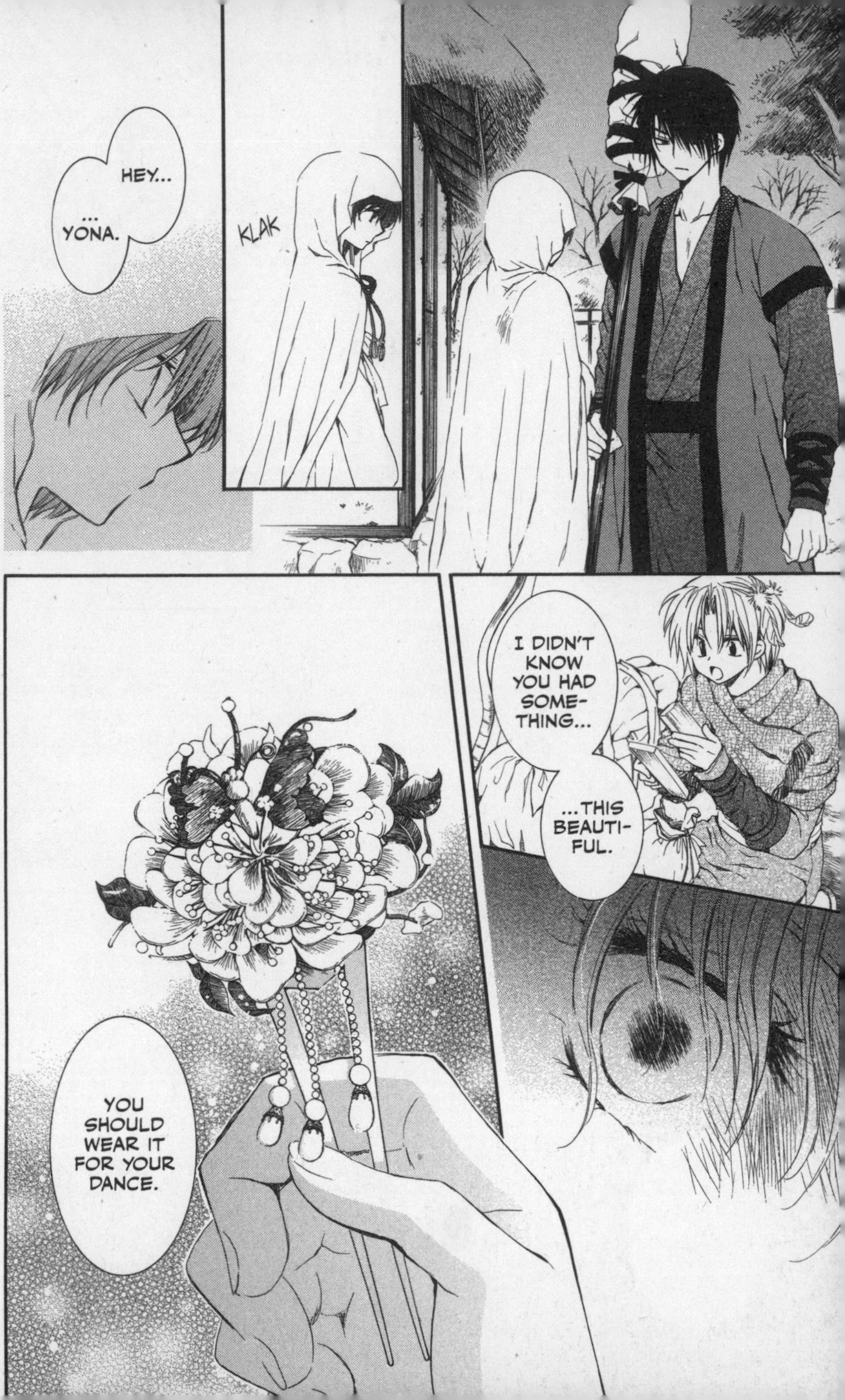
KLAK
HEY...
...YONA.
I DIDN'T KNOW YOU HAD SOMETHING...
...THIS BEAUTIFUL.
YOU SHOULD WEAR IT FOR YOUR DANCE.

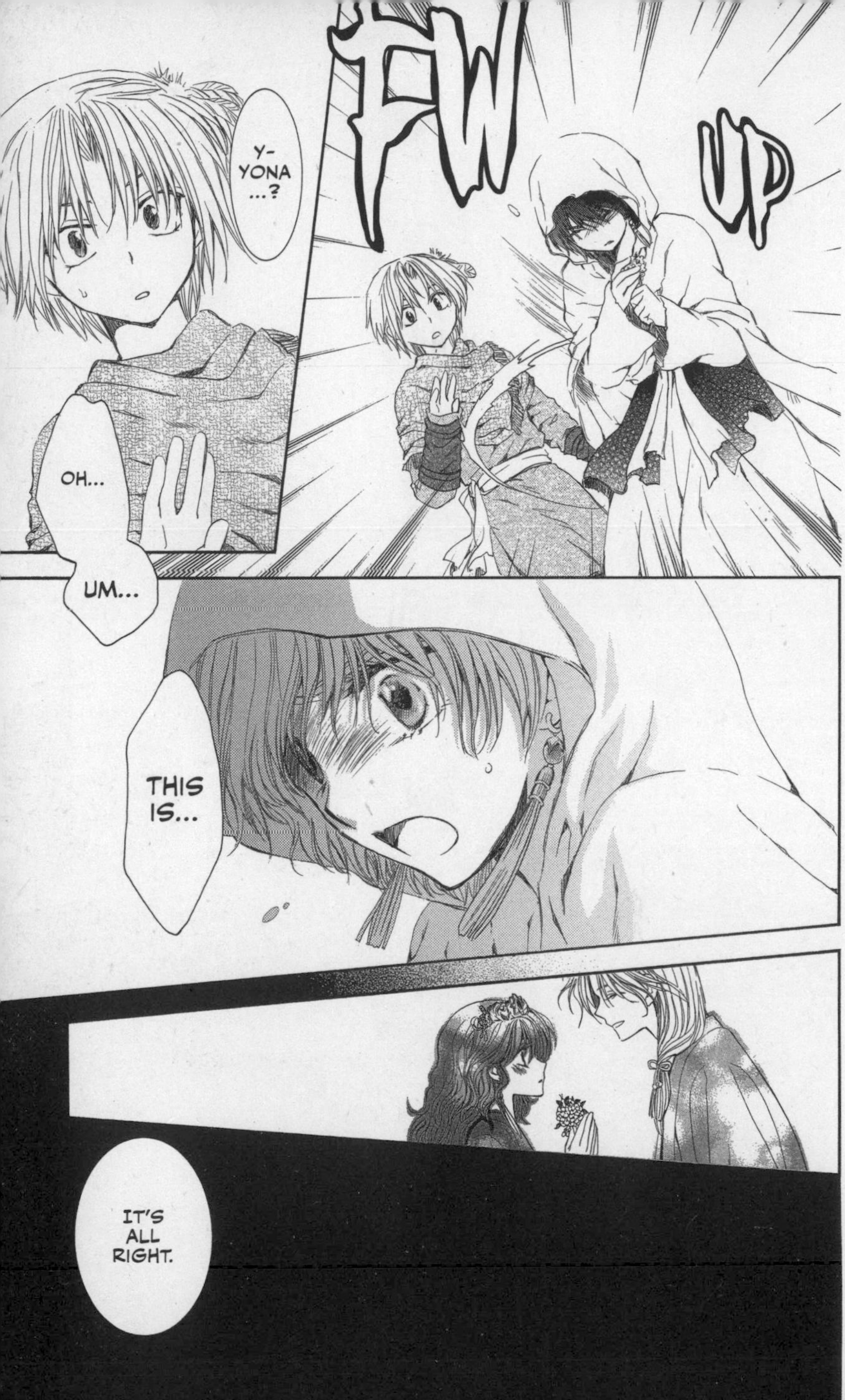
FWUP
Y-YONA ...?
OH...
UM...
THIS IS...
IT'S ALL RIGHT.

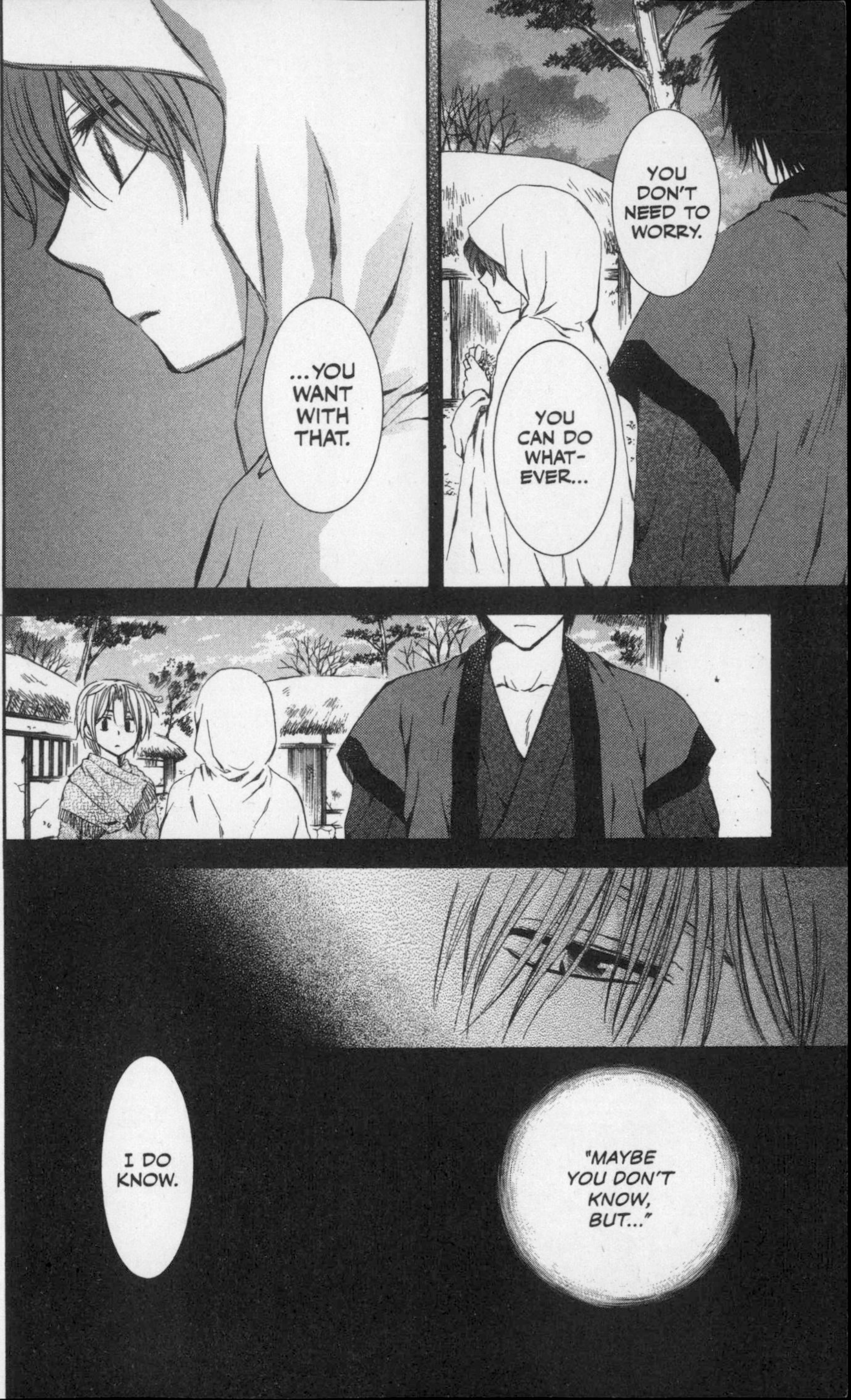
YOU DON'T NEED TO WORRY.
YOU CAN DO WHATEVER...
...YOU WANT WITH THAT.
"MAYBE YOU DON'T KNOW, BUT..."
I DO KNOW.

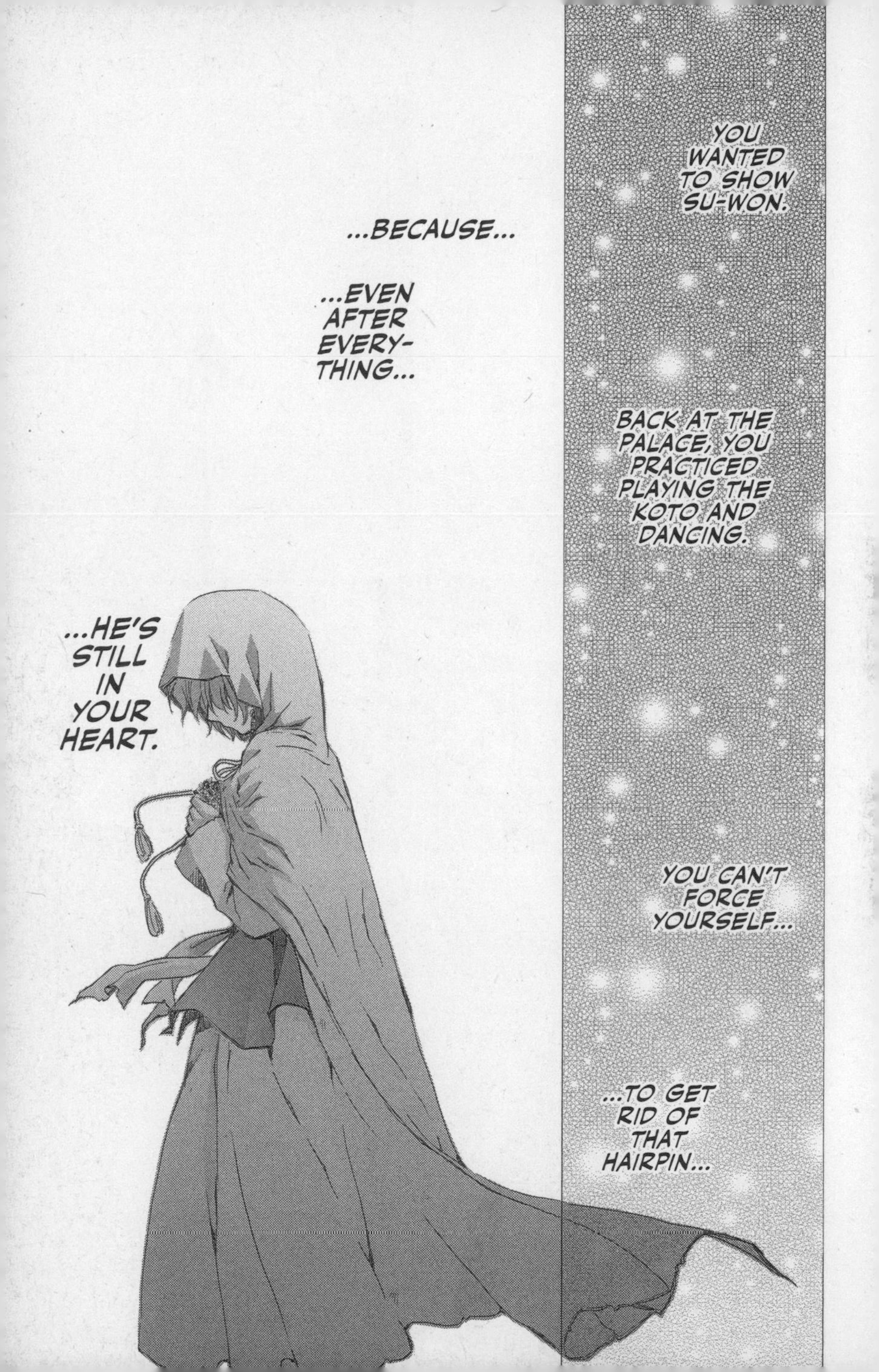
YOU WANTED TO SHOW SU-WON.
BACK AT THE PALACE, YOU PRACTICED PLAYING THE KOTO AND DANCING.
YOU CAN'T FORCE YOURSELF...
...TO GET RID OF THAT HAIRPIN...
...BECAUSE...
...EVEN AFTER EVERY-THING...
...HE'S STILL IN YOUR HEART.

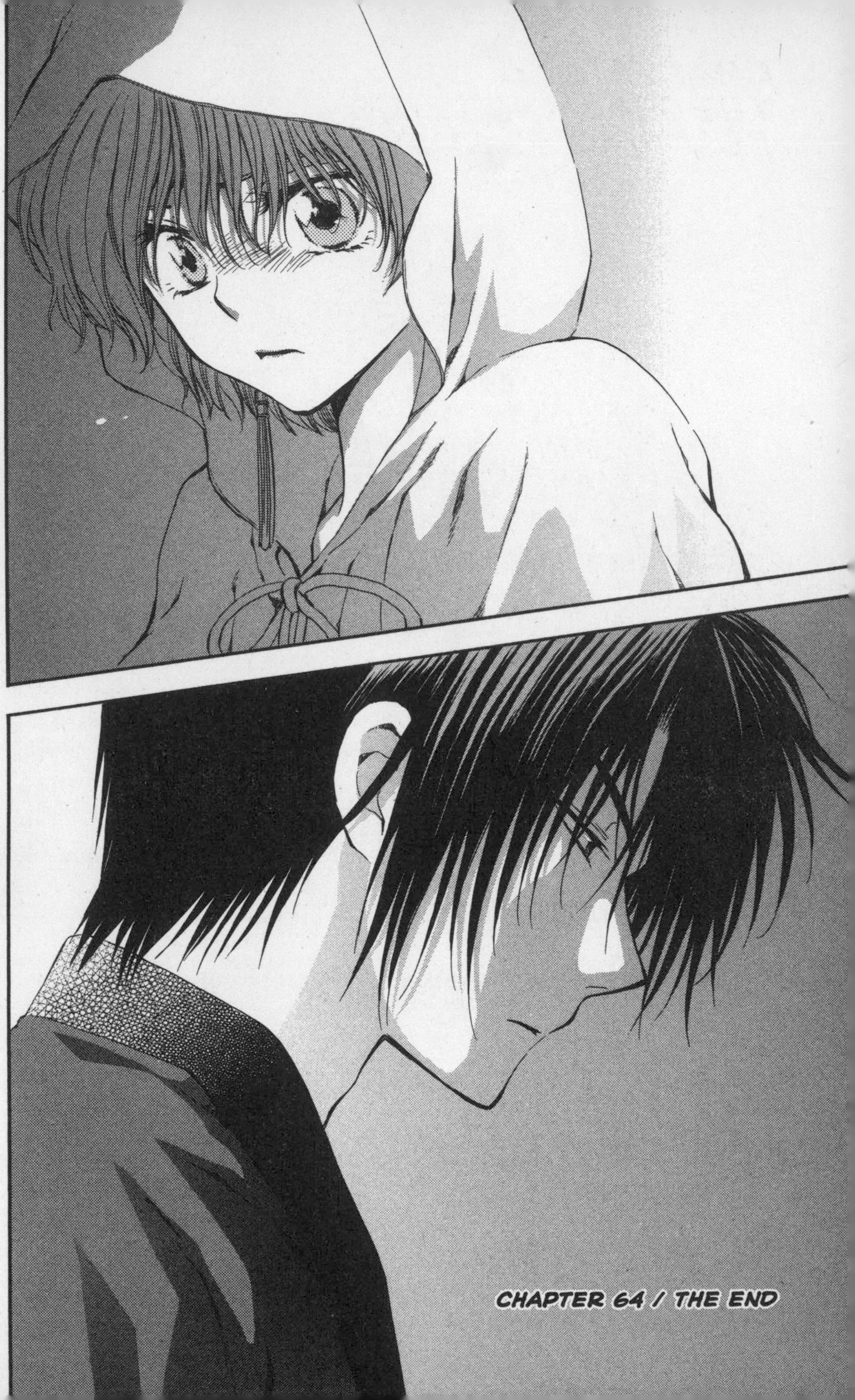
CHAPTER 64 / THE END

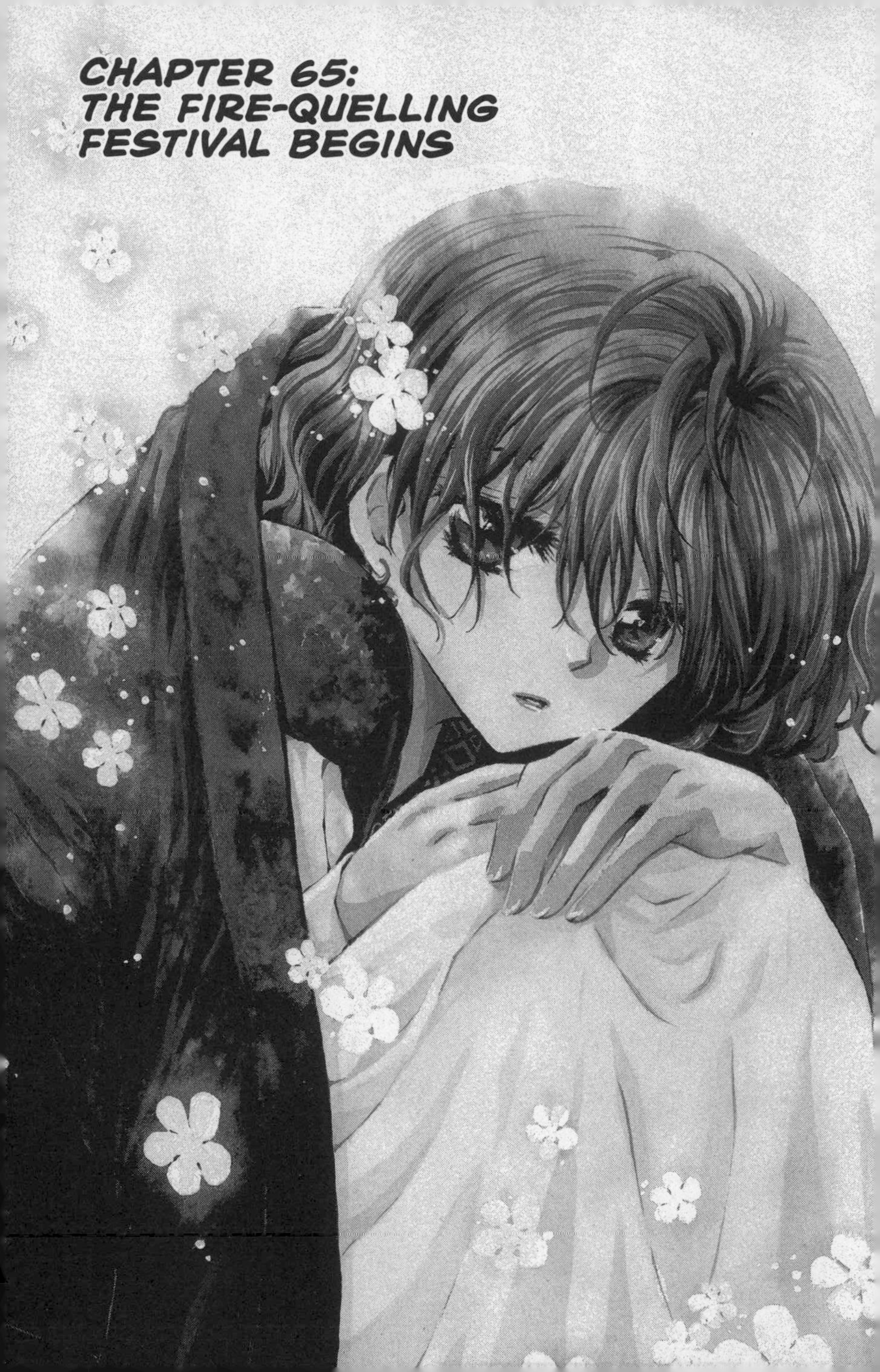
CHAPTER 65:
THE FIRE-QUELLING
FESTIVAL BEGINS

A rejected sketch for the cover of this volume.
It used to have this composition.

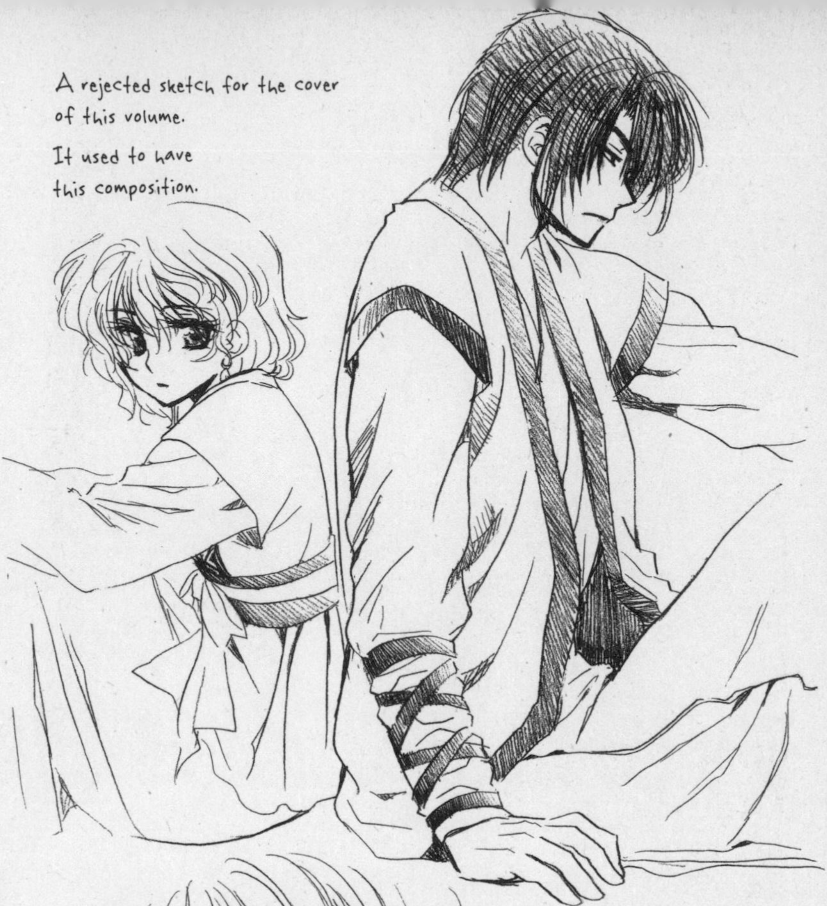

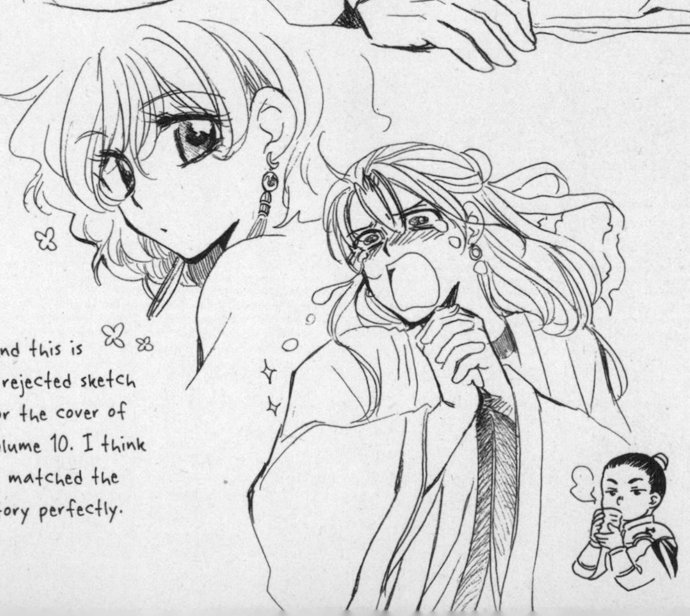

And this is a rejected sketch for the cover of volume 10. I think it matched the story perfectly.

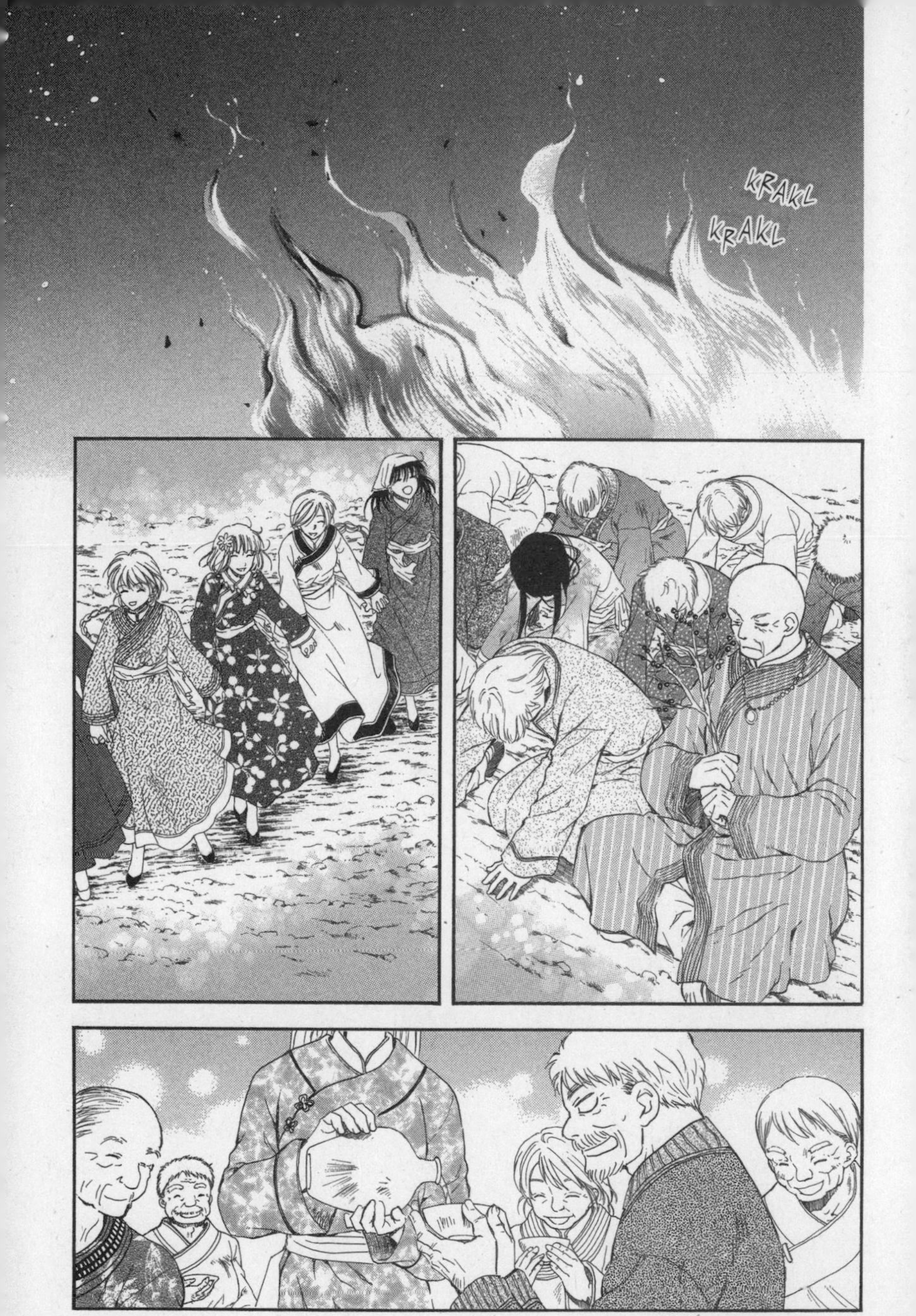
KRAKL
KRAKL

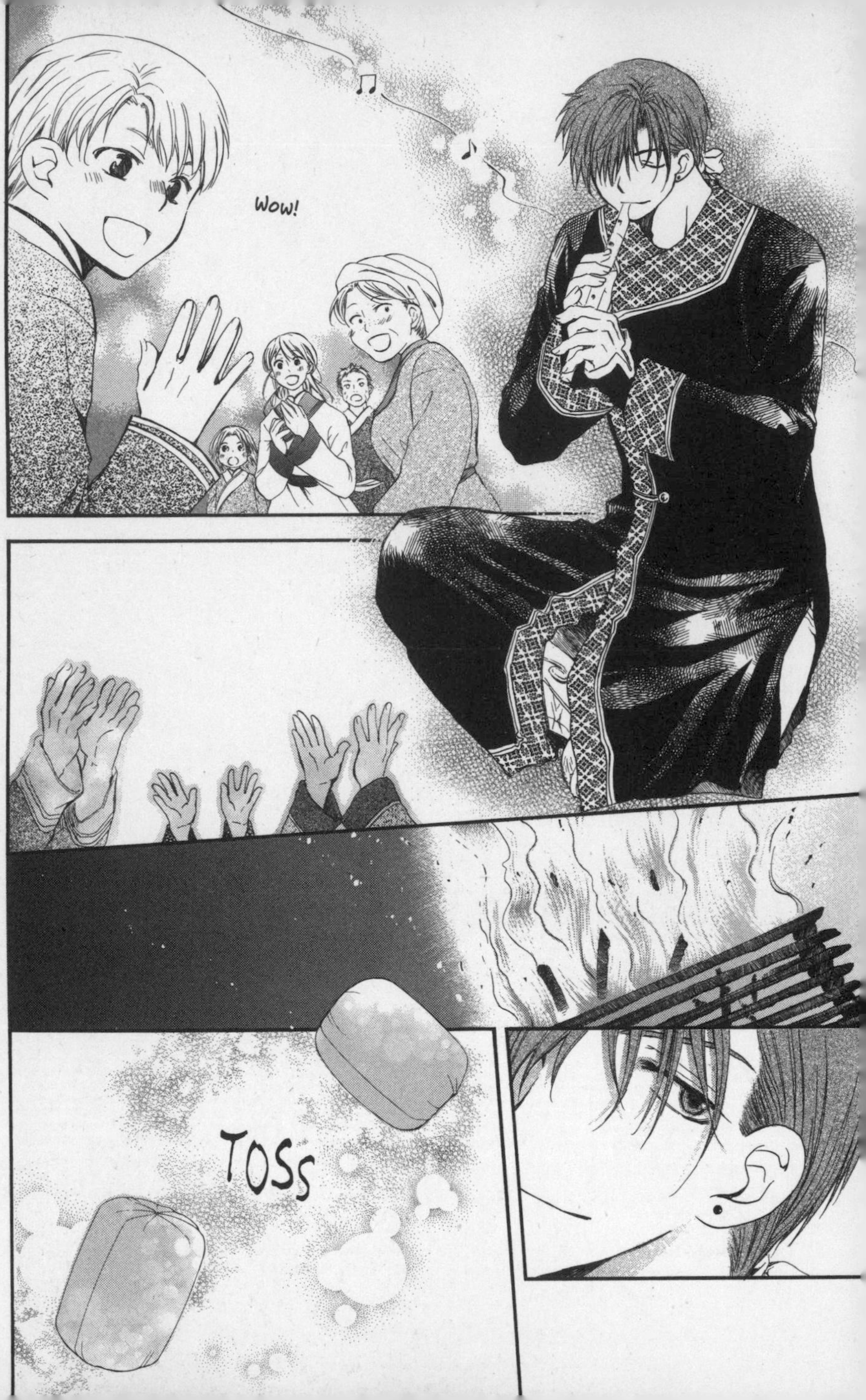
WOW!
TOSS

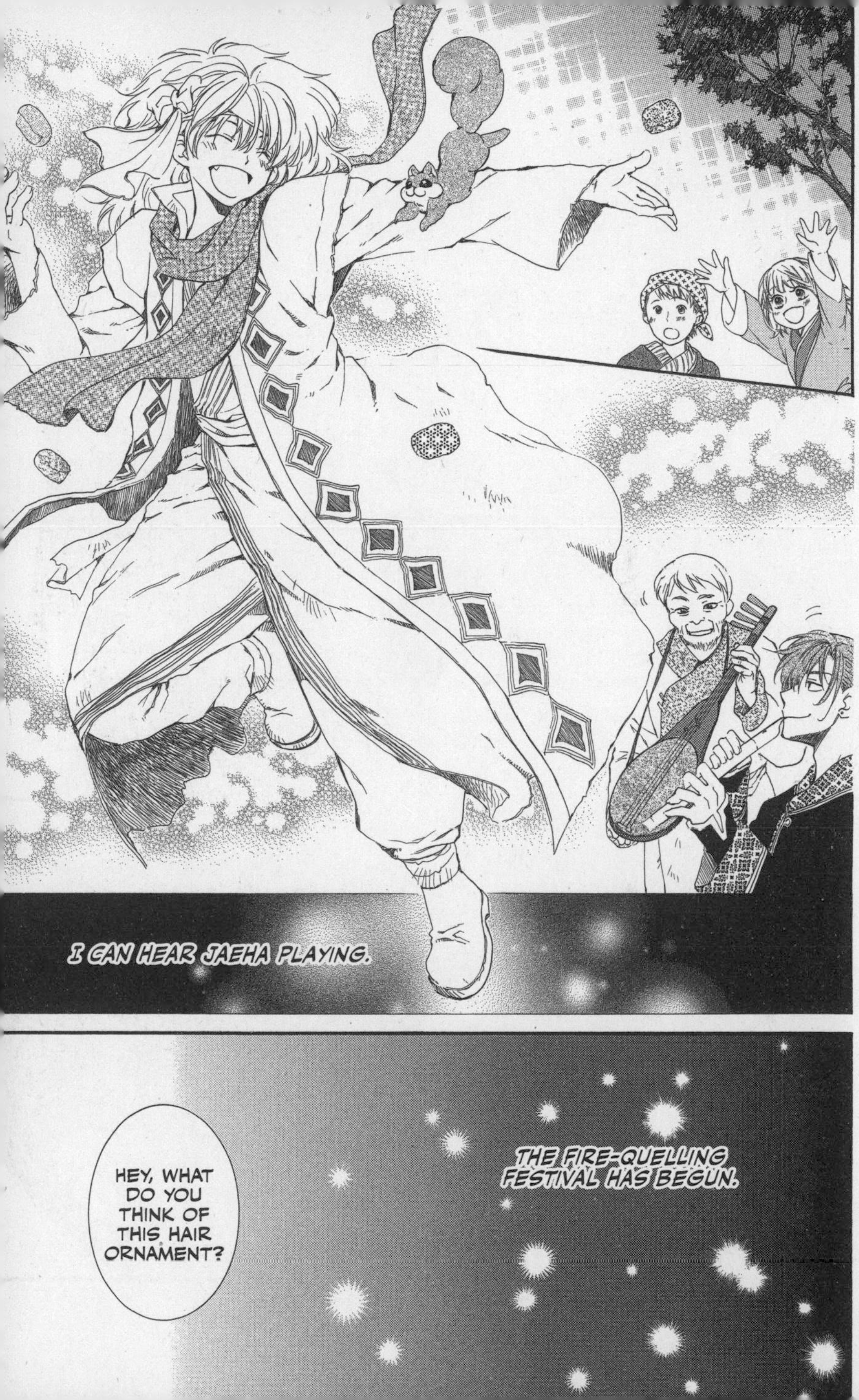
I CAN HEAR JAEHA PLAYING.
THE FIRE-QUELLING FESTIVAL HAS BEGUN.
HEY, WHAT DO YOU THINK OF THIS HAIR ORNAMENT?

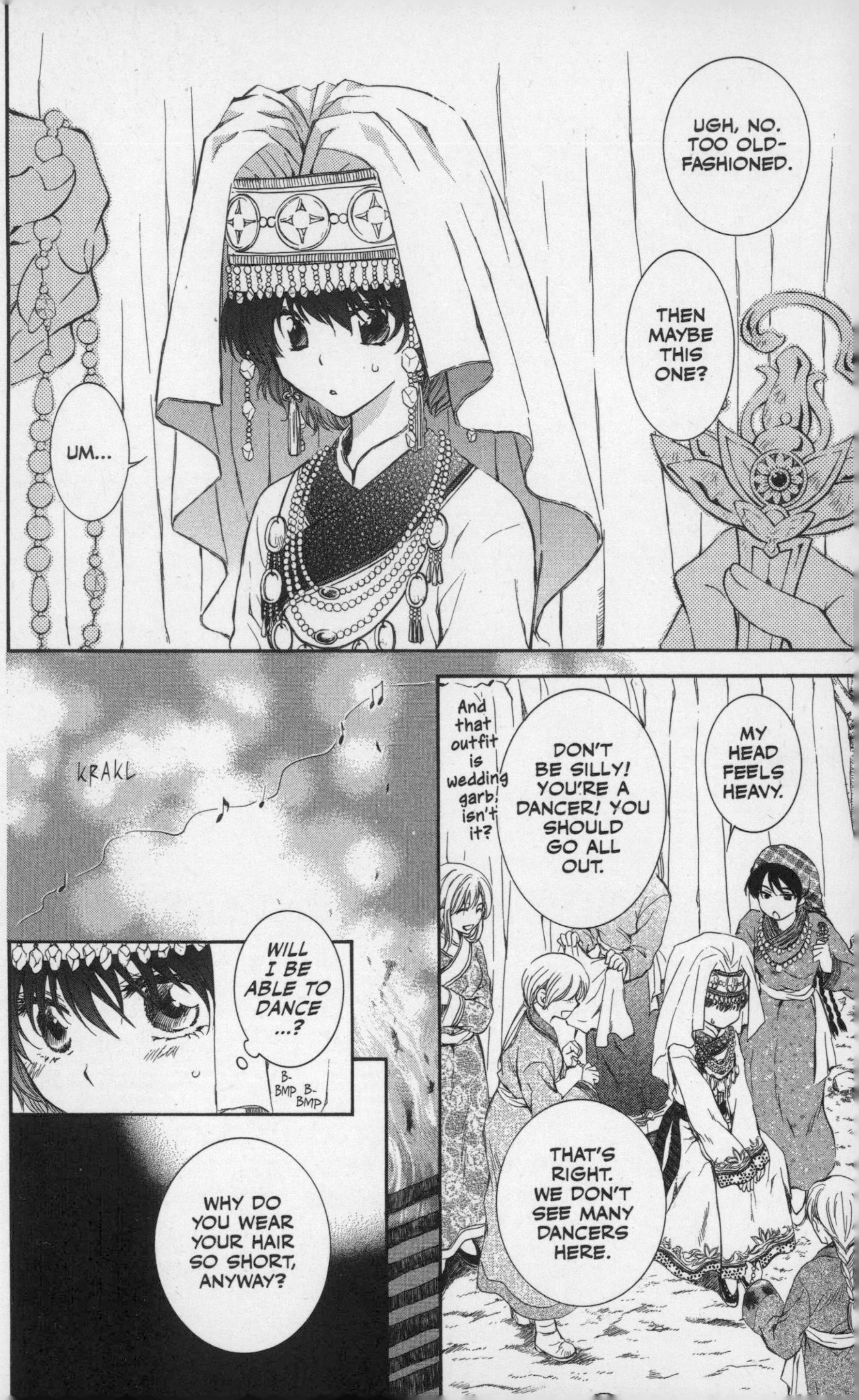
UGH, NO. TOO OLD-FASHIONED.
THEN MAYBE THIS ONE?
UM...
MY HEAD FEELS HEAVY.
DON'T BE SILLY! YOU'RE A DANCER! YOU SHOULD GO ALL OUT.
And that outfit is wedding garb, isn't it?
THAT'S RIGHT. WE DON'T SEE MANY DANCERS HERE.
KRAKL
WILL I BE ABLE TO DANCE ...?
B-BMP B-BMP
WHY DO YOU WEAR YOUR HAIR SO SHORT, ANYWAY?

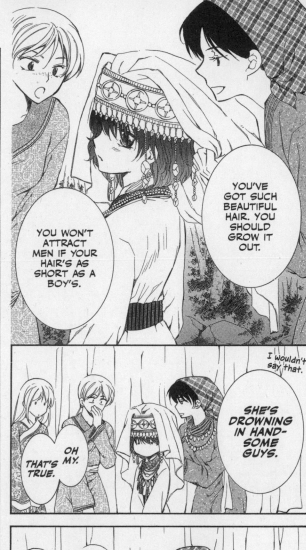

YOU'VE GOT SUCH BEAUTIFUL HAIR. YOU SHOULD GROW IT OUT.
YOU WON'T ATTRACT MEN IF YOUR HAIR'S AS SHORT AS A BOY'S.
I wouldn't say that.
SHE'S DROWNING IN HAND-SOME GUYS.
OH MY.
THAT'S TRUE.

I'm sorry that there aren't many illustrations this time. I was swamped with getting all the art done for the main magazine, so I couldn't find the time to squeeze in much extra art.

I wanted to make the outfits in this volume more elaborate, but this is all I had time to do. One week of illustrations at my drawing speed... Well, let's just say it took forever.

But volume 12 is next up! I'm hard at work drawing the chapters for the main magazine that'll eventually be volume 12.

I'd like to do some stories about the Four Dragon Warriors and the generals. I'd like to have a story about Geun-tae and Yuno, but I probably don't have time, so it'll likely just keep being an idea in my head. Hope to see you in the next volume!

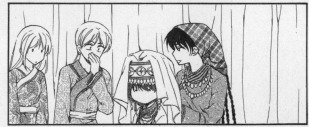

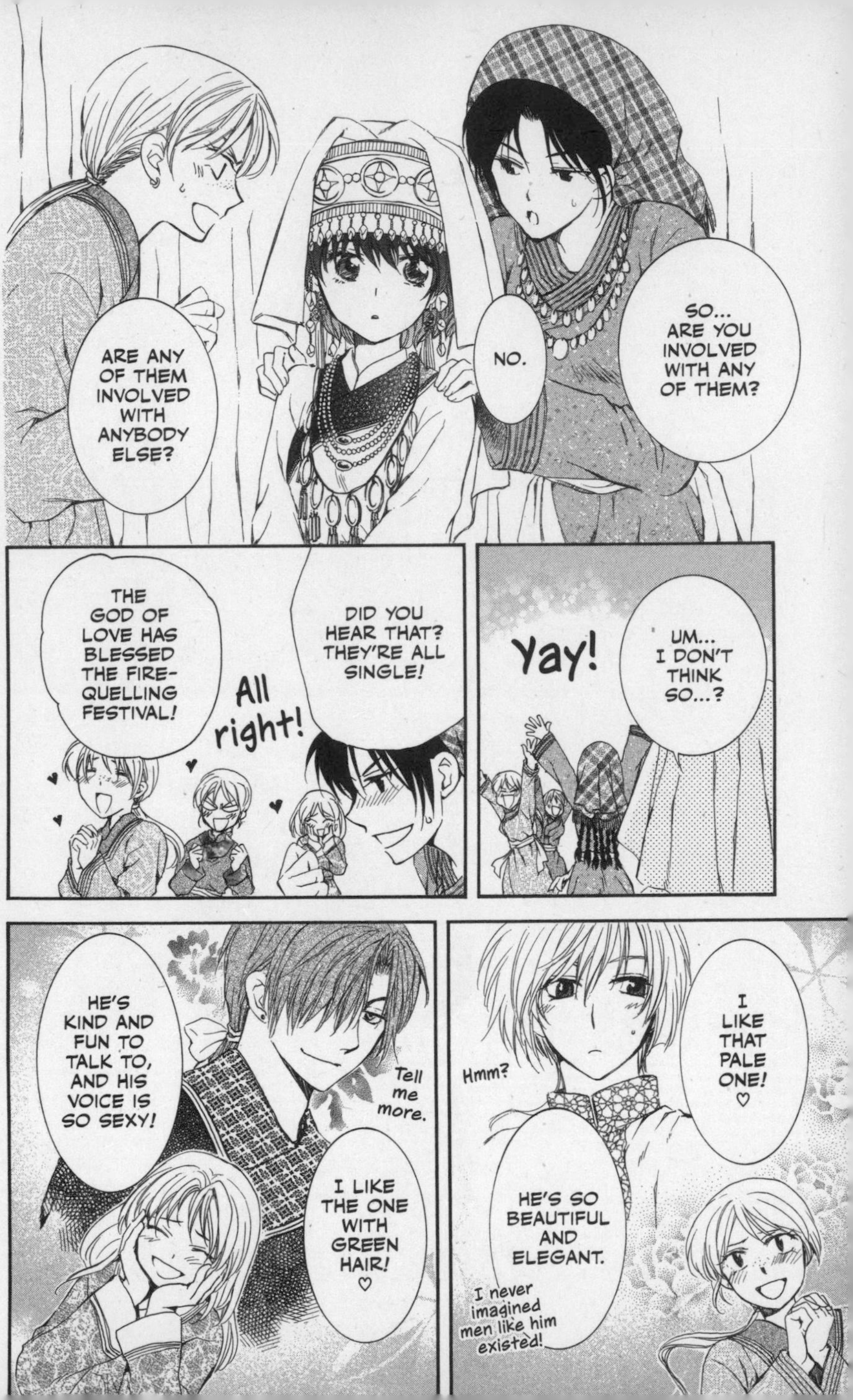
SO... ARE YOU INVOLVED WITH ANY OF THEM?
NO.
ARE ANY OF THEM INVOLVED WITH ANYBODY ELSE?
UM... I DON'T THINK SO...?
Yay!
DID YOU HEAR THAT? THEY'RE ALL SINGLE!
All right!
THE GOD OF LOVE HAS BLESSED THE FIRE-QUELLING FESTIVAL!
I LIKE THAT PALE ONE! ♡
Hmm?
HE'S SO BEAUTIFUL AND ELEGANT.
I never imagined men like him existed!
HE'S KIND AND FUN TO TALK TO, AND HIS VOICE IS SO SEXY!
Tell me more.
I LIKE THE ONE WITH GREEN HAIR! ♡

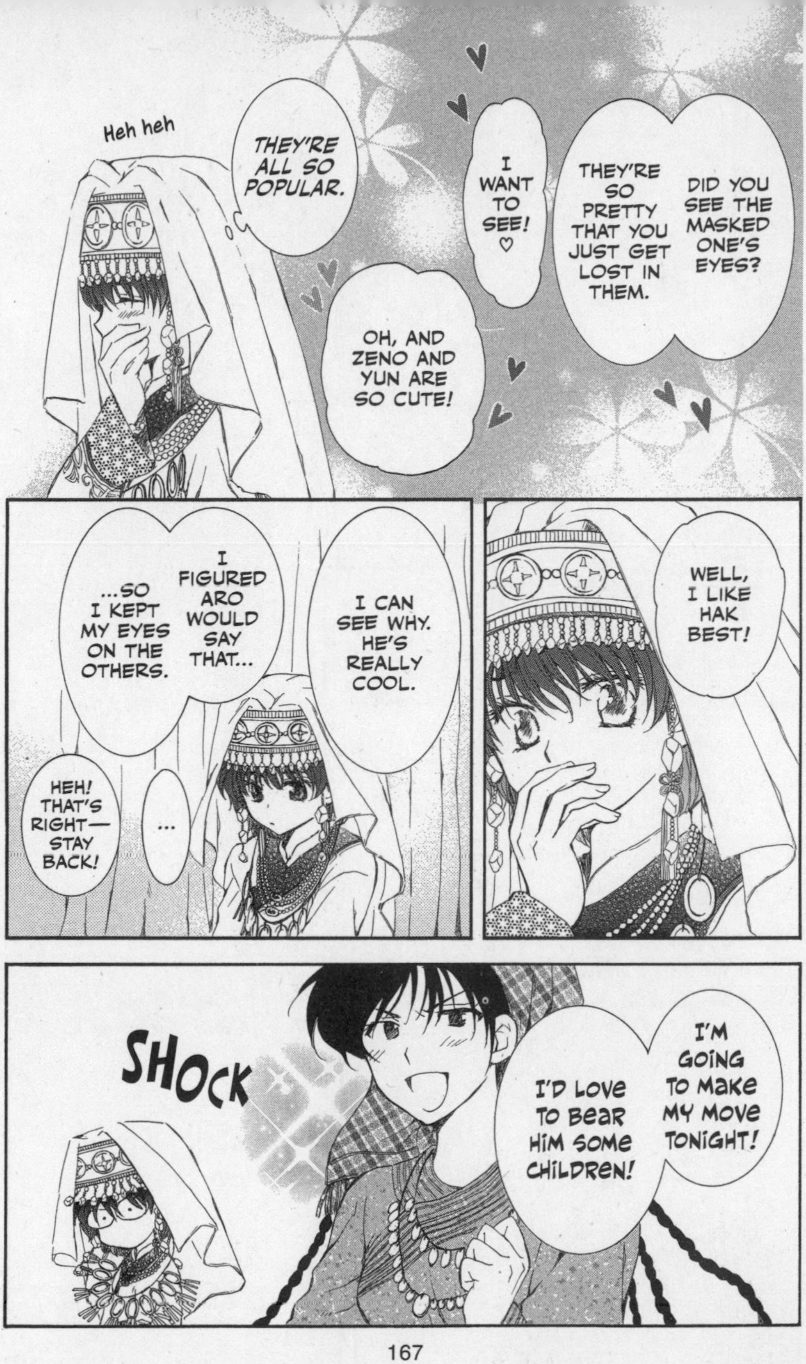
DID YOU SEE THE MASKED ONE'S EYES?
THEY'RE SO PRETTY THAT YOU JUST GET LOST IN THEM.
I WANT TO SEE! ♡
OH, AND ZENO AND YUN ARE SO CUTE!
THEY'RE ALL SO POPULAR.
Heh heh
WELL, I LIKE HAK BEST!
I CAN SEE WHY. HE'S REALLY COOL.
I FIGURED ARO WOULD SAY THAT...
...SO I KEPT MY EYES ON THE OTHERS.
...
HEH! THAT'S RIGHT—STAY BACK!
I'M GOING TO MAKE MY MOVE TONIGHT!
I'D LOVE TO BEAR HIM SOME CHILDREN!
SHOCK

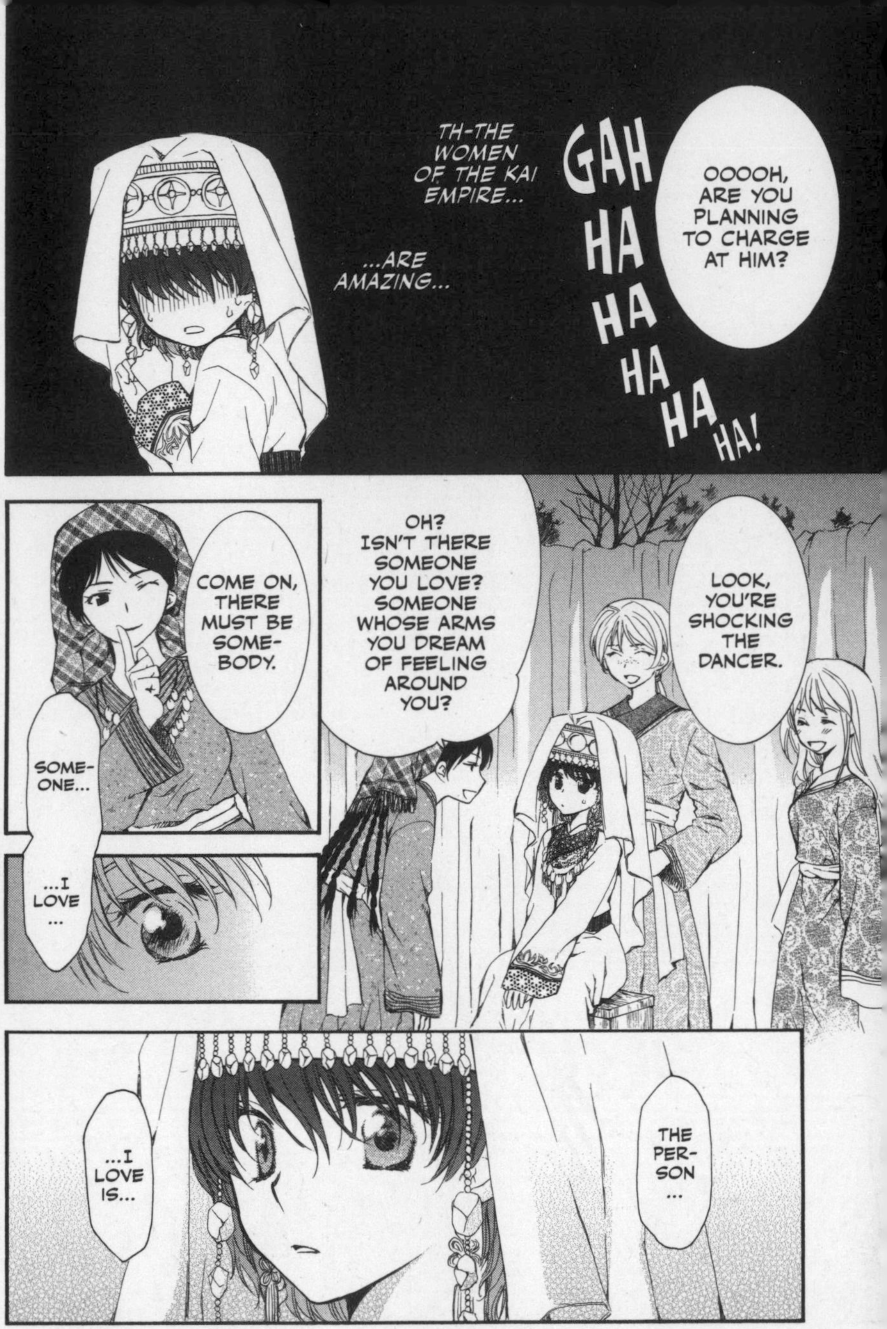
OOOOH, ARE YOU PLANNING TO CHARGE AT HIM?
GAH HA HA HA HA HA!
TH-THE WOMEN OF THE KAI EMPIRE...
...ARE AMAZING...
LOOK, YOU'RE SHOCKING THE DANCER.
OH? ISN'T THERE SOMEONE YOU LOVE? SOMEONE WHOSE ARMS YOU DREAM OF FEELING AROUND YOU?
COME ON, THERE MUST BE SOME-BODY.
SOME-ONE...
...I LOVE ...
THE PER-SON ...
...I LOVE IS...

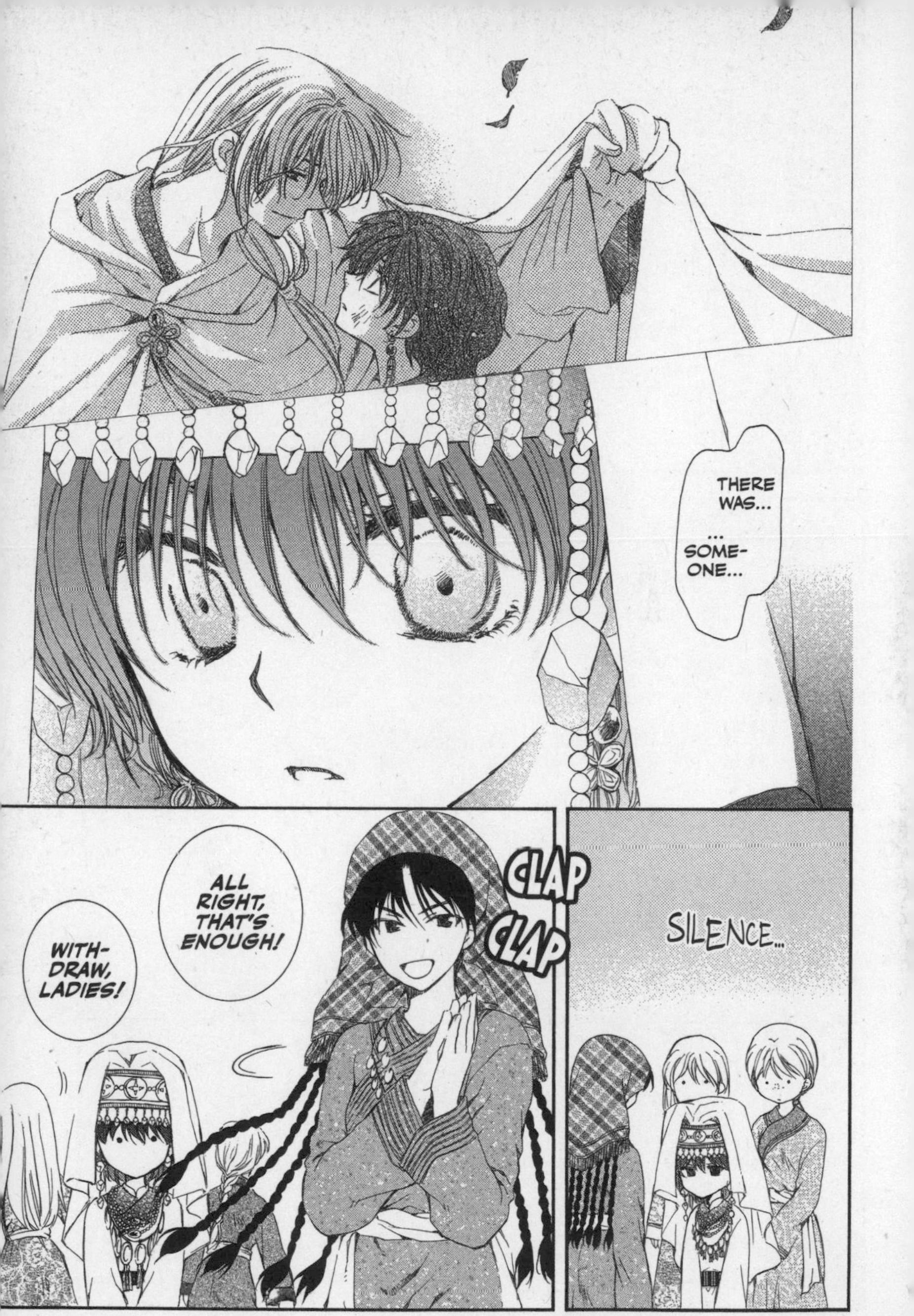
THERE WAS...
...SOME-ONE...
SILENCE...
CLAP CLAP
ALL RIGHT, THAT'S ENOUGH!
WITH-DRAW, LADIES!

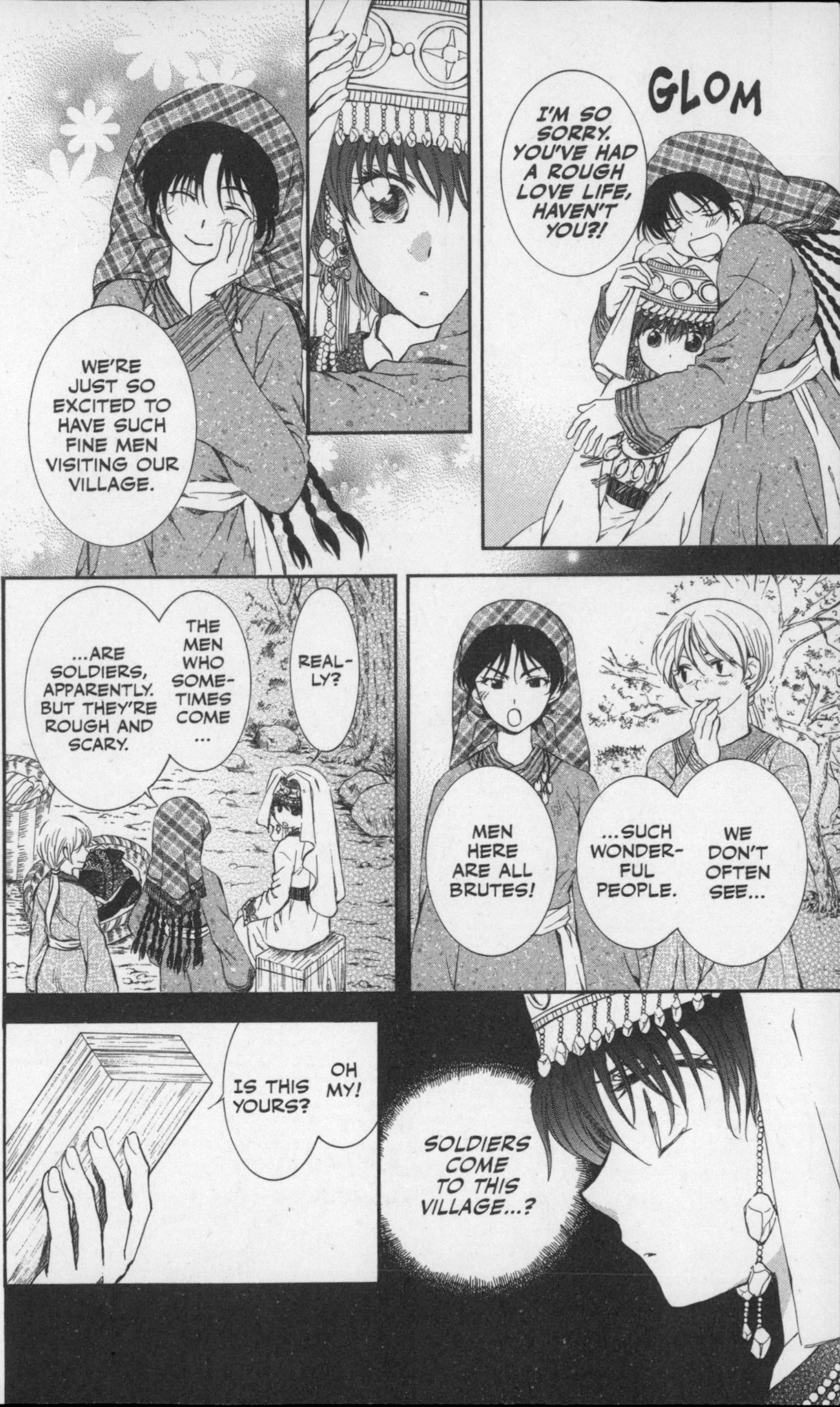
GLOM
I'M SO SORRY. YOU'VE HAD A ROUGH LOVE LIFE, HAVEN'T YOU?!
WE'RE JUST SO EXCITED TO HAVE SUCH FINE MEN VISITING OUR VILLAGE.
WE DON'T OFTEN SEE...
...SUCH WONDERFUL PEOPLE.
MEN HERE ARE ALL BRUTES!
REALLY?
THE MEN WHO SOMETIMES COME...
...ARE SOLDIERS, APPARENTLY. BUT THEY'RE ROUGH AND SCARY.
SOLDIERS COME TO THIS VILLAGE...?
OH MY!
IS THIS YOURS?

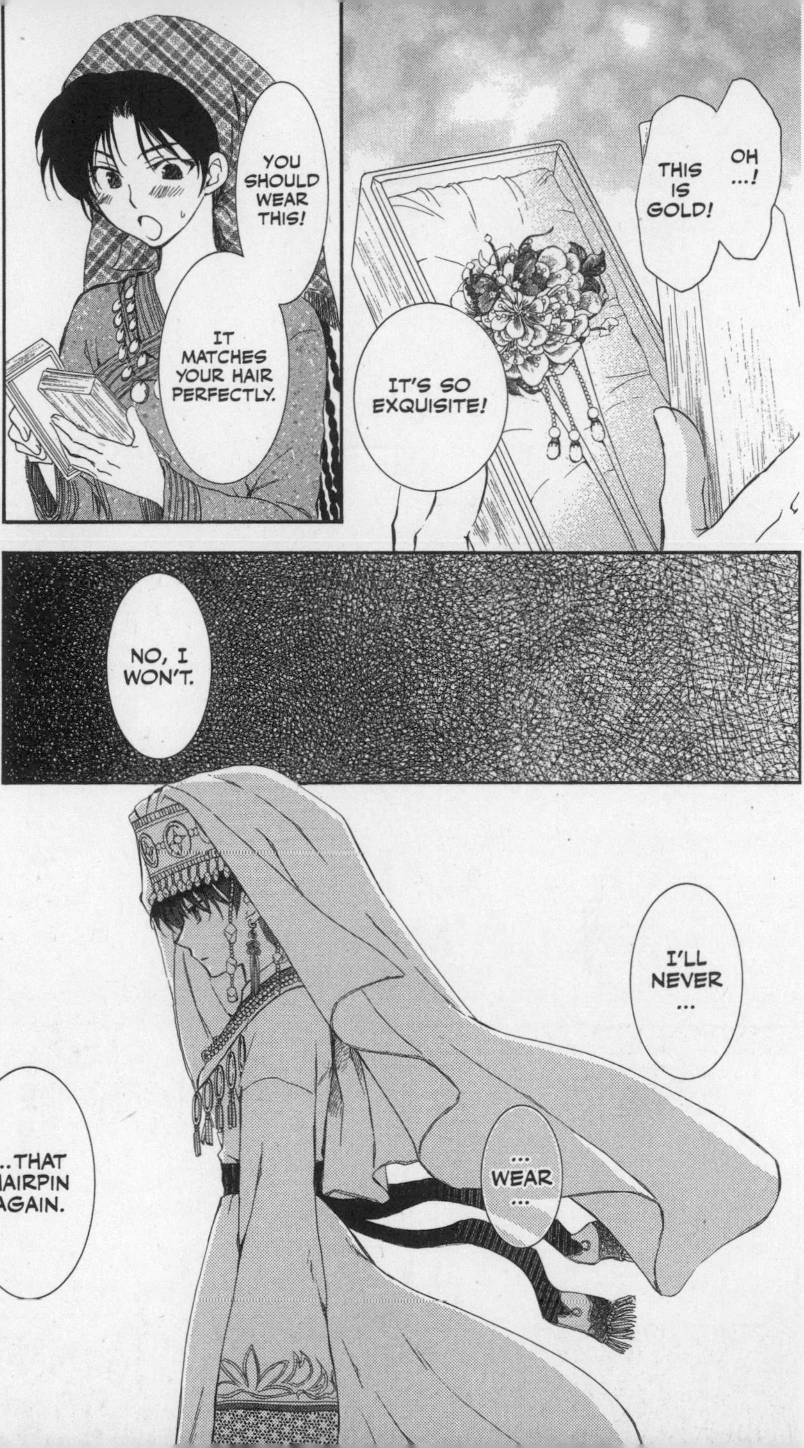
OH ...! THIS IS GOLD!
IT'S SO EXQUISITE!
YOU SHOULD WEAR THIS!
IT MATCHES YOUR HAIR PERFECTLY.
NO, I WON'T.
I'LL NEVER ...
... WEAR ...
...THAT HAIRPIN AGAIN.

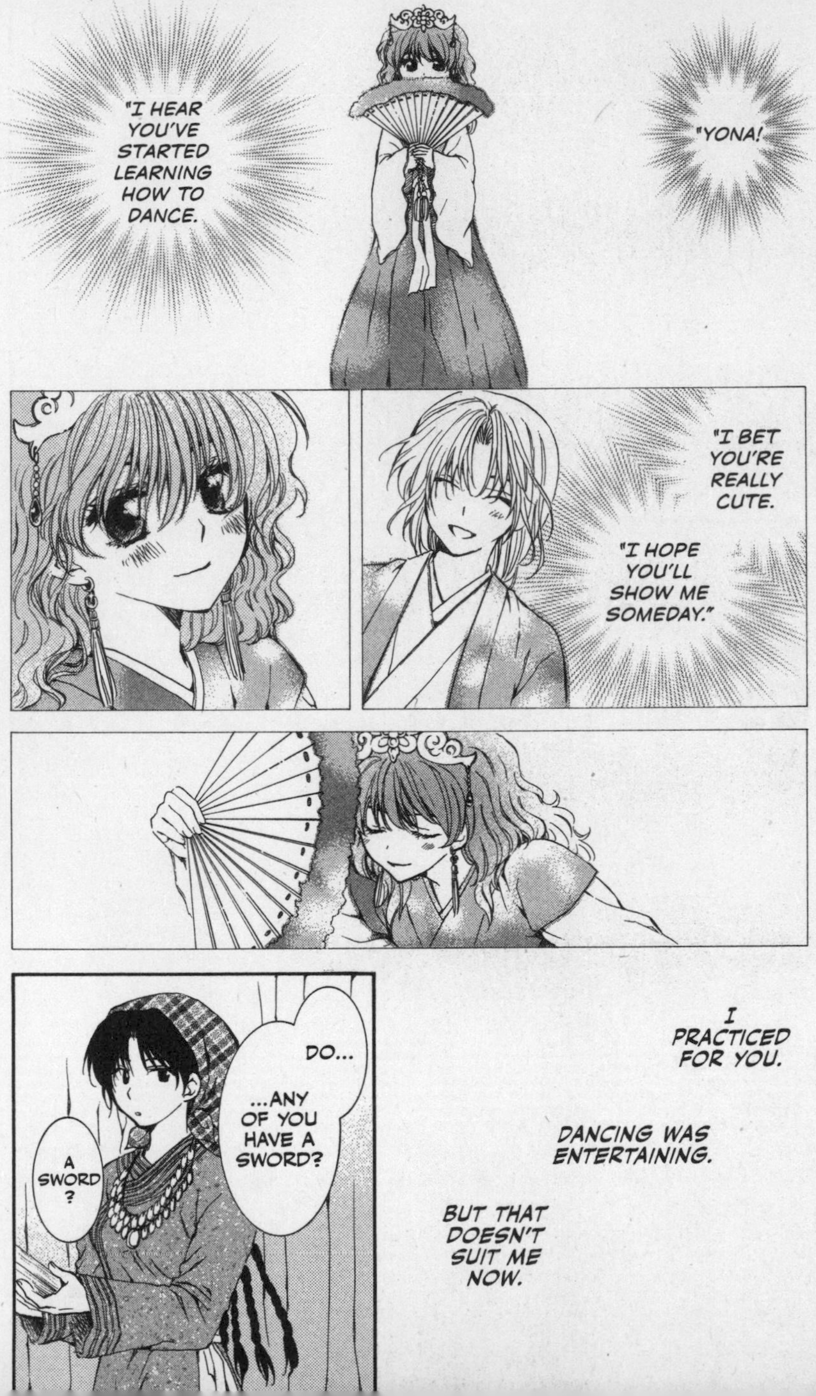
"YONA!
"I HEAR YOU'VE STARTED LEARNING HOW TO DANCE.
"I BET YOU'RE REALLY CUTE.
"I HOPE YOU'LL SHOW ME SOMEDAY."
I PRACTICED FOR YOU.
DANCING WAS ENTERTAINING.
BUT THAT DOESN'T SUIT ME NOW.
DO...
...ANY OF YOU HAVE A SWORD?
A SWORD?

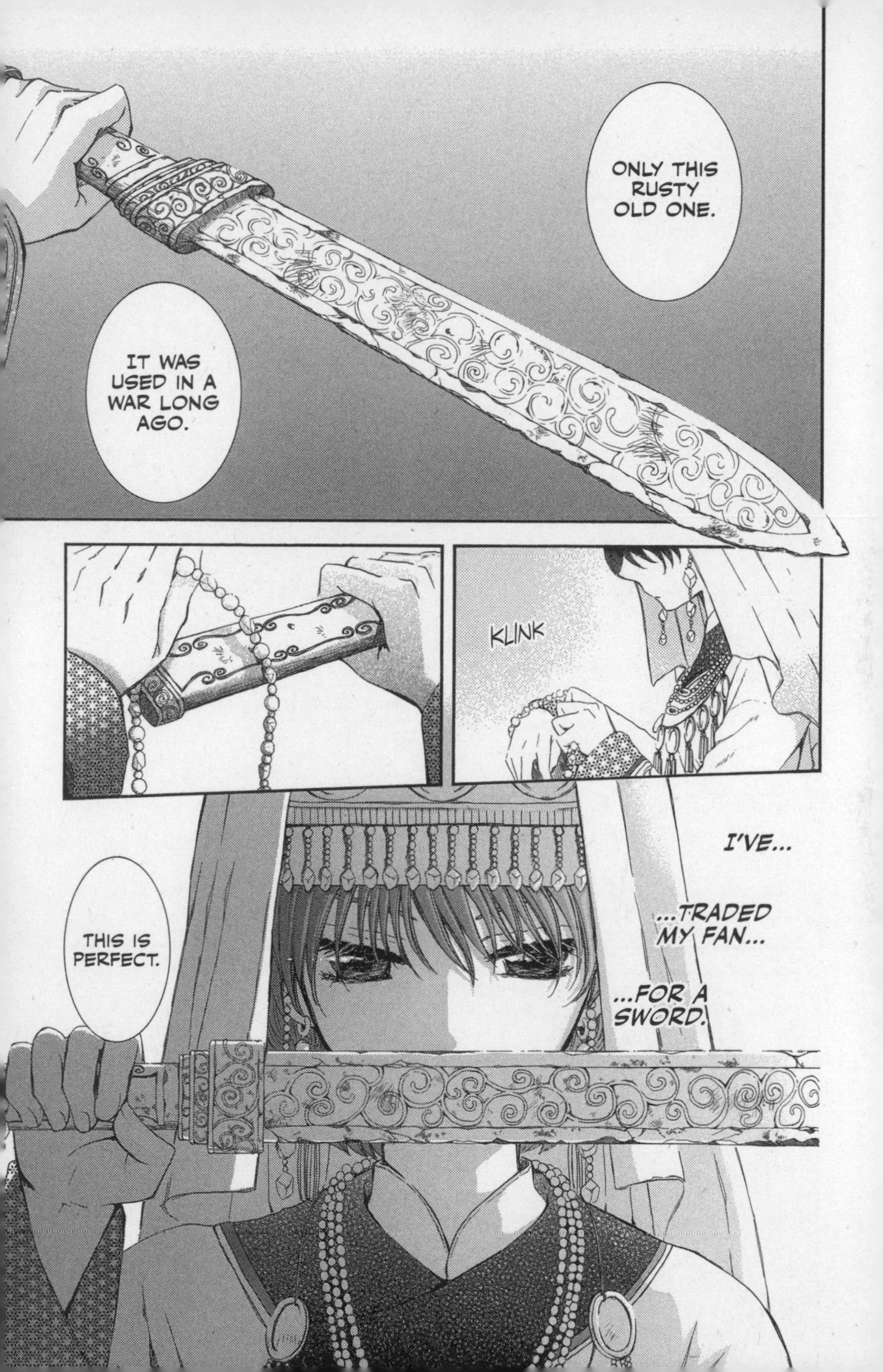
ONLY THIS RUSTY OLD ONE.
IT WAS USED IN A WAR LONG AGO.
KLINK
I'VE...
...TRADED MY FAN...
...FOR A SWORD.
THIS IS PERFECT.

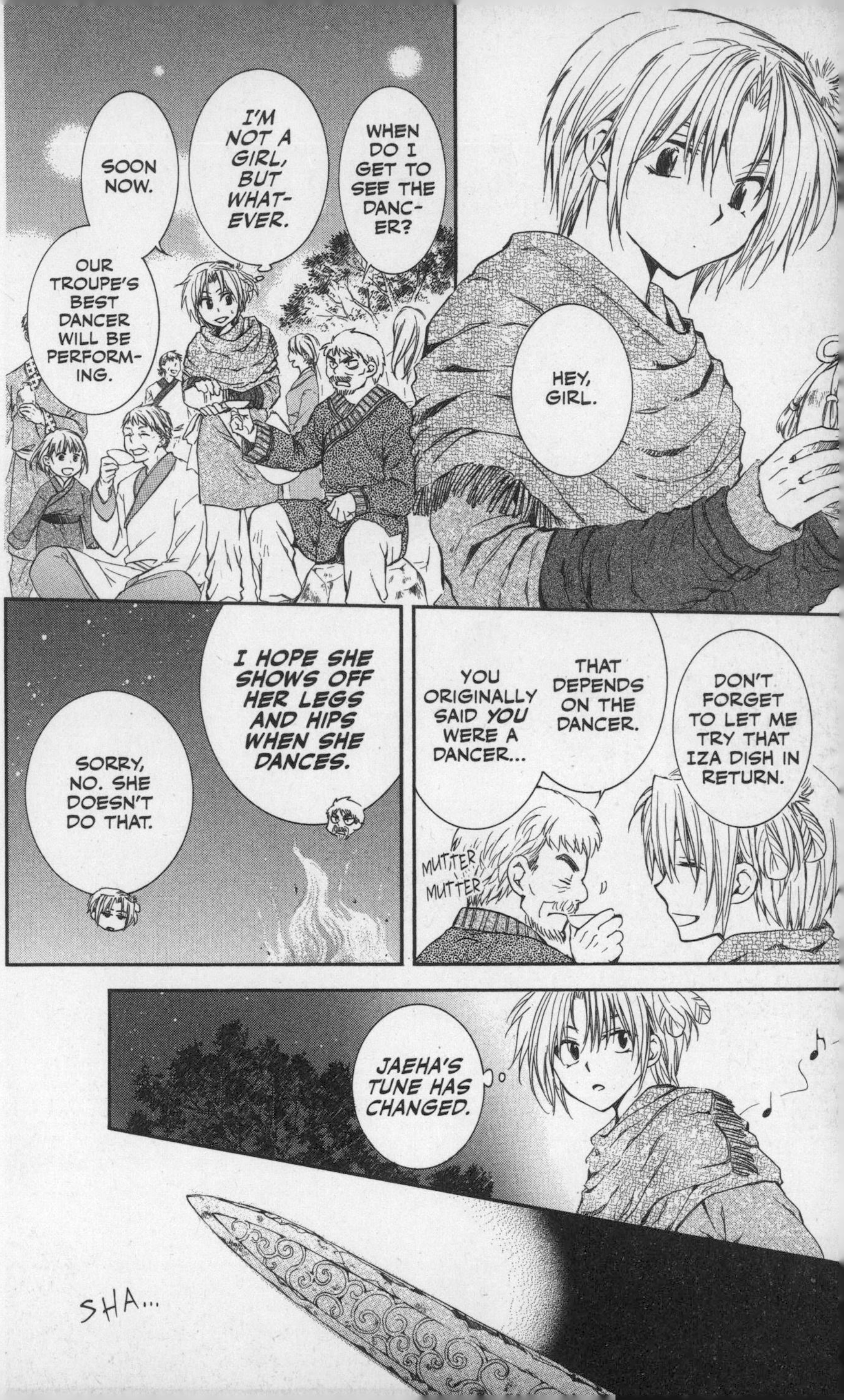
HEY, GIRL.
WHEN DO I GET TO SEE THE DANCER?
I'M NOT A GIRL, BUT WHATEVER.
SOON NOW.
OUR TROUPE'S BEST DANCER WILL BE PERFORMING.
DON'T FORGET TO LET ME TRY THAT IZA DISH IN RETURN.
THAT DEPENDS ON THE DANCER.
YOU ORIGINALLY SAID *YOU* WERE A DANCER...
MUTTER MUTTER
I HOPE SHE SHOWS OFF HER LEGS AND HIPS WHEN SHE DANCES.
SORRY, NO. SHE DOESN'T DO THAT.
JAEHA'S TUNE HAS CHANGED.
SHA...

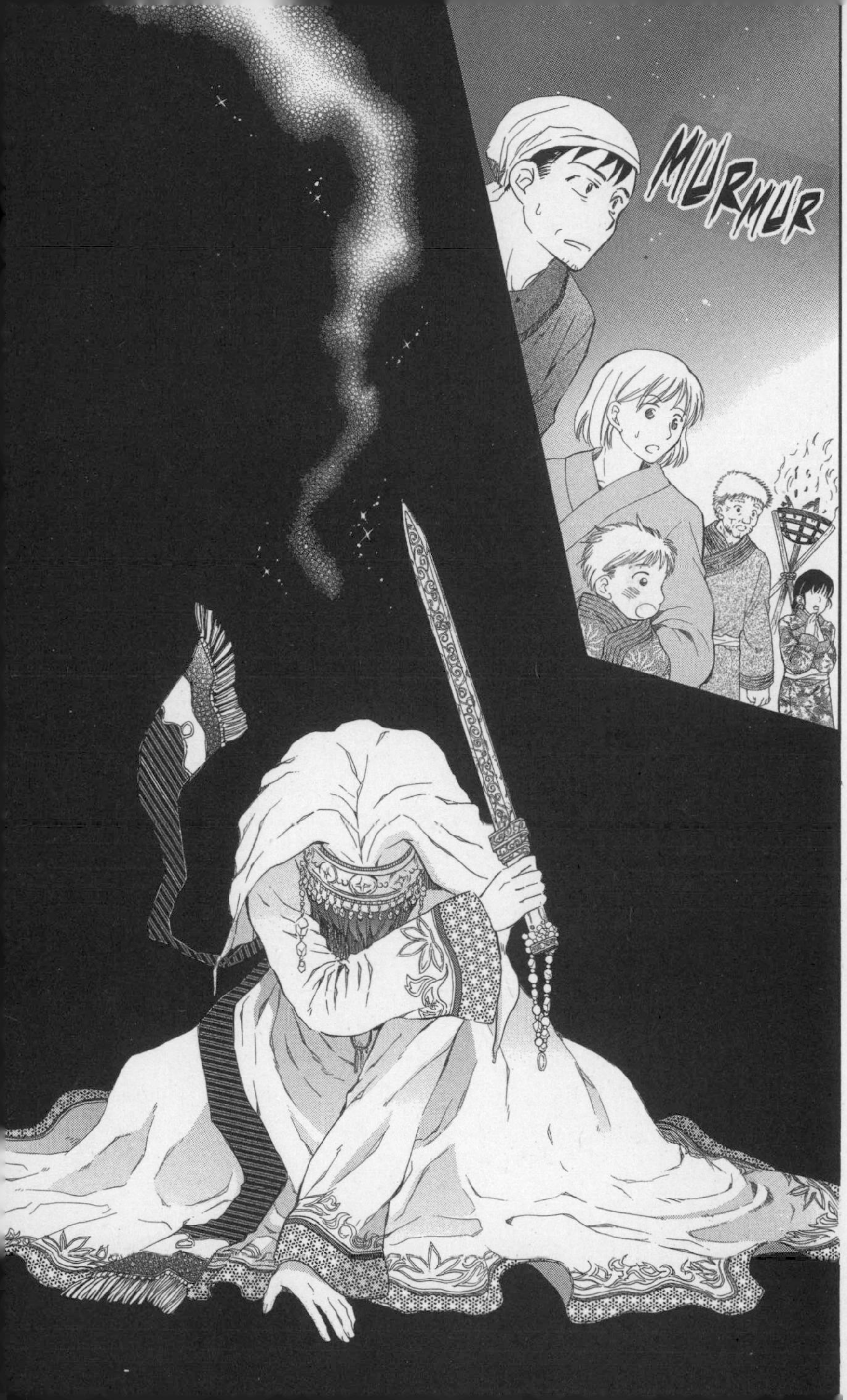
MURMUR

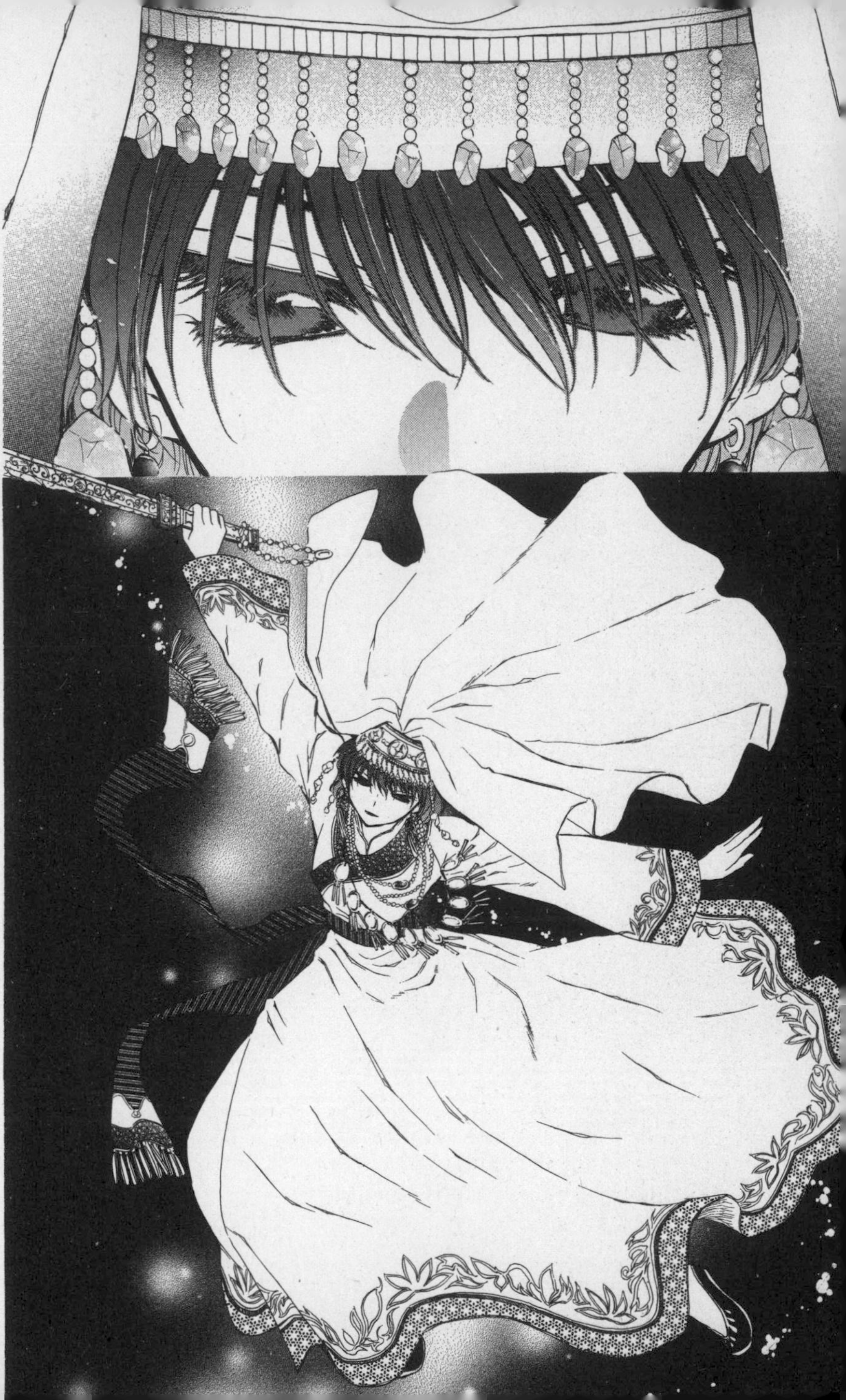

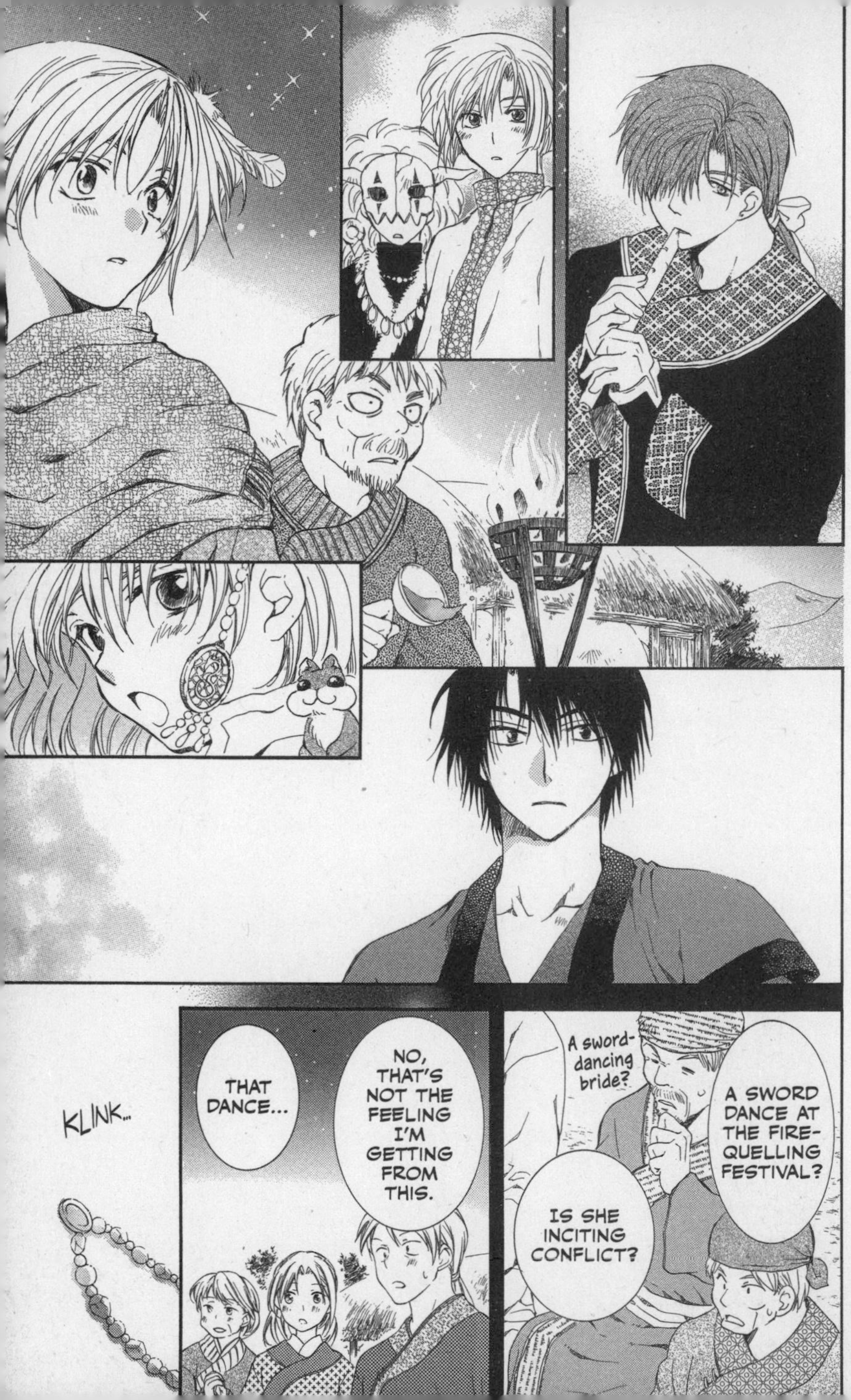
A SWORD DANCE AT THE FIRE-QUELLING FESTIVAL?
A sword-dancing bride?
IS SHE INCITING CONFLICT?
NO, THAT'S NOT THE FEELING I'M GETTING FROM THIS.
THAT DANCE...
KLINK...

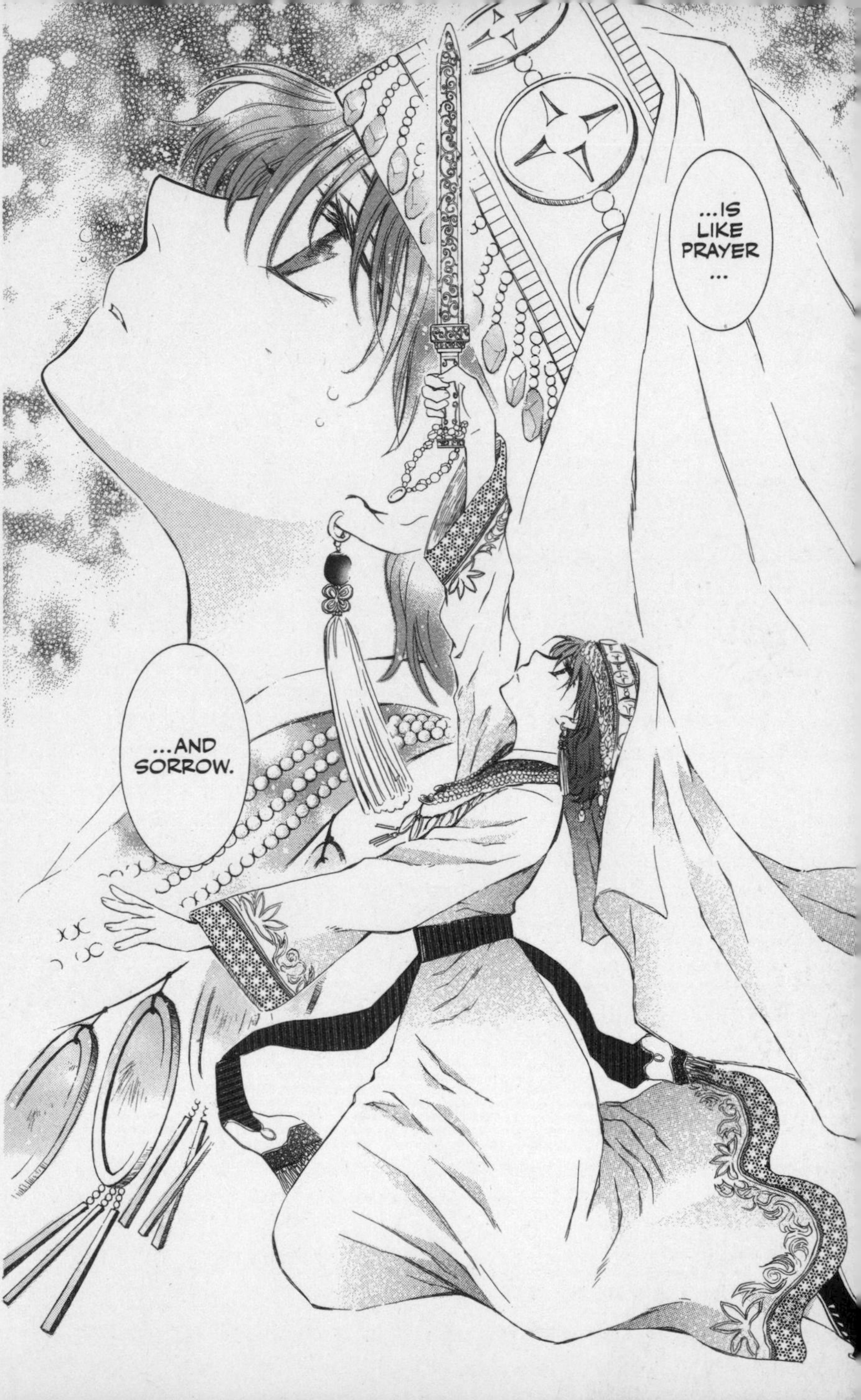
...IS LIKE PRAYER ...
...AND SORROW.

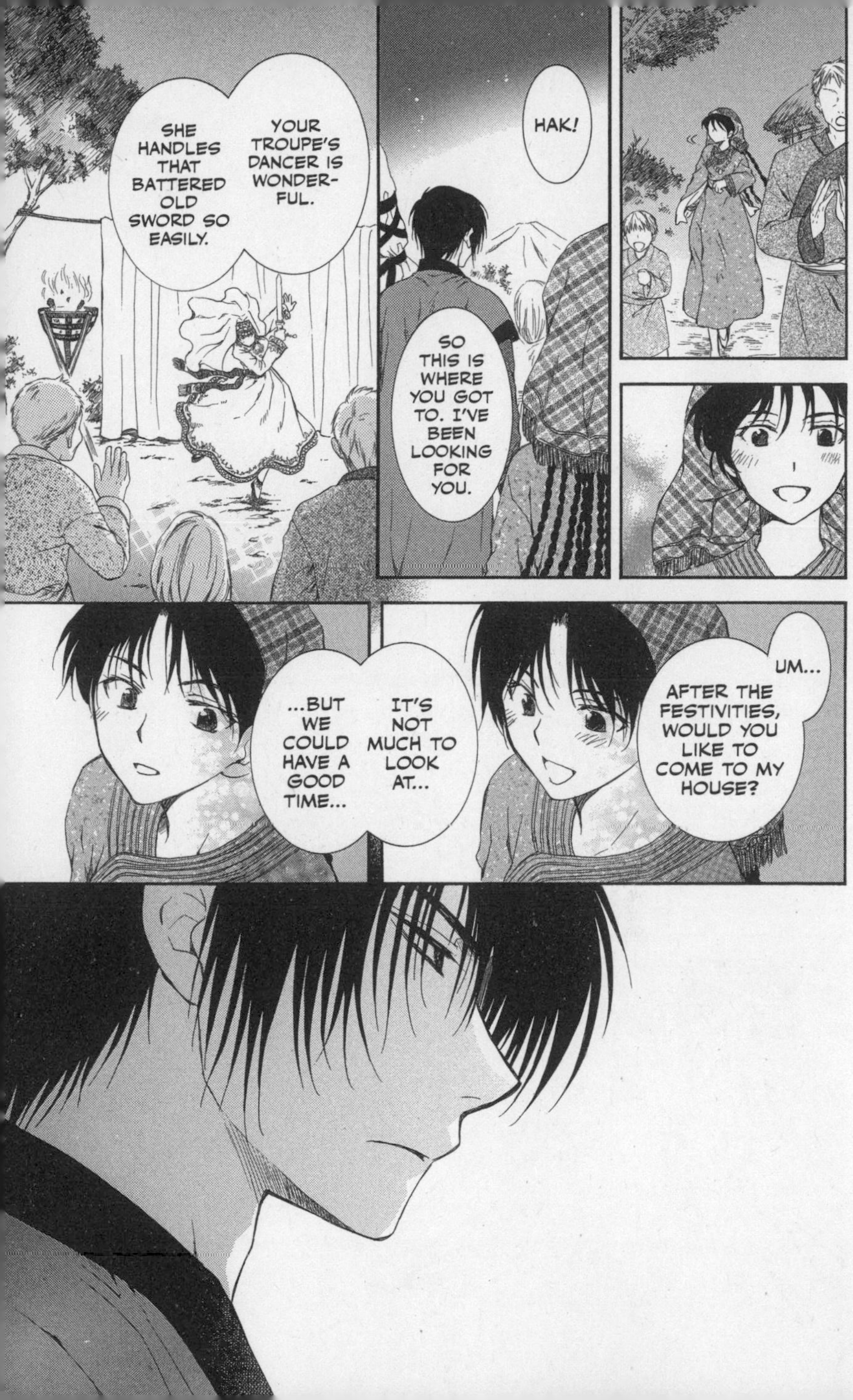
HAK!
SO THIS IS WHERE YOU GOT TO. I'VE BEEN LOOKING FOR YOU.
YOUR TROUPE'S DANCER IS WONDERFUL.
SHE HANDLES THAT BATTERED OLD SWORD SO EASILY.
UM...
AFTER THE FESTIVITIES, WOULD YOU LIKE TO COME TO MY HOUSE?
IT'S NOT MUCH TO LOOK AT...
...BUT WE COULD HAVE A GOOD TIME...

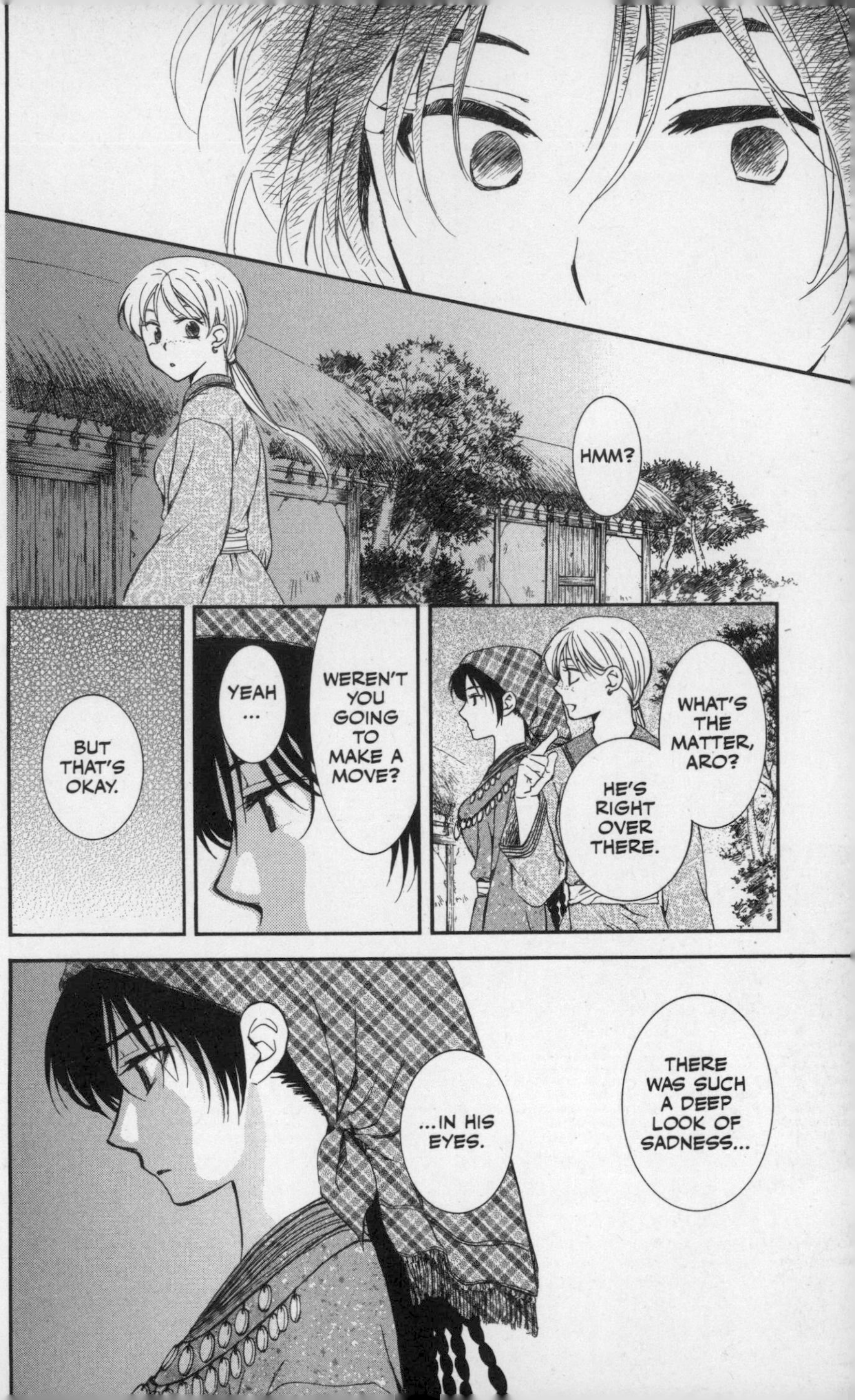
HMM?
WHAT'S THE MATTER, ARO?
HE'S RIGHT OVER THERE.
WEREN'T YOU GOING TO MAKE A MOVE?
YEAH ...
BUT THAT'S OKAY.
THERE WAS SUCH A DEEP LOOK OF SADNESS...
...IN HIS EYES.

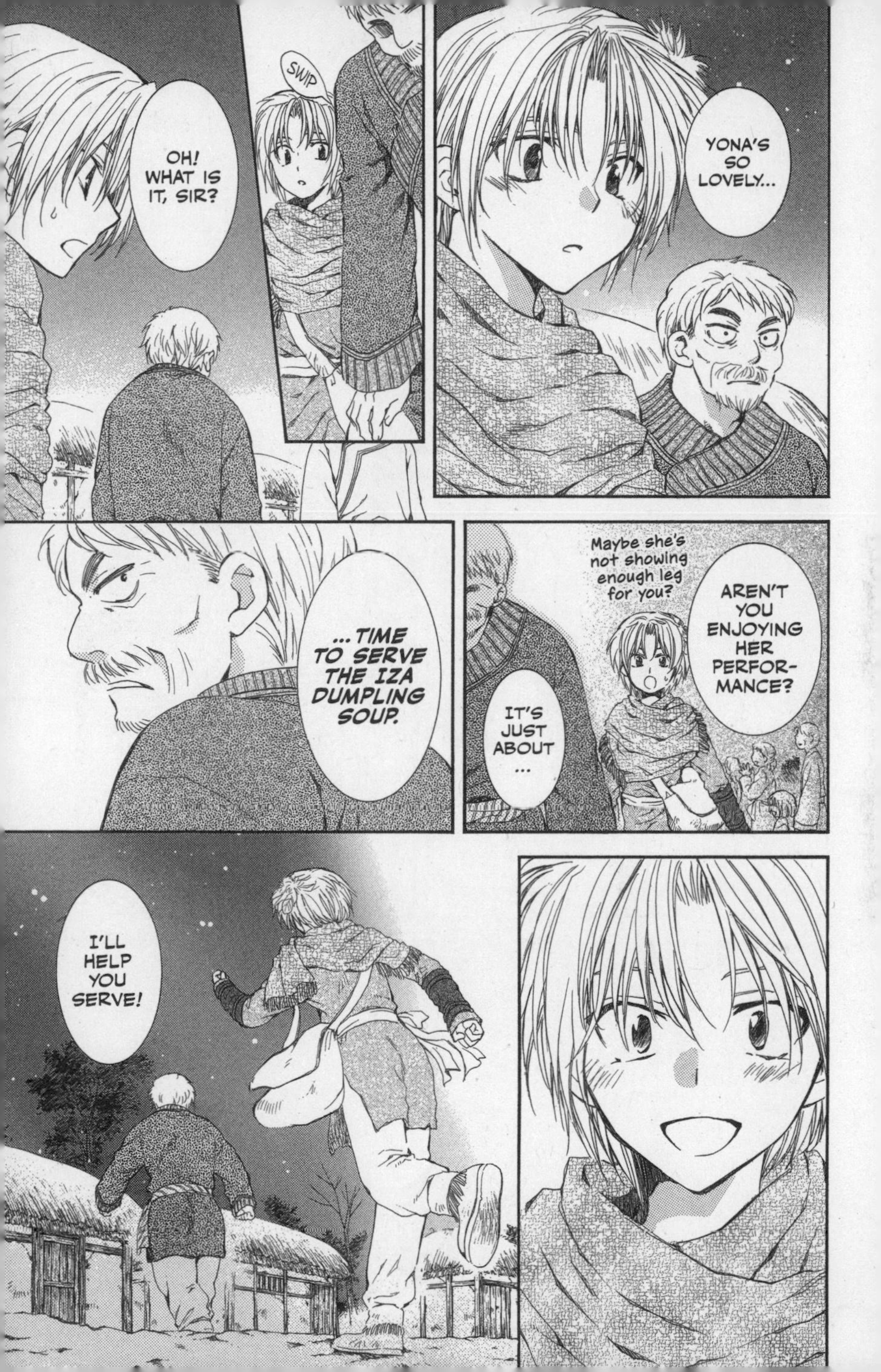
YONA'S SO LOVELY...
SWIP
OH! WHAT IS IT, SIR?
AREN'T YOU ENJOYING HER PERFORMANCE?
Maybe she's not showing enough leg for you?
IT'S JUST ABOUT ...
...TIME TO SERVE THE IZA DUMPLING SOUP.
I'LL HELP YOU SERVE!

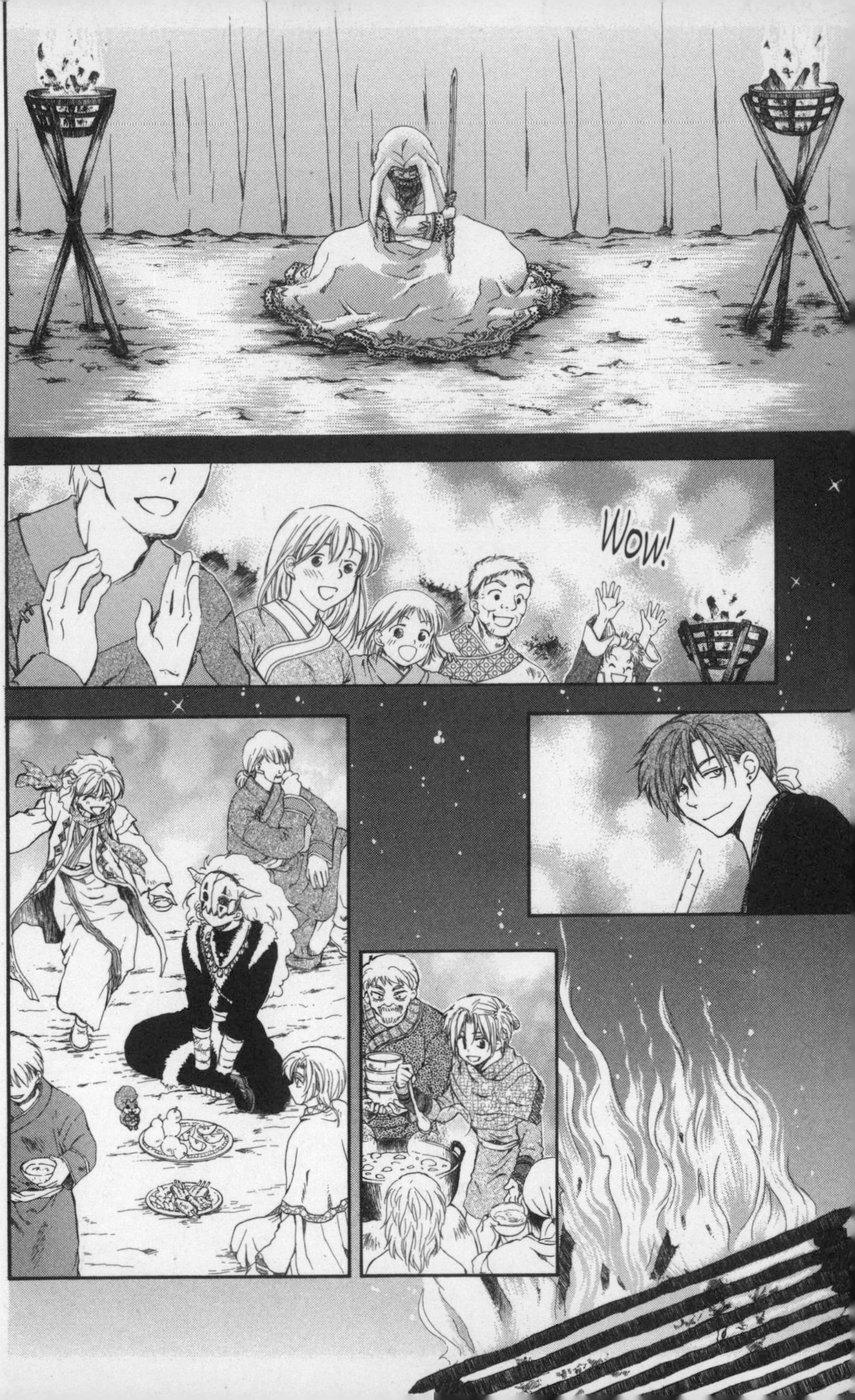
Wow!

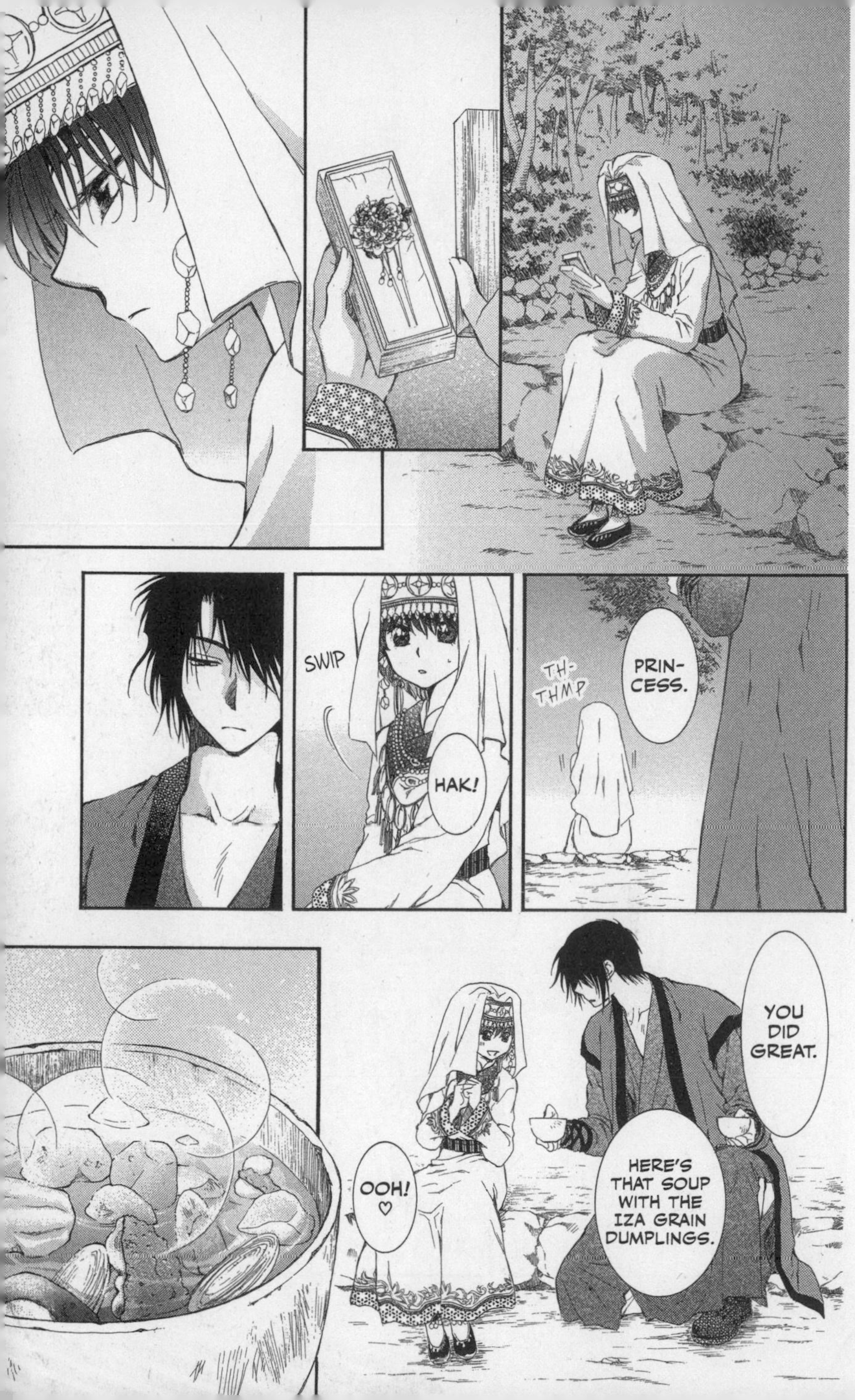
PRIN-CESS.
TH-THMP
SWIP
HAK!
YOU DID GREAT.
HERE'S THAT SOUP WITH THE IZA GRAIN DUMPLINGS.
OOH! ♡

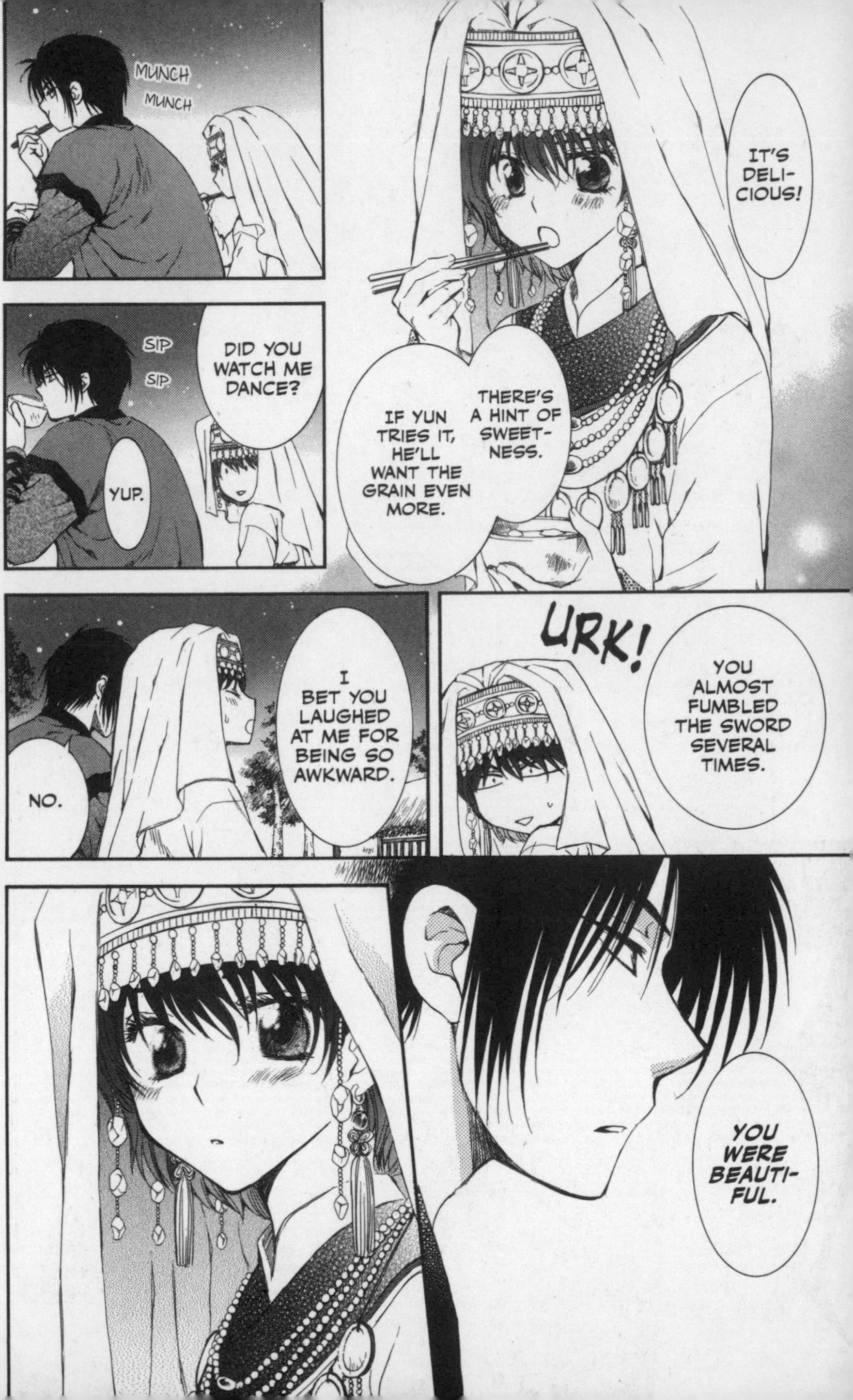
IT'S DELI-CIOUS!
THERE'S A HINT OF SWEET-NESS.
IF YUN TRIES IT, HE'LL WANT THE GRAIN EVEN MORE.
MUNCH
MUNCH
DID YOU WATCH ME DANCE?
SIP
SIP
YUP.
URK!
YOU ALMOST FUMBLED THE SWORD SEVERAL TIMES.
I BET YOU LAUGHED AT ME FOR BEING SO AWKWARD.
NO.
YOU WERE BEAUTI-FUL.

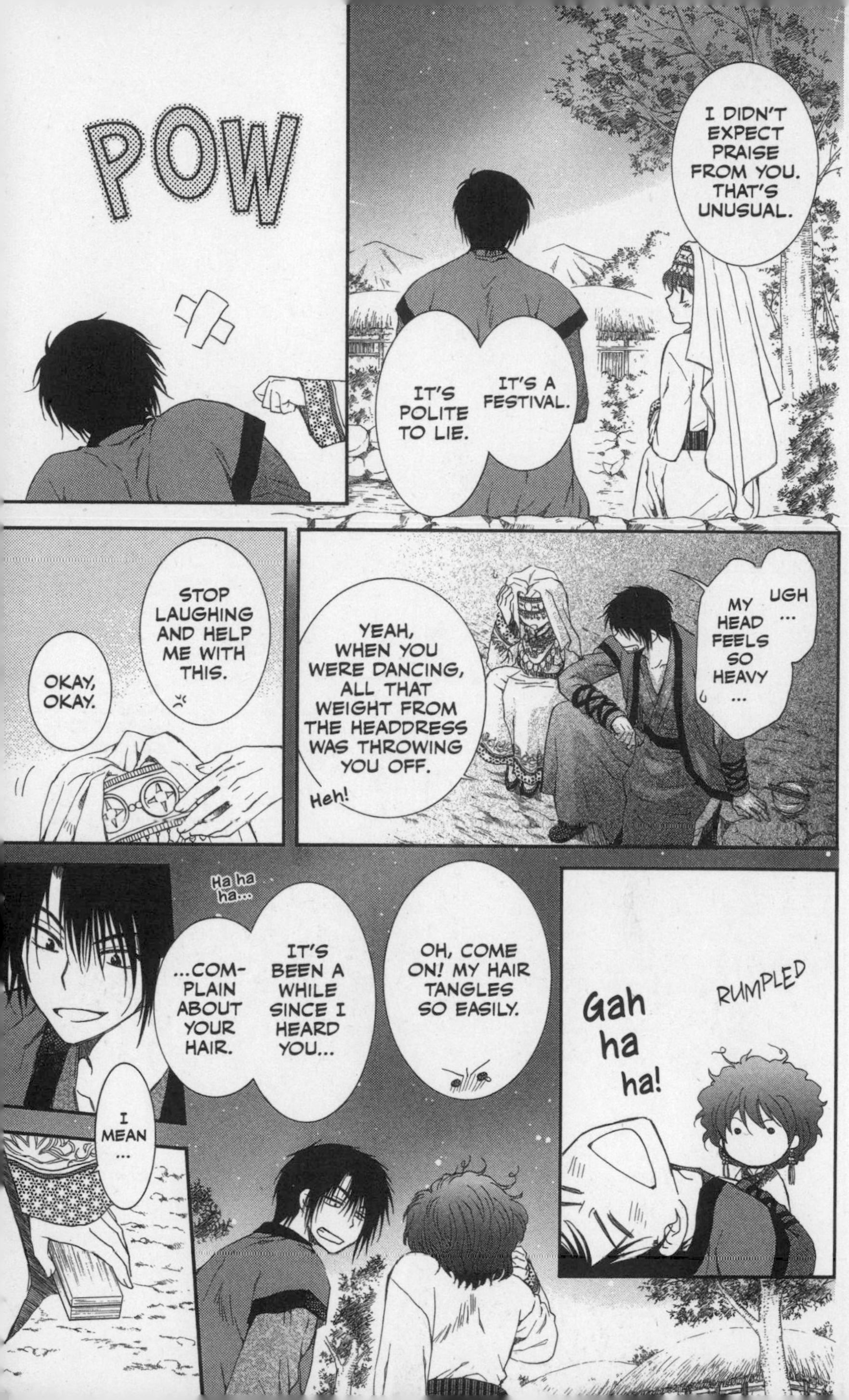
I DIDN'T EXPECT PRAISE FROM YOU. THAT'S UNUSUAL.
IT'S A FESTIVAL.
IT'S POLITE TO LIE.
POW
UGH...
MY HEAD FEELS SO HEAVY...
YEAH, WHEN YOU WERE DANCING, ALL THAT WEIGHT FROM THE HEADDRESS WAS THROWING YOU OFF.
Heh!
STOP LAUGHING AND HELP ME WITH THIS.
OKAY, OKAY.
Gah ha ha!
RUMPLED
OH, COME ON! MY HAIR TANGLES SO EASILY.
Ha ha ha...
IT'S BEEN A WHILE SINCE I HEARD YOU...
...COM-PLAIN ABOUT YOUR HAIR.
I MEAN...

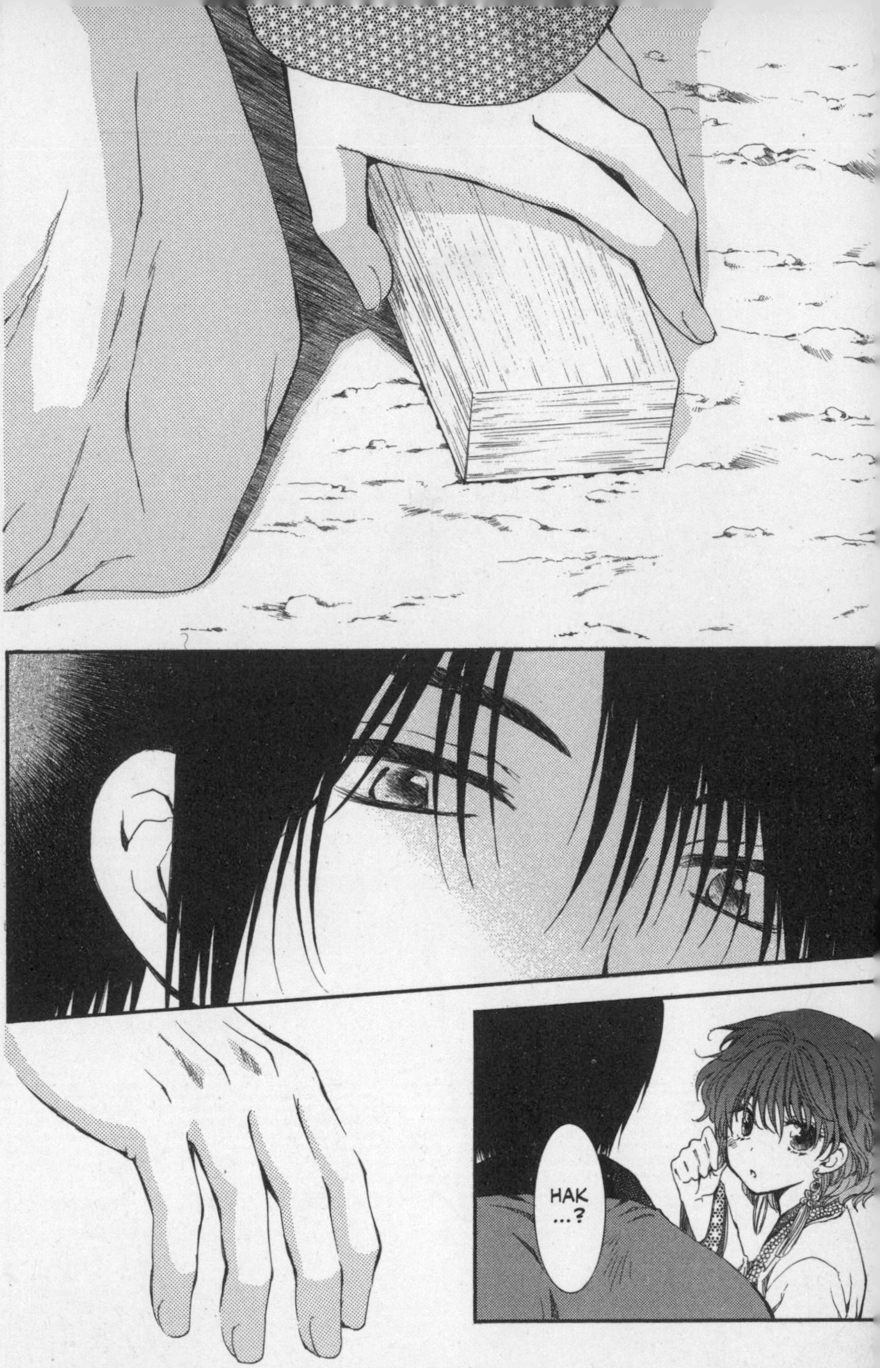
HAK ...?

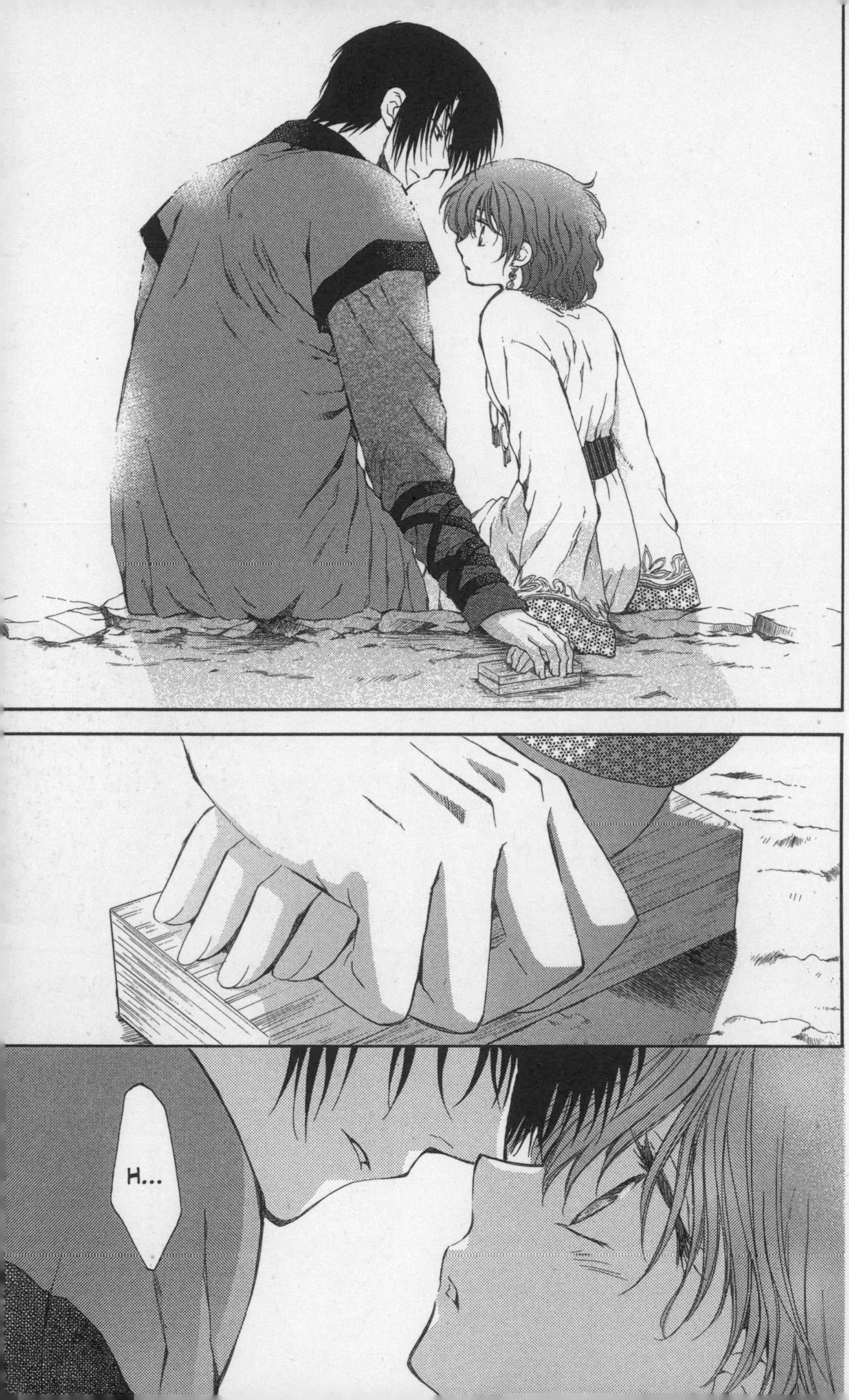
H...

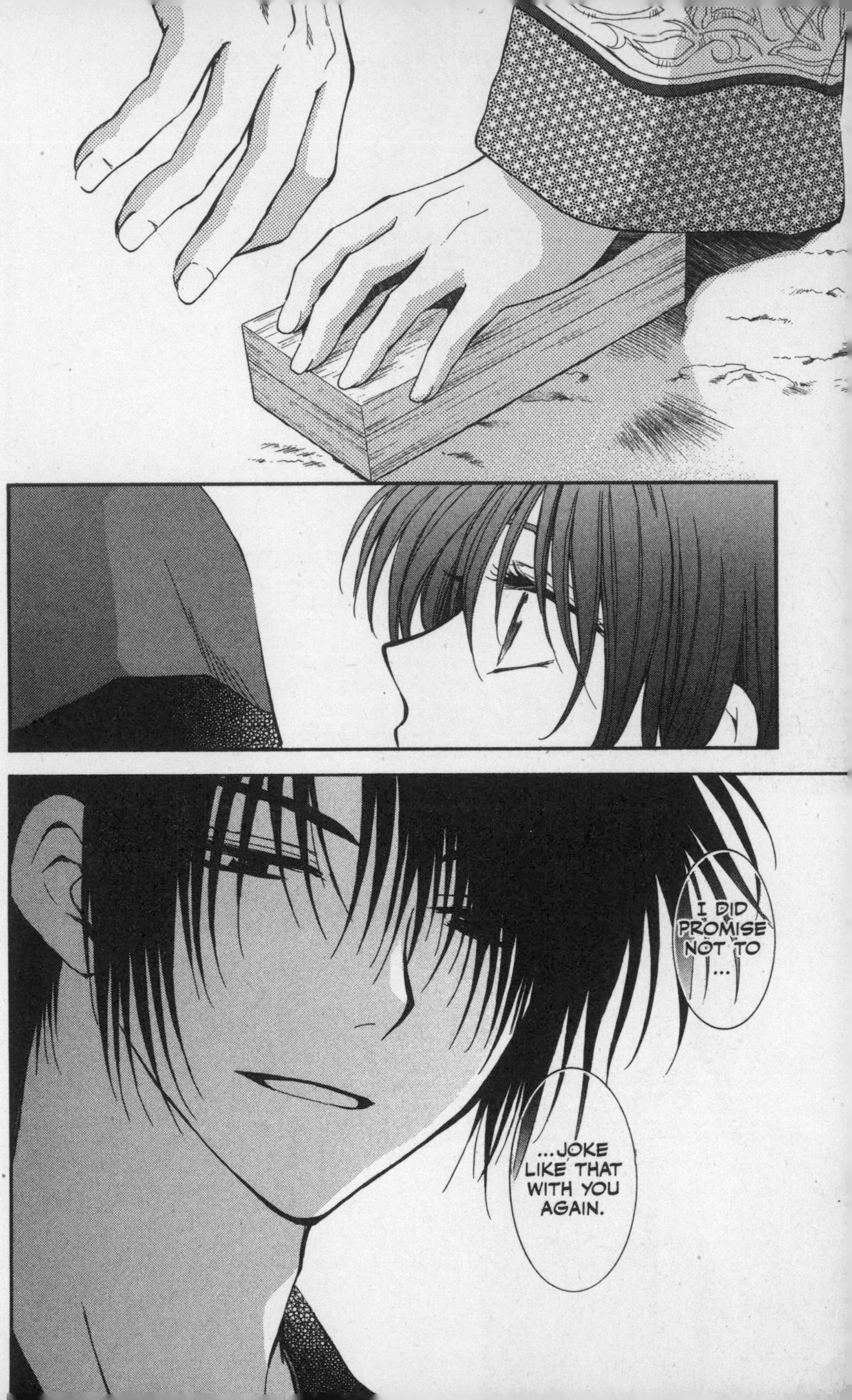
I DID PROMISE NOT TO ...
...JOKE LIKE THAT WITH YOU AGAIN.

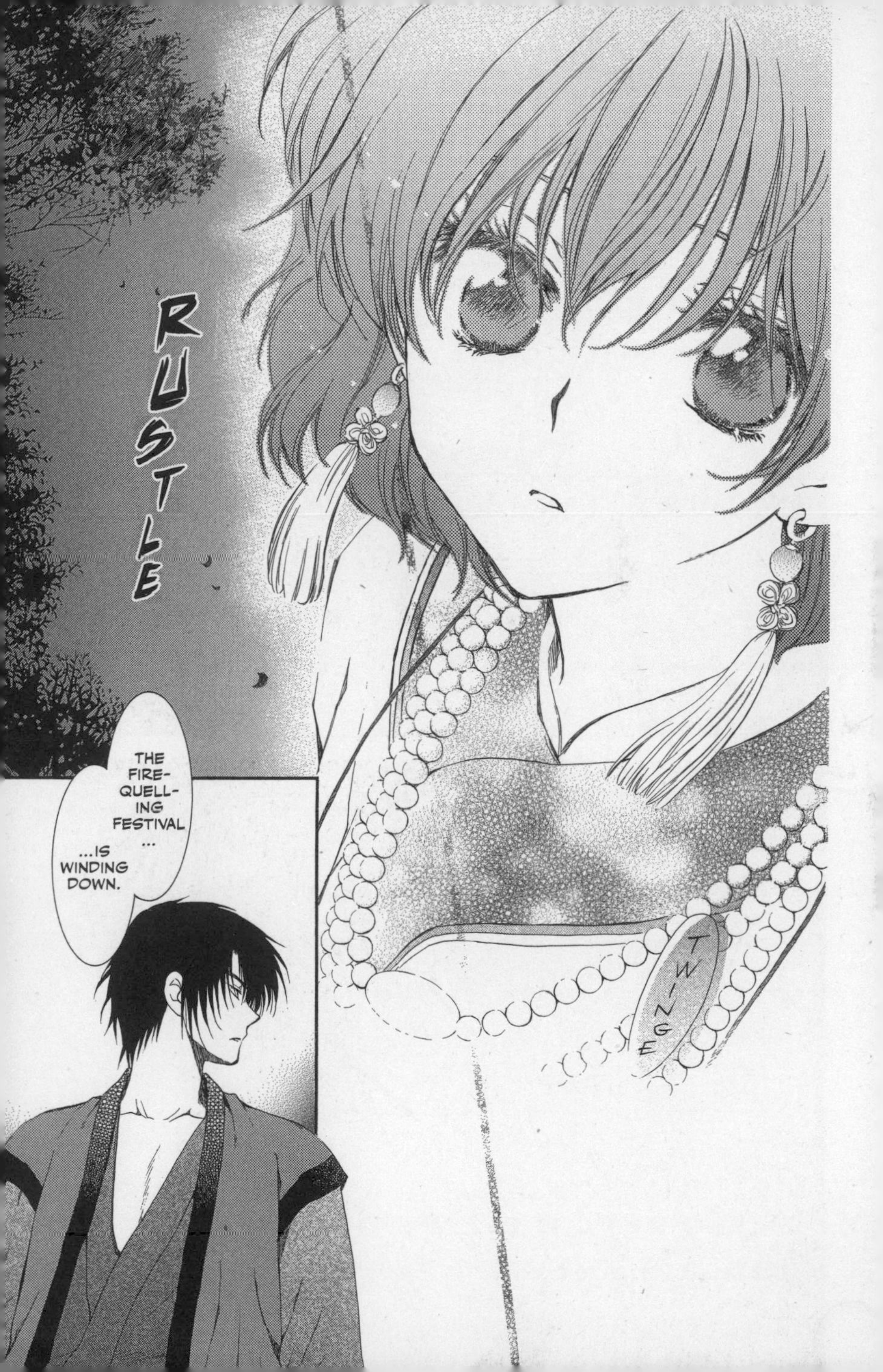
RUSTLE
TWINGE
THE FIRE-QUELLING FESTIVAL ...
...IS WINDING DOWN.

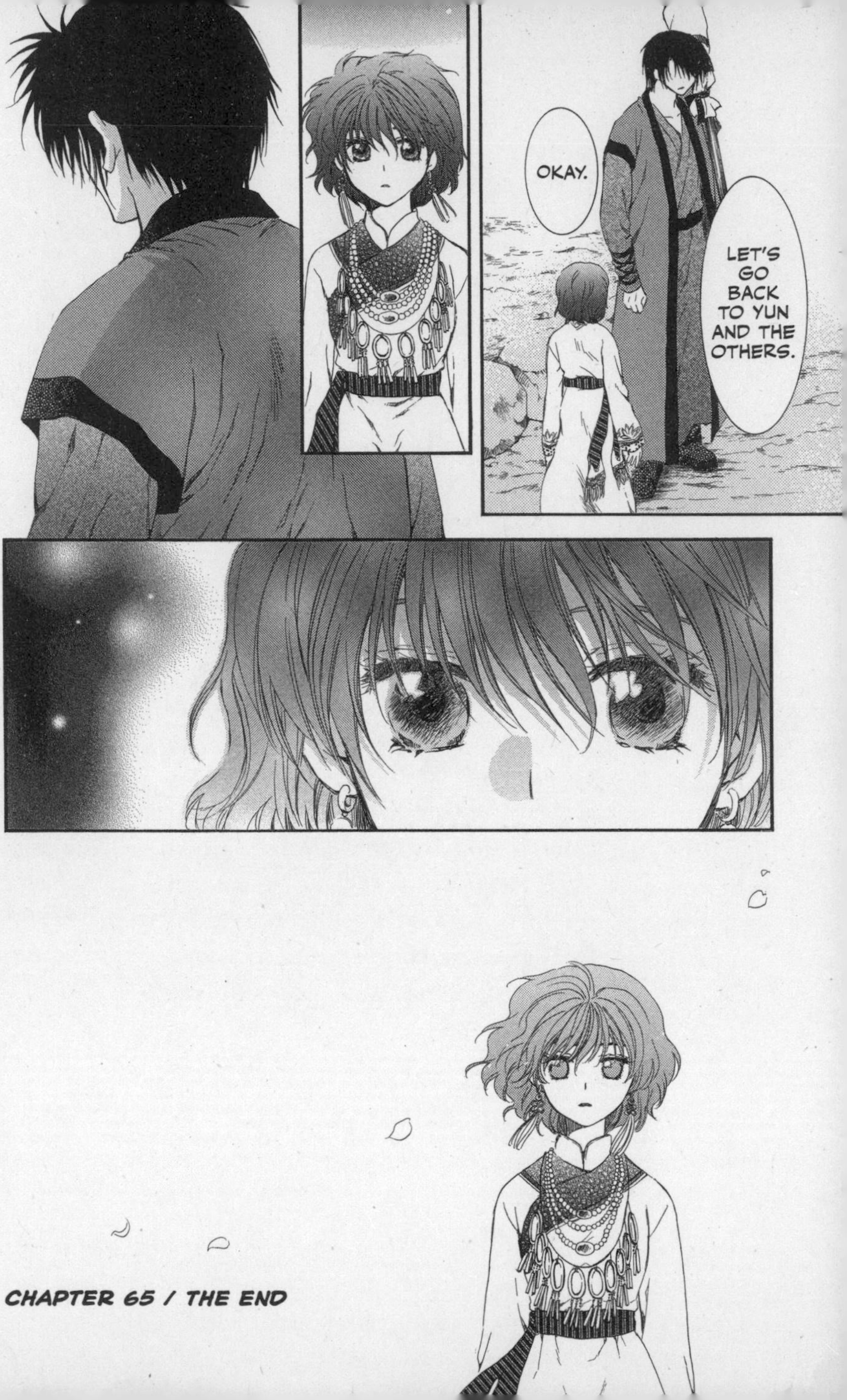
LET'S GO BACK TO YUN AND THE OTHERS.
OKAY.
CHAPTER 65 / THE END